AF657625

Citizenship in a Globalising World

Books by the Author

Tradition and Innovation in Indian Political Thought

Political Theory : Interrogations and Interventions

Critical Theory : The Marx-Marcuse Encounter

Liberalism and the Communitarian Challenge

John Rawls and the Agenda of Social Justice

C.B. Macpherson and Liberalism

Contemporary Political Thinking

Nietzsche After Hundred Years

Citizenship in a Globalising World

B.N. Ray

2007

Kaveri Books

New Delhi - 110 002

First Published in 2007

ISBN 81-7479-082-9

Published by
Rakesh Goel
Kaveri Books
4697/5-21 A, Ansari Road,
New Delhi - 110 002 (India).

Tel.: 011-2 328 8140, 2 324 5799
e-mail: kaveribooks@vsnl.com

Laser Typesetting by
Aarati Computers, Delhi - 110 009.

Printed at
Chawla Offset Printers, Delhi-52.

PRINTED IN INDIA

Preface

The struggle of the disadvantaged and the marginalized for rights as well as improved conditions, and especially the rights of citizenship, is a prominent thread running through the history of the West. Political theorists have been writing about citizenship for over two thousand years, and it has been practiced for even longer. No wonder, therefore, that the concept and status of citizenship have accumulated a complex variety of interpretations. However, no age before ours has had such a widespread and pressing need to understand these narratives. Modern citizenship has developed not only as a consequence of popular democratic pressures, but also in response to the ruling-class's requirements for security, a factor ignored by many theorists of citizenship. Today, citizenship is generally taken to include a universal right to a level of economic and social well-being in addition to the rights of equality before the law and political participation.

The title of citizen (citoyen, citoyenne) was adopted by the French revolutionaries to pronounce the symbolic reality of equality: the titles of aristocratic distinction were expunged. The Russian revolutionaries went one step ahead by replacing even the title of Mr by the uniform title of citizen. Today citizenship is a commonly held status throughout the world, though, true, the title has not persisted; so equality, at least in theory, in principle and in law, might seem pervasive. But explaining that equality – how it has evolved; its variegated elements, including rights and duties; the civic identity it provides; and how far the practice so often falls short of the theory – all this is a much more complicated business than the bland statement of the generalized principle of equality might suggest.

It reminds us that citizenship in the West is more than simply a condition or status; it is a process with identifiable phases in time and with contexts in history which unites it in some degree with other processes such as individualism and secularism. And it is as process in time that citizenship looms up as one of the decisive differences between the Western states in post-medieval times, and the traditional states of Asia.

The great difference between the political state in the West from about the sixteenth century and the traditional state in Asia, such as China and India, has little if anything to do with absoluteness of power claimed by each and almost everything to do with the relation between this absolute power and the masses of people under it.

In the traditional Asiatic state prior to the present era, the state's authority rarely if ever touched the individual directly. Between state and individual lay broad strata of authority – family, clan, village, guild, sometimes caste – which were not often penetrated by the power of the king or emperor. Although bureaucracy was very much a reality in the Asiatic state, it did not often seek to supplant but rather to work with and through the deeply rooted social structures. Marx, as we know, was fascinated by this aspect of political organization in Asia, and indeed he thought the depredation of England upon Indian village, family and caste justified in the long run, however painful they might be to observe in the short run, if only to bring the East into closer correspondence with the West and, hence, to his own theory of historical development.

There was not, there could not have been, in the Asiatic state citizenship as this is understood in the West from the sixteenth century on, for the degree to which individual lives in Asia were contained by clan, village, and caste but not of their political orders. When we look at Western history from the late Middle Ages on, we are struck by processes of political individualization with its "pulverizing and macadamizing" tendencies. Through their operation, in the whole intermediate sphere that had become so strong in medieval times – the sphere of guild, manor, town, monastery, and many other associative ties – the individual and sovereign were brought closer together in legal and administrative terms than would otherwise have been possible. Putting the matter differently, individual and sovereign can be seen from about the sixteenth century on as forming a pair of scissors that cut ever more surely into the corporate relationships which lay within the cutting edges.

This is not proper place to go into the history of the concept of citizenship in the West however, it is necessary to point out that whereas the word *citizen* meant in the Middle Ages simply inhabitant of a town, in sharp contrast to those who were *subjects* under feudal princes and kings in the countryside, what happened in due course was the removal of strictly urban connotations from this word and its gradual utilization first as synonym for, then as replacement of the word, *subject*.

Roman Law, which by the fourteenth century was emerging from the university curriculum and becoming useful instrument to prince and banker alike, did a great deal to rationalize the process of conversion of subject to citizen, for the idea of citizenship is just as luminous in Justinian Code and Digest alike as are the complementary ideas of sovereignty, contract, and not least the concession doctrine that could make perilous the position of all that lay between sovereign and citizen.

It is of course, in the Age of Revolution that we see the final phase of "citizenization" manifesting itself. Appropriately enough, this phase occurs alongside the emergence of nationalism in its strictly modern form. A State became a nation when instead of its members being primarily divided between sovereign and subjects, government and citizenship became a common task, demanding not passive citizenship but active cooperation from all.

Yet, however, difficult the concept of citizenship may be, the effort of comprehension is especially necessary now. For we are at present living through an age that for good reason considers citizenship of cardinal significance. However, as a consequence of this recognized importance, academic enquiry has uncovered the extraordinary complexity of its history and present condition to aid our more accurate understanding.

There have been other ages of heightened consciousness of citizenship, often associated with particular states. Fifth to fourth-century BC Athens, first-century BC to first-century AD Rome, late medieval Florence, late eighteenth-century America and France spring obviously to mind. The present interest is different: it is virtually global in its extent. How then to explain the fascination the subject currently holds? It derives from the confluence of a number of events and concerns in the 1980s and 1990s.

First, in the established liberal democracies the emergence of political and doctrinal dominance of the New Right in the US and UK threw into question the validity of 'social citizenship'. By social citizenship is meant the provision of welfare state benefits as a right. It is a right that was conceded in order to ensure a greater equality for citizens than would be the case if untempered market forces of employment and wages were allowed to prevail.

Secondly, partly because of accelerated human migrations and partly because of enhanced and politicized awareness of ethnic differences within states, the fact that almost all states are multicultural in demographic composition has become an issue related to the definition of citizenship as civic identity.

Thirdly, and closely related to this development, ethnic, cultural and national consciousness have brought about either the loosening or the actual fragmentation of politics hitherto thought of as nation-states. What does it mean, for example, to be a Canadian citizen if one thinks of oneself primarily as a Quebecois, or an Israeli citizen, if a Plasetinian Arab? In potentially fissiparous conditions like these only a stable or strong government could hold a national citizenship in place. In the former Soviet Union and Yugoslavia that stability and strength failed; and the assumed nation-states disintegrated. Furthermore, it was a consciousness among a critical mass of the population of the need and the opportunity to claim an effective citizenship that wrought these changes. Moreover, these states had been autocratic regimes, many of whose successor governments sought to rebuild their political systems this time following the liberal democratic blueprint.

Fourthly, these states have needed to construct fresh constitutions and ways of conducting public life, which could give reality to the legal and political rights of citizenship that had not been thoroughly enjoyed under Communism. The ex-communist countries were not alone in striving to make this transition: South Africa and the states of sub-Saharan Africa and Latin America that had endured but shook themselves loose from military dictatorships, have passed through similar experiences of improving the meanings of citizenship for their people.

Fifthly, we are becoming increasingly conscious that for large numbers of people throughout the world, the idea of citizenship is still hollow and meaningless, deprived as they are of virtually all its attributes and contents.

Sixthly, the validity of the nation-state is itself being vigorously contested. Uniquely, at the sub-continental level, the European Union has created a new, legally defined category of citizenship, namely, of the Union. Meanwhile, economic developments and environmental worries have revived the ancient concept of cosmopolitan citizenship the awareness of being a citizen to be encouraged to behave as such. These trends are part of the increasing recognition that citizenship is a multiple rather than a singular feeling and status.

Modern citizenship, comprising at least universal civil, political and social rights, is not only complex but fraught with internal tensions, as the distinct right which constitute it tend to generate different and sometimes contradictory pulls and pressures. This book explains why an understanding of citizenship rights is important for social and political analysis, and goes on to treat both the relationship between the distinct elements of citizenship and its effects on class inequality, on social and political integration, and on the structure and operation of the state.

Current approaches to modern citizenship began with the publication by T.H. Marshall's of *Citizenship and Social Class* in 1950. This book dealing directly with the historical development of modern citizenship and its social and political consequences, offers a distinctive interpretation and critique of T.H. Marshall's theory, and makes a modest contribution to the debate generated by Marshall.

Structured analytically, the book introduces the reader to all the facets of citizenship. These are illustrated by reference both to a broad range of theoretical writings from Aristotle to the present day, and to the actual provisions of the of citizenship status in a number of countries. The volume explores, in addition, a diverse range of pressing issues, including the differences between the civic republican and liberal styles of citizenship; the origins and current relationship between citizenship and nationality and the issue of multiculturalism; the problems experienced by 'second-class' citizens; the concept of 'multiple citizenship' including the status of EU citizenship; the changing definition of 'world citizenship' in a globalising world; and the role of education in creating citizens.

This book makes an attempt to transform our understanding of citizenship. It piously hopes that it should become required reading in any course in political theory, philosophy, history, international relations and comparative politics that considers this key concept and its practical political and policy implications.

Pondicherry University — **B.N. Ray**

Diwali, 2006

Contents

1

Introduction

The concept of citizenship - the nature of the citizen status and role, its rights, duties, and powers, and the nature of the community of citizens - is much used but little analyzed in social policy analysis. And, outside of political philosophy, it is surprisingly little used or analyzed in social theory in general. Some of the reasons for the relative neglect may have to do with the assumptions that ground the enterprise of political sociology merely a department of sociology rather than a general version of social theory. These assumptions tend to hold that political phenomena like states, citizens, and their activities are dependent variables that can be understood and explained by reference to deeper historical and social forces. In the classic tradition of the social theory, social changes in the mode of production (Marx), in the rationalization process (Weber), and in the development of the division of labor (Durkheim) have all been used to explain political phenomena. Sociology's underlying suspicion of eighteenth century bourgeois individualism and contractarian political philosophy tends to be carried over against the notion of the citizen that may be assumed to embody them. Thus, political sociology tends, when examining the political phenomena of citizen's actions, struggles and movements, to reveal their impotence, dependency, and in any case their ignorance, in respect of the powers of such phenomena as the state's bureaucracy, the ruling groups and elites, dominant and mystifying ideologies, and ultimately socio-economic forces.

However, the political action of citizens can be analyzed as having greater potential rationality and power than such accounts display. And both citizens and states can be treated analytically as having increasing relative autonomy from economic forces. In our approach of citizenship this relative autonomy of citizenship and its context will be as much a focus as their relative dependency on socio-economic factors.

The concept of citizenship is of crucial importance to the social sciences as a whole, although it has a particular prominence in political theory and sociology. It is in fact difficult to separate the debate about citizenship from a range of related issues such as the nature of democratic participation, the analysis of social rights, the legitimacy of the public order and the nature of the state in the human societies. Public debates and philosophical discourses on citizenship reflect this complexity of the concept and its embedded nature in social science analysis and research. It is difficult in fact to distinguish the study of citizenship from the study of rights.

The contemporary analysis of citizenship has to be seen within the broader context of the study of social and human rights, because any inquiry into citizenship necessarily raises questions about the relationship between obligation and right, or between responsibilities and entitlements.

A study of citizenship in contemporary social theory demands that the analysis of citizenship should concern itself with three principal analytical questions: what is citizenship, how does citizenship relate to other major social institutions such as the state, and what historical or causal processes create and develop citizenship as an institution?

We may regard citizenship as a collection of rights and duties, which define socio-political membership, the consequence of which is to allocate collective benefits to social groups, households or individuals. Citizenship is thus defined as a bundle of entitlements and obligations, which constitute individuals as full-fledged members of a socio-political community, providing them with access to scarce resources. This definition of citizenship is somewhat unidimensional and simplistic, and a more elaborate theory of citizenship will require a more sensitive awareness of different types of citizenship. We need to develop more elaborate typologies of citizenship, which will provide us with an analytical tool for more sophisticated comparative and historical research.

Having provided a provisional definition of citizenship, it is possible to give a preliminary analysis of the functions of citizenship in society that is to provide an answer to the question: what does it do? Although the functions of citizenship will vary between different social contexts, it is important to offer a general answer in terms of citizenship as a form of social or legal protection from the vagaries and uncertainties of the market place and related life-cycle disadvantages. Citizenship as a system of individual protection has been in the twentieth century developed in response to such issues as racial disadvantage, market and other forms of economic inequality, sexual and social injustice and differences in power with respect to such groups as women, children and the disabled. A more complex response would argue that social citizenship in modern societies functions to create new types of social solidarity in terms of public relations of reciprocity. In short, citizenship is an aspect of the civil religion of modem society. Citizenship as civil religion is an idea derived directly from the social contract theory of Jean Jacques Rousseau, and this notion of political membership or civil religion has continued to influence the debate about commitment and contract in modern societies, specifically in the context of the American concern about the future of republicanism. With the secularisation of modern societies, citizenship creates new intergenerational bonds of loyalty and obligation outside the family.

There are of course a number of important controversies surrounding this idea of citizenship as secular solidarity, since radical critics of citizenship often argue that it functions, not so much to create emotional solidarity, but to incorporate, through ideological means, subordinate social groups, and in particular the urban working class. From this perspective, citizenship is not an integrated secular religion, but a political means of suppressing protest and opposition. The sociological study of the functions of citizenship has, as a consequence, been tied to the debate about reformism. Scholars like Turner argue that the inequalities of the market place cannot be evaluated by legal and political change within a capitalist system of property. By contrast, right-wing critics of citizenship have argued that the public provision of entitlements through the state has tended to undermine moral loyalties to society, because the provision of benefits to the poor, for example, is now done through neutral, amoral mechanisms which do not require direct commitment to strangers within the public arena. Citizenship in fact encourages cynical indifference to the frail, the marginalised and the weak because, through the mechanism of taxation, the obligations to the poor are distributed through the remote and neutral mechanism of the state. Conservative critics of citizenship suggest that there is very general form of the free-rider problem which breeds indifference to those in need, because our collective generosity is parasitic upon a public agency such as the welfare state. It is further suggested by such critics that the welfare state has in fact contributed to the destruction of the family by obscuring the responsibility of parents, in particular fathers, to their off-spring. In the American debate about citizenship, the growth of female poverty (the so-called feminisation of poverty) and the wide-spread prevalence of single parent households in the poverty trap are both seen to be consequences of a misguided welfare system. Paradoxically public welfare, it is argued, produces private indifference.

The debate about the functions of citizenship is therefore closely connected with the discussion of the nature and functions of social welfare in capitalist societies. The specifically English version of this debate has been associated with the theories and writing of T. H. Marshall, whose work has been widely discussed, debated and defended by a great number of scholars. At this stage, we may simply note that there are broadly two contradictory versions of this discussion. In the work of Michael Mann for example, there is the argument that citizenship is one specific example of a ruling class strategy in which the welfare system functions to integrate the urban working class into the emerging industrial capitalist societies of Europe in the modem period. Citizenship provides a minimal level of social and political participation for the mass of the population but the basic arrangements of the property system are conserved and protected. This view of citizenship has been criticised by a number of writers on the grounds that it represents a narrow Marxist view of citizenship which, apart from anything else, obscures or negates the positive benefits of citizenship in the emergence of modem democracies. This debate has proved useful in generating a typology of citizenship which attempts to transcend this simple dichotomy by showing the variations in the nature and functions of citizenship as between different socio-political systems.

It is now possible to turn to the issue of the historical origins of citizenship. It has been generally argued that citizenship is essentially a product of modem politics, that is the socio-political consequence of the. the French and industrial revolutions. This claim therefore insists that citizenship in the full sense of the word is an outcome of the decline of feudal and slave societies, and therefore directly related to the emergence of the modern industrial capitalist society. In more sociological terms, citizenship is both a constituent of modernity and an effect of the processes of modemisation. Citizenship as an institution therefore presupposes all of the changes which have undermined traditional society, namely urbanisation, secularisation, industrialisation and the modernisation of culture. Following the work of Max Weber and Otto Hintze, political citizenship has a number of preconditions, such as the collapse of feudal estates, the development of the money economy, the emergency of autonomous cities in medieval society, the rationalisation of the legal system and the emergence of certain norms and values which we can broadly describe universalistic. In this kind of reading it is assumed that the development of the citizenship is the product of democratic revolution in modem societies.

This view of citizenship as a modem institution raises at least two significant theoretical and empirical objections. Firstly, this interpretation can be criticised as ethnocentric in that it appears to deny the possibility that non-western societies could have contributed to the universal emergence of citizenship. More directly, it implies that citizenship can only emerge in the West and the argument can therefore be criticised as orientalist. Secondly, the notion that citizenship is a modem development appears to fly in the face of the common assumption that democratic notions of citizenship had their origins in the Greek polis and therefore that the evolution of citizenship occurred over a long historical trajectory which a modernist view of citizenship simply denies. These objections are serious and there are no simple or unambiguous responses to these criticisms.

The modernist interpretation of citizenship does not require a view that the world is fundamentally and irretrievably divided between West and East. Furthermore, the West has developed a number of authoritarian versions of citizenship which may in many respects undermine and deny liberal rights. It has been further argued that, with the globalisation of societies, the importance of citizenship may decline in favour of a more radical and universalistic view of human rights which is based upon the notion of a common ontology. There is a major tradition of Islamic political theory upon which one could draw to identify an Islamic theory of participation in the community, notions of social justice and ideas about political organisation. The claim that Ibn Khaldun is the Islamic fountain of modem political theory is well known. As a result it can also be argued that there is a significant Islamic legacy in political thought, which is not dependent on Greek or Roman politial system. It has to be recognised, however, that Islamic institutions of citizenship and political participation were in fact relatively weak, and this may be itself a function of the specific character of Islamic cities, where there is the lack of independence from the state. It should also be noted that the modem version of citizenship and the concept of citizenship are in the West inextricably connected with the peculiar development of autonomous western cities and the immunities which urban dwellers enjoyed with respect to centralised authority.

It is obviously the case that Western notions of citizenship, democracy and rights are in some respects a legacy of Greek and Roman ideas about politics and citizenship. However, Greek political institutions were highly exclusive, and social membership in the political process was based upon the institutions of patriarchy in which only adult men were thought to be capable of rational participation in the political Community. Thus, Greek political life was grounded in a slave economy which precluded women and slaves from participation in the political process because they were excluded from rational debate. These features of the classical legacy are an important limitation on the use of the term citizenship in reference to Greek social and political conditions.

We present an argument that, although citizenship as an institution and as a theory can be associated with classical Greek and Roman political systems, it is historically and sociologically more satisfying to analyse citizenship firstly as a consequence of radical change in the French Revolution and secondly as an outcome of modernisation associated with the industrial revolution. The intellectual context of modem citizenship has depended extensively on the Enlightenment and liberal traditions. We should regard citizenship as an essentially modern institution which reflects the profound changes which have occurred in western societies following the democratic revolutions in France and America, and as a consequence of broader, more general social changes associated with the industrial revolution, such as urbanisation and secularisation. We may express this in a different but somewhat parallel way that citizenship evolves through the establishment of autonomous cities, develops through the emergence of the nation-state in the eighteenth and nineteenth centuries, and finds it full blossoming in the welfare states of the twentieth century. This is perspective has flourished within the legacy of the writings of the English social philosopher and sociologist, T. H. Marshall.

There are however profound problems with the Marshallian legacy, many of which are analysed in some depth in this book. The fundamental idea behind Marshall's account namely that citizenship is an essential institution of the welfare capitalist system, remains unchallenged. Marshall's contribution was grounded in the liberal response to the problems of nineteenth century capitalism, namely the tensions between a democratic political system and an inegalitarian economic system. Marshall's theory attempted to answer the tensions and contradictions between economic structures and democratic political processes. We might reformulate Marshall's account along these lines to argue that citizenship is not an inevitable outcome of the evolutionary development of industrial democracies, but the effect of contingent social struggles over rights and obligations of individuals and groups within a nation state. Marshall's account need not therefore appear as an evolutionary or optimistic statement of English social history, but a more flexible theory about the contingent consequences of social movements, such as the urban working class and its effects upon the formation of nation-states in the modem period.

These ideas of Marshall's were initially developed in his famous essay on citizenship and social class (1950). They were further elaborated in his idea of the 'hyphenated society' in which he turned his interest more self consciously to the contradictory aspects of a mixed economy in which it is difficult to reconcile the contradictory needs of the economy, the welfare system and a democracy. Although

Marshall's ideas have been often associated with a liberal interpretation of modem social structures, scholars have argued that his ideas have at least some relationship to the critical theories of Jurgen Habermas. In *Legitimation Crisis,* Habermas outlined a view of capitalist society in which there are inevitable tensions between the economy, the state and civil society. In particular, the crises within the economy require some regulation by the state, but the negative effect of this fiscal skim-off has been to reduce the rate of profit in the economy thereby provoking further crises at the economic level to which the regulations of the state are directed. At the same time, the state for its legitimacy depends upon the support of civil society, where the relationship between the state and society depends upon, once more, a contradictory relationship between welfare payouts and voting. In order to secure sufficient legitimacy, the state has to promise extensive welfare payments which have a negative consequence for the economy. Habermas attempted to draw two primary conclusions from such an analysis, namely that the legitimation of capitalism would become increasingly problematic with the dynamic development of these interrelated crises and secondly that the capitalist system could never fully resolve its internal difficulties and problems in a way which would ultimately satisfy this dialectical relationship between democracy within civil society and economic inequality within the property system.

There is a parallel between Marshall's liberal theory of the hyphenated society and Habermas' critical analysis of the contradictions of the economy and civil society. Both social theorists regards citizenship in this context as highly problematic. The institutions of citizenship offer the possibility of a rational resolution of the problems of capitalism, but there is a fundamental incompatibility between the entitlements of democratic citizenship and the economic requirements of a modem society. This tension is also reflected in the relationship between entitlements and obligations. Both Marshall and Habermas have produced a theory, which also has a relationship to the fiscal sociology of Daniel Bell's analysis. *In The Cultural Contradictions of Capitalism,* Bell insists that, the problems of capitalism were centred in the revolutionary growth of entitlements and expectations against a background of significant political and economic constraints. The state within this fiscal sociology is forced to respond to the demand for greater entitlements which are an inevitable consequence of mass democracy, but the state has to respond to these needs within the global constraints of a modem world economy. We could argue that Marshall, Habermas and Bell, from very different political perspectives, have analysed citizenship in terms of these contradictory pressures within an hyphenated society, a set of constraints and contradictions which are not easily resolved. This somewhat pessimistic analysis of the capacity of citizenship to resolve the problems of capitalism has been further reflected in contemporary debate about the so-called dominant model of citizenship. In particular the decline of full employment as a normative objective of governments and the historical erosion of the organised working class in the advanced industrial societies have undermined the basic assumption of the Marshallian tradition, which was that fully employed men would provide the taxation basis, whereby the welfare state would be funded, in a context where married women stayed at home in order to service their men within a nuclear household. The decline of the nuclear family and the traditional household are thus intimately interrelated with the erosion of the urban working class and the political objective of a fully employed labour force. In short, the problem of modem citizenship lies at the very centre of the contemporary debate about how to manage an industrial capitalist system in the late twentieth-century within the context of a globalised economy and profound socio-political changes around individual status, the sovereignty of the nation-state and the continuity of the nuclear household.

These studies of citizenship in the contemporary period draw upon the legacy of Marshall's sociology, but they are forced to recognise fundamental problems and tensions in this legacy. The background assumption is that there are radically different traditions of citizenship in modem social theory, which reflect the profoundly different historical experiences and narratives of the evolution of citizenship in different socio-political contexts. As a consequence the reform of the Marshall legacy will have to take into account the fact that citizenship is not a unitary concept but reflects profound differences in the historical experience of political participation. We can identify three fundamentally different historical experiences of citizenship and distinguish broadly between three separate but obviously interrelated debates about its nature. Firstly, there is the tradition which is centred around the historical relationship between welfare and citizenship within the United Kingdom, and a debate which is focused primarily on the nature of social class. Secondly, there is a North American tradition about citizenship in relation to ethnicity, the core of which has been the relationship between ethnic groups, nationalism and the state. Thirdly, there is a European tradition which concerns the relationship between the state and the citizen. This European debate has focused on the problem of the relationship between the public and the private, or civil society and the individual.

The British model of citizenship has been dominated by a profound concern with the nature of social classes in capitalism. The Marshall view of citizenship saw the institutions of citizenship as a system which attempted to repair the character of liberal society by protecting individuals from the inequalities and vagaries of the market system. Although the development of liberalism had provided individuals with certain political securities, it had failed to address the negative impact of the market on democracy. The subsequent debate about citizenship within the context of British social theory has almost inevitably focused on the question of social class, citizenship and capitalism within the context of a broader concern with the political nature of reformism. This debate has as a result neglected the ethnic and cultural divisions within Britain, such as those, which exist between Scotland, England and Wales, because the focus of research has been primarily, or exclusively on the question of class analysis. Such an approach to citizenship has been easily integrated into the predominant concerns within British sociology between solidarity and schism, that is between the solidity brought about by normative institutions of citizenship and the schismatic impact of economic relationships.

There is a clear and obvious contrast therefore between the British debate and the American one. American citizenship was the product of a revolutionary struggle with the British imperial system in which questions of taxation and representation had become merged with nationalistic and bourgeois aspirations. Within this historical context the development of American democracy as Alexis de Tocqueville recognised was profoundly significant for political change not only in North America but in Europe. Within this Tocquevillian tradition, the revolutionary nature of American democracy lay in the general belief in the equality of human beings in social life. However, this commitment to a radical egalitarianism was, as a consequence of migration and ethnic diversity, challenged by the problem of racism. The civil war and its aftermath were profoundly important for the evolution of citizenship as a set of institutions and as an ideology within the American context. As a result, anxieties about ethnic diversity and pluralism have dominated not only the popular imagination but the scientific perspective of America as a radical society. The continuity of ethnic division, diversity and inequality thus remains a direct challenge to the civil religion of America which is based upon a revolutionary notion of human equality. The North American debate on citizenship has as a result of these historical developments been dominated by the question of an ethnic melting pot, political pluralism and social equality.

Finally, the continental European analysis of citizenship has also had its own specific features. Clearly the two major political events in the evolution of modem Europe prior to the twentieth century were the French Revolution of 1789 and the failure of the liberal bourgeois revolutions of 1848. These two revolutions had a direct impact on the politics and social structure of France and Germany which continue to shape political events in the late twentieth century. The French Revolution, the bourgeois revolutions of 1848 and the unification of Germany were developments which raised basic questions about the relationship between the individual and the state, and between the private sphere of the family and the public sphere of politics. In social historical studies of French and German society, there has been significant concern with the weakness of bourgeois or civil society in continental Europe especially in the case of Germany. A number of historical studies suggest that Germany had a unique social structure in which the land owning aristocracy (the Junkers) continued to dominate the political system, while the bourgeois capitalist class was evolving as an economically significant force with the industrialisation of the Rhine lands, leaving the urban proletariat as an essential weak and underrepresented social group. Caught between the confines of a traditional Junker class and an incoherent working class, the German middle classes developed a particular view which emulated the liberal tradition of Manchester economics and the culture of Paris. Out of this particular combination of relationships, there emerged the idea that the individual is made free by the intervention of the state. Thus the opposition between the state and the individual which was the hallmark of utilitarian liberalism was absent in the German context, where the individual required the protection of the state against the limitations of egotistical interests. In the development of sociological theory this idealistic theory of the state found an important part in the analysis of power within the work of writers such as Max Weber and Karl Schmidt. The educated German classes of the late nineteenth and early twentieth century saw working class democracy as a challenge to the entire leadership of the German nation while they remained profoundly ambiguous about the impact of Anglo-Saxon civilisation on Germanic culture. The consequence of this constellation of factors produced a negative and limited view of democracy, which in the work of Weber was expressed in the theory of plebiscitary democracy.

Any theory of citizenship which is concerned with the historical and comparative problems of the institutions of modem democracies must pay attention to these significant differences in culture and political experience. While we have identified these three distinctive tradition, they have all conceptualised the problems of citizenship within the confines of the city-state and nation-state. There has been an implicit equation between the idea of society and the nation-state which the very term citizenship reflects, namely that a citizen is the inhabitant of an autonomous city. The assumption has been that there is a consistently significant political context for citizenship, namely the organisations and cultures of separate nation states. This basic assumption in the analysis of citizenship has been challenged in contemporary sociological theory by the development of the idea of globalisation. Within the theory of the global system, it is assumed that economic trade, the development of cultural communication and the emergence of global military systems have undermined the sovereignty of the nation-states because within the new world system there are corporations as significant social agents which command greater power and authority than the traditional nation-state. These world changes have once more transformed the debate about citizenship. Modern issues in citizenship theory will increasingly embrace the problems of stateless persons, and refugees, where the question of human rights in relation to citizenship will become highly problematic. In addition, it is difficult to isolate or separate the debate about global responsibility from the ecological crisis, and the issue of animal rights in relation to human and social rights has become inextricably bound up the question of world citizenship and world politics.

The radical nature of citizenship in the context of the French Revolution and industrialization has therefore over a number of centuries been transformed into a radical question about the status of human beings as such in relation to the environment and animals.; there has been a greening of human right and citizenship. The concept of citizenship is enjoying something of a renaissance amongst political philosophers and welfare theorists. Market liberals, welfare pluralists, social democrats and neo-marxists have all laid their claims, and campaigns such as Charter 88, in England, have based their call for a 'Bill of Rights' and for democratic reforms on a reassertion of citizens' rights against the usurpation of power by an increasingly authoritarian state. Authors such as Melucci, Keane, Habermas, Cohen and Arato have become increasingly interested in the idea of 'public spaces' within civil society as locations for the 'democratisation of everyday life'. The idea of individuals forming themselves into voluntary public associations in a space between the state and the market and organising in non-traditional political forms to realise their interests, guaranteed by the 'rule of law' is seen as a basis for promoting active citizenship. In this context, writers like Gorz, Melucci, Tourraine and others, look to the practices of the 'New Social Movements' for progressive models of 'anti-political politics.'

Some authors most notably Keane, have faith in the 'best elements' of the liberal tradition to provide us with a foundation for a theory of citizenship, whilst others are happy to rework Herbert Marshall's classic views on welfare. A different approach is suggested here, however. If the concept of citizenship is to be of any use to progressive politics it must be taken out of its liberal history and inserted into a very different set of theorisations and political practices. Indeed, the liberal tradition of citizenship, resting on an abstract notion of rights and an appeal to universalism has ignored the reality of power. In this context, social relations of power are seen as taking historically varying forms, but most notably those associated with class, gender and race . These historically specific power relations have undermined attempts to realise the liberal ideal of citizenship through either the false collectivism of state welfare or the consumerist democracy of the market. Both these ways of attempting to meet citizenship rights have led to the marginalisation of those excluded from the collective nature of state welfare provision on the one hand, and of those unable to compete as market consumers on the other. Abstract conceptions of rights and entitlements attached to citizenship, then, must come to terms with the underlying structural power relations which underscore practices of both state and market mechanisms.

In addition, the political history of citizenship rights is inextricably linked to the history of Western European nationalism, which in turn must be situated in its world historical context. This history is one in which the consolidation of national states to which citizens belong and have claims against has to be understood in terms of an international division of labour, a particular world distribution of resources and the super exploitation of human labour and the environment by the capitalist core. Citizenship becomes not only a process of a struggle for rights and entitlements in Westem European nation states but also a struggle to reject claims of entitlement by those initially residing outside the core, and subsequently, of migrant and immigrant labour. The liberal history of citizenship, then must be viewed in the context of a set of inclusionary and exclusionary practices, aimed at consolidating a particular set of social relations and of rights and entitlements. A reappropriation of citizenship must not simply be tied to an abstract set of rights guaranteed by the rule of law , but address the deeper bases of social power. This does not entail an abandonment of the idea of social claims against the state, in fact just the opposite. It demands a reconceptualisation of citizenship based on the notion of need. A claim to entitlement abstracted into the form of rights can, however, be anchored in the concept of need. In this respect recent claims such as those by Harris that it is not possible to identify needs objectively, and more general claims that rights form the only universalisable basis for welfare, are not accepted here. Doyal and Gough have attempted a definition of need, which may address some of the problems raised by liberal theorists, and others, have implicitly argued for a universal basis of need in terms of potentiality

- the need of each individual for access to the conditions and resources necessary for a meaningful and creative life.

Equality, rather than citizenship is a core concern of contemporary sociology. Yet citizenship becomes an indirect interest because it connotes the spread of citizen rights designed to enlarge the realm of equality - political, economic, and social. Sociological writings have therefore dealt with citizenship by and large in terms of the spread of citizen rights and the barriers to the equality of rights. Citizenship is a central concept in the development of political democracy and the pursuit of political and social equality. However, citizenship rests on a balance of obligations and rights.

The imbalance in the sociological literature clearly reflects the relative priority on rights versus obligation in the political process of Western political democracies. The longterm trend has been to emphasize and elaborate citizen rights without simultaneously clarifying the issues of citizen obligation. The content of obligation becomes particularly important with the advent of advanced industrialism. The result has been a basic distortion or at least pervasive omission in the sociology of citizenship. It is inescapable that citizenship involves some sort of balance or interplay between rights and obligations. It is impossible to study a polity, especially a democratic polity without assessing the significance of citizen obligation. Our approach seeks to redress this imbalance in the sociology of citizenship.

Clearly the notion of citizenship requires continual conceptual, philosophical, and value clarification. However, it is an institutional analysis of the arrangements of an advanced industrial society which are directly related to the exercise of citizenship. Are the societal institutions organized and articulated so as to make the practice of citizen duties and obligation possible? In particular, do they operate to help or to hinder the exercise of obligation?

A dynamic concept of citizenship must be taken out of its liberal history and rethought. The nationalistic context in which it has evolved is one associated with a set of inclusionary and exclusionary practices based on a variety of forms of social power. Citizenship has not been realised for excluded groups either through the false collectivism of social democratic welfare, or through the consumerist democracy of the market.

The state/market dichotomy is in fact a false one. Neither exist as autonomous spheres but exist only as organisational principles within the totality of social relations. These social relations must be situated in the context of underlying power based not only on class but on race and gender as well. These power relations structure the spaces of the market and the state and thus limit the extent to which either can fulfil the ideal of citizenship. It is not, then, simply to a set of legal reforms based on universalistic concept of rights that we should look in order to promote citizenship, but to a dynamic concept of need.

Fifty years ago, in January of 1950, India was proclaimed a constitutional Republic. With this proclamation, a decision was made regarding India's domestic form of government—a decision which to most people seemed unequivocal. In common parlance, the term republic tends to signify an orderly non-monarchical regime anchored in popularly elected institutions; to this extent, the term shads over into, and is often used interchangeably with, democracy or democratic regime. History provides prominent examples of republican forms of government: from the Roman republic of Florence to successive French republics. No doubt, the framers of the Indian constitution relied on these and similar precedents in choosing the label of the new Indian regime, assuming it to be non-controversial. Many would surely have been surprised to learn that, far from being univocal, the term is constestible and, fifty years later, would find itself embroiled in intense controversy.

A first glimpse of the dispute can be garnered from a glance at the etymology of these terms. As is well known, the English labels derive from the Latin "res publica" meaning the public weal or common wealth. Etymologically, the labels thus establish a demarcation—no matter how porous or tenuous—from the domain of non-public or private life, the later including both the domestic household and private economic or business activities. Matters remain relatively unproblematical as long as private and public domains exist peacefully side by side and do not radically challenge or contest each other. Such constestation, however, arose with the ascent of modern capitalism and its focus on private economic initiative as the central engine of social life—progressively marginalizing the common or public weal. In tandem with the development of market forces, modern liberalism emerged as a political theory celebrating the benefits of individual economic and civil liberties while relegating government to a minimal role as guardian of private property. What is called liberal democracy –in contrast with other forms of democracy—usually designates a kind of regime in which people invest their primary energies in the goal of maximizing their private utilities while paying scant attention to, and perhaps even being apathetic toward the public-political domain. The past fifty years have given a major boost to this system of priorities. With the dismantling of the Soviet Union and the near vanishing of socialist regimes, liberal democracy has achieved nearly global acclaim and predominace. It is against this background that one has to see the contemporary dispute about republicanism.

The resurgence of the public domain, the hence the republican idea in recent times is due to a number of prominent interventions by leading intellectuals and political theorists. In the American context, major credit must be given to Hannah Arendt's *The Human Condition,* a text eloquently portraying the decline of the public domain and public life under the steady pressure of economic-industrial forces and private interests. Arendt's intervention was ably seconded and amplified shortly afterwards by Jurgen Habermas's book *The Structural Transformation of Public sphere* which depicted the progressive retreat and evisceration of public discourse due to the combined impact of industrial managerialism and media manipulation of public opinion.

Since at least the seventeenth century, the discourse of rights has figured prominently in political debate, especially in the English-speaking parts of the world. It is no surprise, then, to find individuals and groups of almost every persuasion stating their cases nowadays in terms of rights. What is surprising is the growing reaction against these ubiquitous appeals to rights. Although few want to deny the importance of individual rights, many political theorists have recently complained that their importance has been greatly overemphasized. The result, as they see it, is an excessive individualism that blinds people to the needs of the community or state to which they belong. We should be less concerned with our rights, in their view, and more concerned with our responsibilities.

This reaction grows out of three different complaints about the superabundance of appeals to rights. If "rights are political trumps," as Ronald Dworkin has said, then it is easy to see how a situation in which everyone is trying to play a trump card is likely to end in deadlock. A related complaints is that the concept of rights is too one-sided and individualistic. We set ourselves apart from others. The appeal to rights encourages us to think of ourselves as apart from a society , state, or government that is constantly seeking to intrude upon or invade our rights. Third complaint is that the ceaseless clamoring for a right to this and a right to that will inevitably weaken all appeals to rights. A kind of conceptual inflation is at work, in other words.

Those who advance this view typically argue against liberalism. This is not a healthy situation. If we are to overcome it, we must find some way to restore a sense of common purpose to civic life. The task is to find a way of strengthening the appeal of duty, community, and related concepts while preserving the appeal of rights. This is what the recent the ries of communitarians have sought to do, by revival of the classical republican or civic humanist tradition. A team of distinguished scholars address issues in contemporary debate over liberalism, communitarianism, civic humanism, citizenship, and democracy. Finding the proper relationship between rights and responsibilities requires us not to choose between liberalism and republicanism, they argue, but to unite them in a republican form of liberalism.

In the confines of professional political theory in America, the resurgence of republicanism is crucially indebted John Pocock's *The Machiavellian Moment,* subtitled *Florentine Political Thought and the Atlantic Republican Tradition.* While acknowledging the growing predominance of liberal democracy, Pocock's book drew attention to an alternative tradition of modern political thought which in many ways challenged or contested Locke's liberal individualism: the tradition of civic republicanism or civic humanism tracing its lineage back to Niccolo Machiavelli and, in Britain, to James Harrington and English country writers. In contrast to the minimalist politics favored by Lockean liberals, republicanism extolled citizen participation in politics and the cultivation of shared public responsibility. Pocock's initiative was backed up at the same time by the work of noted American historians, above all by Gordon Wood whose *The Creation of the American Republic* traced and documented republican influences on the American founding fathers.

In the ensuing dispute about republicanism, the role of political theorists proved to be more significant than that of historians: while the latter focused, and soon got bogged down in retrospective reappraisals of the American revolutionary period, political theorists were more inclined to carry the issue forward into the brewing debate about contemporary liberal democracy. Broadly speaking, one can say that during the last two decades of the twentieth century, republicanism as a theme became entangled and soon formed part and parcel of a broader theoretical controversy waged under the labels liberalism versus communitariansim. While liberals in that contest are usually identified with the legacy stretching from Locke to John Stuart Mill and John Rawls, the label communitarian tends to embrace a broad spectrum ranging from classical Aristotelians and defenders of Rousseau and Hegel all the way to latter-day socialists. Civic republicanism fits awkwardly into this broader discussion—notwithstanding attempts to subsume it under the communitarian label. Despite points of contact, there are several obvious differences. First of all, not all so-called communitarians are democratic republicans. Next and perhaps more importantly, not all communitarians are willing to endorse a differentiated balance between public and private domains, granting due respect to the pursuit of private interests within a framework of public goods –as most republicans are wont to do.

In his recent important book *Between Facts and Norms,* Jurgen Habermas has provided an insightful definition of republicanism and also a useful summary of the main points dividing republicanism from liberalism—as well as from democratic proceduralism. In his succinct formulation, the republican conception of politics refers primarily not to rights of life, liberty, and property that are possessed by private citizens and guaranteed by the state, but preeminently to the practice of self-determination on the part of enfranchised citizens who are oriented to the common good and understand themselves as free and equal members of a cooperative, self-governing community. This republican conception has important consequences for the meaning of democracy and for the relationship between state and society. From the perspective of mainstream liberalism, democracy involves basically the task of programming the government in the interest of society, where government denotes an apparatus of public administration and a system of market and labor relations among private persons. Politics on these premises basically has the function of interest-articulation and interest-aggregation, that is, of clustering together and pushing through private interest against an administration specialized in the employment of political power for collective goals. This view contrasts sharply with republicanism which accords with classical teachings, treats politics as a reflexive form of substantial ethical life, that is, the medium in which individuals become aware of their dependence on one another and, accordingly, shape and develop existing relations of reciprocal recognition into an association of free and equal citizens. From the republican angle, the state-society nexus is radically transformed, in the sense that citizenship and civic solidarity emerge as the connecting link between and even as the architectonic pillar integrating state, bureaucracy and market structures. In Habermas's words: "In the republican conception, the political public sphere acquires, along with its base in civil society, a strategic significance; it should secure the autonomy and intergrating force of the citizens' communicative pratices."

Turning to more specific issues, Habermas singles out four major points of contention between liberals and republicans: the meaning of citizenship; the role of law and legality; the nature of democratic politics, and the function of legitimating procedures. Regarding the first issue, liberals tend to define citizenship primarily in terms of negative rights against the state and other citizens; as rights-bearers, individuals enjoy a broad range of freedom as long as they pursue their private interests within the boundaries set by legal statutes – with political rights simply functioning as a protective shield for the secure pursuit of these interests. Under republican auspices, by contrast, citizenship involves basically the exercise of positive rights and liberties which, instead of preventing external compulsion, guarantee the chance of participating in a common practice through which citizens can first make themselves into what they can be: politically autonomous authors of a community of free and equal persons. For republicans, hence government is not just an appendix of private or pre-political preferences but rather an agency designed to insure public liberty and the civic practice of self-determination. This conflict spills over into the second issue: the role of law and legality. Whereas, in the liberal view, law or the legal order is basically derivative from the aggregation of pre-political, individual rights, republicans tend to regard privately-held or subjective rights as corollaries of an objective or publicly sanctioned legal order that enables and guarantees the integrity of an autonomous life based on mutual respect. In its most adequate normative formulation, republicanism places the integrity of the individual and his liberties on a par with the integrity of the community of free and equal citizens.

In a particularly salient manner, the contrast between liberals and republicans surfaces in their respective conceptions of the nature of politics in a modern democratic context. Politics under liberal auspices is basically a struggle among competing forms of self-interest or group-interest, which ultimately boils down to a struggle for power. Conceptualized as a process of opinion and will-formation, politics here designates the clash of competing strategies pursued by actors or acting groups with the aim of securing positions of dominance. Political success, in liberals terms, is measured by citizens approval quantified as votes, with voting decisions having ultimately the same structure as acts of choice made by market participants. From a republican perspective, on the contrary, politics—both in the public sphere and in parliament—is patterned not on market exchanges but responsive to the demands of public communication oriented to mutual understanding. As a practice of civic self-legislation in the public sphere, Habermas comments, politics for republicans finds its paradigm not in the market but in dialogue. In practical-political terms, this means that public policies pursued by government should be shaped and informed by the continuing public discourse of citizens; the latter, in effect, should be binding on the exercise of public authority—which has implications for the fourth issue of legitimacy. Whereas, in the liberal model, public power is ultimately the result of the utility maximization of competing actors, republicanism has confidence in the capacity of public discourses to yield reasonable outcomes. While patterned on liberal market principles, politics tends to lose "all reference to the normative core of a public use of practical reason," republicans stress the importance of the public sphere as a forum where citizens are able to discuss value orientations and interpretations of needs and wants, including their prepolitical self-understandings and worldviews, and then to change these in an insightful way.

In *Between Facts and Norms,* Habermas does not fully endorse the republican view of politics and democracy. Perhaps assimilating republicanism too closely to the communitarian paradigm, his text prefers to steer a course somewhere between the competing alternatives, along the lines of a procedural or deliberative model of democracy. This is not the place to sort out the complexities of the Habermasian position, not to reach a conclusive settlement of the debate between liberalism and republicanism. Such a settlement—based on a careful weighing of the respective merits and demerits—must ultimately be the task of informed citizens in modern democracies or republics. This task is particularly urgent in a country like India. Fifty years after the establishment of the Republic of India, it surely demands from her citizens to ponder diligently the meaning of republican government and republican politics. This is emphatically true at the time when, under the aegis of economic liberalization programs, the liberal model of politics exerts an increasingly pervasive influence on all levels of Indian social and political life. As it happens, this influence is accompanied today by a pressure coming from an entirely different source: the pressure of a narrowly construed and homogenizing communitarianism. In this situation, it is imperative for Indians to reflect on the meaning and long-range trajectory of the Indian republic which was inaugurated and achieved under such difficult domestic and international conditions by its founders fifty years ago.

Is a marriage of republicanism and liberalism possible? Is it desirable? Has republicanism the necessary cultural and philosophical resources to enable people with conflicting interests and differing faiths to live together in multicultural societies? This book demonstrates how republican liberalism proceeds from a fundamental right of autonomy to the recognition of interdependence and reciprocity, and on to the cultivation of the civic virtues of the public-spirited citizens. Indeed, republican liberalism promises not only to reconcile individual rights and civic duties, but to enhance political deliberation and the sense of community as well. Liberals and communitarians have long criticized each other, but here is a preparative that invites them to listen to one another and enter into a discourse ethics.

2

Rise of Citizenship

The city-states of ancient Greece and medieval Germany and Italy, the chartered and free cities of medieval England and Germany were inhabited by men whose social, financial, professional or trading stature placed them in the class of citizen. The very etymology of the word reveals its association with a city – in English, in French (*citoyen*), in Italian (*cittadino*), in German (*Burger*), for example. A medieval city had its own law and court in the operation of which the citizens participated.

In the nineteenth century the town or city was fully understood to be the cradle of citizenship. Referring to the typical New England township, Tocqueville explained that it was in this local context that the citizen learns to rule society and in the end accumulates clear, practical ideas about the nature of his duties and the extent of his rights. This is an echo here of Aristotle's famous definition of the nature of citizenship in the city-state as 'ruling and being ruled in turn'.

John Stuart Mill, in his *Representative Government,* showed himself to be at one with his French friend. Victorian England in fact provides us with a splendid example of the active municipal citizenship. The growth of industrial cities and the reform of local government led to an extraordinary burgeoning of citizenship at this level. We can cite the extension of the municipal franchise and at least partly as a consequence of this, a devotion to the creation of civic facilities and the flowering of municipal identity and pride. In 1868 the Municipal Franchise Act enfranchised a larger number of men and even some women. As a result, the electorates of Birmingham and Leeds increased to nearly one-fifth of their populations, compared with a figure of about half that for national elections following the Second Reform Act of the preceding year. Birmingham, especially, wonderfully exemplified this style of municipal citizenship. Two men laid respectively the ideological and practical foundation for that city's self-identity and self-esteem. The Baptist minister George Dawson expounded his concept of the municipal or civic gospel. Modeling his combined religious and political zeal on the creed of Mazzini, that arch-exponent of this mode of exultant thinking Dawson preached a kind of republican civic virtue suited to the municipal layer of multiple citizenship: 'a town is a solemn organism', he declared. At the same time, Joseph Chamberlain, mayor from 1873 to 1876, ensured that Birmingham's claim to be the best-governed city in the world was an expression of pride with much validity.

The emasculation of local government by the centralizing policies of the Thatcherite regime of the 1980s accelerated the decline of the municipal values of the high Victorian era. In other countries, however, municipal citizenship remains a vital bottom level in the layered civic system. Some of the cities and township of the USA and the communes of France are obvious examples.

We need to imagine a ziggurat. Layers of citizenship are built up starting with a broad foundation stratum of numerous municipalities. On to that layer is constructed a much smaller number of states or regions. Atop that level is the single State, except in the case of the European Union, where the several States are capped by the Union. Each stratum has its own kind of citizenship.

The idea of cosmopolis

World citizenship is undefinable in theory, non-existent in practice and would be undesirable in any case. Why, then, devote topic to the syllabus? For three reasons. First, the idea that an individual can be a world citizen, or cosmopolite, has survived for two and a half millennia, and is worthy of investigation if only for its staying power. Secondly, the tripartite case against the notion is sufficiently cogent to invite examination in order to test its validity. And thirdly, the positive case is justified on a number of grounds, which are becoming increasingly recognized.

Dominant ideas and practices of the *polis,* Republic and Empire in Graeco-Raoman life and thinking, provided room to contemplate the conception of the oneness of mankind and the existence of a universal Natural Law. This was moral tenet propounded by the Greek and Roman Stoic philosophers in the ancient world, and was later adopted by the Neostoics of the Renaissance. The most famous exponent was the second-century philosopher-emperor Marcus Aurelius. In one of his characteristic syllogisms he demonstrated the existence of Natural law and its connection with the idea of world citizenship.

Eighteenth-century writers and intellectuals – the likes of Voltaire, Franklin and Paine – were proud to own the title of 'world citizen'. Schiller created the character of the Marquis Posa to epitomize this frame of mind, and in this play, the King, repenting Posa's death, declares that, 'He lived to serve the world, and humankind'. Meanwhile, more prosaically, Schiller's German contemporary Kant proposed the principle of a cosmopolitan law.

In the twentieth century the conviction that responsible, thinking people should cultivate a cosmopolitan mentality has been reinvigorated by the horrific tragedies of the World Wars and the grim threats of nuclear and environmental catastrophe. It has been argued that the regime of nation-states has brought humanity to this pass. They moral principle of citizenly allegiance to the state how be complemented, even superseded, by a consciousness of the responsibilities and obligation of world citizenship.

It is quite evident that the term 'citizenship' in the cosmopolitan sense has been used in a way quite lacking the legal and political exactness of the term when used to describe the status of a person in relation to the state. In fact, if we give full recognition to developments in the twentieth century, it is possible to describe a spectrum of meanings shading from the vague to those of some precision. Starting at the vague end, people who have a feeling of identity with the whole of humanity are accorded the title of 'world citizen'. Slightly less vague is the world citizen's acceptance of the moral precept that the individual has some responsibility for the condition of the planet and the rest of its inhabitants, certainly the human ones, even the nonhuman. Finally, the world citizens who live most precisely up to that title are the ones who believe in the need for supra-national political authority and action, and, the most committed, who involve themselves in some activity of this kind.

The conventions of international law and state sovereignty, it is true, supply robust underpinning for the traditional unidemensional concept of citizenship; yet both are flexing beneath the intricate realities of a world being transformed for the twenty-first century.

Legal definitions

Where better to start an answer to our question than with law? It provides an authoritative framework; and it demonstrates the extraordinary confusion that is typical of the whole subject of citizenship. At least we can establish three basic points. First, international law recognizes that each state has the right to define who are or are not permitted to be its citizens. Secondly, legal definitions conflate citizenship and nationality (in the political, of course, not the cultural sense). And thirdly, there are two methods of defining nationality/citizenship, namely, *jus sanguinis zand jus soli*. *Jus sanguinis* means citizenship by inheritance: at birth one acquires the citizenship of one's parents. *Jus soli* means citizenship by state territory: at birth one acquires the citizenship of the land where one is born.

These alternative modes of defining a person's citizenship may appear at first sight both commonsensical and simple; in practice, however, they are not as simple as they seem. *Jus sanguinis* raises several practical questions - what to do about children of mixed marriages, for example. *Jus soli* also raises various detailed questions. For instance, Argentina felt compelled at one time to specify that this rule covered birth in a legation or on a warship or in an international zone under the Argentine flag! Indeed, when one examines the regulations now in use, it is clear that most states, in order to cope with the practical complexities, operate a combination of the two modes. Having adopted such a policy, indeed, some states interpret their own guidelines with such wide discretion as to render easy generalizations rather difficult. The pattern for the USA, Canada, the UK, France and the FRG, is very interesting.

There can be few states with citizenship/nationality laws quite as complex as the United Kingdom's. Indeed, one eminent British lawyer has suggested that many of the provisions of the British Nationality Act of 1981 'are so obscurely drafted that they are unfit to be in the statute book'. The legislation is the combined muddled outcome of, initially, a history of confused British imperialism and, then, concern about a too numerous immigration of coloured people as being productive of racial tension. The 1981 Act defines five categories in the following order: British citizens, British dependent territories citizens, British overseas citizens, British subjects and British protected persons. The first of these alone carries the right of abode in the UK and full civic rights. The four other categories carry very limited rights, decreasing as we move down the list. The production of a graded classification of this kind inevitably raises the question of the worth of the oft-repeated statement that the essence of citizenship lies in the principle of equality.

Equality or elitism?

The principle of equality cannot, in truth, be discounted in any consideration of the nature of citizenship. What we must grasp, however, is that beneath this ideal lies a tangle of reservations and contradictions. It is our task here to try to unravel these complications in order to discover how far in theory and in practice the basic proposition that equality is the very essence of citizenship can be held to be valid.

A fundamental cause of these complications is the wide variety of meanings attached to the word 'equality' that are pertinent to the study of citizenship. Because of its relevance in so many different ways, it is scarcely surprising that equality has been perceived as a powerful characteristic of citizenship. By taking two great defining periods of citizenship, namely fourth-century BC Athens and the late eighteenth-century North Atlantic world, we can easily recognize the strength of the equality principle. In the first era, the constitutional mechanism depended ideally, to repeat the words of Aristotle, on citizens being 'all who share in the civic life of ruling and being ruled in turn', a system in which citizens are 'equals and peers'. In the second era, the assertion of civic equality derived from the ethical principle that all men are created and remain morally equals. It was a proposition which the American Founding Fathers considered to be too 'self-evident' to explain. And if individuals as human beings are by nature equal, then a political system that enshrines inequality is *ipsofacto* unjust. (We may note in passing that the language and ideas of that age are replicated in the present-day Universal Declaration of Human Rights.)

After all, consider the alternatives: a hierarchical society of vassal and lord or of subject and monarch with an intervening aristocracy. These arrangements are ultimately based on the exercise of force from above, not on the will of the people below. In the monarchical age of the eighteenth century the question arose: How could a revolutionary change from royal power to popular will be justified? It was this shift in the basis of authority, the locus of sovereignty indeed, that the political thinkers who set the scene for the American and French Revolutions strove to achieve. And they secured the change through the device of a 'virtual' contract. Rousseau, to take a notable example, was utterly convinced that the concept of the social contract led inexorably to the principle of the equality of citizens.

> Whichever way we look [he wrote], we always return to the same conclusion: namely that the social pact establishes equality among the citizens in that they all pledge themselves under the same conditions and must all enjoy the same rights. Hence by the nature of the compact, every act of sovereignty binds or favours all the citizens equally.

The men of the eighteenth century also spoke in the same breath of freedom or liberty. Without examining here the very real problems of connecting equality with freedom, there can be no doubt that the two are intimately related in the notion of citizenship. Citizenship, equality and freedom were certainly intertwined in Athens in its democratic age. Equality involved not only the obvious rights of voting and holding public office; it also meant the freedom to speak one's mind in the Assembly. Moreover, in the modern world, do we not, in English, use the word 'enfranchise' - make free - for the process of equalizing citizens by conferment of the right to vote? Even more crucially, what price freedom if citizens do not enjoy equality before the law?

There is, finally, the root need for the principle of equality: that is, to sustain the quality and harmony of life in the polity. The operation of a society of citizens relies on their co-operation at least, their altruism and civic conscience at best. This frame of mind needs, above all, fairness, and people are treated fairly if they are treated with at least a rough measure of equality. Discrimination, abuse of power, grossly unjust distribution of wealth and resources corrode equality and destroy any atmosphere of fairness, with the result that the virtues of citizenship are soured into apathy and alienation. Such a deleterious outcome may affect minority groups as well as individuals. Members of ethnic or religious minorities can feel that they are truly citizens only if they perceive an underlying fairness in the social, legal and political systems.

The extension of the status of citizenship from the eighteenth century has indubitably involved a process of mass equalization, however unfinished that process might be. A greater proportion of the world's population now - and especially since 1990 - are treated equally before the law, have rights to participate fully in the political arena and enjoy a modicum of state-provided welfare. In so far as there are blatant denials of these rights of citizenship, they are cause for frequent adverse comment as violating the principle of civic equality.

On the other hand, equal access to and enjoyment of the rights of citizenship have not always been acclaimed as desirable ideals. Let us look at three different kinds of argument: against equality as a delusion; against equality of access to the status; and against equality within the body of the citizenry.

The case against equality as a delusion, our first argument, was famously expounded by Marx in 1843 in his essay 'On the Jewish Question. Modern middle-class man, he argued, has a dual identity. He is simultaneously a citizen and a bourgeois. As a citizen he is equal with others in the state and is endowed with rights attendant upon that status; as a bourgeois he pursues his selfish interests through the market mechanisms of civil society. Living in the bourgeois mode, individuals are anything but equal; yet this is the reality of life in a capitalist society. Living in the citizenry mode, individuals are legally equal; yet this is a spurious equality.

The second case is the reluctance to give equal opportunities for acquiring the title of citizen. For long in the classical world citizenship was a status to be coveted, a privilege to be prized, therefore the possession of a worthy elite. In Greece it was commonly confined to property owners. The Romans, differing markedly from the Athenians, steadily opened the ranks of citizenship to an ever-widening number until, in the early third century AD, the title was available promiscuously to virtually all free men. But even a century before this, Tacitus tartly contrasted the current policy with that, 'Long ago, when the grant was rare and only made as a reward of valour' if the honour was so diluted, it was meaningless. For those who had earned it, its dilution was an insult.

In our contemporary world, we see the concern about and the effects of the watering-down of the status of citizenship in ways typical of modern times. Resistance to a too inclusive policy of naturalization is most often the result of a desire for a country to retain its national-cultural homogeneity. As a consequence, perhaps millions of would-be citizens are denied that status in the country of their choice. The mirror-image of this situation is most evident in the USA. Many immigrants see little point in becoming citizens because successive laws have steadily reduced the distinction between citizens and non-citizens in terms of rights. Benevolent legislation has thus severely weakened the incentive for naturalization. Many thousands of pregnant Mexican women cross the border illegally each year, presumably motivated in part by the desire to confer American citizenship upon the newborn children by the simple expedient of bearing them on American soil.

And so, to our third argument: the felt need to 'grade' those who already have the legal status of citizen. There have been persistent attempts throughout history to retain an elitist quality for political citizenship by the device of ensuring that, while all citizens are equal, some are more equal than others. In the ancient world, as Rome extended her sway in Italy, but reluctant to concede full citizenship to the incorporated peoples, she invented *civitas sine suffragio*. By this device individuals had citizenship without the franchise, legal but not political citizenship. In modern times, the suffrage has in many countries been conceded with slow reluctance. In Britain, for example, it took six Acts of Parliament (1832, 1867, 1884, 1918, 1928, 1969) before all adults aged 18 or over were eligible for the vote.

Perhaps the most tense and detailed debates over the very concept of equality of political rights took place at the time of the drafting of the French Constitution which came into operation in 1791. It fell to the Abbe Sieyes to protect the state from the 'undesirable' effects of the proclaimed Revolutionary objective of equality. By introducing a modest wealth qualification for the franchise he divided the body of citizens into 'active' and 'passive', barring the latter from the right to vote. He justified the distinction by asserting that

> there are men who may be perfectly sound in the physical sense, but to whom all social ideas are remote, and who are hence not in a position to take an active part in the public weal. They should not be personally discriminated against: but who would dare to consider it wrong that they should be excluded to some extent, not, it must be repeated, from legal protection and public aid, but from the exercise of political rights?

Sieyes's criterion of exclusion was indeed relatively humane compared with the 'second-class citizenship' - for this was the origin of the term - of American black people. Moreover, their inferior status extended beyond the political into the civil realm of citizenship. The contradiction of the equality principle, enshrined though it was in the Declaration of Independence, has never been more blatant. For three generations after this seemingly unambiguous statement - until Emancipation in 1863 - millions of Americans were not only non-citizens, they were not even free. And even the post-bellum Fourteenth and Fifteenth Amendments to the Constitution, which provided for equal civil and political rights irrespective of race or colour, were no guarantee against widespread discrimination and physical assault. The black men may then have been, m the words of Senator Sumner, 'Clad in the full panoply of citizenship', but the bitterly hostile whites in the Deep South tore that panoply from him with impunity for a century thereafter.

We may additionally note that Native Americans, subjected to a policy of virtual genocide in the nineteenth century, could scarcely be counted among the ranks of American citizens. Indeed, not until 1924 were they accorded automatic citizenship at birth.

So, does citizenship live up to its vaunted reputation as incorporating the principle of equality? As a concept and arrangement for relating the individual to the law, politics and social structure, there is no room for doubt that citizenship is more equitable than other socio-political relationships devised for large human groupings. What we must be on guard against deriving from this judgement is that citizenship has been or is ever likely to be enjoyed to the level of perfection that an ideal model might suggest. In practice, we should envisage a hierarchy of expressions or experiences of citizenship which blurs any pure equality.

At the top of the ladder are the full and also active citizens, those, depending on the society we are examining, who have the most complete set of rights and who most fully discharge their civic duties. It is important not to forget the second element in this definition: if equality is good for rights it must also hold good for responsibilities. On the second rung down are the full but passive citizens, where we are using 'passive' not in Sieyes's sense, but in the sense of being apathetic about performing duties. Thirdly, there are the second-class citizens. These are the individuals who have the legal status of citizen but, because of discrimination, are denied full rights in practice. For the fourth level we may use the term 'underclass', which became fashionable in the 1980s. These people have the legal standing of citizens, but are so economically and culturally impoverished that they are in effect excluded from the normal style of social and political activity which the term citizen connotes. Fifthly, there are residents, sometimes referred to by the recently revived word 'denizens'. These are persons who are not nationals of the state in which they live; they are therefore not legally citizens and have no political rights, but nevertheless enjoy many civil, social and economic rights associated with citizenship.

Multiple Citizenship

The assumption that citizenship is a singular, bilateral relationship between the individual and the state is deeply embedded in our historical imagination and understanding of the concept. It is a model common to both classical Greek and modern nationalist thinking on the subject. The polis and the nation-state respectively do not completely satisfy the individual's requirement for a political identity. There are always have been complications. And unless we accept the validity of a more capacious and flexible definition of citizenship, we shall be denying the evidence of its history, constricting its theoretical investigation and inhibiting its practical development. For, although the idea of a singular mode of citizenship is useful within its own confines it cannot today be properly construed without the supplementary idea of multiple citizenship.

A brief explanation of what we mean by 'multiple citizenship' will reveal just how pervasive are its various watars. We need initially, by the use of two metaphors, to distinguish between citizenships which coexist in parallel and those which may be described as functioning in layers.

The first is simply stated: parallel citizenship exists in two forms. It is the condition enjoyed by some individuals of simultaneous citizenship or nationality of two different states; it may also be used to describe the relationship between membership of a state and membership of civil society.

The existence of the status of citizenship is more complex. We may identify four main kinds. The most obvious instance is the double level of citizenship operating in a federal constitution, so that individuals are citizens of their component state, in with a lower-case 's' at the lower level, and of the overarching State with a capital's is at the higher. The third instance of layered citizenship recognizes the citizens' additional relationship at the sub-State level, that is, to their town or city. Let us call this municipal citizenship. And, finally, we must cap our layers with the concept of world citizenship at the supra-State level.

The reader may feel disposed to object to the inclusion of the civil society, devolutionary, municipal and world categories as strictly not being forms of citizenship at all.

A brief conspectus of the categories will be useful here. Dual citizenship arose, even as early as classical times, because of the mobility of individuals, the need to take legal cognizance of multiple identities and, in the case of Rome, the mutual interests of provincial notables and the Roman imperium. Federal systems and quasi-federal systems are political arrangements for coping with the requirements of government in States of more than traditional size or complexity. The municipal and civil society styles of citizenship have derived from pre-nation-state forms of administration and bonding, it is increasingly recognized that sub-State citizenship, particularly of the civil society variety, has a vital role to play in preventing or undermining the totalitarian subjection of the individual and thus undermining healthy citizenship at the State level itself. Finally, the concept of world citizenship, almost as venerable as that of State citizenship, has persisted because of the consciousness that humankind is one, inhabiting one planet. Multiple citizenship is therefore a reality.

Parallel citizenship

Let us start with the parallel forms of multiple citizenship. These differ markedly from each other. The one is fully and internationally defined in law; the other might be rated as unworthy of the term citizenship at all. First then, dual citizenship, the least important of the several forms of multiple citizenship because it involves the smallest number of people. None the less, it does raise interesting questions.

During the century from 50 BC the matter of dual citizenship became a live legal and political issue in Rome and its provinces. As Rome expanded its authority throughout the Mediterranean basin she extended the coveted title of Roman citizen with some generosity. But did this, should this conferment of Roman rights involve the enfranchised man in return renouncing his native civic rights?

A famous test case occurred in 56 BC. Cicero denied the possibility of Cornelius Balbus retaining his status as a citizen of Gades after his enfranchisement by Pompey as a citizen of Rome. The principles of residence and allegiance, key elements in the status of citizenship, could not be shared. In expounding his position with characteristic forensic logic, Cicero nevertheless revealed that Roman practice was not as clear-cut as Roman law, and that, in any case, Roman law was out of line with the laws and practices of neighbouring cities.

By 50 BC distinguished persons were openly flouting this incompatibility rule, especially in Italy; by AD 50 dual citizenship was being widely practiced. The best-known assertion of dual citizenship is the response by St Paul on the occasion of his arrest (AD 58). While demanding the judicial rights of his Roman citizenship, he yet proudly proclaimed himself 'a Jew of Tarsus, a city in Cilicia, a citizen of no mean city'.

The question of dual citizenship under the late Roman Republic and early Empire was exceedingly complex. Moreover, we should not be deterred by the simple, strict Ciceronic legal argument of incompatibility from understanding the positive political usefulness of the device. The conferment of citizenship on an alien can be used as a mark of honour; it can be used as a means of cementing the allegiance of aliens to their state of residence; and it can be used to avoid making awkward choices as to which citizenship persons should opt for when the circumstances of their political environment alter. Indeed, although some states pereclude the arrangement, it is not uncommon for individuals to acquire this double status – by conferment; by virtue of being born of parents of one nationality on the territory of a different nation; by the attribution at birth of the nationality of both parents in a mixed marriage; or by naturalization in a second state while retaining their original citizenship.

The political reality and utility of dual citizenship must not, however, tempt us to close our minds to continuing practical difficulties. International lawyers have been forced to frame rules for coping with these, for multiple nationality, the usual term in international jurisprudence is, in fact, a legal inconvenience. What happens if an individual seeks diplomatic protection from a state of which he is also a citizen? And if state A require the individual for military service when he is resident in state B, which has no such requirement, how is the matter to be resolved?

The Hague Convention of 1930 set out some guidelines. Two are of particular importance. One is that 'A State may not afford diplomatic protection to one of its nationals against a State whose nationality such person also possesses'. The second is the principle of 'effective nationality': the citizenship status of the person's usual state of residence takes precedence over any others. Statesmen have also been reluctant to concede the principle in modern times because, by bifurcation, dual citizenship throws in doubt the loyalty of the person with twin identities.

Reality, however, has supervened. Because of the waves of migration in recent years the numbers of persons with dual citizenship have increased, the policies of states, even so, varying quite considerably Historical experience goes a long way to explain this divergence. Thus states with traditions of mass immigration (e.g. USA, Canada) or with considerable post-colonial contacts (e.g. UK, France) tend to be relaxed and tolerant on the matter. For example, it is estimated that by the 1980s, there were in France over one million Franco-Algerians of dual nationality. In contrast, those European countries which either do not have this historical background and/

or have been wrestling with the complication of the status of guest-workers (e.g. Germany, Austria, Belgium, Switzerland) are more resistant to the practice of dual citizenship

The whole discussion thus far has related to the dual civic status of a relatively limited number of geographically scattered individuals. There is no reason, however, why this device should not be used with whole populations. True, the modern tendency to fuse citizenship with ethnic and cultural nationality raises virtually insuperable obstacle.

Even so , there is one obvious example, namely, the convenient fudging of the civic status of Irish people after the creation of the Irish Free State in 1922. The treaty referred to 'the common citizenship of Ireland and Great Britain'. This position obtained until 1935, though from that date until 1948 Irish citizens remained also Commonwealth citizens, admittedly an extraordinarily vague concept. This status was, in turn, removed with the establishment of the Irish Republic and its withdrawal from the Commonwealth. Yet the Irish still retained a form of dual citizenship. In that same year, 1948, the British Nationality Act granted Irish citizens the privileges of British citizenship. Accordingly, today an Irish citizen resident in the United Kingdom can exercise three sets of citizenship rights (such as voting) – Irish, British and European. This last category takes us on from multiple citizenship in its parallel form into the layered style.

Civil society, unlike dual citizenship, is disputed as a form of citizenship in any proper sense of the term. Its claims are none the less sufficiently compelling to justify consideration. Civil society can be interpreted as performing a civic function through its myriad voluntary groupings, organizations, associations, and networks, the members of which Burke vividly described as 'the little platoons'. The kinds of memberships that we now recognize as expressions of civil society are trade unions, churches, environmental group, charities, particularist association for women and ethnic groups, for example; even families are now often listed in the category.

In its modern meaning civil society is a term used to distinguish the identity and activity of the person in bodies such as these that are separate and distinct from the state. In that sense, therefore, we may classify it as a parallel form of citizenship. Hegel was at pains to correct what he believed to be the traditional conflation of the two sets of institutions in political thinking. He argued that individuals join civil society bodies voluntarily and in order to pursue their particular interests. Therefore, 'If the state is confused with civil society then the interest of the individuals as such becomes the ultimate end of their association, and it follows that membership of the state is something optional'.

Yet the belief that civil society offers a useful, even indeed a superior option to the traditional state citizenship became widely accepted in the 1980s. Conditions and events in eastern and central Europe drew attention to the notion. A close look at the communist regimes in these countries made it apparent that conventional citizenship in totalitarian states is a fake citizenship: civil and political rights were severely abbreviated by the oppressive security police system.

Poland showed the way. In 1980 Solidarity was created as a workers' movement independent of state control and, with notable support from the Catholic Church, extracted sweeping concessions – such as relaxation of censorship, the regular broadcasting of church services and promotion in employment irrespective of Party membership. Then, surely, the Solidarity worker were displaying greater civic consciousness and effectiveness, admittedly of a different kind, than they had previously when going through the motions of voting in elections for Communist Party members or of serving in a Warsaw Pact army. A similar, though less dramatic, story can be told about the role of the civil society associations in helping to effect the smooth conclusion of the Communist era in Hungary in 1990.

Meanwhile, in the West, in Thatcherite Britain conspicuously doubts arose concerning the continuing vitality of traditional state citizenship.

The doctrines of the New Right and neo-liberalism directly confronted the very concept of social citizenship and seemed intent on dismantling the welfare state. Furthermore, if there is no such thing society and individualism is all, what price the consciousness of community responsibility that is one of the hallmarks of citizenship? Paradoxically, both Right and Left, discarding and despairing of conventional citizenship respectively, turned to civil society, That charities preached the virtues of 'active citizenship', interpreted as membership of school governing bodies or neighbourhood watch schemes. The Left-inclined young turned Green, forming and joining groups to challenge the immobility and insensitivity of politicians and bureaucrats. Is this realistic, is it even desirable? That very pluralism of civil society detracts from its pretensions to be an alternative school and arena for citizenship.

The nature of civil society as a parallel form of citizenship may be seen to be only partially satisfying on the basis of a quite opposite test. Even when one has acknowledged the civil and social facets of citizenship, that status remains at root political. And in so far as the associations of civil society want to preserve against or accelerate change, they can often achieve their objective only through the political system. Beiner provides a vivid exemplification of this contradiction.

He contends that the solidarity movement in Poland, the most sensational model of the civil society vision, did *not* confine itself to civil society once the totalitarian state collapsed, but went on to turn itself into a political party, quickly assuming the reins of government. This was not a sellout by Solidarity, but a natural response to the 'built–in' insufficiency of the kind of 'localized' citizenship made available to us at the civil society level alone. The parallel lines of civil society and state are in practice therefore sometimes destined to meet.

Federal constitutions

So, from parallel lines to horizontal layers, the clearest example of which is to be found in the federal State. In the eighteenth century federal forms of constitution were a rarity: one may cite the United Provinces and the Swiss Confederation as examples, but they were anomalies. Today every continent has several examples, and hundreds of millions throughout the world consequently experience the status of citizenship at both the State and state levels. The first major nation to adopt the device was the United States of America, which became something of a laboratory for the federalist structure. It therefore provides ample evidence of the difficulties and advantages attendant upon this kind of double-layered citizenship.

In the very process of framing the Constitution, the American draftsmen inscribed an ambiguity at its very heart. The imprecision lies in the apparent discrepancy between the preamble and Art. 7 of the document. The preamble starts with the well-known words: 'We, the people of the United States' Art. 7 required the Constitution to be ratified by separate state Conventions. The questions thus arose whether the Constitution was the product of the will of the nation acting in unity, or of the distinct wills of the separate peoples of the participating states. These alternative readings were indicators of different interpretations of the location of sovereignty; or, to put the matter another way, they raised the question whether primacy between the citizenship statuses rested at the local state level or the overarching State.

In 1857 the Chief Justice gave a ruling in the long-running and controversial Dred Scott case, which underlined the primacy of each state over federal authority in the matter of citizenship. The case was complicated by the fact that Scott had been a slave. However, that aside, the judgment on the conferment of national citizenship was clear. Now single state could make a Negro a citizen of the United Sates, and endue him with the full rights of citizenship in every other state without their consent. By implication this meant that citizenship was primarily a state conferment, not national. It took the blood–letting of the Civil War and the subsequent Fourteenth Amendment to reverse this judgment. Henceforth, in law if not in reality, citizenship was a nationwide status beyond the authority of any individual state to abridge.

The relationship of the political and legal powers of the two levels of a federal State is at one and the same time a cardinal issue for the writers of constitutions to decide upon and an intensely delicate one to resolve in practice. For all their wisdom, the American Founding Fathers left a perilous legacy. However, the precision, justice and workability of instruments of constitutional law are only one facet of the intricacies of layered citizenship. The other major question concerns the level to which the citizenry feel themselves the more attached and at which they feel the more able to participate in civic affairs. Here again, the USA provides a prime example of thinking, observation and practice to help us appreciate the nature of layered citizenship.

The two classic commentaries on the US system of government, *The Federalist* papers and Tocqueville's *Democracy in America,* stress the grater reality of the state government for the average citizen. 'Into the administration of these a greater number of individuals will expect to rise', wrote Madison. '... With the affairs of these the people will be more familiarly and minutely conversant. And with the members of these will a greater proportion the people have the ties of personal acquaintance and friendship, and of family and party attachments' (*The Federalist,* no. 46). This excerpt may be compared with Tocqueville's conclusions drawn from his observation in five New England states half a century later. He declared that 'The central government of each state, being close to the governed, is continually informed of the needs that arise; every year new plans are put forward and published in the press, exciting universal interest and eagerness among the citizens'.

The message is clear. A citizen's sense of identity and bonding, his knowledge and civic competence, and his opportunities and inclination to participate are more effectively nurtured at the lower, state level than the higher, federal level. True, these two commentators were writing about a society with strongly established feelings of local community and with much less pervasive national news media than today. None the les, their observation certain resonance both across the generation and in other countries, finding expression, for instance, in the modern principle of subsidiarity, which has been adopted by the European Union.

The relationship of the citizen to the State must balance this state allegiance and activity. The centrifugal force of state citizenship must be equalled by the centripetal force of State citizenship. Pairs such as local and national patriotism, local traditions and national values, must somehow be kept in harmony.

A tradition of the former slave states of the Deep South has been the separation of whites and blacks, the latter for generation treated as non-or, at best, second-class citizens. A fundamental objective of citizenship is the equality of all those enjoying that status; moreover, the proposition that 'all men are created equal' as written into the American Declaration of Independence. Should, therefore, black children continue to be taught in separate schools in accordance with Southern tradition or schools be desegregated according to the national principle of equal citizenship? This was a live issue in the mid-twentieth century. In 1954 the Supreme Court ruled that segregation was 'inherently unequal'. Nevertheless, when, three years later attempts were made to integrate a few black pupils into the Central High School in Little Rock, Arkansas, agitated supporters of segregation prevailed upon the state Governor to prevent this development by deployment of federal troops to enforce the Supreme Court ruling. He had upheld not just the law, but also the principle of State citizenship over the traditions of state citizenship.

The European Union

Let us consider the concept of 'quasi-federalism': the European Union and the distribution of political authority by means of devolution.

The European Union (EU) evolved from structures for economic co-operation – the Coal and Steel Community (ECSC) and the European Economic Community (EEC). Why, then, should it have developed a from of supra-national citizenship? From the very beginning, the originators of European unity accepted the need for an elected assembly to monitor the executive bodies. Initially indirectly elected by the constituent members' national legislatures, the European Parliament was first directly elected by the citizenry in nationally drawn European constituencies in 1979.

Members of European parliament were soon voicing concern about the 'faceless' unaccountability of the European Commission. In 1998 the Commission noted that 'In its resolutions Parliament has laid particular stress on devising a policy which involves European citizens in the creation of a living Community and on transforming the technocrats' Europe into a people's Europe. It is noteworthy that the phrase rendered into English as 'people's Europe' appears in French as *'Europe des citoyens'*.

Already moves were afoot to build an effective European citizenship. In an effort to encourage individuals to assume a European identity– to think of themselves as 'European' – European passports have been issued, a European flag has been designed and a European anthem adopted. The anthem is Beethoven's version of Schiller's 'Ode to Joy' itself inspired by a reading of the Abbe Saint-Pierre's eighteenth-century Project for European union.

The EU ahs also struggled with the problem of the stratified nature of the Union by declaring adherence to the principle of subsidiarity. This originated in papal political thinking and the path of its transmission to the EU is somewhat misty. It seems to have been channeled to the European Union from the Italian cleric-politician Don Luigi Sturzo via the Christian Democratic parties. The proposition, as enunciated by Pius XI, is that 'it is an injustice, a grave evil and a disturbance of right order, for a larger and higher association to arrogate to itself functions which can be performed efficiently by smaller and lower societies' In 1990, Delors, President of the Commission, declared that subsidiarity should be the 'wathcword' of the European Community.

How does the concept relate to citizenship? Subsidiarity refers to the exercise of power and decision-making at the lowest feasible level in a pyramidal structure. Consequently, if the principle were widely advertised and applied, citizens juggling with their multiple civic identities would know which topics would be handled at which levels; and, furthermore, be assured that their local interests would not be overlooked or overridden by an ignorant or unsympathetic body higher up the scale of authority.

Such ideas and developments were merely tentative steps towards a defined European citizenship. It became a legal status, when the Teaty of European Union came into effect in 1993. The treaty also incorporated the principle of sbsidiarity provided for the appointment by the Parliament of an Ombudsman to receive complaints from citizens and enhanced the powers of the Parliament.

However, citizenship is considered to be not only a civil and political status; there is a social dimension also. The European Union has made some attempt to cater for this. In 1989 the European Community produced its Draft Community Charter of Fundamental Social Rights (the Social Charter). The aim was to provide minimum working conditions throughout the member states. The Masstricht Treaty incorporated these provision in its Social Chapter. But the contribution of the EU to the consolidation of the social rights of the citizen extends beyond the Social Chapter. This process preceded and continues independently of the Maasticht Treaty. European definition of social and employment rights has come about through the issuing of Directives by the Commission and judgments by the European Court of Justice. The work of the latter has had a bearing on the status of European citizen since 1963.

The vigilance of individuals concerned to protect their rights amounts to an effective supervision of the exercise of power by the Community institutions. Since then the Court has built up considerable case law relating to social and especially economic rights, which effectively establishes the superiority of European over national law. The pattern of an evolutionary European citizenship is, in fact, overtly accepted in the Maastricht Treaty. Art. 8e makes it possible for the Council to 'adopt provision to strengthen or add to rights.

The EC/EU has, in practice, been primarily concerned to protect economic rights – understandably because of its mainly economic function. In a complementary manner, the Council of Europe has been primarily concerned to protect civil right. The rights covered by this organization are protected in the European Commission of Human Rights and Court of Human Rights. As membership of the Council of Europe far exceeds in number of states the membership of the European Union, the number of 'European citizen' in the sense of people potentially under protection of the ECHR far exceeds, though of course includes, the numbers of citizens of the European Union.

But not only are the EU states members of the Council of Europe, the Maastricht Treaty formally recognizes the significance of its setting the standards for the preservation of rights. Art. F of the treaty states that the EU 'shall respect the fundamental rights as guaranteed' by the ECHR 'and as they from the constitutional traditions common to the Member States, as general principles of Community law'.

Here, then are the basic bones of European citizenship – the sub continental quasi-federal system which has been developing during the last decades of the twentieth century. What does it all add up to? Potentially perhaps a sophisticated example of multiple citizenship of the layered kind; at the moment, it is a mere shadow of that potential. There is plentiful evidence that the concept and practice of European citizenship is exceedingly weak compared with citizenship as experienced at the national level.

Citizenship is an inert idea if those invested with the status place no value on it or, which is worse, reject it out of hand. Popular support for and identity with the EU, it must be said, has been less than enthusiastic. The very prospect of membership of the Community was greeted with some hostility, notably in Britain and Norway. Even in France, a keen founder-member, the referendum for the ratification of the Maastricht Treaty produced a 'yes' response by the narrowest of margins. Turn-outs in the election for the European Parliament have been very low in some countries: in 1994 in a third of the twelve member states less than half the electorate voted. Nationalism, xenophobia even, especially in Britain, inhibits the growth of a feeling of co-citizenship with other nationalities.

There is, in addition, an institutional reason for the lukewarm attitude of European Parliament. After all, one of the clearest and simplest indicators of citizenship is the casting of one's vote, and the turn-out in an election is often reckoned an index of the strength of a nation's sense of citizenship. But in the case of the EU the relative powerlessness of the Parliament, which has led to complaints about the 'democratic deficit' of the EC/EU, is little incentive to exercise this basic right of political citizenship.

So, what, at bottom, does European citizenship really mean? There is much vagueness and confusion; and it raises fundamental questions about the nature of citizenship. The stress in discussions about European citizenship tends to be placed on the rights which a European citizen can expect to enjoy, the nature of those rights, and the identification of those persons who are eligible to enjoy them. The sphere of political citizenship is clear laid down in the Maastricht Treaty, which also defines a European citizen as 'a person holding the nationality of a Member State'. The trouble arises when one extends the definition of citizenship into the civil, social and economic spheres.

There are four main areas of confusion. One is the existence of a large number of migrant workers in some states of Union – Algerians in France. Yet they enjoy welfare and employment rights. Does that make them 'partial European citizen'? Secondly, different member states interpret the rights to social and employment benefits in defferent ways.

Thirdly, the European Convention of Human Rights recognized by the Maastricht Treaty, provides a comprehensive definition of rights. But these are rights which adhere to a person *qua* human being, not *qua* citizen. Moreover, individuals in the states of central and eastern Europe, not members of the EU, have the same right to live protected by this code as do citizens of Europe as defined by the Maastricht Treaty. Fourthly and finally, much of the EU discourse about citizen' rights is about worker' rights. Workers' rights concern the relationship between citizen and state.

The receptacle that is the concept of citizenship is indeed capacious, but in the case of Europe too much has been poured into it, causing semantic confusion. We would do well, therefore, to keep in mind the unique and experimental nature of the European Union. When Denmark ratified the Maastricht Treaty it appended the following declaration:

> Citizenship of the Union is a political and legal concept entirely different from the concept of citizenship within the meaning of the Constitution of the Kingdom of Denmark. Nothing in the treaty of European Union implies or foresees an undertaking to create a citizenship of the Union in the sense of citizenship of a nation state.

3

The Liberal Tradition

Discourses on citizenship have offered two traditions and styles on the nature of citizenship. These are the civic republican style, which places its stress on duties, and the liberal style, which emphasizes rights. Now, despite the former's origins in classical antiquity and therefore its longevity, it is the liberal tradition that has been dominant for the past two centuries and remains so today. Compared with the republican variant, liberal citizenship is much less demanding of the individual. It involves a loosely committed relationship to the state, a relationship held in place in the main by a set of civic rights, honoured by the state, which otherwise interferes as little as possible in the citizen's life,

Liberal citizenship was the offspring of the liaison between revolutionary upheaval and contractarian natural rights theory, Great Britain playing the role of midwife. True, it was the French Revolution that first established the principle and practice of citizenship as the central feature of the modern socio political structure, but it was the British experience over one-and-a-half centuries prior to 1789 that laid the foundations for the transition from a monarch-subject relationship to a state-citizen relationship. Paradoxically, the actual terms 'citizen' and 'citizenship' were rarely used in the liberal sense in the English-speaking world. Yet the English Civil War and its aftermath, the political theory of John Locke, and the seizing of independence by the American colonies and their transmutation into the United States were all absolutely vital to the evolution of the liberal mode of citizenship and citizens' rights.

A citizen has the right to vote. Colonel Rainborough declared in 1647, '1 do think that the poorest man in England is not at all bound in a strict sense to that government that he has not had a voice to put himself under'. A citizen also has a right to just treatment by the law: the first Habeas Corpus Act was passed in Britain in 1679. In about this year Locke wrote his *Two Treatises of Civil Government*. In the second of these Locke influentially expounded his theory of natural rights, that every man should have the free and equal right 'to preserve his life, liberty, and estate'. The American revolutionaries adapted this formula to 'life, liberty and the pursuit of happiness', and the French, to 'liberty, property, security, and resistance to oppression'. These rights are God-given; but it is the function of the state to ensure their protection. We therefore step from generalized natural rights, which individuals have qua human beings, to specific civic rights, which are assured by the state to individuals qua citizens. Hence the dual title of the French Declaration - of Man and the Citizen.

The distinction could be telling, as Marx recognized. The rights of man are negative, allowing the individual to pursue his own personal life not committing him to a life as a member of a community, a citizen. Marx in *the Jewish Question* declares that the rights of the citizen, on the other hand, have a more defined, positive character. '*The French Declaration* and the *American Bill of Rights* finalized within weeks of each other in 1789, concentrated particularly on a range of legal rights such as freedom of speech and conscience, equality before the law, presumption of innocence, trial by jury.

> The freedom in question is that of a man treated as an isolated monad and withdrawn into himself. None of the so-called rights of man goes beyond egoistic man, namely an individual withdrawn behind his private interests and whims and separated from the community.

Another feature of citizens' rights considered to be crucial in these early days of defining liberal citizenship was the right to property. Locke firmly established this principle. He declared quite trenchantly that 'government has no other end but the preservation of property'. The language of the *Declaration of Rights* is even more forceful, asserting that the right to property is 'inviolable and sacred'. Ownership of property was not only a right, it was, as a universal practice, a requirement for the basic political right of citizenship, namely the right to vote. The political crises of the late eighteenth century threw up the issue of universal manhood suffrage, a cause persistently supported by Thomas Paine. But the mystique of property was too powerful for its implementation.

How, then, may we characterize the concept of liberal citizenship in these emergent years? It is an important question because the consolidation of the basics from roughly Locke to the French Revolution provided a legacy which still shapes our assumptions about citizenship in our own times.

First, the individual remains an individual. The acquisition of citizenly status does not necessitate abandonment of the pursuit of self-interest. Public and private spheres are kept distinct, and citizens are under no obligation to participate in the public arena if they have no inclination to do so. Nor have citizens any defined responsibilities vis-a-vis their fellow citizens. All are equal, autonomous beings, so that there is no sense that the state has any organic existence, bonding the citizens to it and to each other. Citizens perform, unwillingly it is true—mainly the payment of taxes - in return for the protection of their rights by the state. But there is no necessary pride in thinking themselves into the states of citizen. Citizenship largely means the pursuit of one's private life and interests more comfortably because that private life is insured by state protected rights. In short, therefore, the extrapolation of the rights of the citizen from the rights of man may marginally have adapted, but by no means transformed the individual from Marx's 'isolated monad'.

Secondly the liberal citizen is expected to feel only a limited obligation to the state, pari passu the state is expected to invade on the citizen's life in only a feeble way. This is the feature of liberal citizenship as laid down from the late seventeenth century. The state is useful to the citizen as, in Locke's striking image, a 'nightwatchman'. And if any government oversteps its limited powers and interferes in its citizens' activities to the detriment of their life-styles, or, conversely, fails in its protective function, then the citizenry has the right to rouse itself from the quiet pursuit of private affairs and rebel, as the American colonists did in 1776.

Thirdly, are these private affairs that the citizen must be allowed independently to pursue? It is the accrual of wealth. Liberal citizenship is a political expression of capitalism. But the relationship is, in fact, much more complicated than that.

Citizenship and capitalism

We cannot say categorically that the evolution of modern liberal citizenship would have been impossible without the emergence of a capitalist market economy and an accompanying, increasingly powerful bourgeois class. For one thing, pressure for the legal and political rights that were conceded by the three revolutions in England, America and France was spearheaded as much by a lawyer-dominated professional class as by entrepreneurial capitalists, perhaps even more so. Nevertheless, the decay of a feudal or quasi-feudal society and its supersession by a market economy did introduce changes that were at least conducive to the emergence of a liberal form of citizenship. Three kinds of change may be identified.

First, pre-caplitalist society was based on personal subservience - vassal to lord, apprentice to master, subject to prince. In contrast, the free exercise of individual initiative is the very essence of capitalism: Similarly, citizenship grew by the extraction of rights for the individual.

Second, feudal structure was socially hierarchical. The Victorian poet Cecil Frances Alexander unequivocally expressed the distinction between rich and poor: 'God made them, high or lowly, / And order'd their estate.' Capitalism, in contrast, requires social fluidity. Class divisions, it is true, are inevitable - middle class and the lower orders; but not caste rigidity. Initiative, to refer back to our first kind of change, required the partitions between classes to be permeable. The concept of citizenship took this alteration to the logical conclusion of equality of status. A citizen is a citizen is a citizen: no differentiation.

Third, ancien regime society was, to modern minds, unbelievably provincially fragmented. Economically, that is not to be confused with the modern convenience of devolution. Internal customs barriers, even provincially distinct measurements of weights and capacity, were anathema to the capitalist's essential requirement of free and open access to markets. The integration and solidification of the nation-state so essential for the capitalist, made way for citizenship as national identity.

One feature of this transformatory process was the alteration in the relationship between civil society and citizenship. In the Middle Ages citizenship meant being a privileged inhabitant of a city or other municipality, and the status tended to be accorded to members of corporate bodies such as guilds, that is, the component organizations of civil society. The growth of capitalism and the revolutionary changes brought in Europe from the late eighteenth century undermined this localized and fragmented political role of civil society, and citizenship became attached to the national instead of the municipal sphere. The individual's communal identity was therefore bifurcated.

Marx goes further and argues that the collapse of the old structure also destroyed the sense of commitment which had made civil society such a co-operative network. 'The shaking off of the feudal 'political yoke', he explained, 'entailed the shaking off of those bonds that had kept the egoistic spirit of civil society fettered'. Citizenship in the modern, broader sense could only provide a feeling of communal togetherness, stiffened by the ideology of nationalism.

We have a picture of a movement from a hierarchical to an increasingly egalitarian society as the rights of citizenship became democratized. But we must examine this picture more closely because lurking there is the counterbalancing economic inequality induced by unfettered capitalism. This is how Bryan Turner has explained this 'progress'. 'The growth of modernity is a movement from de jure inequalities 'in terms. of legitimate status hierarchies to de-facto inequalities as a consequence of naked market forces where the labourer is defined as a "free" person'.

So in various ways capitalism facilitated the emergence of liberal citizenship. But the connection has not been a one-way process, it has been reciprocal; for citizenship, in turn, has supported capitalism. We have already seen how prominent in the list of citizens' rights as drafted in the early years was the right of property ownership. In times of political upheaval this was a comforting formula for the middle classes. It is quite interesting to note that even the French Declaration of Rights of 1793, formulated by the radical Convention on the eve of the Terror, forcefully asserted this right. The nervousness of the wealthy in the face of social and political upheaval provides another consideration too. The damping down of civil discord by the broad concession of civil and political rights in practice affords a welcome calming of these fears. What is more, the middle classes benefited not just in this indirect manner. Chronologically it was they, not the working classes, who first had access to and made use of these civil and political rights of citizenship.

Nevertheless, the relationship between capitalism and citizenship has by no means been a happy marriage. In some circumstances citizenship has been threatening to capitalism and capitalism has been hostile to citizenship. The basic question has then arisen whether the state can ever, or indeed should ever, be a neutral observer when the interests of capitalism and citizenship are in collision.

One must naturally recognize that the state has an obligation to protect its citizens. In practice, the state has often intervened on behalf of the citizen by curbing the absolute freedom of the capitalist to maximize his profit. This intervention has taken two main forms. One is by regulating the market by laws, for instance, against the formation of cartels and monopolies. The other is by increases in taxation on higher income and heritable wealth in order to fund welfare and educational services for the mass of citizens. Particularly in the twentieth century, the belief that citizenship embodies social as well as legal and political rights has taken hold. Consider one illustration of this. Even in the Reagan—Thatcher era, when the Republican administration in the USA and the Conservative in the UK pursued quite radical neo-liberal free market policies, the amounts spent by the governments on health and social security still increased. From 1979 to 1984 in the UK expenditure on health rose by 16 per cent and on social security by 26 per cent; from 1980 to 1984 in the USA expenditure on health rose by 38 per cent and on social security by 12 per cent. Taxation inevitably increased.

The capitalism-citizenship coin, however, has another side: the threat posed by capitalism to citizenship. We must not forget that the citizenship model presents a state composed of citizens of equal status, equally enjoying their rights and relating to the state by virtue of those rights and concomitant duties. Capitalism weakens this egalitarian political structure by giving primacy to economic relationships.

New class divisions open up, separating the wealthy entrepreneurs from the general populace, a gulf condoned by the liberal virtue of individual enterprise. For the successful, profit in the market place, not civic loyalty, gives social status. For the rest, they are consumers of products and services, not citizens in the proper sense. The Citizen's Charter published by the British Conservative government in 1991 "lets the capitalist cat out of the civic bag:" the text refers in a number of places to 'customer' and 'client' as if these were synonymous with citizen. The danger is that if citizenship is perceived as a set of rights to protect the individual qua consumer against some of the problems exposed by a private or privatized economy, then the need to preserve and improve the core rights of real citizenship will be lost to sight.

Marx, as one would expect, portrayed the hostility of capitalism to citizenship in the starkest of terms, as embedded in the very nature of the state. According to his interpretation, the modern state is a bourgeois state, the expression and protector of bourgeois interests. It follows that the state is incapable of resolving the conflict between capitalism and citizenship because it is not itself a disinterested party. Citizenship as a status and a value is therefore in reality nothing more than a sop, a cloak for the citizen's impotence: 'political man is only the abstract fictional man.'

The societies of western industrial capitalism are essentially contradictory and there is an ongoing dynamic relationship between citizenship and the inequalities of the market place. The dynamic feature of capitalism is precisely the contradiction between politics and economics as fought out in the sphere of social citizenship.

Most people take liberalism as a label for a political philosophy that regards man as possessed of inherent individual rights and the state as existing to protect these rights, deriving its authority from consent though such prominent liberals as Jeremy Bentham and John Stuart Mill, who had little use for the idea of "inherent individual rights."

Similar arguments characterize John Locke's *Second Treatise of Government*, Thomas Paine's *Common Sense*, the *French Declaration of the Rights of Man and of Citizens,* and many other tracts and treatises of the seventeenth and eighteenth centuries. Man, the individual, shorn of status, role, and often cultural identity, had become the center of the moral and political world for these thinkers, and the chief task of government, in their eyes, was to secure his "natural" or "inalienable" rights.

The extent to which Locke, Jefferson, and others conceived of rights as the exclusive property of individuals-as a kind of shield that surrounded each man and protected him against the depredations of others-can easily be exaggerated.

Two of the early critics of rights theories, Edmund Burke and Jeremy Bentham, started from much the same point-condemnation of the French revolutionaries' appeal to natural rights. For both, the danger of the natural-rights approach was its tendency to substitute abstract rhetoric for sensible, practical thinking. "Natural rights is simple nonsense," according to Bentham's judgment on the French Declaration of Rights, and "natural and imprescriptible rights, rhetorical nonsense-nonsense upon stilts." Rights are conventional, not natural, in Bentham's view, and if we enjoy them at all, it is only because we are subject to a legal system, for to have a right is merely to be the beneficiary of a relationship sanctioned by law. Because there are no rights without law and government, law and government cannot possibly be justified by an appeal to rights. Instead, we should look directly to utility, understood most simply in terms of the "two sovereign masters," pain and pleasure, under which nature has placed us.

Burke forcefully argued that the French appeal to natural rights was dangerous not because it was nonsensical but because it was blind to circumstance and tradition. He acknowledged that there are natural rights, abstract rights that do not depend for their existence on government, "but their abstract perfection is their practical defect." The French were elevating a fiction, Man, to the status of a god, and proclaiming a new religion, the Rights of Man, in his name. What they and their sympathizers in other countries should be concerned with, Burke argued, is men as they are, in all their variety and particularity, whether they are French, English, or Chinese, peasants, merchants, or craftsmen, nobles or commoners, masters or apprentices, for "I may assume that the awful Author of our being is the Author of our place in the order of existence,-and that, having disposed and marshalled us by a divine tactic. He has in and by that disposition virtually subjected us to act the part which belongs to the place assigned us." We have rights, then, and they are a kind of property, but a kind that attaches to whatever station in life we may happen to occupy. Those who set the individual against others those who talk of rights against society and government understand neither rights nor the order of things.

The complaint that natural-rights theories are too abstract-that they lift "man" from his social and historical context-became a common ground of criticism in the nineteenth century, uniting writers as different from Burke, and one another, as Hegel, Karl Marx, Green and Macntyre.

Rather than move with Burke toward status concepts and a notion of an objective order, however, Marx looked forward, late in his life, to the transcendence of the rights of man in "a higher phase of communist society," for "only then can the narrow horizon of bourgeois right be crossed in its entirety and society inscribe on its banners: "From each according to his ability, to each according to his needs". Once that horizon is crossed, presumably, human potential will flower forth and the concept of rights, now rendered useless, will wither and die.

For Green, criticism of the asocial and ahistorical views of the natural rights theorists led to an attempt at accommodation. Rights are valuable not in themselves, in his view, but only insofar as they serve to promote the "moral vocation" or "moral personality" of the individual. Yet Green also believed that rights are absolutely necessary to the pursuit of this vocation, so for him rights proved to be very valuable indeed. There ought to be rights. He insisted because the moral personality-the capacity on the part of an individual for making a common good his own-ought to be developed; and it is developed through these rights; i.e. through the recognition by members of a society of powers in each other contributory to a common good, and the regulation of those powers through that recognition.

Green's attempt at accommodation is thus an attempt to tie the rights of the individual to the good of the society to which he or she belongs. Our rights are not merely rights against others; they are also rights to the positive aid of others-aid we need in order to develop our powers so that we may contribute to the common good. Green through that the person with rights and duties is the product of a society, and the rights of the individual must therefore be judged from the point of view of a society as a whole, and not the society from the point of view of the individual.

Where do we stand now, a hundred years after Green and Ritchie, with regard to rights? A survey of the intervening century suggests that two developments have been especially important.

First, philosophers and legal scholars have devoted considerable attention to the analysis of the concept of rights, one result of which is an abundance, perhaps a superabundance of often disputed distinctions: between active and passive rights, positive and negative rights, welfare and option rights, special and general rights. By general consent, the most immpressive of these was set out in 1919 in Wesley Hohfeld's Fundamental Legal Conceptions. Hohfeld's concern as a legal scholar was that the concept of rights and its correlative, the concept of duties, were too broadly and indiscriminately construed. A more careful analysis of rights and duties reveals, he explained, four distinct and fundamental relations under law: rights and duties; privileges and no-rights; powers and liabilities; and immunities and disabilities."

From the standpoint of social and political philosophy, the principal value of Hohfeld's categories seems to lie in the distinction between rights, also called claims or claim-rights, and privileges, now better known as liberties or liberty rights. On Hohfeld's distinction, claim-rights entail a correlative duty on the part of at least one other person, but liberty-rights do not. The difference may be brought out by a pair of familiar. examples. If Atul borrows from Sunil, Sunil then has a claim-right to the return of the money but Atul and Sunil both see a a hundred rupee note in the street and no one else is around, then each has a liberty-right to the money even though neither has a duty, ceteris paribus, to let the other have it. By distinguishing rights from liberties in this way, Hohfeld stresses the relational aspect of rights. Whereas the rights-theorists of the seventeenth and eighteenth centuries tended to regard a right as a faculty or possession, Hohfeld encourages us to conceive of a right as a kind of standing, a relationship between one person-the right-holder and others. It may not have been his intention, but in this sense Hohfeld's analysis reinforces the efforts of the nineteenth-century writers who sought to endow rights with a social dimension.

Much the same could be said for the second notable development of this century in the concept of rights-the popularity among philosophers, political figures, and common people throughout the world of the notion of human rights. As the direct descendant of natural rights, of course, human right is not an entirely new notion. But the shift from "natural" to "human" rights a significant change of emphasis. Arguments from natural rights typically proceeded from the idea of self-possession, from that of a property in oneself that must be defended against others; arguments about human rights. however, usually rest on some conception of a human or a person as a being with needs and interests that must be met if he or she is to live a fully human life. Thus the rights against others of the natural-rights theorists tend to become the claims upon others of the human-rights theorists.

This different emphasis is manifest in the *Universal Declaration of Human Rights* adopted by the United Nations in 1948. There, alongside such familiar proclamations as Article 3-"Everyone has the right to life, liberty, and security of person"-we find such novel assertions as that of the right to marry and found a family, the right to rest and leisure, the right to an adequate standard of living, and the right to participate in the cultural life of the community. Whether these really are or ought to be regarded as rights, human or otherwise, is open to dispute, but the important point here is that these putative rights are put forward as vital ingredients in a fully realized human life. In that sense, the popularity of the appeal to human rights reveals a concern not for what we are but for what we can and presumably should be.

Efforts to secure rights for specific groups of human beings-women's rights, gay rights, the rights of national or cultural minorities, and so on-also display this concern. In each of these cases, the core argument is that the members of the relevant group suffer because they are neither accorded the same respect nor afforded the same opportunities as other persons. They are prevented from realizing their capacities or from acting autonomously and denied the consideration to which human beings are entitled-to be treated with full respect for their dignity as persons.

Perhaps this is why we seem to live in an age of rights. No other concept seems to capture so well the idea that every person, regardless of his or her place in society, is worthy of respect as a person. The concept of human dignity, despite the power of dignitas in ancient Rome, certainly lacks the conceptual force that the appeal to rights now exercises.

Dialectics of rights and duties

There is the idea that one who makes claims is to speak for himself or herself-even when he or she is speaking on behalf of others. There is also the idea that we, as persons, have the potential to make claims, and this potential, like others, requires exercise and cultivation. In both of these respects, the "potential maker of claims" bears a strong resemblance to the autonomous person.

That should not be surprising, for individual rights and personal autonomy are widely associated with liberalism. But there is another aspect of the conception of the person as a "potential maker of claims" that serves to connect rights and autonomy to concerns more often associated with republicanism. For one to be an effective "maker of claims," someone else must be capable of responding, one way or another, to one's claims. A baby's cry may be understood as a claim to nourishment or attention, for instance, but it can be effective only when there are others present who are capable of responding. A person can be a "maker of claims," then, only when others are "responders to claims." Those who respond to claims, of course, will have claims of their own to make, which means that the rights bearing person-the "potential maker of claims"-is entangled in a network of social relationships.

Green and others have rightily argued that the appeal to individual rights can serve to strengthen as well as to weaken these relationships. In keeping with Taylor's account of holistic individualism, the appeal to rights, properly couched, acknowledges the "social embedding of human agents, but at the same time prizes liberty and individual differences very highly." There is no reason to believe, then, that the appeal to individual rights is necessarily hostile to virtue, citizenship, or the common good.

There is some reason to believe that it is going out of control, however. According to Mary Ann Glendon, "rights talk," at least as it is spoken in the United States, threatens to impoverish political discourse "by its starkness and simplicity, its prodigality in bestowing the rights label, its legalistic character, its exaggereated absoluteness, its hyper individualism, its insularity, and its silence with respect to personal, civic, and collective responsibilities." Even some rights theorists now worry about the escalation of rights rhetoric" that threatens either to overwhelm other valuable moral and political concepts and considerations or, by a process of conceptual inflation, to rob the appeal to rights of much of its value. These concerns are well founded. But they should not lead us to conclude that we must attempt to abandon or eradicate the concept of rights. On the contrary, we should appeal to rights more sparingly. We should recognize that the concept of rights has its place and its work to do; just as other concepts—autonomy and civic virtue among them—have theirs.

Even loving couples do not always agree with one another, and their relationships are sometimes strained by tension. This is also true of autonomy and civic virtue. They sometimes pull in different directions, with autonomy leaning toward individual rights and civic virtue toward public responsibility. Yet even this tension is healthy. When autonomy pulls too hard in an individualistic direction, the appeal to civic virtue reminds us that both the development and the exercise of autonomy require the assistance and cooperation of others, when appeals to civic virtue threaten to jeopardize individual rights, the claims of autonomy remind us that the body politic ought to be a cooperative enterprise composed of individuals who have a right to lead a self-governed life. In this way the tension between autonomy and civic virtue leads to a healthy balance. This is the kind of balance that is reflected in the attitude of citizens who are willing to do their part for the common good as long as others are willing to do theirs. These citizens know that they and the other members of the body politic are interdependent: their cooperation helps to enhance others' autonomy, just as the cooperation of others helps to enhance theirs. They have a reason to exhibit civic virtue, then, at least when the body politic as a whole plays a significant part in fostering personal autonomy.

In the liberal tradition, citizenship is defined primarily as a set of individual rights. These rights are said to serve several functions. Most importantly, the possession of rights denotes individual autonomy. Rights give space to the individuals to develop their interests and fulfil their potential free from interference from other individuals or from the community as a whole. The first liberal theorists to assign a central role to rights, such as Locke and Paine, believed that the citizen needed to be protected from the growing power of the state. Without the civil rights of life, liberty and property, the individual would always be at the mercy of arbitrary political power. While the classical liberals of the seventeenth and eighteenth centuries felt the state was required to maintain order, it was in the words of Paine, a necessary evil. Moreover, classical liberals contended that individuals were rational and self-determining before the formation of the state. The basis, then, for the authority of the state is a contract between autonomous actors. The individual consents to give up some liberties in return for the security that the state can offer and guarantee. This abstract individualism means that liberals understand the individual and community as being in opposition and, in part this explains their ambivalence towards responsibilities, democracy and social rights.

The emphasis liberals place upon individual autonomy makes them suspicious of notions of community. The fear is that the community will seek to impose obligations upon the individual that constrain or contradict his or her self-interest. This stands in direct contrast to the holistic approach of the ancient Athenian polis. In the polis, the idea of the individual having a meaningful existence outside of the community was unthinkable. The needs of the community and the interests of the citizen were seen as indivisible. Thinkers who have drawn inspiration from ancient, more participatory models of citizenship have helped expose the incoherence of liberalism. Both socialists and republicans are attracted by the thick conception of citizenship associated with the polis and see the citizenship of liberalism as an impoverished alternative. Liberalism's dualistic approach to citizenship has also drawn criticisms from feminists, postmodernists and ecologists who discern the damaging implications of its assumptions for human relations and the natural environment.

A closely related dichotomy to that of the individual and community is that of agency and structure. Because liberals start with the assumption that the individual is a rational, atomistic actor, they tend towards agency-centred explanations of human behaviour: we shape our own lives through the choices we make. Rights facilitate these choices. The problem with this is that it assumes a very one-dimensional understanding of power. To the liberal mind, power is an individual capacity that is used intentionally and for a clear purpose. This ignores the nature of constraints that structures of power such as race, caste class and gender place upon the individual. Inequalities associated with the class system, caste system patriarchy and racism are deeply rooted in society and are crucial to understanding why the format rights of citizenship are not effective for some groups. An illustration of the way inequalities of power are woven into the fabric of social life, and cannot therefore be reduced to rational choice, is captured in the notion of institutional racism. In 1993, the black, teenager Stephen Lawrence was murdered by a gang of white youths in southeast London. The subsequent investigation by the Metropolitan Police failed to bring the killers to justice and was viewed by the Lawrence family and civil rights activists as grossly incompetent. A public investigation into the affair found that the police were guilty of 'institutional racism', which the inquiry's report defined as an unwitting and unconscious prejudice against ethnic minorities. This particular case is extremely unusual in that we find a rare acceptance by the establishment that structures of power operate in such a way as to deny some people their basic rights.

The way that inequalities shape the practice of citizenship can be further illustrated by a consideration of the public-private divide, which liberals defend. In liberal theory, market interactions and the pursuit of personal interest characterise the private realm. Civil rights protect this sphere from interference from the public realm. Liberals are therefore keen to justify such rights as liberty and property in the strongest terms Locke for example considered such rights as natural.

By this, he meant that men (not women) possessed rights that were inalienable and could not be taken away by any political authority. The public realm was to serve the interests of individuals and to provide defence and security for private interactions. There is no necessary connection between liberalism and democracy because as long as the sovereign, whether it be a monarchy or democracy, does not seek to undermine civil rights, then its rule can be seen as legitimate. However, as the economic power of the capitalist class grew in the eighteenth and nineteenth centuries, the bourgeoisie demanded political rights as well. These were initially extended to property owners who sought to oversee the protection of their possessions by controlling the state through political representation.

Feminist commentators have exposed the apparent neutrality of the public-private divide as a sham. In fact, the 'freedom' of the private sphere is premised upon a highly unequal relationship between men and women. Virtually all prominent liberal commentators have a gendered view of citizenship. Thus, Paine believed that the only natural inequality with humanity was between the sexes, while Locke describes man as the 'master' of his family. Social liberals like Marshall and Green also either ignore important differences between the experiences of men and women, or seek to naturalise those differences. For example, T. H. Green attacks the practice of polygamy as an infringement of the right of the wife, who is morally lowered by exclusion from her proper position in the household and by being used, more or less, as the mere instrument of the husband's pleasure'. Green assumes that monogamous marriage is a condition of women's morality. But, he considers men to be the rightful heads of their households and therefore a woman's position within the family, as well as in the public sphere, is inherently subordinate to that of her husband. It is clear, then, that women are not considered by Green to be rational political agents, capable of practising citizenship. Such patriarchcal attitudes pervade liberalism and make a mockery of the alleged neutrality of the public private divide.

Pateman, in a perceptive critique of liberalism, argues that the social contract that classical liberals see as forming the basis of political authority, is in fact built upon a predetermined sexual contract. The use of the term contract in this context is somewhat misleading since the source of male power is violence and the oppression of women. There is, therefore, no sense of agreement on behalf of women. Nonetheless, the thrust of Pateman's argument is insightful. In liberalism, men are seen as political and economic actors, whereas women are seen as carets rather than citizens. Patriarchal attitudes run through the history of political thought and clearly are not confined to the liberal tradition. However, this blatant inequality is particularly hard to justify through liberal principles. It is only with the development of liberal ideals that patriarchy and other restrictive structures of power could begin to be challenged. Walby has developed this point in her discussion of the transition from private to public patriarchy. Walby shows how, partly through the expanding power of the state, and partly because of the struggles of women themselves, women have managed to gain greater access to the workplace and political institutions, particularly in the twentieth century. In a private system of patriarchy, through their control of economic and political institutions, and as masters of their families, men are able to dominate the women in their lives very effectively. With the onset of public patriarchy, the ideals of citizenship now begin to be extended to women and enhance the opportunities women have to develop separate economic and political lives. The public profile of women has undoubtedly increased in the twentieth century and this marks a considerable progression. However, women are still very much underrepresented in the most important positions of power. It is, therefore, a mistake to draw too sharp a distinction between these forms of patriarchy since it is true, as Walby's own work shows, that women still lack important rights and suffer from oppression. As Lister has argued, for citizenship to have greater meaning for women, we must address the problem of how the egalitarian values of citizenship can be translated into the personal relationships of the private sphere, and how the resources can be made available to enable women to participate fully as citizens, free from the unequal burden of care for children and other dependants. The crucial point is, however, that the ideal of equality, so central to the liberal tradition, has been essential in providing the impetus towards greater opportunities for women.

The public-private divide is also central to socialist critiques of liberal citizenship. Marx's essay *On the Jewish Question* remains the most penetrating. The key to understanding this divide is to consider liberalism's perspective on the relationship between equality and liberty. For Marx, the liberal doctrine of equality is important but limited. This is because in the liberal state, individuals are considered equal only in the public sphere, when they are participating politically as citizens. In their private lives, as workers or capitalists, individuals are subject to the market laws of supply and demand, which liberals consider the most effective method for generating prosperity and distributing resources. These market interactions inevitably result in serious inequalities that, for Marx, undermine the significance of formal rights. What does it mean to have civil rights if one is subject to job insecurity, exploitation or the threat of unemployment due to a downturn in the economic cycle? Thus, for Marx, citizenship in its liberal form represents a false universalism that masks the real sources of domination and exploitation.

It is true that liberals are sceptical about the role politics can play in determining the distribution of resources. The market is seen as the true guarantor of individual freedom. The conditions of a market economy, particularly private property, must therefore be protected through civil rights. This is why classical liberals seek to naturalise civil rights and treat them as existing prior to the formation of the state. In effect, liberals seek to restrict the legitimate scope of democratic decisions. Even radical liberals like J. S. Mill were wary of the extension of political rights to the masses in the nineteenth century. Mill feared the development of a 'tyranny of the majority' where the masses would impose restrictions upon the liberties of the private sphere. As Marshall contends, 'the political rights of citizenship, unlike civil rights, were full of potential danger to the capitalist system .

Neo-liberals, such as Hayek are more intense than Mill in their hostility to political rights. Because Hayek believes that the inequalities of the private sphere are both inevitable and desirable, he considers democracy to be at best a utilitarian device that should be limited strictly to those areas of life that cannot be determined by market forces. Nozick goes even further. Any attempt to seek social justice through the practice of democratic citizenship is an infringement of civil rights. Therefore the state should act as a nightwatchman, providing security, but in the most inconspicuous way possible. The state should not concern icself with the material welfare of its citizens since this would inevitably mean the state interfering in the distribution of resources that is best determined by the market.

As much as political rights present a potential challenge to the market dominance liberals defend, it was with the development of social rights in the twentieth century in many liberal states that citizenship began to pose a potential challenge to the imperatives of the market. Social rights include income support, state-funded education and public health. Because they are funded through taxation, social rights appear to stand in tension with civil rights and in particular the right to property. Marshall considered the development of social rights, which were institutionalised principally through the creation of the welfare state, as having the potential to significantly modify the capitalist system and to offset some of the negative aspects of market inequalities. This is why the social liberalism of Marshall should be considered a step forward for citizenship. Unlike the classical liberals, Marshall was able to discern the limiting effects of capitalism upon citizenship. However, Marshall, like all liberals, is a firm supporter of the market economy and in later writings came to the view that social rights had been detrimental to important freedoms symbolised by civil rights . With this observation, Marshall expresses a common theme in liberalism concerning the inherent tension between different kinds of rights. However, reifying civil rights and assuming they can have a meaningful existence without extensive social rights is to make citizenship vulnerable to dilution. The problem is that in liberalism civil rights and social rights are perceived as very different kinds of rights.

First, civil rights are seen as natural and as protecting the individual from interference. Because civil rights are seen as inalienable in the liberal tradition they are in a sense pre-political rights. Indeed the whole purpose of them is to protect the individual's basic liberties from the potentially damaging implications of political decisions, which may, for example, decide to abolish private property. Social rights, in contrast, are perceived as restrictions on economic freedom and as enhancing the power of the state.

Second, social rights are seen as resource dependent in a way that civil rights are not. This makes them vulnerable in times of economic recession.

Third, for neo-liberals civil rights are inherently positive in their effects for they create autonomy and freedom. Social rights on the other hand can lead to a 'culture of dependency' and destroy the sense of personal innovation and initiative that are essential to the survival of the liberal state. All of these potential problems with social rights allowed the neo-liberal governments of the 1980s and 1990s in countries such as Britain and the USA to roll back social rights in the name of economic efficiency and the enhancement of people's civil freedoms. The problems that the capitalist system experienced from the 1970s onwards were blamed largely upon the growing expenditure on social rights and the associated growth of the bureaucratic and inefficient state that was strangling the freedoms of the market.

However, we should be cautious about accepting neo-liberal arguments at face value. Their claim to have reasserted people's civil rights - by cutting personal taxation, introducing market reforms into the public services, and by freeing up the labour market - is not sustainable. What is very clear however is that the kinds of rights asserted by neo liberals are best termed market rights. By substituting this term for civil rights, we can get closer to understanding the dualism that liberals perceive exists between different types of right. Market rights, which first developed in the eighteenth century, are those rights necessary to the maintenance of a capitalist economy. The primary market right is therefore that of property. Market rights also include the right to accumulate and spend wealth as one sees fit, to assert self-interest in the market place, and to choose between a wide range of service providers. Crucially, market rights have often been asserted at the expense of civil rights as well as social rights. For example, up until the nineteenth century, trade unions were banned or suppressed in many liberal states. Other basic civil rights, such as protest and free speech, were ruthlessly opposed by the state in order to undermine any threats to the development of capitalism that might emerge. Similarly, during the neo-liberal experiment of the 1980s and 1990s, the marketisation of citizenship has been accompanied by growing police powers and restrictions on basic rights to free speech, association and protest. In Britain for example, between 1979 and 1997 the Thatcher and Major governments passed a series of laws that had a negative impact on civil citizenship. The irony of neo-liberal government has been that despite their theoretical hostility to the state, in both Britain and America in particular the state has actually grown in its power. However, because of their scepticism concerning political rights, the democratic accountability of the state has lessened. In Britain, for example, many decisions that were previously taken by democratically elected bodies were transferred to unelected, government-appointed quangos. The main argument here is that there is no necessary conflict between civil and social rights. Rather it is the assertion of market rights that prevents the fulfilment of the egalitarian elements of liberal citizenship. Without the material basis for citizenship that social rights provide, political rights are gravely undermined in their significance. What is more, attempts to weaken social rights have implications for civil rights as well.

The experience of neo-liberal government also exposes a further tension in liberal thinking about the differences between civil and social rights. It is true that social rights are perceived to be costly in a way that civil rights are not. But expenditure in security to safeguard civil rights than they do on social expenditure. Raymond Plant makes a similar point when arguing that all rights require political planning and resources to be allocated to them. Civil rights are no more natural than social rights. Instead, the emphasis upon one at the expense of the other is ideologically determined. Moreover, the nature and content of all types of rights is forever contested. One only has to think of the example of gender here. It is only through the campaigns of feminists that many civil rights could be redefined in the interests of fairness and equality. For example, it is only since 1992 in Britain that men's 'sexual rights' over their wives to force women to have sexual intercourse against their will have been overturned. This means the question of what kinds of rights we should defend is a deeply political question; an argument that is directly opposed to the naturalistic assumption liberals make about civil citizenship.

Another legacy of the recent popularity of neo-liberalism, with its greater emphasis upon market rights, inequality and a coercive state, has been a growing division between active and passive citizens. This division has always existed, at least implicitly, within the liberal tradition. Partly this is due to liberalism's gendered assumptions, whereby men are seen as activists and women as the carers of men and children. The link between property and citizenship was also made clear in early liberal accounts of citizenship. Locke, for example, believed that it was property ownership that gave a person a stake in society, whic is necessary for a commitment to a community's institutions and values. Owing to the liberals' neglect of the impact of social structures upon individual agency, they have also tended towards a harsh attitude to the poor. J. S. Mill, for example, defended the Victorian practice of workhouses because the poor required coercion rather than social rights to help them out of their predicament. The linkage of property to citizenship and the failure to acknowledge the complexity of power inequalities has been evident in neo-liberalism too. During the Thatcherite years in Britain, active citizens came to be seen as those who were able to assert their market rights of consumer choice, inequality and conspicuous consumption. Indeed, many of the Conservative government's policies enhanced the market rights of many. However, the commodification of citizenship also created greater divisions. Material inequality grew sharply during the Thatcherite years. Moreover, those who could not take advantage of the new opportunities were increasingly labelled as 'work shy', or seen as part of a state-dependent underclass.

Such language of exclusion was also closely linked to discourses of nationality. The social disorder that increased as a result of divisive policies was racialised by the government as they sought to blame, in the words of Margaret Thatcher, the influx of alien cultures' for the destruction of 'British' values

The point that the neo-liberals failed to grasp was that without the necessary resources, people are often unable to exercise their rights. This means that when the Thatcherites extolled the virtues of active citizenship in a campaign in 1988, it was unlikely to meet with a positive response from those most in need of the benefits that the government was eroding. Women, the poor and ethnic minorities were most vulnerable to the dilution of their social rights and were more likely to lack the resources necessary to meet the government's demand that they take more responsibility for their own lives and for those of their family and local community.

This was also the case in other countries that fell under the sway of neo-liberalism. In an analysis of the attempt to cut federal welfare budgets in the USA, O'Connor shows how the Reagan administration set out to discredit social rights. This was done by linking social citizenship to rising tax rates, which, it was alleged, were having a detrimental impact upon market rights. The Republicans also argued that it was welfare dependency, not poverty that was the root cause of America's inequalities. Links were also made between welfare benefits, gender and race. Welfare was seen as undermining the traditional family by encouraging illegitimacy and destroying the traditional male role as breadwinner. It also prevented, it was argued, ethnic minorities from exercising their market rights and climbing out of poverty. As O'Connor puts it, like the Thatcherite governments in the UK, the White House utilized stereotypes and overgeneralizations to advance and sustain its own moralistic view of poverty.

The dualisms help to explain why liberals' emphasis is upon rights rather than responsibilities. The potential opposition liberals perceive between the interests of the individual and the needs of the wider community are reflected in their desire to keep the number and intensity of duties to a minimum. Of course, neo-liberal politicians have spoken about the need for responsibilities, but these are chiefly to assert one's market rights and to be self-reliant. The responsibilities asserted by neo-liberals have little to do with citizenship, since neo-liberals are suspicious of the kind of political activism that the responsibilities of citizenship entail. This privileging of rights in liberal thought has attracted substantial criticisms from those who place much greater emphasis on the responsibilities side of the citizenship equation. Briefly, however, both the tensions between sovereignty and human rights and between science and nature are becoming increasingly significant within the citizenship debate. First, globalisation is exposing the contradiction of liberalism's commitment to the exclusive state on one hand and equal rights on the other. Second, liberalism's support of rationalism, symbolised by scientific achievement, is becoming a threat to the most fundamental welfare right of all, namely the right to a healthy and sustainable ecology. This suggests that future conceptions of citizenship will need to give greater emphasis than does liberalism to the question of social responsibilities. This is true not just in relation to the environment. Liberalism has been justly criticised for its neglect of the duties and obligations of the citizen generally.

In recent years, there has been a sharp reaction against liberals' neglect of the responsibilities of citizenship. Social conservatives and communitarians in particular have argued strongly that an overconcentration on rights is detrimental to the quality of citizenship. Individual rights alone make for a thin and defensive form of citizenship that does little to maintain the political community upon which rights are founded. Daniel Bell has identified a crisis in citizenship linked to what he sees as the contradictory processes of modern society:

> The economic dilemmas confronting Western societies derive from the fact that we have sought to combine bourgeois appetites which resist curbs on acquisitiveness, either morally or by taxation; a democratic polity which, increasingly and understandably, demands more and more social services as entitlements; and an individualist ethos which at best defends the idea of personal liberty, and at worst evades the necessary social responsibilities and social sacrifices which a communal society demands. In sum, we have no normative commitment to a public household or a public philosophy that would mediate private conflicts.

This passage captures well many of the concerns of critics of liberalism. The Individualism of liberalism has encouraged a selfish and instrumentalist attitude to democracy and citizenship, which is not seen as expressions of communal life, but as methods for furthering self-interest. Rights are demanded, but no responsibilities accepted. Liberty has mutated into licence.

Social conservatives insist that the way to rejuvenate citizenship is to reconnect rights to responsibilities by making entitlements dependent upon the performance of duties. For example, Selbourne contends that equal rights, without regard to desert or merit, are a 'false equality' that 'cannot serve the well-being of the civic order as a whole'. As in so many social conservative critiques, the main problem is seen as social rights. For Selbourne, the linkage between political and social rights has done much to destroy the sense of service associated with participation. Social rights create subjects, not citizens and have destroyed an ethic of civic virtue upon which the moral order is built. Moreover, state welfare is contingent in a way that political rights are not. Political rights are an expression of the popular sovereignty upon which the community is based and as such are inherent to the modern state. Social provision, on the other hand, should be firmly linked to desert and the performance of duty. Mead advocates a form of workfare, where social rights are dependent upon the recipient performing work that is guaranteed by the state. Both Himmelfarb and Etzioni also highlight the importance of social institutions, particularly the family, as sustaining the values necessary to social responsibilities. Etzioni identifies the 'parenting deficit' as the crucial factor in explaining why young people in particular have failed to internalise a sense of obligation to society. The solution therefore is to legislate for moral behaviour and to pursue social policies that encourage marriage and discourage divorce.

All of these thinkers are to some extent correct to detect problems with the liberal emphasis upon rights. Because of liberals' assumptions about the relationship between the individual and the community, there has been a tendency to see responsibilities as an infringement of liberty, rather than a condition of autonomy. The naturalisation of rights also obscures the fact that all rights and responsibilities are made possible by the political community. There is the danger, therefore, that rights are asserted as absolutes, without considering their consequences for social order. However, there are severe problems with the solutions offered by conservatives and communitarians.

There is a tendency amongst advocates of greater social responsibilities to adopt a cultural critique of modern society, and thereby to neglect the economic and political basis of citizenship. For example, the crisis of citizenship is attributed to a decline in morals. It is telling that Himmelfarb and Bell identify the 1960s as the key decade in explaining the development of a 'normless' society. The sexual revolution and culture of nihilism that developed in this decade has undermined the traditional values that had previously balanced the more acquisitive elements of human personality. Paradoxically this development of individual licence was accompanied by a creeping collectivism, as the welfare state took over many of the functions that had previously been undertaken by responsible citizens, through charity and the performance of good works. The problem here is that social conservatives identify some symptoms of the problems of liberal citizenship but treat them as the underlying cause. Like the liberals they criticise, they have a simplistic view of human agency and understate the role of power inequalities. The lack of a sense of obligation to society is therefore seen as a failing on the part of the individual, rather than an aspect of a wider social problem. Thus the institutions that are the real barriers to the performance of citizenship, principally the exclusive state and the inequalities of the market, are accepted uncritically. This means that in place of the liberals' assertion of an abstract individualism, many conservatives and communitarians assert an equally abstract vision of community.

Such a misdiagnosis can only lead to policies that leave the roots of the problem untouched and create additional inequalities. The fact that many critics of liberalism advocate the reduction of rights, or at least a moratorium on the creation of new rights, is a threat to liberty, particularly for those vulnerable groups whose rights have still to be realised. Many of the solutions offered by communitarians and conservatives risk negating some of the positive steps towards emancipation made by women for example. A return to traditional family structures risks recreating the division between women as carets and men as active citizens. It also risks stigmatising sexual minorities such as homosexuals whose civil rights are still far from certain, even in Western countries. Such policy prescriptions fly in the face of social changes that are unlikely to be reversed, and that have fundamentally changed the nature of gender relations and family structures.

It is to be argued that mass unemployment in Western societies since the 1980s is neither due to individual choice, nor a product of welfare benefits. Rather it is due to structural shifts, in the nature of capitalism that have led to greater job insecurity. Labour markets in the USA and Britain in particular are characterised by an increase in part-time and temporary work, as well as long-term unemployment for many. The problem is that social rights, linked as they are to contributory systems through employment, are dependent upon the vagaries of market forces and as such provide an uncertain base for citizenship. The neo-liberal revolution of the 1980s has shown that growing inequalities are hardly a basis for building citizenship and community. Indeed, the support of many conservative and communitarians for free market capitalism belies their alleged commitment to community. In reality, capitalism, with its emphasis upon short-term gain and the commodification of social relations, is unable to develop the kinds of obligations that conservatives and communitarians advocate.

Since communitarians accept the state uncritically, there is also the danger that an assertion of the needs of the 'community' may result in the promotion of the interests of the privileged majority in the name of the common good. It is also a mistake to attribute the problems of citizenship to 'too much democracy', as conservatives like Crozier have done. In fact, the reverse is true. The elitist structures of government have failed to develop the high level of political participation that is a defining characteristic of citizenship. One of the weaknesses of the social rights defended by Marshall was that they resulted largely from compromises between elites and were dependent upon a centralised and undemocratic state.

Are we left then with a choice between either a rights-based citizenship that fails to encourage responsibilities or an emphasis on responsibilities that undermines the rights of the vulnerable? The only way to move beyond this problem is to approach citizenship more holistically and to see rights and responsibilities not as intrinsically opposed, but as mutually supportive. This means exploring the content of citizenship in terms of the context in which rights and responsibilities are practised.

There are two of the fundamental tensions that liberals identify in citizenship. The first is that between rights and responsibilities. The second is between civil and social rights. In considering these problems we will try to show why a holistic approach to citizenship is required.

Liberals are correct to identify the importance of rights to any meaningful sense of citizenship. Rights are crucial to the successful resolution of the problems of governance, namely the need to distribute resources fairly and to maintain social order. The importance of rights is that they denote political agency and recognise the individual as worthy of respect and consideration. They are invaluable as a way of distributing resources according to the principles of justice and in the recognition of the equal status of each member of the community. Additionally, rights have an important role to play in sustaining social stability. Because of the diversity and creativity of humans, conflicts between them are inevitable. Often these conflicts are highly productive, and conflict certainly does not always involve violence. Indeed, the very purpose of politics, of which citizenship is a constituent part, is to resolve disputes through compromise. Rights play an important role in resolving social conflicts as they are a reminder that each individual is due the utmost respect and cannot be seen as a mere means to another's ends. Rights thereby offer some protection against the republican myth. The primary advocate of this myth is of course Rousseau, who, in his desire to unite the individual interests with that of the community, effectively advocated the annihilation of individual rights. Rousseau's infamous dictums such as the need to be 'forced to be free' or his advocacy of a civil religion to give the state a sacred mystique are methods for undermining the individual's autonomy.

Surprisingly, given his republican credentials, many of the problems of Rousseau's theory of citizenship can be found in his distinctly liberal assumptions. Like Hobbes and Locke, he adopts the concept of the social contract to account for why a political community must be formed. However necessary this community might be, Rousseau believes that by giving up the liberties of the state of nature, individuals surrender their innocence as well. Thus, despite his republican pretensions, Rousseau believes that the community corrupts the individual. It is his mistrust of the individual's ability to shape his or her future democratically that leads him to advocate what amounts to an authoritarian state. His argument that the rules of a society must be determined by 'a superior intelligence' in the person of a lawgiver, for example, indicates Rousseau's reluctance to fully trust the democratic will.

Unfortunately, modern day republicans, who cite Rousseau as inspiration, also adopt his love of paradoxical terminology, which gives ammunition to liberal critiques who fear more responsibilities will come at the expense of individual freedom.

We must also avoid couching citizenship in pseudo-religious terms and theorising the state as an ethically superior entity. Despite the problems of Marx's theory of politics, his great contribution to citizenship theory has been to identify the material base of the state. This stands in contrast to the mystification of the state in writers such as Hegel, Green and Rousseau. The state is no symbol of the ethical life as Hegel believed but is a concrete institution that represents particular interests and bases its authority upon force. The importance of Marx's critique of liberal citizenship is that it begins to show why the rights of the liberal state represent a false universalism. One of Marx's main reasons for rejecting citizenship in its liberal form was that it was essentially a religious concept. In the liberal state citizenship becomes the new 'opium of the people'. He defines the modern state as 'the fake, universal, based not on the expression but on the alienation of people's communal capacities'. This is why communitarianism, without a critique of the state and the market conditions the state protects, amounts to little more than a wish-list of desirable behaviour. The failure of citizenship in liberal societies to generate appropriate obligations is not due to cultural or moral decline but rather to the political failures of the capitalist state. Oldfield has rightly argued that often in liberal theory civic virtue is seen as a threat to liberty, as the denial rather than the fulfilment of self. This is Marx's point too: alienation from oneself as a communal being results not from the performance of responsibility but from the exclusivity of the capitalist state.

While Marx wrote little on citizenship after completing *On the Jewish Question,* he assumed that in a communist society many of the positive values of citizenship, such as reciprocity and equality would be present. With the removal of private property and the withering away of the state, the bases for exploitation and alienation would be removed and the barriers to citizenship lifted. Marx borrowed the phrase 'from each according to his ability, to each according to his needs' to explain how a communist society would be one of cooperation, not competition between atomised individuals as in liberal society

In the *Communist Manifesto* Marx identifies the interdependent nature of citizens when he argues that the free development of each is the condition for the free development of all. This contrasts with

Marx's view of liberal rights, which he saw as encouraging individuals to see in others, not the fulfilment of but the limits to their freedom. Marx then provides a more sustainable communitarian view of citizenship than do presentday writers such as Etzioni. This is because he is willing to look beyond the appearance of citizenship to see how the context of a capitalist state destroys the meaning of citizenship as an expression of communal life. This is why Bernstein considers Marx not to be opposed to rights as such but only to the limits liberal rights place on social and political participation:

> Marx's conclusion, which points to the overcoming of the duality between state and civil society, cannot be construed as recommending the overcoming of rights. On the contrary, the idea of individual man resuming the abstract citizen into himself points rather to individual man taking on in the world of civil society the attributes characterising the present political community. To extend the rights of the citizen to the whole of society is to see that rights are rights to participation in social life as a whole.

There is certainly an element of truth here. It is a plausible interpretation of Marx's early writings to argue that he saw that for political citizenship to have meaning, its influence must reach into civil society. However, we cannot overlook the fact that Marx, especially in his later works, did postulate his own version of the republican myth. By romanticising the proletariat as the vehicle to transform society from the vices of capitalism to the virtues of communism, he failed to see that any revolutionary act that utilised violence and sought to crush a section of society was doomed to failure. Marx's theory contains an anti-political or authoritarian aspect as he underestimates the transformative capacity of citizenship, relying instead upon the teleological forces of history.

Marx is thereby guilty of underemphasising political agency. He did not perceive that even in stateless communism the problems of governance, which citizenship seeks to resolve, would remain. A post-capitalist society could not therefore dispense with citizenship. The irony of actual communist regimes is that they have invariably had even more powerful states than those in liberal societies. The former USSR had a constitutional commitment to rights but these were paternalistic and unconnected to any meaningful system of participation. Communist societies are more pre-liberal than post-liberal since they enshrine a version of subjecthood rather than democratic citizenship. Nevertheless, Marx's critique of liberalism still provides us with significant insight into the false dualisms that liberalism assumes to be inherent to citizenship. This is not only the case with the relationship between rights and responsibilities. It is also true of the conflicts liberals see between different types of rights. There is no necessary conflict between civil and social rights. It is only if we accept liberal assumptions concerning the inevitability of the state and the primacy of the market over politics that certain kinds of civil freedoms appear to conflict with social citizenship. The sanctity of market rights, however, rests upon several myths. The first is that such rights are natural and not political. This simply does not stand up to scrutiny.

Second, the idea of the free market is itself myth. No economy in history has operated outside of a political framework. Modern capitalism is no exception: its development was bound up with the creation of the nation-state. In many cases, such as in Japan and Germany, capitalism was largely created by the state. The question of the balance between economic and political priorities, then, is a question of degree. How many regulations we place upon the economic sphere is therefore a political question and, civil rights require resources in the same way as do any rights.

Third, liberals often defend the market on the grounds that it does not discriminate between individuals. Unlike political decisions, which consciously favour one interest over another, the market cannot produce injustices. However, the fact is that we can predict the outcomes of market interactions and can offset inequalities through social policy. Again, the question is not one of absolutes, but rather of balancing the utility of the market with maintaining the conditions for democratic citizenship.

The emphasis upon limited civil (or market) rights in liberal societies has shaped the way social citizenship has been defined and institutionalised. On this point, Frazer and Gordon have presented an interesting thesis. In an analysis of the apparent contradictions of civil and social rights in the USA, they point to how the dominance of civil citizenship has shaped the approach taken to social rights. The idea of contract, so central to the liberal tradition, has been applied inappropriately to social citizenship. Frazer and Gordon believe that 'the result is a cultural tendency to focus on two, rather extreme, forms of human relationship: discrete contractual exchanges of equivalents, on the one hand, and unreciprocated, unilateral charity, on the other'.

Fred Twine has taken up Frazer and Gordon's challenge by basing his defence of social rights on the fact that human beings are inherently social and interdependent creatures. Twine suggests that the atomistic vision of society that liberals present is an illusion because each individual's life course is intimately bound up with the lives of others. Individuals are interconnected in a number of ways. First, as political animals people can shape common institutions of governance only through collective deliberation. On this point Selbourne is right to argue that political rights are best understood not as ways to protect one's self-interest, but as a reflection of one's interconnectedness with the political community.

Second, through the economic division of labour, individuals also find themselves dependent upon each other for the performance of services and the supply of goods. This means the production of wealth, and indeed the interactions of the market place, do not and cannot involve, individuals as being involved in discrete and isolated market choice. All market exchanges have external effects on others, as well as the buyer and seller. Such externalities have to be managed by the community collectively. This then dispels the liberal myth of atomised and rational consumers.

Third, in our personal lives, we all find ourselves in a position of dependence at certain times in the life course. Sometimes we are carets and sometimes we are cared for. Finally, we exist in an interdependent relationship with nature that demands that we act responsibly towards the environment.

Twine's argument points to the need for a holistic approach to citizenship that recognises that citizenship does not just denote personal autonomy. It is also a status that recognises that our individuality is rooted in the community. Dagger has argued that autonomy and the performance of civic virtue are not necessarily opposed. The purpose of civic virtue, as understood in the ancient polis, was to avoid corruption and passive dependence upon the decisions of others. The performance of civic virtue is therefore an important safeguard of liberty and rights. Selbourne contends that unless we address the lack of obligation individuals feel to the community, we run the risk of a more repressive moral order in the future. We cannot therefore reify one aspect of citizenship, as liberals do with market rights, or communitarians do with responsibilities, and expect citizenship to be effective. A holistic theory of citizenship that sees the interdependence between rights and responsibilities does not mean that we should make one dependent upon the other. Instead, we must work to remove the barriers to the performance of citizenship. Crucial here is recognising the material basis of citizenship and the direct relationship between the resources individuals possess and their willingness and opportunities to perform their rights and responsibilities. This does not of course prevent a society from requiring from its citizens a set of responsibilities. However, for responsibilities and rights to be seen as legitimate they must be linked to a more extensive participatory ethic than liberalism advocates and this ethic must be underpinned by extensive social rights.

Questions about the content of citizenship and the balance between rights and duties are always contingent upon the decisions of community. This is why the notion of a social contract as the basis for citizenship is flawed. The idea of contract is too static. Instead, we need to accept that the requirements and aspirations of a community is dynamic and dialectical. Political participation is therefore central in balancing rights and responsibilities. It is through active campaigns against injustice that rights have been extended to previously excluded groups and the responsibility citizens have to promote justice within the community is exercised. The liberal approach to obligation, which tends to ask only that we obey the law, is too narrow a view of it. Obligation requires us to remain critical of our political institutions and to help those who are alienated from the community develop a sense of obligation and commitment to it. It is useful here to differentiate between different kinds of responsibilities. Duties may be seen as those responsibilities imposed by law and carry some kind of sanction if the individual does not honour and perform them. Obligations, in contrast, may be seen as voluntary and as an expression of solidarity and empathy with others. The mark of a healthy society is its ability to rely upon obligations rather than imposed duties to maintain the conditions of the community. This means that for the foreseeable future we will have to accept more duties if we are to maintain the conditions of our citizenship rights.

It is therefore be argued that the considerable strengths of liberal citizenship are undermined by its dualistic assumptions. A citizenship that is built upon the exclusive state and the inequalities of the market is a thin citizenship indeed. By emphasising the protection of market rights to the exclusion of responsibilities, liberals offer an unbalanced vision of citizenship. However, many critics make the mistake of simply reversing liberals' emphasis upon rights and argue for the dilution of rights and the assertion of duty. But this is to miss the interdependent nature of rights and responsibilities, which must go together if the practice of citizenship is to be enriched, meaningful and transformative.

The Citizen as Consumer

This rival conception derives from the so-called economic theory of democracy. As developed by Joseph Schumpeter, Anthony Downs, and others, this theory attempts to explain politics in terms of economic competition. Political parties compete for votes just as corporations compete for profits. To win elections, parties try to offer the most attractive candidates and the most popular programs. Citizens, following the analogy, are consumers whose votes the parties are trying to gain. If they are sensible consumers, the citizens will spend their votes-or, more precisely, the time and energy required to weigh the alternatives and cast their votes so as to strike the best bargain for themselves. Or they may decide that the political market place offers nothing appealing or that their resources are better invested elsewhere; either way, they will maximize their expected utility by turning their attention away from politics.

This way of thinking about citizenship and politics is far removed from the republican ideal of civic virtue. It is consistent with liberalism, however, or at least with that strand of liberalism, running from Hobbes through Bentham and James Mill, that regards the public as a loose collection of atomistic individuals and politics as simply another way to advance or defend one's personal interests. It is this strand of liberalism that communitarians decry-and perhaps mistake for liberalism in general.

Thinking of the citizen as a consumer is also consistent with the legal dimension of citizenship, since the citizen-consumer enjoys rights and liberties protected by law, including the right to pursue his or her personal interests both in the private and public realms. But there is no room in this conception for the ethical, integrative, or educative dimensions of citizenship. In their view, public-spirited engagement in politics is to make excessive and unrealistic demands on people. It is also dangerous, for it inspires attempts to shape the views and preferences of people in the name of enlightened citizenship. It is both safer and more realistic to assume that people will always act to further their personal interests, that their preferences reveal these interests, and that they enter the political arena if they enter it at all with their preferences already formed. The job of the government is not to decide which preferences are right or good or worth promoting but merely to aggregate the preferences so as to reflect the citizens' will. Rousseau's "will of all," that is nothing more than the sum of their individual preferences. Therefore we ought to regard the citizen as a consumer and to reject any conception, such as that of the republican that smuggles notions of civic virtue into citizenship.

The rivalry between these two conceptions of citizenship-the citizen as consumer and the citizen as republican—stems from two different strands of liberal thought and, perhaps more broadly, two different ways of thinking about politics. Jon Elster captures the difference in his contrast between "the market" and "the forum." According to the first view, the purpose of politics is to coordinate or aggregate individual preferences; hence the economic theory of democracy and the idea of the citizen as consumer. According to the second, the purpose of politics is to transform preferences, just as debate within a forum is supposed to lead the audience to reconsider and perhaps to change their positions. To understand why the republican conception of citizenship is superior to that of the citizen as consumer, some of the problems that beset the "market" view of politics must be identified and examined. One of these is the apparent impossibility of finding an acceptable procedure for aggregating preferences. This problem is also likely to trouble anyone who wants to include democratic voting procedures in a political system that aims at transforming preferences, however, so we shall set it aside and turn to four other difficulties with the market or interest-aggregation view.

First, it is a mistake to think that we face a fundamental choice between taking preferences as given or working to transform them. Preferences are not simply given, except perhaps in the vacuous sense that people typically prefer eating to starvation. That some one prefers baseball to cricket, however, or music to opera must have something to do with the time and place in which one was raised. Preferences are shaped by a variety of factors, from the influence of parents, teachers, and peer groups to that of the marketing experts and advertising agents who make their living by luring the rest of us into the market place. The question, then, is not whether we should subject our preferences to formation or transformation, but how we can best do this. Indeed, the point of the "forum" view of politics is to lead people to examine their preferences so that they may be better able to decide whether these preferences truly square with their interests. Among other things, the resulting enlightenment should include an understanding of how others are already trying to shape our preferences.

The second mistake of the interest-aggregation view is to think that we can or should want to remain absolutely neutral with regard to preferences. At the least, we need to discriminate between genuine statements of preference and those that are the result of manipulation or misinformation. We also need to rule out some preferences, such as those of the person who thinks that only his or her interests should count. If we could ignore or overcome these obstacles, moreover, we would still "need to be assured that all interests will be pressed with equal force." Yet this assurance is precisely what politics as interest-aggregation cannot provide, since it "favours those with the resources and the incentives to press their interests politically."

A third problem is that market politics has little to offer with regard to the integrative dimension of citizenship. If the market view provides the individual with a secure sense of self, it does so less by integrating the roles one plays than by narrowing them until one sees oneself, in all aspects of life, as a consumer. And even this pinched sense of the self is unlikely to remain secure. When everything else becomes a commodity subject to exchange in the market place, people themselves become "human resources." When one's worth is fixed by the market value others set, as Hobbes thought it was, the result will be anxiety, not security.

Finally, and most significantly, politics as interest aggregation is incapable of generating allegiance. If citizens are merely consumers and the political order nothing more than a mechanism for coordinating and aggregating the citizens' preferences, there is no satisfactory answer to the question, "What reason has anyone to accept the decision that emerges from the process of interest - aggregation?" There is no appeal to solidarity or civic virtue, of course. In such a "resolutely individualistic" conception of politics, people are essentially competitors-rivals for space, for resources, for power. The only bonds between citizens are contractual in nature, formed by agreements based on the self-interest of the parties involved.

Perhaps this is too hasty a conclusion. Someone who adheres to the market view can still point out that self-interest can provide two reasons for obeying the rules of the political order. The first rests in recognizing that it is in one's interests, in the long term, to have a system for aggregating preferences, especially when that system gives everyone's preferences equal weight. Some people may not take such a long view of their interests, to be sure, so it is necessary to employ the practice of punishment to secure their compliance. Avoiding punishment thus provides a second reason, rooted in self-interest, for obeying the law.

Neither of these reasons is satisfactory. The appeal to self-interest in the long term does not work because it leaves open the problem of free riders. The political order is a public good, at least when we may reasonably regard it as a cooperative enterprise governed by the rule of law. But public goods are subject to free riders, and someone moved by self-interest-even self-interest over the long term-will look to escape the burdens of cooperation whenever possible. If we take citizens to be consumers looking for the best bargain, then we should expect everyone to disobey the law whenever he or she finds obedience burdensome. This being so, all of the weight must rest on coercion. Yet the more we rely on coercion to secure compliance, the more we shall have to rely on coercion. When obedience seems burdensome, the law and those who enforce it will be resented as obstacles, or even opponents that block the satisfaction of one's desires. Government and law soon appear to be alien forces imposed on one-forces to be circumvented whenever possible, As lawbreaking increases, however, and our own interests suffer, we have no recourse but to call for more police, more jails, and more coercion. The only question is whether we can stop short of Hobbes's Leviathan-state.

Societies, which rely heavily on the use of force, are likely to be less efficient, more costly, and more unpleasant than those where trust is maintained by other means. In the former, resources tend to be diverted away from economic undertakings and spent in coercion, surveillance, and information gathering, and less incentive is found to engage in cooperative activities.

Such inefficiency is both an embarrassing problem for and a telling argument against the market view of politics, for it demonstrates how that view subverts itself. Citizens who think of themselves as consumers will surely prize efficiency. Yet the more citizens think of themselves as consumers, as the more likely they are to rely on the inefficient means of coercion to secure compliance with the laws. On its own grounds, then, the conception of the citizen as consumer is inferior to a their publican conception, that does not rely exclusively on coercion to generate the necessary cooperation.

In short, politics as interest-aggregation simply cannot provide an adequate account of citizenship. It avoids the liberty-constricting features of stringent republicanism, but its narrow individualism deprives it of the capacity to inspire the loyalty of its citizen-consumers.

The Assurance Game

Republicanism promises to generate its own support. But can it do so? Republicanism may be more promising than the market-based notion of the citizen as consumer, but whether that promise can be realized remains to be seen. We still face the question, in other words, of the practical possibility of republican citizenship.

Answering this question requires a return to the problem of collective action and a brief excursion into game theory. The excursion is necessary partly because game theory may indicate that there are certain conditions, not involving coercion, in which self-interested individuals will find cooperation to be in their interests.

The starting point is those problems of collective action in which a pure public good is involved in which the good in question is indivisible, nonexcludable, and nonrival. In these situations, as in the classic examples of clean air and national defense, everyone in the group may either cooperate to help produce the good in question or defect in hopes of enjoying the good without contributing to its provision. Except in special circumstances, one person may get the good without the help of the others, and will find it rational to defect. As in the *prisoners' dilemma,* the outcome will be less desirable to all than the outcome that follows from everyone's choosing to cooperate.

The assurance game differs from the prisoners' dilemma in two key respects: motives and information. In the prisoners' dilemma, whether iterative or not, the assumption is that the parties involved are rational and narrowly self-interested. In the assurance game, the assumption is that the parties are rational and conditionally altruistic. They are altruistic because they take the interests of others into consideration; they are willing to forgo the opportunity to ride free on the efforts of others. But their altruism is qualified or conditional because they are not willing to cooperate when they believe that others will take advantage of their cooperation and play them for suckers. If they are to act cooperatively, however, they must have the information, or the assurance that the others will indeed cooperate. But if there is insufficient reason to believe that others are acting, have acted, or are likely to act cooperatively, the assurance game degenerates into the prisoners' dilemma.

From the perspective of republican citizenship, the assurance game is clearly more promising than the prisoners' dilemma. Because the difference between the two rests on motives and informaribon, though, the question is whether we can encourage the motives and provide the information necessary to the assurance game. Can we assume that people are conditional altruists, or is it safer to conclude that human beings are irrevocably egoistic? On the basis of experience and the criticisms directed against Hobbes and other proponents of the egoistic or economic conception of human nature, no reason to believe that all people have been, are, and must be narrowly or strictly self-interested. Yet all that needs to be said on this point is that people may be either egoists or conditional altruists, and perhaps both, at different times. If this is the case, then there is no reason to reject the possibility that conditional altruism may be cultivated, thus establishing the basis for the assurance game.

That is a lengthy string of "is," however, and we cannot simply leap to the conclusion. First it is necessary to determine what cultivates conditional altruism. The answer seems to be prolonged interaction and interdependency, a sense of common condition, and the bonds that grow with familiarity. These are, as Elster notes, the same conditions that generate the information needed for the cooperative solution to the assurance game. "Affection for others and information about them tend to grow pari passu."

Five factors should be considered in this light: size, stability, fairness, communication, and participation.

Montesquieu seems to have perceived the importance of size when he wrote, "In a large republic, the common good is sacrificed to a thousand considerations; it is subordinated to exceptions; it depends upon accidents. In a small one, the public good is better felt, better known, lies nearer to each citizen; abuses are less extensive there and consequently less protected." In recent years both formal studies of collective action, such as Taylor's and Mancur Olson's, and the experiments of social psychologists have borne out the observation that size inhibits cooperation. The larger the group, the less likely are its members to cooperate for the good of the group. Small groups encourage solidarity and reciprocity because the individual's contribution is more visible and more meaningful not the mere "drop in the bucket" as it is in a large group.

The stability of a group is the second factor related to its ability to encourage cooperation, although the relationship is positive rather than negative in this case. The more stable the group the greater the continuity of its membership over time. The more likely it is to resemble an assurance game. One reason for this is that the members of a stable group know they are engaged in an ongoing enterprise, which should lead them to lower the rate of discount for future goods. Social psychologists' experiments confirm this reasoning. According to a survey of experimental studies of the conditions that foster and inhibit cooperation, "one important consideration for subjects is whether or not they view the interchange from a short term or a long-term perspective. Stability thus enables the actors to develop the ties of affection that promote conditional altruism: the desire to do one's part in a cooperative effort as long as others are doing theirs. Solidarity and stability go together.

The populations in these locations have remained stable over long periods of time. Individuals have shared a past and expect to share a future. It is important for individuals to maintain their reputations as reliable members of the community. These individuals live side by side and farm the same plots year after year. They expect their children and grandchildren to inherit their land. In other words, their discount rates are low.

It is equally important that considerations of fairness also play a part here. Those who believe they are being suspected for their efforts in the cooperative enterprise as genuine contributions to the well being of the group will not work for common good. Even conditional altruists are not likely to work to produce a public good when they suspect that others arc enjoying a disproportionate share of that good or simply failing to contribute to its production. This suspicion in turn generates claims of exploitation and, along with these claims, the selfish motives associated with the prisoners' dilemma. What counts as playing fair will vary with the circumstances, but it is always related to the idea of equality.

It is difficult, to be sure, to say exactly what is involved in treating people as equals. But it means at least that the interests of every member of a practice are to be taken into account and that no member's interests automatically count for more or less than any other's. In politics this translates into two familiar maxims: what touches all should be decided by all, and one person, one vote. Political equality in this sense is an essential ingredient in the civic community that Robert Putnam takes to be a successful democracy. According to his study of Italian politics, "the more that politics approximates the ideal of political equality among citizens following norms of reciprocity and engaged in self-government, the more civic that community may be said to be.'

Vital as it is, equality in this formal sense may not be enough to ensure conditional altruism. If there is reason to believe that formal equality merely masks an inequality of power or influence that gives some people's interests greater weight than others', then those with less influence may see themselves as locked in an exploitative relationship rather than a reciprocal one in which everyone is playing fair. When this happens, cooperation will collapse. Absolute equality of resources is not necessary certainly, but something like a distribution according to Rawls's 'difference principle', which holds that social and economic inequalities are justified when and because they work to the benefit of the worst-off members of society, will probably promote solidarity.

Communication, the fourth factor, is essential because no one will cooperate in the assurance game unless he or she has reason to believe that others will also cooperate. This information is easiest to gather in small, stable groups, where it grows naturally out of the "direct and many-sided relations" that Taylor takes to be an essential attribute of community. The knowledge that rules exist and are enforced, for instance, provides the individual with some basis for confidence in the cooperation of others.

Finally, the greater their participation in the affairs of the group, the more likely the members are to act cooperatively. Those who take an active part in the life of a group or community tend to develop an attachment to it and to identify their interests with the group's. This identification promotes solidarity, and it follows that one way to encourage solidarity in the body politic is to enable, or even to require, more people to participate in public affairs. In this way, as Mill recognized, those who are citizens in name only may transform themselves into active, public spirited citizens.

Communitarian critics like Charles Taylor, Maclntyre, Michel Sandel, Michael Walzer, Robert. N. Bellah, and Willian Sullivan have mounted powerful attacks on liberal tradition of citizenship. They argue that America is losing the institutions that help to create the kind of person who could sustain a connection to a wider political community and thus ultimately support the maintenance of free institutions. They fear that "individualism may have grown cancerous—that it may be destroying those social integuments that Tocqueville saw as moderating its more destructive potentials, that it may be threatening the survival of freedom itself."

Proponents of the liberal free market order should take seriously the concerns communitarians of that citizens of a liberal regime cannot live by exchanges alone. Liberal constitutionalism depends upon a certain level and quality of citizen virtue. That analysis serves, moreover, as the springboard for a radically transformist argument that seeks, not so much to elevate and shape, but to transcend and deny the self-interestedness that the free market exercises. Habits, for example, is a lament about "modernity" that often sounds like MacIntyre at his most dire attack: "Progress, modernity's master idea, seems less compelling when it appears that it may progress into the abyss." Taylor charges that modern individual is at his most "atomistic" existence and Sandel, warns that "in our day separation and individuation have reached a kind of culmination."

MacIntyre claims that modern Western societies are characterized by basic moral disagreement. "The most striking feature of contemporary moral utterance," says MacIntyre, "is that so much of it is used to express disagreements...". And this is, in part, because all we have are "fragments" of genuine morality : the "language and appearances of morality" without the "integral substance." MacIntyre's main evidence for his disintegration thesis is the rampant disagreement among moral philosophers and others about how to justify correct positions on issues such as just war and abortion. These disagreements seem to come to a head in metaethical disputes among "incommensurable" moral paradigms : deontology, the varieties of consequentialism, perfectionism, and so on.

One leading complaint shared by many communitarians is that ends and purposes tend to be regarded as matters of choice, matters about which liberalism posits an "unencumbered self" : "the values and relations we have are the products of choice, the possessions of a self given prior to its ends."

MacIntyre, likewise, bemoans what he terms the "emotivist" moral character of our age : "the self as presented by emotivism... cannot be simply or unconditionally identified with any particular moral attitude or point of view including that of those characters which socially embody emotivism just because of the fact that its judgments are in the end criterionless." Lacking any ultimate criteria of choice, "the self is 'nothing', is not a substance but a set of perpetually open possibilities." Without objective and impersonal criteria of morality, people come to hold that any moral principle is in the end an expression of the preferences of an individual. And so, even when Americans are bound up in valuable associations and personal relationships they tend to regard these as basically "arbitrary." Because they consider the ends of purposes of life to be arbitrary, Americans pursue mere "means" such as material prosperity.

Loking in substantive justification, communitarians further suggest, personal commitments rest on a "fragile foundation....it lacks a language to explain what seem to be the real commitments that define one's life, and to that extent the commitments themselves are precarious." The stability of shared commitments and associations requires articulateness about real human goods.

It can be argued that the communitarian critique of liberalism is misguided. Middle-class Americans are, apparently, capable of reflecting upon and revising their moral values and commitments, they are not "unencumbered selves" choosing in abstract isolation. An American is not unencumbered by his values and ends, but he does lack an articulate account of ultimate human goods but does this imply that he lacks any sense of real goods? Simon Weil and Iris Murdoch aruge that apprehending the good is more a matter of "seeing" than "saying," a matter of loving attention to "a magnetic but inexhaustible reality." Inarticulateness is not necessarily a sign of the arbitrariness of one's commitments : real human goods may be hard to articulate.

Communitarians generally tend to avoid objective moral claims, favouring instead the local route to community provided by our shared "social identity." And so they argue that our preferences are "detached from any social or cultural base that could give them broader meaning." Our problem, apparently, is that "American cultural traditions" live "suspended in glorious but terrifying isolation."

The isolation of the self is exhibited in our public life by the dominance of managerial expertise, and in private by a therapeutic model of relationships. Modern liberralism's moral condition is, as another communitarian has put it, a "mixture of private Romanticism and public utilitarianism."

Relationships, are modelled on a "therapeutic" quest for self-clarification, self-acceptance, and self-expression : the therapist takes "each person's values as given or self-defined," as "self-set value."

The task of therapy is simply to achieve "clarity" about one's "personal preferences" so that they can better be realized. communitarians worry that this conception of "healthy" personal relationships implies an ultimately isolated self-reliance.

Bellah, MacIntyre and others, are concerned to emphasize the importance of understanding our choices as choices among options defined by inherited ideals and traditions. Perhaps culture does elevate self-expression at the expense of tradition, but traditionalism becomes mere conventionalism unless it is supported by a critical account of which among our many inherited practices have real value.

4

The Civic Republican Tradition

Although liberal discourses of citizenship have in the main dominated our current civic style, the alternative civic republican tradition has emerged as a powerful alternative tradition and retains its relevance. Moreover, many of the really significant thinkers who have written on the subject of citizenship adhered to the civic republican mode. First of all, a word of explanation about the use of the term 'civic republican'. By 'republic' is meant a constitutional system with some form of sharing out of power to prevent concentrated arbitrary and autocratic government; and civic means the involvement of the citizenry in public affairs to the mutual benefit of the individual and the community.

Sixth to fourth-century Sparta and Athens and Rome's half millennium of Republican rule set the scene. Of all the classical political theorists and historians who wrote about citizenship as defined by and experienced in these states, Aristotle and Cicero each typified his age, expounded the subject thoroughly and exerted a great influence on subsequent thinkers.

Sparta and Athens at the pinnacle of their fame are the archetypes of opposed political principles - stern authoritarianism and free democracy. Yet as exponents of the classical institution of citizenship, they were really not so very far apart. Indeed, it is instructive to view Spartan citizenship as an intensification of the Athenian notion of public service. Both of these city-states were proud of their citizens, commitment to their civic duties, though whereas Athens is famed for the ready participation of her citizens in governmental and juridical functions, Sparta is renowned for the selfless devotion of her citizen-soldiers.

How does this background relate to Aristotle's treatment of the subject of citizenship? The topic features in his *Politics*, and appears in a few relevant passages like the *Nicomachean Ethics*. In the *Politics* he explains the great variety of practices at different times in history and in different states, leading him to declare that 'The nature of citizenship is a question which is often disputed'. However, Aristotle was not only a political scientist, he was a political theorist as well: he therefore also expressed his views on what citizenship ideally should be.

What, then, is particularly characteristic about Aristotle's conception of citizenship? Size of population is important for him. The body of citizens should be sufficiently compact as to enable them to 'know one another's characters'. Only by means of this intimacy could the necessary communal bonds of true fraternal citizenship - 'concord' be tied. Athens, where he spent just over half of his life exceeded his absolute maximum. Another of his ideal characteristic of citizenship, for which in fact Athens did provide an apposite model, was that citizens should 'share the civic life of ruling and being ruled in turn'. There is no room for apathy, citizens are expected to be publicly active.

But the crucial requirement was that citizens must possess of and display arte, goodness or virtue. By this Aristotle meant fitting in social and political behaviour, to the style of the particular constitution of the polis. In a sense, therefore, civic virtue was for Aristotle a relative quality. Even so, a basic moral calibre was essential in whatever polis: the good citizens were those wholly and efficiently committed through thought and action to the common good. Moreover, by living such a life the citizen benefited himself as well as the state : he became a morally more mature person. There was, indeed, no other way of becoming a fulfilled human being because, Aristotle asserted, 'man is by nature an animal intended to live in a polis'.

Two problems arise from this conception of *arte*. One is that men who must work full-time for a living cannot have the leisure to study or participate fully in public affairs; so, although in some city-states such men were enrolled as citizens, it was difficult for them to be good, 'proper' citizens. Aristotle's model citizenry was a leisured, propertied elite. The second problem concerns those who, although by all other criteria are citizens, are deficient of the ideal virtuous qualities. After all, good citizens are not born. Aristotle was fully aware that good citizens are the product of education. He was convinced that the state provision of education is absolutely essential, and admired Sparta as being almost the only polis to undertake this responsibility.

Aristotle provided the classic exposition of the civic republican form of citizenship. From him the ideal was passed on through Zeno, the founder of Stoicism., to Roman thinkers such as Cicero. And although Machiavelli and Rousseau do not overtly mention Aristotle, there can be little doubt that through the deep study of classical writers that dominated Renaissance and eighteenth- century education and literature, they did absorb his teaching. Absorption does not necessarily mean total acceptance, of course. For instance, Cicero, while admiring Aristotle's stress on morality , rejected his elitist definition of citizenship, even though he wrote primarily to remind the Roman oligarchy of their state's honourable tradition of civic virtue.

Cicero lived in disturbed times – for he was 62 when Julius Caesar was assassinated. Nor did he personally escape the turmoil, He was a lawyer, a politician and, by philosophical conviction, a Stoic. Moreover, he lived by his beliefs. And as he lived by his beliefs, so he died by them, paying the ultimate bloody price for his civic moral standards. On the death of Caesar, Cicero warned against the danger posed to the Roman Republic of the power being amassed by the contemptible Mark Antony, the very antithesis of Cicero's concept of a virtuous citizen. Caught in fight from Antony's agents, he was murdered and his severed head and hands were sent to Mark Antony and his wife.

Cicero's education had given him a splendid foundation for thinking about citizenship: he studied political theory in Athens and law in Rome. Cicero's staunch commitment to the Stoic ethic gave his interpretation of citizenship its weighty influence. Basing his arguments on this demanding philosophy, Cicero explained that man must use his gifts of speech and moral and rational thought for virtuous actions. If a citizen, by withdrawing into the ease of a private existence, denies his fellow men, his community and his state the benefit of his conscientious involvement in public work, he is betraying his nature as a social animal.

Only the higher ranks of Roman society, of course, had the opportunity to commit themselves really fully to public service; as a consequence, the responsibility of living the life of a good citizen fell most heavily upon them. Thus, Cicero asserted that a worthy and truly brave citizen, and one who deserves to hold the reins of government, will shun and detest civil dissensions, tumults and civil wars; and will give himself so to the service of the public, as to aim at no riches or power for himself and will so take care of the whole community, as not to pass over any, part of it and will rather part with his life itself, than do anything that is contrary to the virtues.

Through the exposition of his high moral principles and his clear, elegant prose, Cicero remained the most influential of all moral philosophers in Europe down to the nineteenth century. His influence was especially marked in Renaissance Italy. Here an awareness of the ancient practice and ideal of citizenship was also enlivened by the study of Roman historians. Among these, and of incomparable stature, was Livy, who had laboured for forty years to produce his *History of Rome* from its foundation in 142 'books'. The first ten of these were used by Machiavelli as a platform on which to muse about the nature of politics, including citizenship.

Like Cicero, Niccolo Machiavelli was disturbed by the turbulence of his times, viewed from the perspective of engagement in public affairs - as minister, diplomat and soldier for the city-state of Florence. Following military defeat and a change of regime, he was dismissed from office, imprisoned and tortured. On his release, he retired to the exiled sanctuary of his farm some miles south of the city. There, in the evenings, closeted in his study, he settled to a new life as a writer. And in so doing he gave a new impetus to the civic republican conception of citizenship.

Machiavelli was a realist. His studies and experience led him to believe that violence and war are more common than peace, that despotic government is more common than republican, and that corrupt and self-seeking behaviour is more common than good citizenship. Yet good citizenship is essential for sustaining a militarily secure state and a republican form of government; indeed, citizenship is possible only in a republic. But for Machiavelli good citizenship had necessarily to be of a hardened, tougher moral fabric than even the classical writers had commended.

And so, as with Aristotle and Cicero, civic virtue is central to Machiavelli's thinking on citizenship. However, his use of the word virtu, though conveniently translated as 'virtue', carries many overtones quite absent from the English word. Of its rich content, one of Machiavelli's recent English editor Crick lists then as courage, fortitude, audacity,, skill and civic spirit. Virtu is the quality of mind and action that creates, saves or maintains cities..'Civic spirit' is probably the best simple translation - if by 'spirit' one means spirited action.

How are such men made in Renaissance Italy, all too rare quality of virtu? By an education steeped in a vigorous civic religion, Machiavelli believed. Here lies the difference between pagan Rome and Christian Italy, he argued, the one strengthened by the virtue of stout-hearted manliness, the other weakened by the virtue of Christian humility.

The good citizen, effectively educated in the precepts of virtu, must lead an active life, whether civilian or military. In civilian life the citizen must take a positive interest in public affairs and, above all, refrain from according priority to a private life of wealth, luxury and ease over a commitment to the general public good.

But it is the role of the citizen as soldier that Machiavelli especially emphasizes. Military service provides the discipline necessary to convert the naturally wicked man into a virtuous, patriotic citizen and patriotic citizen-soldiers will serve the state so much more effectively than mercenaries. Politics and military organization are, in fact, to Machiavelli's mind, interrelated. In the *Discourses* he declares that where military discipline 'does not exist, there can neither be good laws nor anything else that is good'. The truth of the necessity for this discipline, he explains, 'is apparent on every page of Livy's history'. Only by deploying its citizens as soldiers aggressively can the republic ensure that its citizens as civilians can enjoy the benefits of a stable polity.

Machiavelli and other Renaissance thinkers revived the classical concept of citizenship and when, in the eighteenth century, a new intensification of classical studies came about, the writings of the Italian political theorists reinforced the civic republican message. According to an influential thesis by J. G. A. Pocock, the political thinking which led up to the American War of Independence and Constitution was largely coloured by this shade of transmitted citizenship theory. It has been argued by 'Pocock that Americans are the ultimate beneficiaries of a classical republicanism recodified by Machiavelli'.

Jean-Jacques Rousseau is not likely to be the first candidate of anyone who canvasses the history of political thought in search of exemplars of republicanism. Rousseau's republican credentials are good enough, to be sure, as a number of recent studies attest. The problem is that they may be too good to allow much hope of finding a significant strain of liberalism in his thought. Certainly his willingness to invoke a legislator who "should feel that he is capable of changing human nature," his call for a civil religion that requires "a purely civil profession of faith, the articles of which are for the sovereign to establish," and his declaration that people may "be forced to be free" seem to put him outside the bounds of most definitions of liberalism.

In the end, one may decide that other important political philosophers—Montesquieu or Tocqueville, perhaps, or John Stuart Mill or T. H. Green -are better exemplars of republican liberalism than Rousseau. Yet none of these thinkers combined a republican commitment to civic virtue with the analytical device of the social contract-a device usually associated with liberalism. Rousseau did this, of course, and he did it in a brilliant way that is doubly valuable for practice of citizenship.

Rousseau's peculiar contractarian republicanism is valuable, first, because it suggests that republican ideals and liberal devices are not strictly incompatible. Quentin Skinner may be correct when he remarks that "the ideals of classical republicanism had largely been swallowed up by the rising tide of contractarian political thought" by the time of Montesquieu, at which point "the concept of individual rights attained that hegemony which it has never subsequently lost."If contractarian thought did have this general effect, however, it was despite Rousseau's efforts. Rousseau saw the "rising tide of contractarian political thought"presenting an opportunity to advance republican ideals, not engulf them. The idea of the social contract may have encouraged people to think of government as a guarantor of their individual rights and liberty, but Rousseau saw that the idea also offered a means of deepening their understanding of their duties and common interests.

By using the contractarian device in this way, Rousseau pointed to the reciprocity that should obtain between the members of a body politic. This concern for reciprocity is the second respect in which his brand of republican liberalism is worth exploring here. Rousseau recognized the need to make people aware of their reciprocal rights and obligations and to help them see the connection between their individual interests and the common good. He hoped to accomplish these goals and thus to promote citizenship by appealing to the idea of the "general will." Whether he succeeded or failed, there is much to learn about the plausibility of republican liberalism from a study of his attempt.

Rousseau's attempt to formulate the general will is an attempt to provide the foundation for a body politic as a cooperative venture in which all citizens are treated fairly. More than that, Rousseau's polity would secure a substantial measure of autonomy for citizens in the form of "moral liberty." Whether they will recognize this, however, and sense that their rights and obligations are reciprocal that their liberty as citizens rests on their duties as subjects-is another matter. As Rousseau remarks in his Letter to D'Alembert,

> 'When our interest is involved, our sentiments are soon corrupted.... Is it not a necessary effect of the constitution of things that the vicious man profits doubly, from his injustice and the probity of others? What more advantageous treaty could he conclude than one obliging the whole world, excepting himself, to be just, so that everyone will faithfully render him what is due him, while he renders to no one what he owes? He loves virtue, unquestionably; but he loves it in others because he hopes to profit from it.

The General Will and Moral Freedom

The idea of the general will rests on a fundamental distinction between two aspects of a person. In Rousseau's terms, every person may be thought of as a man-an actual, identifiable person and, at least potentially, as a citizen. Insofar as we are men, we are each unique; each of us has a particular identity and set of interests. Insofar as we are citizens, however, we are alike in that we are members of the public, and as members of the public we share a common interest in the welfare of the body politic. Everyone, consequently, has both a particular interest as a man and a general interest as a citizen.

From the distinction between man and citizen, Rousseau moves to a corresponding distinction between the particular or private will, on the one hand, and the general will, on the other. The private will aims at the fulfillment of the particular interest of a man, of an actual individual, while the general will seeks to further the interest of the citizen. Because the interests of all citizens are the same, the object of the general will is the common good or public interest-the interest all share as members of the public. Rousseau distinguishes the private from the general will in this manner: "The private will tends by its nature toward preferences, and the general will toward equality". As men with private wills, we naturally move to our own interests and desires. The private will is partial both because it is the will of an identifiable individual, one who is only part of the body politic, and because it places a higher value on one's personal interests than on the interests of others. The general will, in contrast, tends toward equality because it necessarily grants equal consideration to the interests of every member of the body politic. Because it focuses on the common interest we share as citizens, the general will is impartial: it considers only the interests of the abstract person, Rousseau calls, the citizen. Because we are all the same qua citizen, the general will is devoted equally to all.

A man who has the ability to be an adept burglar, for example, may well find it in his interest, as a man, to put his burgling skills to use. His private will may then be to steal from others in order to satisfy his own desires. The general will, however, directs the potential burglar to obey the law. As the will of the citizen, the general will requires us at times to ignore our particular interests and personal attributes our possessions, our position in society, our abilities and to think of ourselves only as members of the public. Laws against burglary are in the interests of all citizens, if not all men, and if our potential burglar thinks of himself only as a citizen, he will recognize that he ought to respect the law.

As the example illustrates, the general will performs much the same function as John Rawls's "veil of ignorance," which deprives the parties to a hypothetical social contract of most information about their personal identities. Behind the veil, the parties do not know what their social or economic positions are, what abilities or disabilities they have, what religious or philosophical views they hold, or even what their ages, vaces caste or sexes are. The veil thus forces the parties to the contract to adopt a common, and presumably morally neutral viewpoint. In Rousseau's terms, it leads the parties to promote their common interest as citizens rather than their private interests as men.

There is also a moral dimension to the general will, just as there is to the veil of ignorance. Rousseau does not invoke the general will simply as a counterweight to selfish interests. This would be futile, for one's interest as a man may well outweigh one's interest as a citizen. An industrialist may find, for instance, that it is not in his or her interest to install pollution-inhibiting devices in the factory's smokestacks, all things considered, even though it is in his or her interest as a citizen to reduce air pollution. Rousseau's claim, however, is that in some cases we ought to consider only our interests as citizens. The purpose of the general will, then, is to provide a principle that will lead to just public policy. If we consider the interests of citizens and not those of men, in other words, we will reach decisions that establish laws and policies in accordance with the common interest. From the standpoint of citizens-as members of the public-we share the same interests. Considered abstractly, as citizens, the burglar and his victim share a common interest in the enforcement of a law against burglary, just as the industrialist and the person who lives downwind of the factory share a common interest in eliminating air pollution. What Rousseau suggests, in sum, is that only the general will of the citizen and not the private will of the man should determine public policy.

Understood in this way, the general will operates as a moral imperative or principle; its purpose is to guarantee that the claims of no particular individuals are given preference. Everyone receives equal consideration because public decisions take into account only the viewpoint of the citizen. Any other perspective is at best morally irrelevant. Here we see the emphasis on equality that is such a marked characteristic of Rousseau's political philosophy. The social compact, according to Rousseau, established an equality between the citizens such that they all engage themselves under the same conditions and should all benefit from the same rights. Thus by the very nature of the compact, every act of sovereignty, which is to say every authentic act of the general will, obligates or favors all citizens equally, so that the sovereign knows only the nation as a body and makes no distinctions between any of those who compose it.

A further implication is that laws established in accordance with the general will do more than grant equal consideration to everyone: they truly are in everyone's interest, for a law sanctioned by the general will promotes everyone's interest qua citizen. Such a law may not be the first choice of many individuals, but it is acceptable to all because it makes some contribution to everyone's well-being.

According to Rousseau, moreover, the general will applies only to laws, not to decrees. A law is a general policy, a rule that governs the conduct of every member of the body politic, while a decree is an act that refers to particular, identifiable individuals. The general will "loses its natural rectitude when it is directed toward any individual, determinate object. Because then, judging what is foreign to us, we have no true principle of equity to guide us". There is no principle of equity in these cases because flesh-and-blood men, in all their particularity, are involved, not abstract citizens. Instead of appealing to the general will, then, we must decide on the merits of the particular case-and these decisions are best left to executives and judges, not to the sovereign people as a whole.

Understanding the general will as a principle meant to guide public decisions is also consistent with what Rousseau has to say about groups within the body politic. There is a sense in which each of these groups, or "partial associations," has its own general will, for the individuals who compose each group share a common interest in their capacities as members of that association. These groups, in other words, may be considered publics. When we regard them from the perspective of the body politic, however, it is clear that the will of each association is a private will-one that may be antagonistic to the general will of the community as a whole. Rousseau consequently disapproves of these associations because he fears that they will divide and divert the loyalty of the people, who will be more likely to think of themselves as merchants or farmers, Catholics or Protestants than as citizens. When this happens, Rousseau warns, the private wills of these groups will prevent the general will from prevailing when the people vote. "In order for the general will to be well expressed," he concludes, "it is therefore important that there be no partial society in the State, and that each citizen give only his own opinion."

There is also a close connection between the general will and Rousseau's conception of moral freedom. There must be, if the social contract is to solve the "fundamental problem" that Rousseau sets himself: " 'Find a form of association that defends and protects the person and goods of each associate with all the common force, and by means of which each one, uniting with all, nevertheless obeys only himself and remains as free as before"

How can a man who enters 'into a contract to place himself under law be as free as he was before the contract? Rousseau's answer relies on distinction between three kinds of freedom: natural, civil, and moral. The man who enters into the social contract may surrender the natural freedom of the state of nature, but he gains civil freedom and the opportunity for moral freedom in its place. Civil freedom which secures "the proprietorship of everything he possesses," is "limited by the general will"; moral freedom which overcomes the "impulse of appetite" and requires "obedience to the law one has prescribed for oneself," is expressed through it.

This solution to Rousseau's "fundamental problem" is not free of difficulties. Nevertheless, it is a remarkable attempt to square autonomy with authority. For Rousseau, as for Kant, there is a close connection between freedom and law. Moral freedom consists of self legislation, of obeying laws that one gives to oneself. Natural freedom is freedom from restraint, but moral freedom requires self-restraint. In order to formulate the laws that are to govern one's conduct, one must reflect on one's appetites, needs, and circumstances. To follow "the impulse of appetite alone is slavery," but the moral freedom that comes with self-legislation "makes man truly the master of himself ". Moral freedom, then, is a form of self-government or self-mastery or autonomy that is available only to those who belong to a polity in which men act as citizens by following their general will. In the state of nature, man may be free in one sense, but he is subject to the impulses of his appetites and the attacks of others. In the just society of the Social Contract, the individual enjoys a different kind of freedom-the kind that allows him to obey only himself, as a citizen, while uniting with others in a cooperative, law governed enterprise.

In this way the social contract and the general will, understood as a principle akin to Kant's categorical imperative, represent what may be called the liberal side of Rousseau's political thought. On the one hand, the contract and the general will justify political authority by showing how it can reconcile "what right permits with what interest prescribes, so that justice and utility are not at variance"; they also show how the individual who enters the contract "obeys only himself and remains as free as before". Yet political authority is justified, on the other hand, only when the general will is operative and citizens are obeying laws that they prescribe for themselves. Thus Rousseau conjoins autonomy with authority, moral freedom with political obligation.

There are, however, well-known problems with Rousseau's contractual argument, especially where freedom and obligation are concerned. There is, first, the complaint that he is self-contradictory, and perhaps tilts toward totalitarianism, when he claims that someone may be "forced to be free." How can one be forced to be free when freedom is the very absence of coercion?

The obvious answer is that Rousseau is talking about moral freedom here, and he merely means that one may be compelled to obey a law to which one has consented. But this explanation does not meet all objections, for why should one have to be forced to obey a law to which one has consented? Here the answer lies in Rousseau's distinction between private wills and the general will. The private will of the lawbreaker-of a man who cheats on his taxes, for example-is likely to be in conflict with his general will as a citizen. The cheater may "view what he owes the common cause as a free contribution, the loss of which will harm others less than its payment burdens him," and consequently "wish to enjoy the rights of the citizen without wanting to fulfill the duties of a subject" These two wills are in conflict because the cheater wants to enjoy the benefits of the social order-"the rights of the citizen "-without contributing his share to the maintenance of that order-"the duties-of a subject."

Therefore, in order for the social compact not to be an ineffectual formula, it tacitly includes the following engagement, which alone can give force to the others: that whoever refuses to obey the general will shall be constrained to do so by the entire body.

The body politic, according to the view set out here, is supposed to be a cooperative enterprise, and the citizens are all pledged to share its burdens. Only those who try to evade this obligation-those who "wish to enjoy the rights of the citizen without wanting to fulfill the duties of a subject"must be "forced to be free." These individuals are free riders. Like the tax cheater, they want to receive the benefits of social cooperation without contributing their fair share toward the provision of those benefits.

The just state grants equal rights and protection to all, thereby helping to secure everyone from personal dependence. Any man who accepts and follows social rules whenever they favor him, only to break them when it serves his purposes, is contributing to the destruction of that realm. Such a man is a parasite whose actions threaten his own freedom-his moral freedom-as well as that of others. That is why Rousseau says that the free rider must be "forced to be free"-forced, that is, to act in accordance with his own will as a citizen.

Assuming that this response is satisfactory, there is still a second problem confronting Rousseau's attempt to join right and interest, freedom and obligation. This problem arises out of Rousseau's endorsement of majority rule, which appears to lead hirn again into a contradiction: How can someone remain as free as before he entered into the social contract if he is now subject to the will of the majority?

Rousseau is aware of this problem, as his brief discussion of majority rule makes clear. He begins by acknowledging that the social contract requires unanimous consent: "Since every man is born free and master of himself, no one can subject him without his consent". But he soon goes on to say that "except for this primitive contract, the vote of the majority always obligates all the others". The problem is obvious- how can the opponents be free yet subject to laws to which they have not consented? Rousseau quickly offers this resolution. He argues that when a law is proposed in the assembly of the people, what they are being asked is not precisely whether they approve or reject the proposal, but whether it does or does not conform to the general will that is theirs. Each one expresses his opinion on this by voting, and the declaration of the general will is drawn from the counting of the votes. This is an important distinction, almost unmarked in Rousseau's writings, between 'the' general will and 'a' general will. The proposal is to be approved if it conforms to the general will, that is, the principle that everyone should act as a citizen, not as a man; but a general will, a specific policy that satisfies this principle, is discovered only by counting votes. Votes are irrelevant to the general will, for principles are not discovered by voting, but a general will often need counting of majority votes.

Making Citizens of Men

Beginning with the liberal device of the social contract, Rousseau's argument leads to conclusions usually associated with republican theorists and occasionally, some critics claim, with totalitarians. His definition of citizens not as mere bearers of privileges and immunities but as "participants in the sovereign authority" already points in the republican direction. So does his argument that people must sometimes "be forced to be free" in order to prevent them from disobeying laws they have prescribed as citizens for themselves. That no one can enter the social contract on these terms, for no polity could survive if it allowed its members to disobey the laws whenever it suited their personal interests to do so.

Rousseau's argument thus rests on his conception of the political order as a cooperative practice subject to the principle of fair play. He does not use these terms, to be sure, but the logic of his argument clearly points to this conception of the political order. One important aspect of this conception is his desire to promote the spirit of cooperation by encouraging people to think of themselves as subjects who have an obligation to obey the laws they make as citizens.

Rousseau's abiding concern for equality is evidence of this desire. The great possibility of a political society, according to Rousseau, is that it "substitutes a moral and legitimate equality for whatever physical inequality nature may have placed between man." Equality thus promotes freedom, largely by securing people from personal dependence. Throughout his writings, Rousseau makes plain his hatred for personal dependence, which, in true republican spirit, is a form of slavery.

Rousseau's devotion to the small community and his hatred of big cities also play a part here. More than mere nostalgia for the Geneva of his youth or for the city-states of antiquity, this concern reflects his underlying conception of the political order as a cooperative practice. As the size of a cooperative practice grows, each person's contribution seems less and less significant, just as "the share of each member of the State" in "the sovereign authority" decreases.

Rousseau's discussion of education in the *Emile* and elsewhere also aims at cultivating the cooperative attitude of the citizen-subject, as do his supposedly totalitarian remarks on the legislator and civil religion in the Social Contract. However unappealing it may seem, the civil religion is "a purely civil profession of faith, the articles of which are for the sovereign to establish, not exactly as religious dogmas, but as sentiments of sociability without which it is impossible to be a good citizen or a faithful subject. Indeed, the doctrine of the civil religion exemplifies Rousseau's attempt to combine the republican emphasis on civic devotion with a concern, subsequently associated with liberalism, for tolerance and freedom of thought:

> Now it matters greatly to the State that each citizen has a religion that causes him to love his duties; but the dogmas of that religion are of no interest either to the State or to its members; except insofar as these dogmas relate to morality, and to the duties that anyone who professes it is obliged to fulfill toward others.

The 'legislator', this extraordinary person who drafts the fundamental laws and establishes the basic institutions should feel that he is capable of changing human nature, so to speak, of transforming each individual, who by himself is a perfect and solitary whole, into a part of a larger whole from which this individual receives, in a sense, his life and his being; of substituting a partial and moral existence for the physical and independent existence we have all received from nature.

Although he cannot himself enact the legislation he recommends, the legislator should feel capable of transforming human nature because such a transformation is necessary to replace the natural life of men with the moral life of the citizen. The legislator's task, in a sense, is to complete the passage from the state of nature to the civil state. This passage from the state of nature to the civil state produces a remarkable change in man, by substituting justice for instinct in his behavior and giving his actions the morality they previously lacked. Only then, when the voice of duty replaces physical impulse and right replaces appetite, does man, who until that time only considered himself, find himself forced to act upon other principles and to consult his reason before heeding his inclinations. Although in this state he deprives himself of several advantages given by nature, he gains such great ones, his faculties are exercised and developed, his ideas broadened, his feelings ennobled, and his whole soul elevated to such a point that if the abuses of this new condition did not often degrade him beneath the condition he left, he ought ceaselessly to bless the happy moment that tore him away from it forever, and that changed him from a stupid, limited animal into an intelligent being and a man.

The legislator's task, then, is to provide the legal and institutional foundation that will prevent the abuses of the civil state that degrade people below their natural condition. By doing this-by directing people toward the general will-the legislator will complete the transformation of human nature begun when people first left the state of nature.

Through these and other measures, Rousseau sought to encourage men to act as citizens to seek and follow the general will. If some of the measures seem excessive, it is probably because Rousseau regarded the challenge reconciling "what right permits with what interest prescribes," as extraordinarily difficult. Some of these measures may now seem out of place or anachronistic-the invocation of the legislator, for instance-and others, such as the call for a civil religion, may fit better with a strong form of classical republicanism than with liberalism. There are other problems with Rousseau's theory as well, notably his exclusion of women from the public realm. This exclusion is objectionable not only for what seems to be his repugnant attitude but also for the way it condemns women to the personal dependence he so frequently abhors.

In addition, some problems associated with Rousseau's formulation of the general will persist even when we understand it as a principle that requires us to act as citizens rather than as men. First is the question of how the general will is to be applied. What does it mean to say that public policy must attend to the common interest of citizens and ignore the private interests of men? Is the viewpoint of the citizen always readily apparent? Consider the case of a city that finds its fortunes tied to a single industry. Cities of this sort often find themselves on the horns of a dilemma. There may be reliable evidence that pollution from the industry is hazardous to the health of those in the community, but eliminating that hazard may involve the loss of the industry with all of the money and jobs it directly and indirectly provides. Everyone in the community will suffer if the hazard is not eliminated, yet it is also conceivable that everyone will suffer if the industry leaves. In this case, is there a single viewpoint that is distinctly the citizen's?

By altering the example slightly, we can produce yet another problem for Rousseau. Suppose that many people in this city will suffer severe economic hardship if the industry leaves and that a few, for one reason or another, will not suffer at all. In this case all of the members of the community share an interest in eliminating the hazard, but all do not share an interest in keeping the industry in town. The general will, presumably, would require the elimination of the hazard because that would be in the interest of the citizens, even though it might spell disaster for most of the men in the city. Given possibilities of this kind, is it clear that we should always ignore the private interests of men when deciding matters of public policy?

Rousseau's views on citizenship were drawn, however, from Plutarch rather than Livy, and from the history of Sparta as much as Rome. His early absorption in Roman history at his father's knee led him later to proclaim that 'I was a Roman before I was twelve'. Even so, it was the small-scale compactness of the citystate that he, like Aristotle, felt to be the best-suited context for an ideal polity: hence part of Sparta's attraction for him. He was also influenced by his admiration for the citystate republic of Geneva, where he was born: he signed *The Social Contract* 'J.J. Rousseau, citizen of Geneva'. In his political writings, he gave considerable attention to the topic of citizenship.

These ideal arrangements, in effect a utopia, would not be easy to apply in eighteenth-century circumstances. Rousseau was forced to address this problem because he was asked twice to advise countries in difficulties, namely, Corsica and Poland. He saw that one of their needs was a boosting of patriotism, and suggested that, in these modern conditions, unlike those of classical antiquity, the bonding force could most effectively be provided by a sense of nationhood. Thus he wrote to the Corsicans: 'The first rule that we have to follow is national character: all people have, or should have, a national character; if it is lacking in this, it would be necessary to start by giving it one'

Rousseau was breaking the classical mould, and his fame and influence as a political thinker derive as much from innovative ideas as his continuation of tradition, probably more so. Yet his true self was surely happier in the old tradition. Seven years before he wrote *The Social Contract* and ten years before his work on *Corsica* he epigrammatically assured his readers that, 'The country cannot continue to exist without liberty, nor liberty without virtue, nor virtue without citizens'.

Rousseau's political ideas had little impact before the French Revolution. Then they caught on. 'The law is the expression of the general will', proclaimed the Declaration of Rights. No one was a more pious disciple of Jean-Jacques than Robespierre. His ardent desire was to make France a nation of virtuous citizens. The difficulty was how to achieve this end. Rousseau advocated the moral force of education as the normal method; Robespierre was convinced of the educational morality of force in the abnormal times of crisis: virtue must be supplemented by the propagandistic use of terror -virtue without which terror is squalidly repressive, terror without which virtue lies disarmed'. But, then, did not Rousseau insist that obedience to the General Will was the way to true freedom and that anyone who disobeyed it 'shall be forced to be free'.

Yet the civic republican version did not die. It was sustained in the nineteenth century alongside the new liberal interpretation by such figures as Hegel and Tocqueville; while more recently its qualities have been recognized and attempts been made to use them as a counterbalance to the perceived defects of liberal citizenship. Accordingly, the distinguished writers in the classical tradition are not just of historical interest. They still have contributions to make to our own understanding of the basic principles of civic republicanism.

Purpose of citizenship

All institutions must serve a purpose. A purpose may, however, be complex, it may be controversial, and its operation in practice may not live up to ideal expectations. In these very common circumstances, theorists and commentators expound, elucidate, judge and defend. The objectives of citizenship have been clarified and promoted by such processes; and from this work we can derive a short definition which might run along these lines: The purpose of citizenship is to connect the individual and the state in a symbiotic relationship so that a just and stable republican polity can be created and sustained and the individual citizen can enjoy freedom. Thus, the individual can be truly free only in a republic; a republic can exist only through the support of its citizens.

'Man was born free, and he is everywhere in chains', Rousseau famously declared. How to resolve the antithesis? One way is by a revolutionary breaking of the chains of tyranny - the liberal way of asserting the citizen's rights, including the right to a private life free of state interference. But Rousseau did not want to break the chains; he wanted to make them legitimate, to achieve their mutation into a linkage that would provide mankind with a moral, positive form of freedom: the republican way.

Rousseau, whose work is a particularly good exemplar of the civic republican view of freedom, distinguished between natural liberty as freedom through the pursuit of self-interest, and civil liberty as freedom though the merging of self-interest with duty. He asserted this principle pungently in negative form while proclaiming its absolute primacy: To renounce freedom', he declared, 'is to renounce one's humanity, one's rights as a man and equally one's duties'. This kind of freedom is the prerequisite for a life of happiness and virtue; and it can be enjoyed only as a citizen. In a polity devoid of citizenship, men are subject to the arbitrary will of others; outside a political structure men are subject to their own whims.

One is free in a republic because qua citizen the 'them and us' opposition of government and subject is dissolved. In Rousseau's theory this is achieved by his ingenious device of the General Will. The basic concept, however, was already present in the thought of Aristotle, who said, 'Liberty has more than one form. One of its forms consists in the interchange of ruling and being ruled'.

So, one of the purposes of citizenship is to secure freedom; the other is to underpin the republican state. What kind of polity is best suited to the effective discharge of this citizenly function? Two characteristics are especially desirable, perhaps essential. One is a mixed constitution, the other is compact size.

Citizenship does not imply democracy: this form of constitution is not conducive to stability, so many of the theorists argued. Citizenship produces the best kind of state, a republic, when that status operates through a constitution in which different forms are mingled. Aristotle established this desideratum. What he advocated was the avoidance of extremes - the golden mean of a mixture of aristocratic and democratic elements.

Montesquieu, in his *Spirit of the Laws,* provided the solutions in his theory of 'confederation' which combines 'all the internal advantages of a republican, together with the external force of a monarchical government'. What is crucial is that the component republics preserve their happiness and probity. This device was found especially attractive to Alexander Hamilton, who contributed so significantly to the civic republican thinking in the American colonies. Tocqueville, also, in the nineteenth century, was convinced that the pyramidal structure of the United States - from township to state to federal government - successfully retained the republican style of active citizenship.

Nevertheless, citizenship can neither preserve freedom nor sustain the republican state if citizens do not live it in the republican style of a sense of community, of friendship and concord.

Style of citizenship

The republican style of political thinking places great emphasis above all on the necessity for the state and its citizens to be a community, an organic society, not merely a collection of individuals. Constitutions and laws, it is true, lay down the rules by which a group of individuals live together in a state; but constitutions and laws cannot by themselves make a community, only the propitious conditions in which a group can get into a community. That gelling process requires the essential ingredient of social friendship and harmony.

It was Aristotle who analysed this idea particularly thoroughly in the course of his survey of different kinds of friendship in the *Nicomacbean Ethics.* Here he makes the basic observation that 'friendship is an expression of community, and continues by claiming that all friendship associations 'may be regarded as parts of the association we call the state'. However, he felt the need to introduce a special word to distinguish the particular kind of friendship that exists at the state level, at least in well-ordered polities. This word, a sort of catchword among Greek writers for a century before Aristotle, was homonoza. It carried the dual meaning of peace between the city states and social /political harmony within them: the antonym respectively of war and civil strife. The usual translation is 'concord'.

Concord is something more than agreement in opinion, for that might be found in people who do not know one another. Neither do we call it concord when people agree in theory about a speculative matter. But we say there is concord in a state when the citizens agree about their interests, adopt a policy unanimously and proceed to carry it out. This implies that we have concord only where a practical end is in view - an important end capable of attainment by the interested parties concord is friendship between the citizens of a state, its province being the interests and concerns of life. Citizenship connects the individual to the state, certainly; but it also connects individuals to each other. Citizenship is teamwork; citizenship is shared activity in a spirit of mutual goodwill. Rousseau, too, understood that, though concord is crucial, it does not appear spontaneously. One of the methods he advocated was the use of theatre, festivals and spectacles to imbue the citizenry with 'public fraternity, in the tradition of the ancients.

Citizenship requires independence of mind, else manipulation or corruption will destroy its very essence. Citizens must therefore be socially and economically independent in order to be able to resist attempts at manipulating or corrupting their free political or juridical judgement. They must also be disinterested, be independent in the sense of having the capacity to be objective. Moreover, they must have enough time to allocate to their civic activities. Only owners of a reasonable amount of property can fit to this description. But the case goes even further. Because it is so difficult to identify who is likely to be a virtuous, active and conscientious citizen, as a rule of thumb, ownership of property was taken to be as good a practical index and guide as any.

Nevertheless, not all property is associated with civic virtue, only land. It is owners of land who have been thought to be a reliable and stabilizing influence, though admittedly this feature of the class was often said to relate to self-interest. The argument is that investment in land gives the owner a tangible stake in the state, a vested interest therefore in its preservation and strength. In the republican tradition, however, the matter of motive was of lesser moment than the source of the property. Owning wealth was a sign of virtue; making wealth was civically questionable. Remember the slogan of the rebellious citizens of *Animal Farm*: 'landowners good, merchants bad.'

But there is a problem in all this. By identifying civic virtue with landed wealth, the civic republican thinkers were praising and supporting inequality in the economic realm while, at the same time, advocating and promoting citizenship as a means to equality in the political realm. This contradiction was of more than theoretical concern, as some writers were aware; for extreme disparities of wealth can lead to usurpation of power by the rich . Rousseau consequently concluded that 'the social state is advantageous to men only when all possess something and none has too much'.

Aristotle, as one would expect, also argued against extremes. Assuredly, he put his faith in landowners as against traders: 'The natural form of the art of acquisition is always and in all cases, acquisition from fruits and animals,' he asserted; in contrast to 'retail trade which is justly censured, because the gain in which it results is not naturally made from plants and animal, but is made at the expense of other men'. In political terms, 'the land should be owned, in our ideal state, by the class which bears arms and the class which shares in the conduct of government'.

The very wealthy, however, should not be dominant. It is the middle ranks who should dominate in order to achieve the best state, for they neither provoke envy nor are envious themselves. As a consequence, 'where the middle class is large, there is the least likelihood of faction and dissension among citizens'.

The issue of the source of wealth in relation to citizenship occasioned particularly lively debate in Britain from the mid-seventeenth to mideighteenth centuries, a debate which, in turn, influenced political thinking in the American colonies. Britain at this time was, after all, not only one of the few states with effective representative political institutions, it was also one of the leading mercantile nations. In addition, Parliament was controlled by the landed aristocracy. From the years of the Civil War and Interregnum the questions of the possible reform of the electoral system and composition of the House of Commons and the balance of powers between the Crown and Parliament were hotly argued. By the early eighteenth century a group calling themselves the Commonwealth men - a kind of radical wing of the reformist Whigs hostile to royal power - were speaking the vocabulary of civic republicanism. In particular, they presented the virtue of the landed interest as an essential counter to the power of the monarch exerted through patronage. England before the Conquest, they insisted, was a land of virtuous freeholders. Daniel Defoe was one who turned his literary talents to supporting this political position. He put the case against the trading class rather more pungently than Aristotle: by giving a worraing that to attempt to fill the House with "mechanicks, tradesmen, stock-jobbers, and men neither of sense nor honesty, is tricking at the root, and undermining the nation's felicity at once."

Qualities of Citizenship

Who are the good citizens of classical tradition? Take two stories from Livy. First, about Lucius Junius Brutus, who played a major role in expelling Rome's tyrannical royal family and became consul in the new republic. Then his sons became involved in an abortive plot to restore the monarchy. Their father was presented with an appalling dilemma: as consul he had the responsibility of passing sentence and witnessing their flogging and beheading. He did not flinch from performing his civic duty-, even though on his face 'a father's anguish was plain to see'. The second story concerns Cincinnatus, who, after a period of public service, lived modestly working his three-acre farm. A desperate crisis arose. Cincinnatus was offered supreme political and military power for six months. He defeated the enemy, and finally resigned after holding office for fifteen days. He then returned to his plough, turning his back on both power and riches. Self-interest, however tempting, must give way to the higher, indeed supreme requirements of selfless civic duty. That is the mark of the model citizen.

These stories are therefore exemplifications of civic virtue. The Greeks believed that there were four particular forms of goodness: these were temperance, justice, courage and wisdom, or prudence. The Greek word arte, the Latin word virtus and the Italian word virtu, all significantly carry in their complexity the meaning of manliness. The very etymology of the Latin and Italian words reveals this, deriving as they do, from the Latin vir, man. Civic virtue also implies successful assertiveness; indeed one authority has even suggested that 'The Greeks would have regarded Napoleon as a man of preeminent arte'.

Civic virtue, whether as understood' by Aristotle, Cicero, Machiavelli or Rousseau, was applied to a man who displayed martial patriotic devotion. Both Aristotle and Machiavelli made it clear, however, that pure courage was hardly to be expected of the citizen-soldier. Aristotle explained that the soldier's courage, while positively inspired 'by the desire of a noble thing, honour is also negatively prompted by 'the wish to escape reproach'. Machiavelli believed that the courage of the citizen-soldier was the product of military training and religious indoctrination. The virtue of courage was not, therefore, exactly altruistically self-motivated. Yet, once instilled, it led to the ultimate sacrifice for one's country.

This is what is entailed in being a citizen-patriot. As the Roman poet Horace, 'the educator of citizens', wrote: 'It is sweet and fitting to die for one's country.' Even so, just as courage needs the spur of influences outside the individual citizen's conscience, so patriotism needs deliberate cultivation. Rousseau believed that this process does, and rightly should start at birth. 'Every true republican', he wrote., 'takes in with his mother's milk the love of the fatherland. This love forms all his existence; he sees nothing but his fatherland'. This patriotism nevertheless has to be constantly refreshed through the virtuous mores of the community and, particularly, through the messages transmitted by the civil religion which Rousseau thought so essential for the political health and success of the state. Machiavelli also believed that religion, and more especially military discipline, was required to keep up the patriotic spirit.

Tocqueville, however, held that such devices produced a synthetic kind of patriotism, bland and unreflecting. He made two significant points. First, he linked the sentiment with his fundamental observation of the USA as a state operating in several strata. American patriotism, he was convinced, was rooted in the township and the several states rather than the Union, because citizens could more readily identify with and participate at these levels. Related to this interpretation is his second point, his distinction between 'instinctive' and 'we considered' patriotism. Citizenship involves making judgements about public affairs, and that reflective style of life should inform the citizen's patriotism as much as any other aspect of his civic role.

Patriotism, therefore, has not just a military meaning; it has a civil one also. For judgement is to the citizen-as-civilian as courage is to the citizen-as-soldier. In considering the quality of judgement it is wise again to start with Aristotle. The reason is that he shows how this capacity is connected with so many other features of citizenship. These linkages start with concord. Political judgement involves individuals contributing their wisdom and considered opinions on what is prudent action to the compilation of a collective view. This collaboration cannot take place in an atmosphere of enmity, it requires friendly discussion. Judgement, therefore, is the outcome of deliberation.

There is, however, little point in the citizen exercising his wisdom and understanding in order to formulate his contributory judgement if the process ends there. The whole purpose of exercising judgement is to forward the procedure of decision-making. Judgement leads to action, whether juridical, legislative or executive.

On the other hand, if citizens are to be encouraged to use their judgement in order to help shape decisions, can the calibre of their judgement really be relied upon? Despite Aristotle's thinking that the process of aggregation would produce a reliable outcome, Machiavelli and Rousseau were not so sure: Machiavelli because of his belief in innate human wickedness; Rousseau because of his belief in man's corruption following his emergence from the state of nature.

Machiavelli' strongly believed that the political judgment of neither senate nor plebs is to be trusted on its own, that is, without support. Each needs to be checked by the other, or to be disciplined by religion and military codes. Rousseau wrestles with the tension between his democratic instincts and his lack of trust in the general populace. His skepticism becomes loud and clear: Listen to his intellectual tussling:

> How can a blind multitude, which often does not know what it wants, because it seldom knows what is good for it, undertakes by itself an enterprise as vast and difficult as a system of legislation? The general will is always rightful, but the judgement which guides it is not always enlightened.

In other words, the General Will in the heart is not matched by the judgement in the head. Rousseau's solution is the availability of a 'lawgiver' to guide the translation of the General Will into detailed practical effect in order to support a somewhat frail faculty of judgement, which is all that the citizenry can be expected to muster.

And yet, with all their doubts, neither Machiavelli nor Rousseau would deny that citizens should exercise their Judgement, however assisted. For using one's judgement is part of the condition of being a citizen. It is a quality, however limited its supply at its best, that must be fed into the political system. In short, its exercise is a duty.

Role of the Citizen

Citizenly duties are civic qualities put into practice. The whole republican tradition is based upon the premise that citizens recognize and understand what their duties are and have a sense of moral obligation instilled into them to discharge these responsibilities. Indeed, individuals were considered barely worthy of the title of citizen if they avoided performing their appointed duties.

Military service was a central feature of Greek citizenship. We know, for example, that Socrates was called upon to fight in two battles, the second when he was 45. A middle-aged philosopher might seem an unlikely infantry but he performed his duty. A century later, the Athenian statesman Lycurgus introduced a two-year course of compulsory military training.

Drawing lessons mainly from Roman history, Machiavelli was convinced that the citizen's military duty was paramount. A valorous and disciplined citizen army would be generally beneficial to the health of the state, so different from the effects of professional troops. Regiments of mercenary ruffians, having replaced the cities' citizen-militias, which had been common in the Middle Ages, were wreaking havoc in Italy in Machiavelli's own day. In both *The Prince* and *The Discourses* he vented his hatred of mercenaries. Only citizen-soldiers would dutifully and loyally protect their state and keep it free.

The Athenian democratic system of citizens' duties to act as politicians/ legislators in the assembly and as jurors in the courts of law is the classical model. Rousseau was especially keen on assemblies of the sovereign citizenry. Participation in both juridical and political matters is, therefore, a fundamental citizenly duty.

There is also another political duty and right and this is to act as a watchdog on the government. Eternal vigilance is the price of liberty. Aristotle gives 'the calling of magistrates to account as one of the sovereign rights of the deliberative element in the constitution. 'The election of magistrates, and their examination at the end of their tenure, are the most important of issues,' he declares. Rousseau, too, considers such a function to be vital. He allocates the task to 'the assemblies of the people, which are the shield of the body politic and the brake on the government'. He adds that consequently they 'have always been the nightmare of magistrates'.

Forming the Citizen

It is, in fact, quite a tall order. And that is because what is being asked is scarcely a natural human activity. The cynic may think that all virtue is a bit of an effort; civic virtue certainly is. It requires the acquisition of knowledge and the development of skills; it requires considering the interests of others, not just one's own, even preferring them. Self-motivation being rare, it must accordingly be bolstered by techniques devised and provided by society itself. Some theorists of civic republicanism identified two as being especially efficacious: education for the young, novice citizens, and a civil religion as an educative device for all.

On the matter of education, Aristotle's considered advice might seem contradictory. In *the Ethics* he states categorically that 'political science is not a proper study for the young'. Yet in *the Politics* he asserts that 'The citizens of a state should always be educated to suit the constitution of their state'. How, then, are we to explain this apparent discrepancy in relation to the motivation of citizens to live the civic life?

The answer lies in distinguishing two elements in the notion of civic virtue-moral behaviour and efficient performance of duties. Aristotle's prime concern was to advocate the state control of education in order, through a liberal curriculum, to produce a good man, the necessary framework on which to shape a good citizen. It was Plato, however, who expressed the idea with succinct clarity. He wrote that the state shall impart education from childhood in virtue, a training which produces a keen desire to become a perfect citizen who knows how to rule and be ruled as justice demands.

And this order of priorities was picked up by eighteenth-century writers. Montesquieu, for instance, asserted that in a republic inspiring 'love of the laws and of our country ought to be the principal business of education'. However, it was Rousseau who, like Plato, distinguished himself almost equally as an educational theorist as he did as a political theorist. .

Yet Rousseau's treatment of education is ambivalent. Unlike his Greek predecessors he allows for a private style of education for personal development which has no civic purpose. Even so, his parallel views on education for citizenship do reveal a role for the educative process every bit as vital for the success of the ideal state as Plato and Aristotle envisaged.

At the same time, he was very alert to the limitations of education: human beings had enough elemental, natural resistance to being bent to the needs of political society to render civic education only a partial success. Other devices were needed to combine for the formation of citizens. Absolutely essential was a civil religion.

Religion may be, as Marx asserted, an opiate, numbing the critical faculties of the people; but for civic republicans it also has its use as a stimulant, helping to arouse citizens to a positive allegiance to the state. The policy of Augustus, faced with the task of pulling Rome out of the depressing turmoil that brought about the collapse of the Republic, provides an illuminating example. He restored the old gods, both Olympian and domestic and familial, to greater public consciousness by refurbishing decayed temples and shrines and reviving ancient ceremonies and rites.

Machiavelli, calling upon the evidence of an earlier age in Rome's long history, was impressed with the way in which the Romans managed their religious observances. He tells his readers that it was religion that facilitated whatever enterprise the senate and great men of Rome designed to undertake. Religion helped in the control of armies, in encouraging the plebs, in producing good men, and in shaming the bad.

The Romans, he explains, were fortunate in their pagan religion because, unlike the Christian focus on the after life, it provided the state with a powerful reinforcement of civic purpose. Worship of the Roman deities encouraged men to magnanimity, bodily strength, and boldness. It also had a vital educative role: unlike the debilitating effect of Christian education, the Roman cults upheld republicanism and liberty.

Rousseau had even firmer opinions on the relationship of religion to citizenship, partly from personal experiences. He thought atheism 'intolerable', Christianity 'bizarre', and clergy politically 'dangerous'. His positive recommendations were for an overtly civil religion. This faith would consist of 'articles, not strictly religious dogmas', that are 'sentiments of sociability, without which it is impossible to be either a good citizen or a loyal subject'. Following closely Rousseau's prescription, Robespierre, his most earnest politician-disciple, attempted, and abortively, to establish such a civil religion in his 'cult of the supreme being'.

Tocqueville, in contradistinction to Machiavelli and Rousseau, accepted, indeed welcomed the civic good of Christianity. This form of religion, he believed, is an essential concomitant of liberty. It encourages a sense of community and therefore patriotism; it gives moral tone to the community. Above all, his belief in the positive, benign influence of religion enabled Tocqueville to temper his own fear of the political tyranny of the majority in a democracy. He identified these civic qualities in the Christian religion by his study of the history of the American colonies and the evidence of his own ears and eyes on his visit to New England. Writing particularly of the Puritanism practised in these states, he explained that 'Religion is considered as the guardian of mores, and mores are regarded as the guarantee of the laws and pledge for the "maintenance of freedom itself".

Revival and arguments

From the late eighteenth century the civic republican interpretation of citizenship steadily gave way to the liberal style of citizenship. In recent years, however, interest in the older tradition has revived, partly because of perceived weaknesses in the liberal style, and partly because of the putative intrinsic values of civic republicanism.

Scholars and public opinion in the USA have led the way. Several explanations may be offered for this American interest. First, the American Revolution was partly inspired and sustained by the classical ideals, particularly during the war; and the shift in focus to the liberal stress on individual rights in the Constitution, some argue, changed the balance too radically away from feelings of obligation and community. On the other hand, and secondly, as Tocqueville reported, the structure is in place for realistic participation in public affairs: township and state could replicate something of the intimacy of the city-state if a greater proportion of citizens seized the opportunities. Thirdly, a strengthening of a sense of community and of responsibility to contribute to communal harmony is felt to be imperative in a nation with so many social problems.

One of the most distinguished of recent American scholars in the field of politics, Hannah Arendt, was convinced of the value of active citizenship as construed by the classical writers. She expressed her ideas on the subject most fully in *The Human Condition*, published in 1958. She expounds Jefferson's idea of the ward system of 'little republics'.

It was not, indeed, for another two decades that work to revive civic republicanism really got under way. Two features of what is sometimes referred to as 'neo-republicanism' are of cardinal importance and may be illustrated by quotations from two of the leading exponents. One is disillusionment with the American democratic system: so few even bother to vote; even fewer participate politically in any other way. Benjamin Barber describes this condition as 'thin democracy' which yields neither the pleasures of participation nor the fellowship of civic association, neither the autonomy and self-governance of continuous political activity nor the enlarging mutuality of shared public goods - of mutual deliberation, decision, and work.

The other feature of neo-republicanism derives from the criticism that liberal citizenship has led to a weak feeling of community. The belief that a restored sense of neighbourhood, or indeed national 'togetherness', is essential has produced the word 'communitarian' to describe this thinking.

The liberal form of citizenship tends to focus on individual freedom and rights. But there should be, in all conscience, some balance, however rough it might be between freedom and rights for the individual on the one hand and commitment and duties to the community on the other. Without such a balance, civic virtue is submerged by selfishness.

A society of selfish individuals is, at its extreme, no society at all, nor does it have citizens, properly speaking - it is nothing more than an agglomeration of competitive egoistic monads. And self-seeking competitiveness generates stresses and resentments - that are the very antithesis of the republican vision of a harmonious, co-operative community, in which self-interest and the interest of the community are in some sense identical. Moreover, the concord of mutually agreed strivings and achievements minimizes anti-social behaviour and thus reliance on coercive policing for maintaining the peace. In addition, of course, when the individual citizen's commitment to the community is turned from sustaining internal harmony to the requirements of external security, the civic republican ideal expects unquestioning patriotism and self sacrifice.

The picture is assuredly an attractive one, and although composed of contributions from centuries long ago, may well fit the needs of our own times as readily as those of Aristotle, Cicero, Machiavelli and Rousseau. The civic republican ideal contains perennial values. Or is this the complete picture? Are there not weaknesses that some might find positively distasteful?

Even the proponents of civic republicanism accept that their expectations are very demanding. Citizenship is not an easy life; it requires conscientious application. Most people lead a very full life with their family commitments, leisure pursuits and above all, employment, for we are not Greeks with slaves to work for us. Yet the republican citizen must, in addition, allocate time, summon up the energy and generate commitment to an involvement in public affairs. It is obvious, however, that there is a limit to the elasticity of a person's life-style, and in order to accommodate active participation in public affairs something has to give. Serious questions arise from this requirement. How many individuals are prepared to make that adjustment? Is it fair and is it desirable that the demand should be made? If harmony and happiness are the intended outcomes of civic republicanism - as they certainly are - it can be plausibly argued that this infringement of private life would have precisely the contrary effect.

The direction of individuals into involvement in the public arena and mobilizing the resources of education and religion to this purpose smacks of paternalism. By incorporation into this kind of civic regime the individual suffers a loss of personal freedom, autonomy and the power of fully independent critical thought. So speak the opponents of the republican school, arguing that the prospect of true freedom, autonomy and judgement through the blending process of identification with the community is little more than a philosophical sleight of hand.

This has at least three unfortunate consequences. One is that citizenship properly speaking becomes an elite activity, the rest of the populace relegated to a merely nominal citizenly status. The reason for this is that normally only the well-educated and the adequately wealthy have the inclination and time to participate in formal politics. Secondly, this narrow definition of public participation excludes the whole broad range of civic society activities, such as pressure groups, trade unions, charities.

The third unfortunate consequence is that, generally speaking, men find it easier and more congenial to involve themselves in formal politics while women find it easier and more congenial to involve themselves in civil society. It is unsurprising, therefore, that feminists are often aligned against civic republicanism. Moreover, the spurning of civil society is not the only cause of feminist resentment. Civic republican citizenship has been an essentially male concept because it was devised by men for male-dominated societies; it would be anachronistic to expect otherwise. And one of its evident male features is the requirement to be possessed of the virtue of military valour.

Oldfield has suggested that modern citizens lack all three prerequisites for acting in the republican manner; these are resources, opportunities and motivation. A convincing case can be made to support this contention. Few people have the resources of information, time and energy for effective political participation. Political affairs in the modern world are exceedingly complex and often technically difficult, especially in the field of economics, and so mastering this material in order to make informed, detailed judgements is difficult. It has even been argued that the mass media, particularly in the USA, by trivializing their news presentations, obscure rather than facilitate the comprehension of the major issues.

It has been argued that are the devices envisaged by the mainstream writers for motivating individuals to citizenly activity are not available in modern states. A Rousseauean civil religion is scarcely a common feature. The 'secular religions' of Communism and Nazism have had their day, but, in any case, were not exactly epitomes of the virtues of republicanism. Islam remains a religio-political force, particularly in Iran and Taliban Afghanistan, but not at all replicable in western societies. The use of military discipline as an alternative for welding a collection of men into a community of citizens is no longer an option in a world of technically sophisticated professional armies. Even France, with a long tradition of conscription, has abandoned its military national service. There is a widespread belief that schools could and should educate their pupils to be good citizens. Defining precise objectives and methodologies is, however, very hard, and the effectiveness of what is being attempted is highly questionable.

We must conclude, therefore, that there are many objections and difficulties surrounding any attempt to restore a civic republican mode as a strong feature of citizenship in the modern world, yet at the same time there is still a recognized hard-core value in the ideal. The key question to be addressed, then, is how to create the habits of the heart for its acceptance, appropriately adapted to present-day circumstances and conditions.

However, today the Civil vepublican tradition has been appropriated by political theorists and politicians to define a socio-political position, which was emerging in the 1980s. The word itself was, in fact, formally adopted by a small group meeting of American social scientists in 1990. A number of very distinguished scholars in the USA have associated themselves with and worked on the concept of communitarianism, albeit with slightly different personal nuances of interpretation: they include Amitai Etzioni, William Galston, Alasdair MacIntyre, Michael Sandel and Charles Taylor.

Communitarians are fundamentally, reacting against both the credo of liberal individualism and the interpretation of citizenship.

The communitarians argue that appeal to human rights, when couched in terms of the right of autonomy, does not dissolve the bonds of community. In fact, it should strengthen these bonds insofar as it leads people to recognize that a special relationship obtains between them and the cooperating members of their political community. Those who recognize this relationship are also likely to agree with William Galston when he suggests that every community represents a cooperative endeavor in pursuit of shared puposes. Each term of this proposition offers a key ingredient of community

"Cooperation" presupposes mutual benefit, rather than the exploitation of some members by others through force or fraud; "endeavor" implies that the good must be created, rather than passively received or consumed; and "shared purposes" define a common good the community seeks to bring into being and to sustain, not merely private individual advantage.

As this sketch of the argument from reciprocity indicates, reciprocity connects the right of autonomy to the bonds of community. Yet the sketch will have to be filled in and some serious objections overcome before the connection is truly established. One kind of objection concerns political obligation. The argument from reciprocity traces political obligation to the principle of fair play, but several philosophers have argued that this principle cannot provide an adequate account of political obligation. Some philosophers have even gone so far as to claim that there is no general obligation to obey the laws of any state, no matter how just the state may be.

Another objection might be that the argument from reciprocity succeeds in connecting autonomy to community, but only in a formal, legalistic, and attenuated sense of "community." Michael Sandel provides the best example of the objection when he criticizes the "weak" conceptions of community in liberal theory. According to Sande, liberal views of community have been "weak" because they are either " instrumental" where individuals regard social arrangements as a necessary burden and cooperate only for the sake of pursuing their private ends or "sentimental". Against these "weak" conceptions, Sandel proposes what he takes to be a truer conception of community.

On this strong view, the members of a society are bound by a sense of community. It is not simply to say that a great many of them profess communitarian sentiments and pursue communitarian aims, but rather that they conceive their identity-the subject and not just the object of their feelings and aspirations as defined to some extent by the community. For them, community describes not just what they have as fellow citizens, but also what they are, not a relationship they choose but an attachment they discover, not merely an attribute but a constituent of their identity. In contrast to the instrumental and sentimental conceptions of community, this strong view offers the constitutive conception.

Although Sandel makes no mention of obligation here, his constitutive conception of community implies that those who are "bound by a sense of community"-a community to which they "discover" an "attachment"-certainly do have an obligation of some sort to the community and its members. But the sense of obligation seems to be more important than the obligation itself. That one has an obligation to follow the customs, norms, or laws is, in these circumstances, something that goes without saying.

Part of the reason that considerations of obligation are otiose in a strong community is that the members of the community are unlikely to regard themselves as being burdened when they act for the common good. In an instrumental conception of community the members of the cooperative endeavor bear the burdens of cooperation in order to receive its benefits. In a strong community, by contrast, the members identify so thoroughly with the community that they hardly think in terms of personal gains or losses, benefits or burdens.

This vision of a constitutive community that simultaneously promotes and rests upon the "enlarged self-understanding" of its members is appealing in some ways but not in all. Its appeal resides two features. One is that individual identity does in some sense depend upon community. No one is an entirely self created person, and the constitutive conception of community recognizes and builds upon our social or communal nature. The second source of its appeal is the bond the constitutive community forges between the purposes of the individual and those of the community.

The person whose identity is so closely bound to the community that he or she is virtually incapable of questioning or challenging the community's norms, as seems to be the case with Troglodytes, whose rational faculties are stunted. Such a person may be happy-or at least satisfied, as John Stuart Mill argued-but he or she is stunted nonetheless by the inability to realize a capacity for rational thought and self- reflection, for this capacity cannot be fully employed unless a person is able to see himself or herself as somehow apart or separate from the community.

The constitutive conception of community is too closely to Montesquicu's untutored and unreflective Troglodytes. Sandel probably prefers a more Aristotelian or Hegelian form of community than Montesquieu portrays. Yet he cannot justify this preference simply by appealing to the constitutive conception of community. An Aristotelian community would constitute the identity of its members in one way, the Troglodyte community in another. Both would be constitutive communities, however, and judged by that standard one is as desirable as the other. Even communities that have become notorious for smugness, intolerance, and superstition seem to be models of constitutive community.

A possible response to this complaint is in the appeal to membership that Sandel makes in the introduction to *Liberalism and Its Critics.* There he says that "the civil rights movement of the 1960s might be justified by liberals in the name of human dignity and respect for persons, and by communitarians in the name of recognizing the full membership of fellow citizens wrongly excluded from' the common life of the nation."" In this case, Sandel says, communitarians and liberals agree on the policy to be followed, but the liberal conception of "unencumbered selves" misses the dimension of membership that communitarianism, with its conception of 'situated selves', captures. He is right about this dimension of membership, as African Americans' complaints of being defined as "second-class citizens" suggested at the time. But there is another dimension of membership that does not support his position.

Membership is usually defined not only inclusively-that is, in terms of who the members are-but also exclusively, by ruling some people out. Thus one may appeal to membership in an effort to exclude as well as to include people. A self can be so situated, so imbued with a sense of membership in a community, that he or she will fail to acknowledge the claims to membership made by those he or she considers to be outsiders. Slavery and segregation laws encouraged people to think in this way in the United States, just as apartheid has done in South Africa. Thinking in terms of membership is thinking in terms of "we" and "they," in other words, and there is nothing inherent in the idea of membership that leads one to believe that "we" ought to be expanded to include "they."

Sandel's theory must be open to either internal or external criticism or both. This seems to leave Sandel on the horns of a dilemma. If a community is tightly knit, as it presumably must be to satisfy the constitutive conception, its standards and practices will likely admit little or no challenge. This will leave little room for freedom, or for self-development in any rich sense of the term. The situated self may thus be as cramped and crippled

But if the community is open enough to allow or even encourage free and critical thinking, its standards and practices will be constantly challenged and possibly undermined. The unencumbered self may thus cut itself off from its moorings in community.

Is there an escape between the horns of this dilemma? Is there a way to encourage free and critical thinking-the kind that autonomy requires within a community that fosters devotion to the common good? Such an escape may be possible by way of "holistic individualism "-a view that Charles Taylor associates with thinkers as diverse as Wilhelm von Humboldt, Machiavelli, Montesquieu, and Alexis de Tocqueville.

Taylor's sympathies with communitarianism are evident, but his unwillingness to abandon the liberal concern for liberty, autonomy,, and rights is equally clear. His strategy, it seems, is to show liberals how the realization of their hopes for individual rights and liberties fundamentally depend on certain social and cultural conditions. Moreover, he endorses these liberal aspirations, at least when they are understood as he thinks they should be. In "Atomism," for instance, Taylor rejects what he calls "the primacy of rights," but he does so not to dismiss or discount their importance. Instead, his purpose is to show that a commitment to the value of individual rights entails an obligation to belong. This will be as fundamental as the assertion of rights, because it will be inseparable from it. So it would be incoherent to try to assert the rights, while denying the obligation or giving it the status of optional extra which we may or may not contract. Furthermore, in "Atomism" and in "What's Wrong with Negative Liberty," he makes the same move with regard to freedom. His argument is based on the notion, first, that developed freedom requires a certain understanding of self, one in which the aspirations to autonomy and self-development become conceivable; and second, that this self-understanding is not something we can sustain on our own, but that our identity is always partly defined in conversation with others or through the common understanding which underlies the practices of our society.

Taylor's emphasis on rights and liberty is not so much mistaken as misplaced. Liberals are right to value individual rights and liberty, but they need to see that these rights and liberties cannot be grounded in atomism and the "utterly facile moral psychology of traditional empiricism, according to which human agents possess the full capacity of choice as a given rather than as a potential which has to be developed." On the contrary, the value of rights, liberty, and autonomy can only be grounded in and sustained by a community or culture that enables the individual to develop his or her capacity of choice.

Taylor is communitarians of a decidedly liberal cast. Whatever we call it, the important point is that Taylor's "holistic individualist" approach promises an escape from the dilemma that seems to confront Sandal. Taylor's attempt to reconcile community and liberty is especially significant for what it implies for political obligation. Taylor does not speak directly to the question of whether there is an obligation to obey the laws of one's community, but he does invoke the language of obligation more often and more explicitly than Sandel, Alasdair MacIntyre, and other communitarians. Thus he speaks, of "an obligation to belong" that is "inseparable" from the assertion of rights. "I am arguing," he says, that the free individual of the West is only what he is by virtue of the whole society and civilization which brought him to be and which nourishes him; that our families can only form us up to this capacity and these aspirations because they are set in this civilization; and that a family alone outside of this context-the real old patriarchal family—was a quite different animal which never tended these horizons."

Taylor's belief in this "obligation to belong" is, then, quite clear; the source and nature of this obligation, however, are not. The furthest Taylor goes toward answering questions of this sort is in "The Nature and Scope of Distributive justice," in which he says, "To the extent that we think of ourselves as already formed by the past development of these institutions and practices that protect and sustain the sense of liberty, our obligation to maintain them springs from a principle of justice between generations, that the good we have received we should pass on'. This is helpful, but it hardly counts as a satisfactory answer to the questions raised above.

We could follow Karl Marx and Friedrich Engels here and distinguish true from illusory communities by looking to see whether socalled communities provide their members with "the means of cultivating their gifts in all directions.

Liberal citizenship is nevertheless so firmly embedded, certainly in western political culture, and has so much to be said in its favour, that it would be surprising if communitarians had not come under attack. Critics have worried on academic grounds that communitarians have failed to proffer a clear definition of what they mean by 'community'. However, whatever the precise meaning, their stress on communal bonding raises several problems.

Integration of a community involves an implied rejection of the 'strangers' who are not members. It also implies that all who are members have the same interests, yet that is not necessarily so: what about the interests of women compared with men, or of ethnic minorities compared with the cultural majority? The whole reality of multiple identity, indeed, would seem to be underplayed. Communitarianism also has the smack of an authoritarian defence of the status quo, even a retrogression. Feminists are especially unhappy and worried about some unjust and illiberal practices of communities. Even so, the communitarians' case for recognizing the value of community life and the need to stem the selfish abuse of liberal values has appeared sufficiently cogent to have been adopted by a number of politicians. The most influential writer to achieve this practical effect has been Etzioni. The titles of some of his recent books reveal the thrust of his work: The *Moral Dimension*, The *Parenting Deficit* and, of widest impact, The *Spirit of Community*. Etzioni diagnoses the imbalance between rights and responsibilities and the decline in the two-parent family, the decay of religious faith and the collapse of a sense of neighbourhood as afflications causing a serious distemper in western democracies. He deeply regrets the 'millions of latchkey children' and, echoing Tocqueville's 'habits of the heart', urges a 'change of heart' among citizens. From an early position of academic sociological analysis, Etzioni has come to adopt the posture of a campaigner. Communitarianism is not just a set of principles, but a movement.

By 1990 the doctrines of both the traditional Left and the New Right were discredited. As a consequence, politicians such as Clinton in the USA, Berlusconi in Italy and Blair in the UK, searching for some principles with which to clothe their scantily clad pragmatism, bought communitarianism off the peg. In Britain New Labour's policy statements have been replete with references to 'community' and 'responsibility': communitarianism has been the intellectual foundation of the 'Third Way'. In 1994 Gordon Brown declared that 'people must accept their responsibilities as individuals and as citizens, and community action should never be a substitute for the assumption of personal responsibility.' Three years later, Tony Blair stated: 'I am utterly convinced that the only way to rebuild a strong civic society for the modern world is on the basis of rights and responsibility going together'

There may well be signal advantages in the communitarian vision. On the other hand, we have journeyed some way from the classical republican concept of the citizen. Where is the legal status? Where is political participation? If anything, we need today a broader, not a narrower definition of citizenship than even civic republicanism can offer. Being a citizen is now an extraordinarily complicated business, as the next chapters will reveal.

5

Marshall's Theory of Citizenship

Debates and discourses on citizenship rights refer almost inevitably to T. H. Marshall's famous lectures given at Cambridge in 1949 and published in the following year under the title 'Citizenship and Social Class'. In these lectures, T. H. Marshall reflected on the progress of what he called the rights of citizenship and addressed the main question of whether or not this progress was compatible with the maintenance of a market economy and corresponding social inequalities. Marshall was delivering the Alfred Marshall lectures and he used the occasion to present his own topic of citizenship with the assistance of Alfred Marshall's paper on 'The Future of the Working Classes'. It is worth recalling the main issues at stake in these reflections of the two great scholars.

'The Future of the Working Classes' was a paper read by Alfred Marshall also in Cambridge, at the Reform Club in 1873. Alfred Marshall was quite clear on the question he wanted to address, as well as on the answer he wanted to uphold.

> The question for us to-night he is not whether all men will ultimately be equal-that they certainly will not-but whether progress may not go on steadily if slowly, till the official distincion between working man and gentleman has passed away; by occupation at least every man is a gentleman. I hold that it may, and that it will.[6]

In 1949, T. H. Marshall addressed the same problem but he introduced two alterations. Where Alfred Marshall had used the term 'gentleman', T.H. Marshall proposed the term 'civilzed', 'for it is clear that Alfred Marshall was taking as the standard of civilized life the conditions regarded by his generation as appropriate to a gentleman'. Then T. H. Marshall adds to enjoy these conditions of a civilised or a gentleman's life ais a claim to be admitted to a share in the social heritage, which in turn means a claim to be accepted as full members of the society, that is, as citizens.'

Having thus introduced the concept of citizenship, T. H. Marshall embarks upon an historical survey of the evolution of the concept and its application in the last 250 years. His three-fold scheme of citizenship rights and their corresponding institutions is now well known. The emergence of civil, political and social rights would have roughly corresponded to the eighteenth, nineteenth and twentieth centuries; their institutional counterparts would have been the courts of justice (civil rights), parliament and councils of local government (political rights), and finally the educational system and the social services (social rights).

Civil rights, according to T. H. Marshall, are composed of 'the rights necessary for individual freedom - liberty of the person, freedom of speech, thought and faith, the right to own property and to conclude valid contracts and the right to justice'. Political rights, on the other hand, include 'the right to participate in the exercise of political power, as a member of a body invested with political authority or as an elector of the members of such a body'. Finally, social rights involve 'the whole range from the right to a modicum of economic welfare and security to the right to share to the full in the social heritage and to live the life of a civilzed being according to the standards prevailing in the society'.

Alfred Marshall postulated that there is a kind of basic human equality associated with the concept of full membership of a community or, of citizenship, which is not inconsistent with the inequalities, which distinguish the various economic levels in the society. In other words, the inequality of the social class system may be acceptable provided the equality of citizenship is recognised.

Seventy-six years later, again in Cambridge, T.H. Marshall addressed the same problem and posed his predecessor's question afresh. 'The basic human equality of membership', he observed, 'has been enriched with new substance and invested with a formidable array of rights'.

The questions stemming from this evolution go without saying:

Is it still true that the basic equality, when enriched in substance and embodied in the formal rights of citizenship, is consistent with the inequalities of social class? Is it still true that basic equality can be created and preserved without invading the freedom of the competitive market?

T.H. Marshall's answers to these questions were both qualified. He thought that equality of citizenship compatible with class inequality but only with certain inequalities: 'citizenship, he maintained, has itself become, in certain respects, the architect of legitimate inequlities.'

As for the market system, Marshall thought that the advancement of citizenship had transformed it into a 'socialist system', although, he added, 'it is equally obvious that the market still functions within limits'. Marshall saw this conflict as a creative one, giving rise to what he called a hyphenated society, the welfare-capitalist society. This is mainly characterized by a progressive divorce between real and money incomes. Social service provide individuals with the access to goods which are not directly proportionate to their purchasing power in the market. The advantages obtained by having a large money income do not disappear, but they are confined to a limited area of consumption, Marshall concluded.

This conflict between social citizenship and the market-a conflict of pronciples which, Marshall asserted, 'springs from the very roots of our social order in the present development of democratic citizenship'.

T. H. Marshall's influential essay, "Citizenship and Social Class" prepared in 1949, examines these trends in the content of citizenship in Western democratic nation-states. He argues that the long-term historical extension of citizenship rights has supplied the basis for overcoming or at least tempering the gross injustices of social inequality. Citizenship is a source of equality. Citizenship is a status bestowed on those who are full members of a community. All who possess the status are equal with respect to the rights and duties with which the status is endowed". Marshall argued that the implication for social stratification and social inequality is clear. "The equality implicit in the concept of citizenship, even though limited in content, undermined the inequality of the class system, which was in principle a total inequality"

Marshall's historical narrative emphasizes that in the eighteenth century, civil rights were institutionalized. Then, in the nineteenth century, civil rights supplied the basis for achieving political rights. In turn in the twentieth century, on the basis of the exercise of political rights, social rights were developed. Cumulatively, the extension of these citizenship rights has produced significant economic development and change - both in improving the material standard of living of wide segments of the working strata and in raising the level of well-being of those with the lowest incomes.

Marshall argued that civil rights undermined the economic forms of feudalism and made possible the contractual relations essential for the emergence of capitalism with its resulting economic growth. This process of economic growth supplied the material basis for the expansion of the welfare system. The historical process was complex and its course as well as its consequences hardly self-evident. In short, civil and political rights were the precursors of social rights and of the trends toward greater equality. It is an argument which rejects rigid economic determinism. Marshall focuses on the experiences of Great Britain, but his observations supply the basis for comparison among modem Western parliamentary regimes in general.

Marshall's argument is of particular interest because in explaining the nature of citizenship in post-World War Britain, it also provides an account of the emergence of citizenship in the modern nation-state in terms of the historical development of capitalist society. Marshall is able to advance this case by distinguishing between parts or elements of citizenship, and in doing so he offers a new characterization of citizenship which lends itself to an analysis of the relations between citizenship and society which is absent in other approaches.

The general understanding of citizenship in Marshall is entirely conventional. He says, firstly, that citizenship is a status attached to full membership of a community, and secondly, that those who possess this status are equal with respect to the rights and duties associated with it. Marshall adds that different societies will attach different rights and duties to the status of citizen, for there is no universal principle which determines necessary rights and duties of citizenship in general. It is by going beyond the conventional idea that membership of a community is predominantly a political matter that Marshall is able to contribute to the study of citizenship. Three distinct parts or elements of citizenship are identified by Marshall which may or may not be present in any given constitution of citizenship: these are civil, political and social rights.

The principal point in all of this is that the different elements of citizenship have different institutional bases, and in significant respects different histories. This is to say that citizenship comprises elements which are not necessarily cut from the same cloth, and bear different relations with distinct social groups and with each other.

It should be mentioned here that Marshall's approach to citizenship is novel not simply in stressing its distinct elements. Indeed, a germ of the idea that citizenship comprises three parts can be identified in a series of lectures given by Leonard Hobhouse at Columbia University in America in 1911, and subsequently published. Hobhouse refers to political and civic inequalities in the principles of modern citizenship, and in discussing the Old Age Pensions Act of 1908 refers to the 'duty of the community to provide the bare minimum necessary to an independent life' and of a responsibility of the state for the individual. The influence of Hobhouse on Marshall's thought is generally acknowledged, and was no doubt readily facilitated by the fact that Hobhouse was professor of sociology at the London School of Economics when Marshall first went there to teach in 1926. Marshall's more developed treatment of the elements of citizenship is not the same as Hobhouse's adumbration. First, he differs from Hobhouse on many fundamental issues. Marshall fundamentally departs from Hobhouse, and from liberal thought in general in the idea that not all citizenship rights are logically derivable from civil rights and especially property rights. Liberal theory holds that social rights, for instance, and also political rights are explicable in terms of the market rights of private property. These rights can be extended to persons in non-property classes when labour is regarded as the property of its possessor, as it has been in liberal theory since John Locke in the seventeenth century. Marshall has no need for such teleology as he sees that while some rights might arise as a secondary product of other rights they can also attach directly and independently to citizenship as such. In addition to this account of the basis of citizenship rights Marshall does not agree with Hobhouse that the development of citizenship is simply an outcome of the development of the state. According to Marshall changes in the nature of citizenship are achieved through conflict between social institutions and possibly between social groups. These ideas are not fully developed in Marshall's discussion but they are widely held to be a real contribution to the theory of citizenship.

Second, Marshall's theory of citizenship directly and explicitly addresses the question of the relationship between citizenship and social class. Marshall notes that the development of the institutions of modern citizenship in England coincided with the rise of capitalism. He regards this as anomalous because while capitalism creates class inequalities between those subject to it, citizenship is a status through which its members share equal rights and duties. Thus Marshall concludes that it is 'reasonable to expect that the impact of citizenship on social class should take the form of a conflict between opposing principles'. Marshall's account of this relationship is particularly compelling because it is able to explain ostensibly opposite outcomes without itself being contradictory.

In the early phase of the development of capitalism citizenship tended to undermine the customary privileges of class which were a legacy of the feudal past, whilst at the same time it consolidated incipient capitalist class relations based on commodity production and exchange. During this period the class system was encrusted with hereditary privilege, customs and legal rights which derived from the earlier system of feudal estates. The development of modern citizenship, from the middle of the seventeenth century, weakened and eventually undermined these aspects of class, and permitted the emergence of a class system based on a set of relations coterminous with the institutions of private property. During the period of the eighteenth and nineteenth centuries the rights of citizenship were entirely harmonious with the class inequalities of capitalist society. According to Marshall such rights were 'necessary to the maintenance of that particular form of inequality', because at that time citizenship rights were basically civil rights and civil rights 'were indispensible to a competitive market economy'. The reason for this is that civil rights bestow on those who have them the capacity to enter market exchanges as independent and self-sufficient agents. Capitalists and workers are indistinguishable from the perspective of civil rights in having the same right to enter into market exchanges and contracts with each other. Civil rights as the core of citizenship, will consolidate class inequalities.

When citizenship comes to incorporate political rights, and also social rights, then its relationship with the class system is more clearly conflictual than it is when it consists only of civil rights. Marshall argues that the full potential danger to the capitalist class system from the political rights of citizenship was deflected during the nineteenth century in England only because the newly enfranchised working class was too inexperienced to effectively wield the political power provided by the nineteenth-century Reform Acts. But this is not the end of the story, for while the working-class movement was not able to effectively mobilize political power during the closing decades of the nineteenth century, it created trade unionism as 'a secondary system of industrial citizenship parallel with and supplementary to the system of political citizenship'. Trade unionism, and the collective bargaining with employers it permits, became a means by which the economic and social status of organized workers was raised. In other words, the collective exercise of rights by members of the working class in creating and using trade unionism established 'the claim that they, as citizens, were entitled to certain social rights'

Marshall argues that the addition of social rights to the constitution of citizenship brought citizenship and the capitalist class system to war. It must be made dear that Marshall does not suggest that the war has had, or is likely to have, a fundamental outcome. Social citizenship has not destroyed class nor even removed social inequality. Indeed, the development of citizenship, including social citizenship, has given rise to new inequalities. Marshall contends that social citizenship has tended to reduce certain social inequalities, and especially those associated with the operations of the market, the market value of individuals is no longer determinant of their real income because of the provision through state administration of economic goods and services as a right. Marshall does not argue that class has been abolished by citizenship, but that citizenship has imposed modifications on class. The precise nature of these modifications is subject to interpretation certainly. It seems to be beyond dispute, that changes in the class system have occurred through the exercise of citizenship rights by the working class movement.

It will be evident that in Marshall's account of citizenship and social class is a theory of social change. He says that the growth of citizenship is 'stimulated both by the struggle to win those rights and by their enjoyment when won'. As the enjoyment of citizenship rights in their civil and political phases involves the exercise of liberty and political power, an element of potential conflict is inherent in the exercise and not simply in the origins of citizenship rights. This is especially so in a society divided by class inequality ties in which citizenship rights are given to persons across class lines and in which the principle of citizenship and its components are opposed to class inequality. Marshall's approach to citizenship and social class entails not only that citizenship modify class, but also that class conflict is likely to be an expression of the struggle for rights and especially citizenship rights.

In summary then, Marshall sees the development of citizenship and of the class system in terms of the interactions between them. Through their antagonistic relationship citizenship and class inequality each contribute to changes in the other. Unlike most theorists of class structure, Marshall recognizes the possible impact of citizenship on aspects of class inequality and therefore on class loyalty and class resentment. Marshall sees such possibilities because he understands citizenship in terms not only of its legal and political dimensions, but also of its social component. It follows that from Marshall's perspective citizenship is not simply a status, which detracts from class inequality but is in some tension with it, so that class conflict may possibly be about the nature and scope of citizenship rights. Any understanding of citizenship in the modern world, and in social and political theory, must therefore pay serious attention to Marshall's contribution.

During the late 1950s and early 1960s Marshall's essay exercised a considerable influence on sociological thought, and from the late 1970s to the present time, there has been a revived interest in his work. In the literatures associated with these periods quite different, almost opposite interpretations of Marshall's argument can be found, emphasizing certain aspects of it at the expense of others, and therefore in the least fortunate way revealing its complexity. The earlier interpreters argued that Marshall accepts integration of the working class into capitalist society through the development of citizenship and a subsequent decline of class and class conflict.

More recently, after relative neglect, possibly because the interpretations of the 1960s were taken for granted, Marshall has again become the subject of sociological interest Giddens, Gold Thorpe, Lockwood and Turner contend that the systems of class and citizenship exist in tension with each other, and that the quest for citizenship might promote rather than reduce class conflict. Not all interpreters in the same period shared the prevailing view of Marshall. Lipset for instance, says that Marshall 'kept alive the perspective that society requires conflict'; and Barry Hindess tends to regard Marshall as a theorist of social integration rather than anything else. The strength of Marshall's theory is partly in its complexity, in its ability to proffer almost opposite possibilities without being contradictory.

Marshall says that the civil, political and social rights which make up the separate elements of modern citizenship were woven into a single thread under the feudal constitution. The amalgamation of feudal rights reflected the cohabitation of civil and political functions in feudal institutions. With the demise of estate society and the rise of market exchange unrestrained by customary and religious precepts, the economic and political spheres became institutionally separate and independent. As a consequence of this departure 'the institutions on which the three elements of citizenship depended parted company, and it became possible for each to go its separate way, travelling at its own speed under the direction of its own peculiar principles'. The separation of the elements of citizenship is significant not only in terms of the analytical distinction between rights but also in the fact that the practices associated with each set of rights have quite different effects on social relationships and on the economic and political organization of society.

Citizenship can be characterized as both a status and a set of rights. This association of rights and status is not accidental. The political importance of rights derives from the social nature of status. In the most general terms rights are significant because they attach a particular capacity to persons by virtue of a legal or conventional status. That is, persons may have certain capabilities or opportunities for particular actions - certain powers - as a consequence of their status. A person's rights derive from their attachment to a status because in a meaningful sense one's status indicates what one can do, what capacities one has.

Status, Marshall contends, emphasizes the fact that expectations exist in the relevant social groups. These include expectations about appropriate behaviour not only from those who share a particular status but also from those who do not. The status of a particular category of persons is typified by how others relate to those in it. It is only when others come to accept a person's expectations as not only reasonable but legitimate that their status has any authenticity. The compliance of others in one's expectations can seldom be attained through persuasion alone. Perhaps this is why some writers have placed so much emphasis on the attainment of rights through struggle. The normative expectations of status not only sustain but are the mirror image of the rights and capacities attached to it.

It would be a mistake, however, to assume that status is simply achieved through struggle. It can be held only because it is publicly recognized as legitimate. In this sense the expectations, capacities and entitlements associated with a status and which therefore define social positions are a part of the very fabric of society. They possess a certainty, a naturalness and incontestability which social life require and assumes.

It follows that any infringement of a right will be perceived by those involved as a uniquely serious threat. 'Rights', says Marshall, 'are not a proper matter for bargaining'. Directly associated with the idea that rights provide a minimum of social capacities and entitlements is the notion that the violation of a right is sufficient justification for the use of force in correcting the situation, for this latter is the ultimate recourse of defending itself. This, then, is a third aspect of the political importance of rights.

Rights provide persons with capacities or capabilities and opportunities and that they can do so with a measure of security. This is because as attributes of status or position in society rights define an ultimate boundary and their contravention will be subject to sanction. This characterization raises a number -of questions, especially issues of the relationship between rights and the distribution of social resources, power and interests.

Different rights attach different capacities to persons. Some rights, such as welfare rights, which entitle persons to a minimum level of material well-being, provide access not simply to opportunities but also to conditions. The distinction between opportunity and condition is easy to make but the practical relation between them is complex. It is frequently remarked, for instance, that equality of opportunity leads to inequality of outcome or condition. This arises because abilities of one sort or another, or other means through which opportunities are taken, are themselves unevenly distributed through a population. 'A property right', Marshall remarks, 'is not a right to possess property. But a right to acquire it, if you can, and to _protect it, if you can get it'. Thus paupers and millionaires possess the same capacities through property rights without the distribution of property being in the least degree affected. The capacities exercised in the right to vote, however, or to strike, provide opportunities, which are closer to the shaping of material conditions, and in the absence of such rights material conditions would be less likely to change in a direction favourable to those without social power. With some qualification, then, it is possible to say that certain rights may serve as a means to the social acquisition of material conditions, which might not otherwise be available.

Since Thrasymachus's dialogue in the first book of Plato's *Republic* the idea that 'might is right' has enjoyed a good deal of prestige. It is true that certain rights are means of organizing the interests of the powerful, property rights being a particular case in point. But it is necessary to add that rights are especially at issue when they provide capacities, which simply would not otherwise be available. Rights are thus much more significant for those without social and political power than they are for the powerful. Rights provide access to opportunities and possibly to conditions that may otherwise be achieved only through the use of power. In this case rights are an alternative route to social resources and material conditions. Generally speaking this is why those who struggle for rights tend to see themselves as socially disadvantaged and powerless.

Not all rights and not even all legal rights are citizenship rights. This may seem obvious but is necessary to make the point forcefully because some confusion surrounds it. Bryan Turner, for example, believes that the advent of rights for animals modifies the nature of citizenship. Marshall, on the other hand, demonstrates that the provision of certain rights is precisely to compensate those who are excluded from the status of citizenship. Citizenship is a status bestowed on those who are full members of a national community, and citizenship rights, therefore, are those which derive from and facilitate participation in this 'common possession',

Citizenship rights, as the rights of persons in the community of a nation-state, will ultimately be secured by the state, but this is not their unique feature. Generally rights involve duties for any person exercising them. But certain rights exact duties from others. Citizenship rights impose certain limitations on the state's sovereign authority. Greaves says that citizenship rights 'may be better called the duties of the state to its members'. Not all rights which constrain the state are ipso facto citizenship rights, all citizenship rights share this property. The different specific rights of citizenship do so in different ways, however. This partly explains why citizenship rights which are universal, and therefore in principle satisfy the interests of all who share them, in fact tend to serve distinct social differently.

The different rights which are components of modern citizenship are not cut from the same cloth, and, under certain circumstances serious tensions may develop between them. Marshall tends not simply to underplay but to ignore this fact. This is because he is more interested in discussing the historical development of the three elements of citizenship than the relations between them. This is connected to a second point. As citizenship rights tend to be seen by Marshall as developing sequentially, so that civil rights, for instance, might sponsor other types of rights, the relationship between rights is assumed by him to be one of logical compatibility, Finally, Marshall is concerned with the antagonisms between citizenship and social class rather than with the contradictions within citizenship itself.

Yet Marshall's exposition must raise a doubt about the coherence of modern citizenship rights. He argues that not only are civil rights in citizenship compatible with capitalist inequalities, they are required for their maintenance. He goes on to say that the political rights of citizenship, on the other hand, 'were full of potential danger to the capitalist system'. And with the advent of social rights of citizenship the threat to the inequalities of market and class is most pronounced. It is in this respect that there is at least, a potential for practical incompatibility in the effects of the elements of citizenship.

Civil rights include not only property rights and the right of contract but also right to the freedoms of thought and speech, religious practice, and of assembly and association. They are in principle unified as civil rights in so far as each is a right permissive of human action. But they are more than this. Marshall says that 'civil rights, though vested in individuals, are used to create groups, associations, corporations and movements of every kind'. In this sense, Marshall continues, civil rights are a form of power. In sharp contrast to civil rights, social rights 'are not designed for the exercise of power at all. He goes on to say that while social rights are strongly individualistic, they refer 'to individuals as consumers, not as actors'. Ontologically the difference between civil and social rights could not be greater.

It is true that citizenship rights constrain the state. As elements of citizenship both civil and social rights perform this task but in different ways. This fact is nicely captured in C. B. Macpherson's statement that civil rights are rights against the state whereas social rights are claims for benefits guaranteed by the state. This distinction highlights the difference between civil and social rights from the perspective of the state's obligations to its citizens. For persons to act as citizens there must be freedoms the state cannot invade and therefore actions which the state cannot perform. This distinction raises a further difference between the two types of rights. The provision of benefits by the state means that social rights require not only an extensive administrative apparatus but also certain conditions of expertise and professionalism in the delivery of social benefits which are unnecessary in the practice of civil and political citizenship.

Though these two rights are different they are not apposed. Under certain circumstances, however, civil and social rights do find themselves in antagonism. The constraint exercised by social rights against the state is direct and imposes costs on the state and therefore taxes on citizens. There is therefore a structural budgetary basis for a potential threat to social rights. And the nature of social rights, as those of consumers rather than actors, means that they are necessarily vulnerable. During periods of economic decline there may arise a contradiction between the need for the maintenance of the institutional basis of social rights through taxation and the requirements of capital accumulation. At such times a pressure against social rights may take the form of a reassertion of civil rights, not simply as property rights but as an independent source of economic action and power. Marshall's comment that civil rights were essential to a competitive market economy because they gave to each person 'the power to engage as an independent unit in the economic struggle' is followed by his observation that for this reason civil rights made it possible to deny social protection on the ground that a person was equipped with the means to protect himself.

It would be imprudent to assume that the different component rights of modern citizenship are equally guaranteed by the state. Not only are civil and social rights founded on different principles and bases, they may exist in some tension with each other. This situation is complicated further by the different involvement of distinct sectors of the state in the operations of citizenship rights. Ralph Miliband warns us that the courts have traditionally attempted to annul or at least limit the scope of industrial rights granted by Parliament. The tension between the different rights of citizenship has led Nigel Young to suggest that the concept of citizenship is essentially artificial in so far as it postulates the articulation of elements of a unity which are in reality contradictory and antithetical.

It will be clear that the threat to social rights from civil rights is ultimately a class threat. While citizenship rights can be exercised by all who possess them, they in fact tend to serve members of different classes differently. Marshall was well aware that civil and social tights each have a clear class bias in their principles and operation. But he failed to seriously consider the logical relationship between rights, and the associated problem of the propensity of the state to defend the different elements of citizenship unequally. Certain civil rights are central to the foundations of capitalist economies and their operation. For these reasons they have the potential to undermine social rights.

In focusing on the evolutionary development of citizenship in which the support of one right was provided by another, Marshall tends to emphasize a quite different aspect of civil rights, namely their role in the development of the working-class movement and its political and industrial opposition to aspects of capitalism.

The full complexity of the relationship between the elements of citizenship can be most clearly demonstrated in a discussion of industrial rights. Questions of the role of civil rights in the formation of and their relationship with other rights, of class bias in citizenship rights, and of the constituting elements of modem citizenship, are all raised by the concept of industrial citizenship and Marshall's treatment of it.

Marshall refers to the 'present phase of the development of democratic citizenship' in a manner and context which suggests that he believes a subsequent phase is imminent. Indeed, his discussion of the development of citizenship in which new political and then social elements are added to civil rights conveys more-that there has been an historical progression of phases of development than that the development must be limited to the evolution of only these three components and no more. Certainly this is how others have interpreted Marshall. Dahrendorf, for instance, in a brief comment on Marshall's work, refers to the 'gradual expansion of citizenship from the legal to the political and social sphere', and adds that this process 'is still unfinished' as 'new dimensions of citizenship' may be discovered by political organizations and social groups. It is particularly odd, then, that 'industrial rights' are mentioned by Marshall in his account of the development of modern citizenship, but are not included by him as an authentic component of citizenship along with civil, political and social rights.

Marshall's discussion of industrial rights is briefer and less clear than his treatment of civil,, political and social rights. Industrial rights, the rights of employees to form trade unions, to collectively bargain and to strike, are ostensibly treated by him as civil rights. It is this characterization of industrial rights to which Anthony Giddens takes strong exception. His argument rests on the assumption that rights might be distinguished by their class bias. The rights of individual freedom and equality before the law were fought for and won by the rising capitalist class against feudal privilege and restrictions on commerce,

Giddens argues that the importance of civil rights to the bourgeoisie was to strengthen the power of employers over their workforce. The rights to form unions and strike, on the other hand, were not simply extensions of existing civil rights, but were achieved in struggle by the working-class movement against the resistance of employers and the state.

Giddens' conclusion about the independent status of industrial rights in modern citizenship is entirely acceptable, but his arguments are not adequate. It is true that Marshall treats industrial rights as though they emerged gradually through the enlightened development of market institutions. But Giddens is wrong to distinguish the civil rights of bourgeois liberties from the industrial rights of labour unions on the grounds of who fought for what. Not only was the involvement of the lower and working classes crucial in winning bourgeois freedoms in mid eighteenth century England, but precisely these freedoms of the press, of opinion and of assembly, were central to the struggle for trade unionism and the right to strike, and therefore essential to the emergence of industrial citizenship.

Marshall's discussion of industrial citizenship is not entirely what it appears to be; it is necessary to go through it carefully to see exactly what it claims. The obvious point is that Marshall saw the nineteenth-century advent of collective bargaining as a strengthening of civil rights rather than the creation of a new right. But the contradistinction here is not between civil rights and industrial rights but between civil rights and social rights. Collective bargaining requires an acceptance of market exchange but modifies the units entering the exchange so that associations or combinations of workers rather than individual workers enter into agreements over wages and conditions with employers. Marshall's point is that this development was a means of strengthening the hand of labour and thus securing minimum. But this situation was entirely transitional because the. collective use of civil rights was, according to Marshall, precisely to 'assert basic claims to the elements of social justice'. During the twentieth century these claims have become accepted as full and genuine rights of social citizenship.

The instrument through which civil rights were used to establish social rights as Marshall puts it, was trade unionism. Marshall's argument is that trade unions exercised the civil rights of their individual members collectively. He adds that this is entirely anomalous, for civil rights 'were in origin intensely individual'. With the more recent developments of incorporation, collectivities are 'enabled to act legally as individuals'.

Marshall does not leave the matter here but goes on to argue that 'the acceptance of collective bargaining was not simply a natural extension of civil rights.' At this time workers either did not possess or did not know how to use the political right of the franchise. Marshall describing the situation more accurately argues that trade unionism has 'created a secondary system of industrial citizenship parallel with and supplementary to the system of political citizenship'. Here is Marshall's argument about industrial citizenship: it is a secondary system of citizenship, based on the institution of trade unionism, which is responsible for collective bargaining as a means not so much of seeking market equilibrium as of laying claim to certain basic rights of social justice.

Marshall argues that while citizenship in nineteenth-century England did not have a political component, because the electoral franchise was the privilege of a limited economic class, it did not follow that citizenship at this time was politically meaningless. At this time no citizen, apart from the insane and the criminal, was excluded by personal status from voting in elections. The civil rights of citizenship entitled men to enter the market and purchase property or rent a house, and to take advantage of any political rights which went with such economic achievements. Thus nineteenth-century citizenship 'did not confer a right', 'but it recognized a capacity'. In this sense nineteenth-century political rights were a 'secondary product of civil rights'. In the twentieth century, of course, this situation no longer obtains and political rights are attached 'directly and independently to citizenship as such'. In this account civil rights have a role only in the historical origins of political rights, but no relevance for an understanding of their function and operation.

Given the analogous secondary nature of political and industrial rights in the nineteenth century, could it be argued that political rights in the twentieth century also be said of industrial rights? Marshall seems to think not, but his arguments are highly tendentious. Marshall holds that whereas in the past trade unionism asserted social rights by 'attacks delivered from outside the system in which power resided', from the mid-twentieth century 'it defends them from inside, in cooperation with government'. This defence of citizenship rights by something like a joint discussion of policy by the unions and the government. An appreciation of these duties includes what he calls a 'lively sense of responsibility towards the welfare of the community'. 'The mark of irresponsibility in this context is a high incidence of unofficial strikes, unofficial because of the breach between trade union leaders who understand and accept their responsibility and the rank and file who do not. The implication of Marshall's account is. that with the political incorporation of trade union leaders industrial citizenship which existed in the nineteenth century as a secondary system of rights supplementary to the system of political citizenship, is in the twentieth century rendered redundant. Marshall's grounds for believing that are questionable, and his general characterization of industrial citizenship dubious.

It is of interest that Marshall accepts that strikes will be justified by those who engage in them through an appeal to the status rights of industrial citizenship. The recognition of a capacity is the recognition of a right. But in addition to the claims of strikers it is possible to point to a body of legislation in all advanced capitalist countries which in fact does confer industrial rights. These are not equivalent to or logically connected with social rights, as Marshall suggests, although they have been used to defend the social and economic conditions of trade unionists and their families before social rights had been put in place. Industrial rights are not individualistic, obligatory, or consumption-orientated but the rights of individuals permitting and enabling their collective action and organization. The institutional bases- of industrial rights are trade unions and similar associations of employees. Industrial citizenship is a status limiting the commodification of persons in employment and therefore includes the right to influence the terms of employment, the conditions of work and the level of pay, and is therefore also the right to develop and sustain the independent means of achieving these things through the organization of combinations or unions. Industrial rights share with civil rights a permissive quality and an enabling capacity, but the suggestion of Reinhard Bendix that the industrial right to combine is more or less continuous with the civil right of association ignores crucial differences between them. Individual rights are paramount in civil citizenship, and any collective action can only be justified as an expression of civil rights if the right of the individual in them is preserved. This requirement extends to the correlative duties and responsibilities of civil rights which attach to the individual participants in unincorporated collectivities or to the artificial corporate individuals. These conditions do not necessarily obtain in the case of industrial rights.

Trade unions can only function properly if the rights of their individual members are subordinate to the rights of the collectivity, and in their operations they frequently infringe the rights of property and contract by preventing manufacture and trade through strike action. Even when routinely influencing wages and conditions, the exercise of industrial rights modifies property rights by encroaching on the prerogatives of management. Thus the exercise of industrial rights may be injurious to the civil rights of individual workers, possibly including trade unionists, and employers alike. Unless this is accepted and accommodated in law, industrial rights are without legal sanction and industrial citizenship will remain a secondary system of rights. In the history of British unionism the legislation of 1871 and 1896, which recognized the legality of unions, was useless in protecting industrial rights until the passage of the Trade Disputes Act of 1906. Industrial citizenship in Britain can be dated from the 1906 legislation, which declared that a trade union could not be sued 'in respect of any tortious, act alleged to have been committed by or on behalf of a trade union', and removed it from civil conspiracy, breach of contract and prevention of picketing restraints. Industrial rights are not only distinct from civil rights but in their application may be opposed to them.

Given the obvious class bias of industrial rights their incorporation in citizenship may appear problematic. Although in practice industrial rights directly serve one class, and, it could be added, potentially injure members of another class, they remain universal. They do not require that everyone be an employee, but offer some protection against commodification to all those who find themselves in the employment of another. In this respect industrial rights are entirely analogous to property rights. They are universal in being available to all who through their material situation need to draw upon them. But there is another aspect to industrial rights which clearly brings them into the orbit of citizenship. Industrial rights are used by organized workers against employers. But in doing so they follow set limits for the purpose of common participation in a unified functional system. In this sense industrial rights are premissed on what Marshall calls a 'loyalty to a civilization which is a common possession'. It is arguable that in the absence of industrial rights the vast mass of employees would not be able partake in the industrial civilization of modern capitalism.

Marshall believes that the balance has moved too far toward rights in contrast to obligations. It was indeed bold for a sociologist oriented toward British socialism to offer such an assessment in 1949 and to imply that a better balance was required for a democratic polity. But British socialist thought, if not practice, has a long tradition of concern with obligation. Therefore, Marshall offers a list of citizen obligations whose appropriateness and consequences he seeks to assess. These obligations conform generally to the conventional actions of civic duties. His list includes, for example, paying taxes, educating one's family, military service, and promoting the welfare of the community.

A survey of the critical judgement on Marshall reveals a formidable list of identified faults. These may be clustered into five categories: that his study was temporally and geographically too myopic; that his notion of citizenship was too exclusive; that his vision was optimistic, that his triad of rights was too simplistic; and that his interpretation was too unhistorical. However, despite this range of apparent failings, covering both detail and the core of Marshall's thesis, some of the commentary has overstepped the boundary into unfairness. A review of this critical work is, indeed, worthwhile not merely for the light it sheds on Marshall's interpretation, but also as a formative commentary on the liberal version of citizenship, particularly in England.

First, Marshall's myopia. In his enthusiasm for the achievements of welfare state. Marshall, so his critics aver, underestimated the perhaps tentative nature of the social citizenship which he saw the welfare state as consolidating. He gave no thought to the possible future need to advance the social element in the citizenry status, let alone defend it against retrogression.

Furthermore, if his model of an evolutionary tripartite form of citizenship was intended for general application, he was culpable of ignoring not just all other countries, but even the relationship of England with the rest of the United Kingdom. As to Britain, if civil rights had been as solidly established in Northern Ireland as in England, the troubles that burst out in the 1968 might have been averted. And even a superficial survey of other countries reveals wide variations in the phasing of and manner in which citizens' rights have been won.

Secondly, the exclusive nature of Marshall's picture of the development of citizenship. Most noticeable, it is centred on the achievement of male citizenship: his patter falls apart if the experience of women is incorporated. Marshall describes the position of women in the nineteenth century with regard to civil rights as in some important respects peculiar. Only by making this rather ungracious concession to the fact that the condition of half the population invalidated his sequence of civil rights as preceding political rights could Marshall pretend to sustain his evolutionary thesis. After all, women were enfranchised in 1928, yet not until 1990, for instance, were they automatically taxed separately from their husbands. Only very gradually they have approximated to a position civil equality with men. By casting his discussion of citizenship in relation to class differences, Marshall omitted the differences between the sexes which cut across class divisions.

But women are not the only groups who have failed to keep pace with Marshall's historical design of the gradual achievement of full citizenship status. Still today many people are in reality only partial citizens: members of racial and ethnic minorities, the very poor underclass, and the various individuals who are incapable for one reason or another of complete self-determination-children, the mentally incapable, elderly infirm. Such people clearly cannot participate on equal terms with the rest of the community in the enjoyment of a common civic culture as Marshall envisaged citizens able to do; yet he makes no reference to the possibility of some individuals being citizens in only a second-class or partial sense.

Thirdly, Marshall's optimism. This accusation has several strands. He is charged with assuming too readily — caught up as he was in the general enthusiasm for the welfare state that progress in social rights would continue. It has even been suggested that his optimism was an expression of his naivety. Looking back from a standpoint in the 1990s, critics can indicate a number of features in British history during the second half of the century which have counteracted the egalitarian thrust of social citizenship described by Marshall.

Society has not become more homogeneous and egalitarian in socio-economic terms. A number of reasons have been presented as having contributed to this disappointment of Marshall's hope. Education has not yet become a means of providing equal opportunities for all. Nor are the social services, including health, equally accessible to all. Capitalism has been more resistant to the spread of social citizenship than Marshall allowed for. And the state has not been neutral as he implied in the citizenship versus, class competition for the distribution of resources. For instance, because of government policy the gap between rich and poor in Britain actually widened to a marked degree in the 1980s. In short, if the creation of the welfare state was something of a social revolution, Marshall can be interpreted as not allowing of the resilience of the old regime or the counter-revolution of the neo-liberalism of the New Right.

Fourthly, his plan of a triangular shape of citizenship was overly simple. This criticism can itself be broken down into three subdivisions. Basically, it is argued, citizens rights do not neatly fall into three compartments; and to try to force them into this pattern is misleading. A number of proposals for sub-dividing, reallocating content and adding to the categories have been made. The most cogent criticism is that the category of civil citizenship really contains quite distinct sets of rights. One of these is the right of individuals to pursue their own interests — the bourgeois establishment of equality before the law and of market rights such as the freedom to trade and make contracts. The other is the right of acting to achieve collective aims, notably through trade unionism — what Marshall calls economic civil rights. The first entailed a confrontation with the state; the second, with the state and employers.

Another weakness detected in Marshall's tripartite pattern is his failure to recognise that social citizenship is different in kind from the political and, especially, civil varieties. Civil citizenship establishes rights against the state; social citizenship establishes rights provided by the state. Social citizenship consequently involves expenditure and hence taxation on a considerable scale. But taxation invades civil rights in their capitalist form of the sanctity of property. So, civil and social citizenship, which in Marshall's scenario are complementary components, are in fact potentially at loggerheads.

And there is yet another problem with the idea that citizenship comprises three sets of rights: the simplicity of the pattern ignores the differences between entailments and provisions, between formal and substantive rights. Entitlements are the rights which in theory citizenship should have; provision is what in practice citizens are allowed to have. Marshall was more interested in defining the former rather than the latter. Similarly, he was more interested in substantive citizenship, involving what citizens could expect in the way of rights, than he was in formal citizenship, involving who had the right to be citizens —a matter that proved difficult and contentious in the face of pressure for immigration from other Commonwealth countries.

Fifthly, there are accusation that Marshall's sequential pattern of civil followed by political followed by social citizenship does violence to the historical facts; a serious charge given that Marshall had originally been a trained and practising historian. Related to this concern are other opinions that his understanding of the relevant historical processes also left something to be desired.

The trouble with Marshall's phases is twofold: it is too neat for Britain and it is not applicable to some countries at all. In Britain, the real pattern was much more confused and overlapping. Even discounting the exclusion of women from his pattern, critics have listed what they hold to be unfortunate exceptions to his periodisation. His allocation of the achievement of civil rights to the eighteenth century ignores the very important struggle for trade union rights in the nineteenth century. His allocation of the achievement of political rights to the nineteenth century underplays the lateness of the concession of full manhood suffrage in 1918 and his allocation of the achievement of social rights to the twentieth century underestimates the value of the old, admittedly paternalistic, system of employment and poor relief which persisted into the eighteenth century.

When one turns to the development of citizens rights in other countries, one may note two examples where criticism have pointed out that social rights preceded civil and political rights. One is post-1871 Imperial Germany. There, Bismarck introduced social insurance schemes in a politically authoritarian state. The second example is the strength of social rights in the post-1945 Soviet bloc prior to the acquisition of civil and political rights consequent upon the collapse of Communism.

Not only has it been suggested that Marshall's sequential pattern is faulty, the very notion of a smooth evolutionary process has been challenged. By portraying the development of rights in tidy stages — political rights from a platform of civil rights, political rights then in turn providing a platform for achieving social rights — Marshall obscures the historical reality of conservative resistance at all times and the often intense struggle necessary to overcome this resistance. Nor are causes and connections evident in Marshall's narrative. What conditions were propitious for the extraction of rights? What was the role of war? What was the role of the economic health of the country? He does not say.

Moreover, the struggle to achieve citizenship rights cannot be adequately understood merely in terms of the relationship between citizenship and social class. Different groups and individuals have campaigned for rights without necessarily acting for or against class interests, As one British academic has stressed, the very meaning of particular rights cannot be adequately understood if the range of concerns and pressures which have given rise to them is not properly grasped.

The neo-liberal antipathy to social citizenship finds expression in a number of constituent arguments, both pragmatic and ideological. We may start with the key assertion that the underlying objective of social citizenship, namely, the shaping of a more equal society, is a forlorn hope for the simple reason that people are inherently unequal: this fact of human nature should be accepted; the state should not try to tamper with it.

But the task of levelling up is more than otiose, it has decidedly deleterious effects. Because the social liberal promise of a bettering of the life style for all the poor is impossible achievement, the realisation of this fact could well lead to social discontent among those with disappointed expectations. And the more the egalitarian principle of citizenship is broadcast, the deeper will be the resentment.

Alternatively, the welfare state system may foster a weal-willed docility, as the poor lapse into a resigned acceptance of their inferior condition —or recklessly allow themselves to lapse, in the view of the harder of the New Right. Because of the very existence of state-provided social security, these 'partial' citizens lose all self-esteem and consequently any initiative for self-improvement to full citizenly status. One of the results is actually to increase poverty because of the lack of incentive to work. One of the reasons advanced in the neo-liberal case for this impoverishment of the human spirit, leading to material impoverishment, is the extensive and daunting impersonal bureaucracy with which the welfare state is managed.

In turn, this bureaucracy has to be founded; and so, together with the costs in the form of cash payments and services for welfare, health and education, the total bill is so large that a substantial proportion of GDP must perforce be allocated to meeting it. Drawing money from taxpayers for this purpose has, to the neo-liberal mind, two infelicitous effects.

One is that personal wealth is diverted from its potential use for improving the country's economy. The other effect is to foreclose individuals' choices by taking their wealth and directing them to the state-provided welfare, health and education service. Free and autonomous citizens should be able to keep that portion of their income and spend it how they judge best for themselves and their families. What is more, because of the earlier argument that there can be no end in sight to the social liberal's programme of raising all to a notional full citizenship status, there can be no calculable ceiling to the required tax burden for reaching that chimerical goal.

Finally, there is the moral issue, which takes the neo-liberal reasoning to the heart of the citizenship ideal. This is the immorality of accepting rights — in this case social rights — without honouring reciprocal obligations. To put the matter curtly: it is unethical to expect hard-working citizens to meet their obligations to pay a high rate of tax in order that listless citizens shall enjoy their rights to social welfare payments. Those rights should be conditional, not automatic, be earned through evidence of genuine attempts at self-improvement. Marshall's analysis of the concept of citizenship into three elements - civil, political, and social, was "dictated by the British, history even more clearly than by logic."

Marshall's analysis of the concept of citizenship, its rights, and, as he later emphasizes, its duties also, is not exhausted by the list of the three elements. Later in his discussion he adds the notion of "industrial citizenship" and its duties, and this seems to sit rather awkwardly across these three main elements. Another difficulty with Marshall's list of elements is their conceptual or logical interrelationships, if any.

Taking Marshall's analysis as a jumping-off point, a more adequate theory of citizenship would seem to require at least some kind of explicit analytic ordering of the elements and assessment of their relationships. Such an assessment could not ignore the fact that civil rights and social rights are licensed and produced by political communities, and are particularly tied to the emergence of nation-states and democratic political orders and ideologies. Citizenship, then, is first a political status. What does this imply for civil and social citizenship? It implies at least that we theorize the nature of the political life and of its preconditions, when considering the nature and purpose of social citizenship and its welfare institutions in particular. Any analysis of citizenship's elements must make general philosophical assumptions about political phenomena, principally the nature of the citizen and the state. In his discussions of civil, political, and social rights Marshall presupposes, justifiably, an ontology of the citizen. This is a notion of the citizen as an entity in principle capable of recognizing, khowing about, and acting appropriately in respect of rights and duties - a notion of the citizen as a moral subject, a rational actor, and as the possessor of relevant and effective powers and skills. In his discussion of the judicial, political, and social institutions that correspond to these rights Marshall presupposes a version of the being of the state as both democratic and authoritative. That is, it is an entity capable on the one hand of empowering citizens, recognizing their rights and developing their skills, and also, on the other, of exacting the performance of duties and of subjecting them to legitimate power.

Marshall's three elements to be of much use in a theory of citizenship must need to be capable of illuminating the important matters of the being of "citizen" and "state" as such. Marshall's "political" element, and probably also his "civil" element, would seem to have some priority in any ordering of the elements in his schema. But Marshall's sense of the nature of the "political" or the "political civil" dimension is assumed and is probably narrower than what is required. What follows is an initial effort to explore and expand basic notions of the political actor and the political community underlying notions of citizen action, its powers and skills, its rights and duties.

We need some discussion of the being of the citizen as a free moral subject and rational actor. This in turn requires a theoretic conception of, and also a commitment to, both the notion and the good of individual autonomy and also the notion and the good of autonomy's needs, preconditions, and their satisfaction as occasions for good public actions by a political community and its members.

Marshall's normative position in his 1949 lectures could loosely be called "social liberal." He implies a justification of the state's welfare duties, of the citizen's social and other rights and of a limited notion of social equality. All this tends to be assumed and is not made thematic. His overriding aim and style is that of sociological and historical description of the fact of the emergence of the welfare state etc., and its probable effects on the structure of social class and inequality. But his concept of the citizen, with its associated meanings of full "member"/'gentleman" and "civilized way of life," clearly carries a moral and evaluative loading - and arguably quite properly so. It is up to political theory or political philosophy to clarify both the logical structure and normative dimensions of the concept further.

Marshall seems to have assumed that not only were there no particularly important and noteworthy logical connections between the three elements of his concept, but also that there was little in the way of ultimate normative conflicts of value and principle between them either. Similar assumptions are arguably also evident in the more philosophical post-war tradition of social liberal justifications of notions of egalitarianism, social justice, and social rights. As against this, New Right conservative and neo-liberal political philosophy, in the light of the post-war development of the welfare state and of the social rights, have argued that there is a conflict of principle between civil and social rights, and in general between social equality and freedom as competing political aims and ideals. Extreme proponents of this view, like Hayek, Nozick, and Friedman, in support of a notion of freedom, have helped propagate a view and a politics that would deny that the constitution of modem states ought to include state welfare duties, and that the concept of citizenship be thought to include such things as social rights.

The terms of contemporary political debate require that social liberalism clearly acknowledge the special status of the concept of freedom and thus the special status of civil rights, the law and political rights as embodiments of this. Recent discussions of the concept of "autonomy," by social demonatic theorists of the welfare state and of social citizenship, are significant here in that they argue that an interest in and commitment to freedom carries with it commitments to freedom's social preconditions. Thus civil rights and liberties in principle imply and require social rights, and are not opposed to them.

Social liberals, such as Plant and Weale, strengthen the case for a welfare role by the state by expanding its reasonable and legitimate interest in, and conception of, the citizen beyond that of legal and political rights and duties, and beyond even membership of the nation or society. They argue that any modern state must take account of the common humanity of the citizen and associated human needs and rights. This is to consider the citizen basically and in the first instance as "autonomous," as a "moral subject," a status understood to be shared by all human beings.

Plant contends that the state and its activities are to be assessed in terms of their "morality" anti 'legitimacy," which are understood in terms of their satisfaction of "basic human needs" that consist of the needs for "survival" and "autonomy. " The satisfaction of the basic need for autonomy requires that the slate act to minimize i) the arbitrary exercise of its own and others' power, ii) mental and physical ill health, and iii) ignorance. Weale, insists that all governmental social policy ought to be subject to "one overriding imperative" or' "principle," that of "equal autonomy." This principle of autonomy asserts that all persons are entitled to respect as deliberative and purposive agents capable of formulating their own projects, and that as part of this respect there is a governmental obligation to bring into being or preserve the conditions in which this autonomy can be realized." Social and economic security provides members of the community with the material preconditions of the freedom with which they can participate in public affairs.

Unlike some of the earlier social liberal thinking neither Weale nor Plant acknowledge the normative validity of Marshall's "social rights" as such. They acknowledge only the utility of "the language of rights" regarding social and welfare claims. They argue that the proper basis of these rights lies in a rational conception of autonomy and its preconditions and implications rather than in non-rational notions of benevolence and altruism, even of the collective and socially evolved kind pictured by Marshall and other welfare state theorists such as Richard Titmuss.

As far as the concept of citizenship goes, then, its evolution in Britain, Marshall's chosen territory, may be treated as a "leading case" for the understanding of the "evolution" of citizenship in general in modern societies, But there is a cost involved in looking at the general evolution through the eyes of the British case in particular. And that is that some other nation-state histories that may be equally as important in world-history and conceptual - theoretical terms in various ways, for instance those of the United States, France, Germany, and Russia/USSR will tend to get marginalized or even, as in Marshall's account, excluded altogether.

Marshall's theory of citizenship is criticized for being Anglocentric and evolutionist. Comparative historical analysis of industrial societies reveals not one but at least five viable strategies for the institutionalization of class conflict : liberal, reformist, authoritarian monarchist, fascist and authoritarian socialist. Many in explaining the origin and developmentof citizenship *emphasise* the strategies and cohesion of ruling classes rather than upon those of the rising bourgeois and proletarian classes. In explaining their durability emphasis should be placed upon geo-political events, especially the two world wars, rather than on their internal efficiency. Man further argues that Marshall's third stage of citizenship as a reasonably accurate description of contemporary Europe, is primarily due to the military victories of the 'Anglo-Saxon' powers.

The major classes of modern capitalism, bourgeoisie and proletariat, institutionalized their struggles with each other. Citizenship and capitalism were still at war, Marshall declared, but it was institutionalized, rule-governed warfare. Such was the model developed in his famous 1949 lecture. It has continued to seem true and important. Major sociologists like Reinhard Bendix, Ralf

Dahrendorf, Ronald Dore, Halsey, Lipset, David Lockwood and Peter Townsend have acknowledged his influence. It remains strong today. This is for a good reason: Marshall's view of citizenship is essentially true - at least as a description of what has actually happened in Britain is entirely about Great Britain. There is not a single mention of any other country.

Did Marshall regard Britain as typical of the capitalist West as a whole? He does not explicitly say so. Yet the most general level of the argument explores the tension between economic inequalities and demands for popular participation, both generated everywhere by the rise of capitalism. This certainly implies a general evolutionary approach, and indeed he does intermittently use the term evolution. Mann argues that the British strategy of citizenship described by Marshal has been only one among five pursued by advanced industrial countries the liberal, reformist, authoritarian monarchist, Fascist, and authoritarian socialist strategies. He maintains that all five strategies proved themselves reasonably adept at handling modem class struggle. They all converted the head-on collision of massive, antagonistic social classes into conflicts that were less class-defined, more limited and complex, sometimes more orderly, sometimes more erratic. Thus evolutionary narratives are wrong. There has been no single best way of institutionalizing class conflict in industrial society, but at least five potentially durable forms of institutionalized conflict and mixes of citizen rights.

In explaining how such different strategies arose, stresses Mann the role of ruling classes: a combination of the dominant economic class and the political and military rulers. As a ruling class possesses most power, its strategies matter most. In fact, many anciens regimes could survive the onslaught of emergent classes with a few concessions here and there. Neither the bourgeoisie nor the proletariat has been as powerful as has been argued by the dominant schools of sociology, liberal, reformist and Marxist. Indeed, ruling class strategies tended to determine the nature of the social movements generated-by bourgeoisie and proletariat, especially whether they were liberal, reformist or revolutionary. We generally exaggerate the transformative powers of the Industrial Revolution. That Revolution was preceded by centuries of structural change - the commercialization of agriculture,, the globalization of trade, the consolidation of the modern state, the mechanization of war, the secularization of ideology. Others have also stressed the survival of tradition through the Industrial Revolution -classically Moore and Rokkan, more recently Mayer and Corrigan and Sayer. Mana further argues that the durability of regime strategies has been due less to their superior internal efficiency than to geo-politics - and specifically to victory in world wars The geopolitical and military influences on society have been considerable but neglected in sociological theory.

In retrospect, Marshall's assessment of citizen obligation in the arena of industrial citizenship appears naive, as it deals with the British scene and increasingly so for the United States. He concludes that, by and large, national trade unions are responsible and meet their obligations. He fails to present criteria for judging performance. However, there is sufficient evidence for him to point out that there is a lack of industrial citizenship among local trade union leaders.

Marshall's analysis of industrial relations is hardly adequate for Great Britain. The long term trend in national performance hardly conforms to his assessment, while local trade union citizenship has become dismal. Moreover, he argues mainly as if obligations of industrial citizenship are a matter of good will and good faith. He is oblivious to the consequences of different trade union structures and different patterns of collective bargaining in stimulating or frustrating the expression of industrial citizenship. He fails to highlight the pervasive adversary form of labor-management in Great Britain with its decisive liabilities for industrial productivity and effective conflict resolution. He wrote without reference to the alternative forms of industrial citizenship, as for example the system of codetermination in the Federal Republic of Germany which, allocating elements of industrial decision-making to the trade unions, has produced greater trade union responsibility.

Likewise, Marshall's analysis does not pay sufficient attention to the organization and consequences of national elections as mechanisms for channeling citizen obligations. For him, the importance of partisan politics has receded, and instead the real issue of institution building rests in industrial democracy, in the arena of collective bargaining and the internal management of the productive and service sectors of society. While the enlargment of industrial citizenship is required, it is hardly sufficient. The obligation of responsible collective bargaining cannot resolve the full range of issues linked to economic growth as well as to the management of social services and the welfare state. In addition, crucial issues of international relations and national defense transcend industrial democracy. Contrary to Marshall, citizen obligations must be effectively expressed in the electoral arena.

From the point of view of citizenship obligations, at stake is the strategic effectiveness of competitive elections in insuring political democracy and political control of economic relations. Drawing on the writings of Joseph Schumpeter, there has been a body of theoretical and empirical analysis which highlights the limitations of the competitive election system especially in the aggregating of decisive political majorities. Under a competitive election system, the crucial obligation of the citizen in the electoral arena is to calculate and implement his enlightened self-interest and simultaneously, the national interest. In other words, his operative obligation is to be judged by his contribution to the outcome of the electoral process; that is, by the decisions and mandates which elections produce. It is our view that the growth of social services and the welfare state makes it more difficult for people to calculate their enlightened self-interest, and the corresponding national interest. They must calculate the relative advantages and disadvantages of particular policies of economic growth versus -the complexities of alternative programs of social welfare. These are calculations which need to be made in terms of relatively enlightened selfinterest and broad national interest.

After a century of growth of the welfare state we are witnessing a fierce and intense political debate about the scope of social welfare and in particular about the appropriate balance between the market place and the allocation of grants and subsidies. The effort to handle the tension between market place value and social rights has led to a massive increase in formalized relations between occupational and economic groups, a kind of modern scientific version of guild regulations. But the formalisms are not adequate since they will always be insufficient and the source of chronic discontent.

Current discourses on the rise of citizenship points in contradictory directions. On the one hand citizenship is seen as an expansive sphere in which new rights are added to a growing body of rights as new social forces are included in the national community. On the other hand there is the idea that the exercise of citizenship rights can never be guaranteed and is often precarious. Recent trends in Western capitalist societies have led Anthony Giddens, for instance, to argue that Marshall's evolutionary account of the development of citizenship can conclusively prove that the battle for civil and political rights has been won. In a complementary vein Bryan Turner has emphasized the 'contingent nature of the process through which citizenship develops, and cautioned that such a development has 'no necessary historical logic or unfolding process'

It is true that a new development of citizenship might come to threaten established interests, and that these in turn could attempt to shrink the practice of citizenship back to earlier limits. But it is difficult to believe that any assault on citizenship rights could be total, except through revolution. While the operation of citizenship rights is ever subject to contemporary influences, the advent of the institutions of citizenship and their consolidation have a clear historical a reality which must play a role in the continuing development of rights. It follows that the career of citizenship is indeed contingent, but also that it has a history which unfolds through time. And while the course of history is never teleological, it is set by social conditions and determinants.

One well-established approach to the historical development of rights holds that democratic citizenship arises out of the evolution to industrialization, or from the civic progress of nation. More recent historiography, on the other hand , emphasizes the role of the "contest of interests, of struggle, compromise and containment", in the extension of citizenship rights to previously excluded groups, and especially the working class. Marshall's place in relation to these approaches is surprisingly ambiguous. Bryan Turner says that 'Marshall can be interpreted as saying that social violence has the potential for expanding the universalistic definition of the citizen', whereas Anthony Giddens claims that Marshall 'failed to emphasize that citizenship rights have been achieved in substantial degree only through struggle'. Other commentators tend to support Turner's interpretation against Giddens'. S. M.Lipset says that Marshall 'kept alive the perspective that society requires conflict', and A.H. Halsey maintains that 'Giddens' criticism cannot be fully sustained when Marshall describes class and citizenship as principles or social forces which have been "at war in the twentieth century" and this conflict of principles "springs from the very roots of our social order". Marshall saw conflict as a permanent and indeed desirable feature of a dynamic society.

Marshall does say that the growth of citizenship is stimulated 'by the struggle to win those rights'. But he goes on to add, virtually in the same breath, that the 'familiar instruments of modern democracy were fashioned by the upper classes and then Marshall refers to here is not necessarily social struggle between groups or classes of people, but principally struggle against established ways of doing things. Elsewhere, of course, Marshall refers to conflict, as Lipset and Halsey indicate; this is a conflict between the opposing principles of citizenship, on the one hand, and class or capitalist society, on the other. Use of the term 'conflict' in this context however, is ambiguous and misleading. Marshall's discussion of conflict here does not point to social struggle type of relationship between social actors. The conflict which Marshall refers to is between sets of institutions or the parts of a social system, as opposed to the actors within it has shown, in a quite different context, that the term 'conflict' properly refers only to struggle between actors or groups expressed as actual social practices, whereas the term contradiction should be used to refer to the disjunction of structural principles of system organization. Marshall's conflict is more contradiction than struggle.

The conflict of principles to which Marshall refers is precisely the contradiction between the equality of status in citizenship on the one hand and the inequality of class in market society on the other. This conceptualization encourages the view that citizenship develops through the rise of secondary rights on the basis of civil rights. While civil rights are entirely compatible with class inequalities, the political and social rights are opposed to class inequality. Thus the development of citizenship is through the conflict, or more properly through the opposition and contradiction between the principles of citizenship and of class. This account does not itself address the question of whether the relationship between social groups caught up in this process will be antagonistic. Marshall's arguments on his matter are too few to permit a conclusive interpretation, but the bias of his account seems to be toward bargaining and conciliation rather than social conflict struggle or violence.

Marshall's account is primarily concerned with the effect of the development of citizenship on the structure of class inequality. Some writers have seen in Marshall an explanation of the rise of citizenship. An explanation of the development of citizenship in terms of the application of existing rights in the creation of new ones is incomplete if it fails to indicate the facilitating conditions under which such things occur and the social groups involved. It is for this reason that an account of the social determinants in the historical development of citizenship is not particularly assisted by a reading of Marshall.

Historical trajectory suggests that rights are not given so much as thought and won. Giddens puts it, the 'extension of citizenship rights in Britain as in other societies, was in substantial degree the result of the efforts of the underprivileged to improve their lot'. He goes on to explain that in order to attain citizenship groups previously excluded from its scope have had to struggle against the resistance of those who have been opposed to its extension. Such struggle does not occur in a vacuum, and striving for a goal does not imply that it will be achieved. It is necessary therefore to identify the conditions under which struggle for citizenship rights might succeed.

Modern democratic citizenship has a history which parallets the growth of Western capitalism. But citizenship rights do not simply arise out of capitalist tendencies themselves. Industrialization, the creation of a propertyless working class, the formation of a professional middle class, and the development of scientific technologies can all occur without requiring or creating civil, political, social or any other types of citizenship rights. Nevertheless capitalist development has tended to create a social structure and especially a class structure which provides elements of the necessary context in which democratic citizenship might arise.

The first thing which should be mentioned as relevant to this consideration, and which is most frequently neglected, is the way in which capitalist development is likely to remove from the social structure class forces which would otherwise inhibit the progress of modern citizenship. In particular the rise of capitalist relations through the commercialization of feudal agriculture began a process which displaced the peasantry from the social and political landscape. This tendency was given added impetus in England by the Civil War of the 1640s and the parliamentary enclosures of the eighteenth century. According to Barrington Moore the Civil War 'eliminated the king as the last protection of the peasantry against the encroachment of the landed upper classes.' Moore goes on to say that the enclosures served the interests of the larger landlords and 'broke the back of the English peasantry, eliminating them as a factor from British political life'. The destruction of the peasantry was crucial for the development of bourgeois democracy, and therefore for modern citizenship, because it eliminated a 'huge reservoir of conservative and reactionary forces'. Societies in which a large peasantry remained significant in the class structure, such as Germany and Japan, failed to achieve modern, democratic citizenship through internal processes as consequence.

A further aspect of the commercialization of English agriculture, but one which refers to more positive outcomes of capitalist development for the rise of modern citizenship, is that during the eighteenth and nineteenth centuries the hereditary landed upper class shared common capitalist interests with the rising industrialists of the period. In more general terms it can be said that capitalist development creates competitive intra-ruling class relationship within the context of a unified sovereign state. In the early stages of capitalist development and by the eighteenth century these things were associated with the development of civil rights as the core of an emerging national citizenship. By the nineteenth century competition within the ruling class, especially between landed and urban capital, had led to a parliamentary rivalry for popular electoral support. This division within the unity of the ruling class for appeal to a wider public not only led to the Factory Acts of the 1840s, with the landed interests supporting pressure from labour against the manufacturers, but also to the extension of the franchise through the 1867 Reform Act in an attempt to increase the parliamentary power of the Tories over the Liberals. This same ruling class configuration of rival parties seeking mass support, led to the pioneering social legislation of 1908-11. In other words, the structure of intra-ruling class competition, which tends to be sponsored by capitalist development, provides a necessary context for the creation of modern citizenship and its expansion.

It will be clear from the above account that modern citizenship in England can be described, as Marshall describes it, as moving through three stages in which the civil element is established by the eighteenth century, and the political and social elements are added in the nineteenth and twentieth centuries. Gidden disagreement with this chronology, insisting that civil and political citizenship rights developed together, derives from a confusion between power and rights. Civil rights in citizenship consolidate capitalist relationship and therefore of political participation without limitation by economic status, could only be added to the general status of citizenship when a class emerged in the social structure which was prepared and able to fight for such rights. This of course is Giddens' more general point; but it too requires qualification.

A third aspect of capitalist social structure, then, which serves as a condition under which modern citizenship might develop, is the rise of the working-class movement. Goran Therborn argues that the positive tendencies of competitive capitalism have not themselves led to democracy; rather it has been the basic contradiction between the classes of capital and labour which has promoted the rise of democracy beyond the dominant class and its immediate supporters. In recognizing the importance of the rise of the working class as a condition for the development of democratic citizenship, Therborn offers three very important qualifications. The first is that pressure from the working class has never directly led to the gaining of citizenship rights 'in the heat of battle'. Therborn goes on to say that the common patterns is for the dominant class to initially resist pressure for reform, and to offer concessions only after a period of such resistance. Not only are working-class struggles for democratic citizenship never directly or immediately successful, they seldom successful by themselves. Therborn's second point, namely that the labour movement has never been strong enough to achieve bourgeois democracy on its own, without the aid of victorious foreign armies, domestic allies more powerful than itself, or splits in the ranks of the class enemy.' The third point Therborn raise is that while protracted struggle in alliance with others may lead to an expansion of citizenship, the initiative has always rested with the dominant class, so that 'the critical questions of timing and form – of when and how democracy was to be introduced' have never been the prerogative of those struggling for rights. The point to emphasize here is that it is insufficient to point merely to struggle as the basis of rights because the outcome of such struggle must be understood in terms of a larger context.

Whilst an appropriate class structure is necessary for the development of modern citizenship, it is itself an insufficient platform for to with and development. Other facilitating conditions are required. The most obvious is a material basis of economic prosperity. In the context of a world-dominant and expanding capitalist economy, demands for reform placed on the English state have historically been relatively easy to accommodate. In this explanation of the rise democracy in England Moore ties this to the fact that the repressive capacity of the English state was underdeveloped. Moore argues that the relative weakness of the state repressive apparatus in England, a legacy of the Civil War, the evolution of the Monarchy, and England's island form leading to reliance on a navy rather than an army, meant that non-repressive means were used to ameliorate and control expressions of discontent. This was possible largely as a consequence of national economic prosperity and well-being. In economically less favorable circumstances, such as those of nineteenth-century Germany, popular discontent led not to political and economic reform but to forceful repression. It needs to be added here that the relationship between state repression and citizenship rights will almost certainly always be negative. For instance commentators frequently notice that the exercise of military force in Northern Ireland is part of a process which threatens civil rights in Britain.

Another important although frequently ignored factor in any account of the expansion of national citizenship is the condition of the international order. Dominant classes and political states which feel themselves to be risk and under threat from foreign powers are not likely to grant concessions and reforms at home. On the contrary, any struggle for new rights under such circumstances is likely to lead to repression. The 'recession' of 1919–20 in the United States of

America, a reaction justified by antipathy to the communist revolution in Russia, were directed against civil rights, political dissent and industrial citizenship. Much earlier and in many ways more serious, the effect of the French Revolution on the development of citizenship rights in England was to introduce a phase of repression which lasted nearly twenty years. Moore goes so far as to say that if the Battle of Waterloo had not removed the 'menace' of revolution 'it is highly unlikely that England would have resumed in the nineteenth century those slow and halting steps toward political and social reform that she had given up at the end of the eighteenth century.

The paramount importance of their security to ruling classes means, however, that unnerving foreign regimes and developments do not necessarily lead to domestic repression. Security may be achieved by removing the temptation of a foreign revolutionary example by offering democratic reforms to subordinate classes and dissident forces at home. In an insightful polemic on British history and politics Leon Trotsky argues that the fear of European revolution led the English capitalist class to accept the legalization of trade unions, the extension of the suffrage, and the introduction of social reforms. These developments had been possible, according to Trotsky 'so long as the English bourgeoisie, owing to its world leadership, still had in its hands great resources for its maneuvers'. Trotsky's observations suggest that economic prosperity and foreign revolution, for instance, have quite different consequences for the development of democratic citizenship when they appear together than when they do not.

The discussion here suggests that struggle is important in the advancement of citizenship, but significantly because it disposes the dominant class and the state to accommodation and conciliation, if it is to their advantage to be so disposed. If the extension of democratic citizenship is not in the interests of the powerful, then struggle is as likely to lead to repression as to the gaining of rights; indeed, more likely. Thus the interests of the dominant class and the state are as important as lower-class struggle for an understanding of the rise and extension of modern citizenship. In a sense Giddens for instance, acknowledge, the need to qualify his proposition that citizenship rights have been achieved only through struggle when he goes to note that it is surely not accidental that, in various European countries, the universal franchise was only achieved in the shadow of the First World War. The war helped to break down some traditional sources of resistance to social change. But governments also needed the commitment of the population to national objectives; the new citizens became cannon fodder on the battlefields of Europe. Yet Giddens fails to recognize how seriously his general position is compromised when he accepts that government expedience and not only class struggle can extend citizenship rights.

Turner's qualifications of the idea that citizenship is attained through struggle are of quite a different order. Without disclaiming the significance of struggle and conflict, indeed social violence, in the developments in democratic citizenship, he wishes to change the emphasis away from class antagonism. Turner argues that while class formation and relations have been crucial to an understanding of modern capitalism as an outcome of the demise of feudalism, a number of modern societies have no feudal history and have instead developed through colonial settlement and migration. According to Turner the preoccupation with class has led 'to the neglect of other components of modern social change such as war migration which are also crucial determinants of modern citizenship.

The idea that warfare promotes citizenship which has come to be widely accepted, is based on at least three propositions. In order to wage war states require the commitments of their populations, and this can be bought with an extension of citizenship. Secondly, warfare promotes social change through mass mobilization and state intervention; and under these conditions there emerges a new appreciation of collective and shared responsibility and the means are created whereby meaningful participation in the national community can be achieved through the expansion of citizenship, especially social citizenship. That is, in wartime people come to realize that if the dangers a country faces are to be shared, then its resources should also be shared. Finally, warfare promotes full employment and tight labour markets. Under these circumstances labour struggles are likely to put great pressure on employers and government and lead to gains for labour, including an expansion of citizenship rights.

There is another aspect to the relationship between warfare and citizenship. In seventeen OECD countries Goran Therborn refers to 'the war democracies proper', that is, countries in which modern democratic citizenship was instituted as a consequence of military defeat. Democracies by defeat included Austria, Finland, Germany, Italy, Japan and Sweden. Therborn is not suggesting that this is the only war-led route to modern citizenship, for he goes on to say that war time national mobilization has also been an important factor in the development of democratic citizenship, but largely in accelerating processes already under way. But in none of the cases that he considered was it possible to say that it was a necessary condition of an expansion of citizenship. In fact the suggestion that warfare can be held responsible for the extension of citizenship is speciously overdrawn, except in the case of democracies by defeat.

Historically there have been few wars which could arguably lead to an extension of citizenship through the need to recruit a population to patriotic objectives and through a consolidation of resistance to pre-war privilege. Such cases typically involve universal military conscription, extensive state control over economic organization and labour allocation, and a general societal mobilization for the war effort. Only the two World Wars, of 1914–18 and 1939–45, satisfy such requirements. Other wars have crated citizenship rights for large categories of the populations of combatant nations, especially revolutionary and civil wars, but few could have done so as a consequence of social and political processes set in motion as a secondary effect of societal war mobilization.

Duncan Gallie has shown that during the First World War, in all major belligerent countries, societal war mobilization is likely to have contributed to the working-class radicalism which at the end of the war sought a society more egalitarian than it had been before and during hostilities. But unlike Turner, Gallie does not draw general conclusions from these finding, for the war-promoted demands for extensions of democratic citizenship, among other things, were not met in significant case. Gallie's comparison of the different situation of Britain and France is highly instructive for an understanding of the role of the war in the development of citizenship.

Gallie notes that while the governments of France and Britain shared the same objectives in the immediate society in the face of a fear of impending revolution, they adopted 'very different strategies towards their respective labour movements'. The French government of the day, according to Gallie had no programms of social reform, and not only excluded the labour movement from national political life but by 1920 had also facilitated the destruction of its influence in industry. The British government, on the other hand, brought in legislation which extended the political and social citizenship of the working class.

The measures introduced by the British government after the war were partly in return for promises made during the war by the trade union movement and the Labour Party for support of the war effort. Why the British government felt that it should so commit itself when the French government subject to no such compulsion is to be found in the strength of the British labour movement prior to and during the war and in the weakness of the French labour movement during the same periods. Gallie argues that 'a critical factor that appears to have weighed heavily on the British government's preferences for an accommodative strategy was its assessment of the potential disruptive power of organized labour in a war situation'. No similar threat faced the French government. This conclusion strongly suggests that it is misleading for Giddens and Turner to regard the attainment of citizenship through war mobilization as an alternative to its achievement through class struggle. Gallie's discussion shows that the level of class conflict is crucial to the context in which the state may need to manipulate popular commitment by the extension of citizenship rights.

We must go deeper to understand this process because it suggests that warfare, together with class struggle does expand citizenship. But warfare, above all else, has generally diminished the rights, including the citizenship rights, exercised in pre-war times by the population of belligerent nations. The requirements of organization for war, including the mobilization of personnel (through military conscription and civilian work-force planning), of information (through propaganda and censorship), all encroach on civil, political, industrial and social rights. A return to normalization in the post-war period may involve an expansion of citizenship rights relative to war time limitations on the rights of citizens, but this hardly amounts to a causal influence of warfare on the development of citizenship. Pat Thane argues that an element in the development of social citizenship following the First and Second World Wars was to 'retrieve the losses in health-care, housing and education which occurred during the war'. In those countries in which post-war expansions in citizenship rights ware real the war interrupted developments which were already under way. In Britain, for example, the foundation of industrial and social rights was firmly established in legislation passed during the period from 1906 to 1911, including the Workmen's Compensation Act of 1906, the Old Age Pensions. Act of 1908 and the National Insurance Act 1911. The expansion of citizenship rights through such post-war legislation as the Representation of the People Act of 1918 and the Unemployment Insurance Act of 1920 can be more readily explained by the processes which led up to the earlier developments than by the war which came between them.

What about the third proposition of the idea that war promotes citizenship? It is true that war creates labour shortages and that tight labour markets give workers an advantage in collective bargaining. Labour's gains under these circumstances may go beyond increases in pay and improvements in conditions and include an expansion of rights, especially of industrial citizenship. These possibilities have materialized in certain cases and in particular have been very important for the American labour-movement, which historically has enjoyed only the most limited industrial rights. It must be added that what American labour achieved during both World Wars were lost within two or three years of a return to post-war normalcy. This fact may be used to indicate the causal significance of war, but in the context its temporary effect cannot be used in favor of the notion. Here again war does not replace class struggle as an influence on the development of citizenship, but is simply a factor which affects a set of conditions, the shortage of labour in particular, which may enhance the bargaining power of workers. This is a very inadequate ground from which to argue that warfare expands citizenship.

It will be clear from the brief discussion here that war relates to citizenship in a number for quite different ways. First, the actual waging of war requires a diminution of citizenship rights. Second, democracy may be imposed on countries militarily defeated in war.

This is not a necessary consequence of defeat, of course, but has been the cause of democratic citizenship in some significant cases. Third, the argument that war creates citizenship through social processes it sets in motion has been advanced by constructing the most 'precarious generalization on slender evidence'. At best the proposition applies to wars in which societal mobilization has occurred, but certainly not to all nations subject to such mobilization. Any expansion of citizenship through war mobilization cannot be regarded as an alternative to its achievement through class struggle, and the introduction of a context of the pre-war situation tends to enormously reduce the importance of warfare to post-war developments of citizenship. In addition to war, Turner holds that migration, and also egalitarian ideologies, are responsible for modern democratic citizenship. Turner identifies two quite distinct roles for migration in the development of citizenship. First, migration out of traditional rural cultures promotes a secularization which in turn supports the struggle for citizenship rights; and second, modern citizenship in British dominion societies, including America, has to be understood in terms of the migrant nature of those societies. The significance of a migrant basis in the development of democratic citizenship in America, Australia, Canada and New Zealand, for example, is not explicitly indicated by Turner. Any consideration of the historical development of such societies will in fact point to the importance of class relations in the rise of democratic citizenship in migrant societies.

Colonies of white settlement in which the original population was either sparse at the outset or largely eliminated during colonization are likely to share two further features: first, a chronic shortage of labour and second, a significant capitalist farming sector. The high wage structure created by the first of these reinforces the high technology and productivity of the second. The resulting class structure, free of a cash-cropping peasantry and a native underclass, mark the capture of the colonial state by the settler population politically feasible. It is important to stress that it is not migration so much as the class formation of the migrant society which leads to democratic citizenship in dominion societies. Other colonies of white settlement, especially those which typically contain mining and plantation sectors drawing upon cheap indigenous labour and a peasant subsistence sector, such as Kenya and Rhodesia, have been much less successful in the development of democratic citizenship. In these cases the dominant colonial class maintains links with and indeed could be seen as a direct extension of the dominant class of the colonizing power. The settler population under these general circumstances is not able to wrest control of the state from colonial rule, and in its relations with the indigenous labour-force and peasantry has little interest in a struggle for democratic citizenship.

Dahrendorf shows that because Marshall leaves 'entirely untouched the problem of power or authority and its social distribution, the conflicts and tension he refers to are 'essentially random phenomena'. Dahrendorf continues by saying that this is because Marshall 'excludes the problem of power and authority from social analysis, and he therefore abandons the possibility to trace social conflicts back to structural conditions'.

We have argued that while the integrative role cannot be ignored, it far from exhausts all the possible consequences of citizenship. By designating membership in a national community, citizenship also defines non-membership. Those excluded from the citizenship status may find it necessary to fight for inclusion. Thus citizenship may be a source of conflict as well as integration. But conflict is too narrow a category to cover the non-integrative aspects of citizenship. The obverse of integration is not disintegration nor even conflict but movement.

At the most general level social movements can be said to arise out of collective social action. Social movements, unlike political movements, are not directed to capturing political power but express the aspiration, interests, values and norms of social change through modification of the expectations and mores which influence social relationships. As a means of cultural change social movements redefine what social participation may consist of.

While social movements may advance the development of citizenship, citizenship rights facilitate the emergence of social movements. Given the two-way relationship between citizenship and social movement it is appropriate to a framework which poses the questions concerning citizenship in terms of social class.

There is a comprehensive involvement of various civil rights in the formation and performance of social movements. As a form of collective action drawing upon persons of diverse background social movements are composed of members legally and socially constituted as private individuals. Persons are linked to social movements through a shared self-consciousness of purpose which is supported by the freedoms of association and expression. Thus it is with some reason that Marshall is able to say that civil rights 'might usefully be regarded as form of power' because they provide the persons for the emergence of social movements. Marshall argues that 'civil rights, though vested in individuals, are used to crate groups, association, corporations and movements of every kind'.

The conditions for the formation of social movements and other social collectivities cannot be reduced to civil rights, of course. Social organization in this sense requires members who can draw upon material and interactional resources, in addition to norms and rights. Ralf Dahrendorf goes so far as to say that in the absence of the right to association the other conditions are unlikely to produce social organization or movement. However, the suppression of movements through the absence of civil rights and even their repression through police force does not necessarily mean that their prospects are impossible.

In 'Reflections on Power' Marshall argues that in the effective absence of civil rights, social movement itself can be an alternative source of power in providing a capacity for successful action. Marshall refers to the Black Power Movement and the Students Movement in particular, but the point is applicable to social movements in general. What is not available as a right may be achieved through usurpation and the mobilization of numbers.

The development of citizenship has two analytically distinct aspects: there is the inclusion of new categories of persons into existing citizenship rights, and there is the advent of new types of rights in citizenship, the creation of new components or elements of citizenship. These different processes may historically occur together, although they need not. While an expansion of the numbers of citizens seldom in itself leads to changes in the structure of citizenship, the creation of new types of citizenship rights frequently inducts previously excluded sections of the population into a national community, as when the nineteenth century creation of national citizenship brought sections of the working class into the operations of European societies for the first time.

The inclusion of migrants into a host-nation's citizenship structure is the most obvious case of the development of citizenship though increases in the numbers of persons meeting existing criteria of membership rather than through the advent of new rights as components or elements of citizenship.

In this account the defining characteristic of social movement is its capacity to mobilize resources, and the cultural definition of both the structure of citizenship and, therefore, the host community on the one hand, and the excluded or aspirant group on the other, are taken for granted or assumed to be given. An aspect of the American Civil Rights movement in particular, however, is that it not only served to mobilize resources for social change by insinuating negros into locations in the social structure previously denied to them, but also culturally redefined Blacks in a manner which in turn led to a reappraisal and redefinition of American institutions in general.

A quite different understanding of social movements regards them principally as the basis and source of cultural transformation in society, as being responsible for changes in the way that society, its members and their relationship, are defined and understood. Alain Touraine, who is particularly associated with this understanding of social movement, says that 'a social movements is constantly occupied with challenging the social definition of roles, the functioning of the political arena, and the social order'. Form this perspective social movements are a form of action which transform historically given cultural patterns. It is in this sense that the nineteenth-century English labour movement provides an excellent example of social movement as its emergence not only destroyed the liberal understanding of human nature but among other things also led to an entirely new conception of society and its animus.

The relevance of the conception of social movement as a mediator of cultural change to the question of citizenship has recently been emphasized by Bryan Turner. Turner argues that as the redefinition of society and therefore social membership is the intention or outcome of social movements. Social movements are 'inevitably movements about the rights of citizenship'. In this way it is possible to describe the historical developments of citizenship not only in terms of the consequences for the definition of social membership of successive occurrence, incidents or episodes of social movement. Turner says that there have been four such 'waves' in the development of modern citizenship: the first had the consequence of removing property from the definition of the citizen; the second removed sex; the third wave redefined the significance of age and kinship ties in the family for citizenship rights; and a fourth wave, is currently expanding citizenship by ascribing rights to nature and the environment.

There is no need to dispute that it is possible and frequently useful to recognize the relevance of social movements to the development of citizenship. The women's movement in particular has not only been instrumental in increasing the numbers of persons who can count as full members of society, but has also influenced the nature of the rights exercised in social participation. It is not entirely clear, though, why this fact undermines the validity of the concept 'social class' in the discussion of citizenship, among other things, as a number of writers, including Turner, assume. What has to be considered is the relationship between social movement and social class.

Some of these matters are elaborated by Claus Offe in an important contribution to the discussion of social movements. According to Offe the pattern of social and political conflict expressed in the new social movements is 'the polar opposite of the model of class conflict'. This is because, firstly, social movement conflict is conducted by an 'alliance that consists, in varying proportion, of elements coming from different classes and "non classes". The imputation here is that class conflict, on the other hand, is staged by one class against another. Also social movement demands are either more or less inclusive than class-specific demands, that is, they tend to be either strongly universalistic or highly particularistic. It will be shown that these points are insufficient to distinguish social movements conflict from class conflict, and they fail to demonstrate that the two are polar opposites.

In making the first point above Offe seems not to appreciate the role of social alliance in class conflict. It has been observed that in its struggle for citizenship rights the working class has always relied on alliances with others, including elements of other classes and non-class social forces such as victorious foreign armies. The idea that the agents of class conflict are something other than class alliances is in fact difficult to discover in the relevant literature. In Marx's historical writings, for instance, and in the *Communist Manifesto,* and in practically all of Lenin's relevant works, class conflict is always treated as conflict between sets of alliances. The composition of these alliances is held to be different in different social settings and at different stages of class struggle, but typically in these works the working-class struggles in alliance with sections of the ruling and middle classes and peasantry; and , for its part, the ruling class allies itself with sections of the middle class and the lumpen proleteriat.

Although neither Offe nor Turner mention it explicitly, others doubtful about the political relevance of the class concept argue that if class is an aspect of social structure, then classes as such cannot act, and therefore cannot struggle, form alliances, and so on. Again, such views are based on a limited appreciation of the class concept. Max Weber's discussion of class conflict, for instance, emphasize the fact that the actors in class struggle can never be classes as such, because the basis of all class action is in the formation of a 'group' drawn from but not equivalent to the aggregation of common class situations. Although Weber intended this formulation to be an alternative to the Marxist treatment of class conflict it is in this regard similar to it. Marx distinguishes between class as an objective circumstance (class-in-itself) and class as a political force based on association formed through recognition of a consciousness of shared conditions (class-for-itself). The general point here is that for Marx, as for Weber, actors in class struggle are not classes as elements of social structure but are social groups formed on a basis of common class-identity.

Turner does not wholly reject the use of the class concept for social analysis when he acknowledges that social movements 'have a complex class composition'. This is a view which Offe also accepts. He describes the social-structural composition of the new social movements as being significantly 'rooted in major segments of the new middle class' This is important in the present context because a leading characteristic of the new middle class is that while it is 'class-aware' it is not 'class-conscious'. This means that the demands shaped by the core of the new social movements 'are highly class – unspecific, dispersed, and either "universalistic" in nature (e.g. environmental, peace, and civil rights concern) or highly concentrated on particular groups (defined, for instance, by locality, age, or their being affected situationally by certain practices, laws, or institutions of the state)'. To insist in this context that class conflict be characterized by 'class' demands and that social movement conflict be characterized by non-class demands thus becomes entirely arbitrary when it is acknowledged that the social structure of each can readily be treated in terms of their social class composition. Offe shows that the nature of the demands made in conflict situations will vary with the class-basis of the dominant faction of the social alliances involved.

The identity of social groups or movements may be based on class loyalty or on religious, ethnic, national, sexual, or some other attachment. In this sense 'class' and 'ethnicity' for example, can be said to be in competition with each other. If the predominant type of social identity in any given situation takes a non-class form it would follow that 'class' has been displaced by some other social force. But, such a statement ignores a dimension of the class concept which is in fact prior to class identity.

Unlike Turner, Alain Touraine insists that classes and social movements are quite different types of phenomena which bear a non-contradictory relationship with each other. In a characterization interestingly similar to Marx's distinction between a class-in-itself and a class-for-itself, Touraine characterizes classes as social situations or conditions and social movements as collective actors. While collective action is not possible for classes as situations or conditions, the membership of social movements is drawn from persons with clear and distinct class backgrounds, although social movements need not be defined in terms of the social class composition of their membership.

In his analysis of citizenship Marshall is concerned with the consequences of the expansion of rights on class structure as an objective situation in something of the manner indicated by Touraine, and also on the level of class resentment. Class resentment relates to the propensity of conflict rather than to the identity to which one subscribes when engaged in conflict, or any other form of group involvement and membership. Marshall has very little to say about the role of class or social-movement conflict in the expansion of citizenship.

The notion that class is no longer a useful category encourages the more general view that class is a less valid notion for understanding the expansion of citizenship than social movement. A strong caution against this conclusion is warranted because it is not at all clear that even the full development of social citizenship negates social class. The development of social participation may indeed diminish class resentment; but it cannot dismantle the pattern of class inequality in the social structure. The self-identify of the movements which seek to modify the patterns of both social participation and social inequality are inevitably different at different times, but the conclusions to be drawn from this fact should not be exaggerated. It must be added that the suggestion that 'class conflict' has been displaced from the Western political arena by 'social-movement conflict' is both premature and misleading.

The concept of class is crucial for such an analysis, a fact Marshall appreciated through a very strong sense of the concrete historical reality of capitalism as a social system.

Giddens versus Marshall

While Anthony Giddens affirms the significance of Marshall's analysis of citizenship for contemporary social and political theory, he has a number of criticisms to make. In the first place, he is critical of what he sees as the teleological and evolutionary elements in Marshall's analysis. Giddens criticizes Marshall for treating the development of citizenship as if it were something that unfolded in phases according to some inner logic within the modern world. In Giddens's account, Marshall tends to overstate the extent to which citizenship rights can be understood in terms of a threefold staged process. In addition, Giddens sees in Marshall's account an oversimplification of the role of politics and the state. Marshall, according to Giddens, understood the unfolding of citizenship rights from the eighteenth to the twentieth century as a process which is supported and buttressed by 'the beneficent hand of the state'. In

Giddens's analysis, Marshall seriously underestimated the way 'citizenship rights have been achieved in substantial degree only through struggle'. Furthermore, Giddens argues, Marshall underestimated the degree to which the balance of power was tipped to the underprivileged only during times of war, particularly during the periods of world war.

These criticisms are, misleading in a number of respects. Far from suggesting a general evolutionary framework for the explanation of the development of citizenship rights, Marshall, takes a more contingent view of historical change. There seems little, if any, evidence to suggest that Marshall's schemes rests on the assumption of an evolutionary logic. Marshall emphasized that institutions and complexes of rights developed at their 'own speed' and under the direction of varying forces and principles. The development of rights by no means followed, he stressed, a linear path in any one time-period; there were often losses as well as gains. Further, the chief factor which Marshall saw underpinning the development of rights was, in fact, struggle—struggle against hierarchy in its traditional feudal form, struggle against inequality in the market-place, and struggle against social injustice perpetuated by state institutions. Rights had to be fought for, and when they were won they had to be protected. At the root of these processes was the delicate balance between social and political forces. When Marshall discussed citizenship and class, and when he described the relationship between the two as one of 'warfare', he was addressing himself explicitly to some of the major social movements which have shaped the contemporary world. In writings after 'Citizenship and social class', Marshall is even more explicit about the formative role of political and social conflict.

A second area of criticism voiced by Giddens concerns Marshall's treatment of the expansion of citizenship rights as a purely 'one-way phenomenon'. Marshall is criticised for regarding the development of citizenship as an 'irreversible process'. There are passage in Marshall which certainly justify this criticism. However, it seems in general to be misplaced. For instance, Marshall documented the way in which primitive forms of social rights—rooted in membership of local communities and funcational associations (guilds) existed prior to the eighteenth century and yet practically vanished in the latter half of the eighteenth and the early nineteenth centuries. He argued that their revival began with the development of public elementary education, but that this process of revival itself had by no means a stable history, and depended on the particular strength of the various social movements supporting reform. More fundamentally, Marshall pointed to the emergence of nationalism—'modern national consciousness', as he put it, as a critical factor in the stimulation of the demand for the recognition of equal social worth. Nationalist movements inspired a direct sense of 'community membership' and the aspiration that all nationals become full and equal members of the community. Marshall did not develop this insight, and he did not provide a detailed analysis of the international context within which the demands for citizenship rights developed. None the less, he did not ignore this context and in various writings stressed the significance of nationalism and warfare to the history of rights, particularly social rights. Moreover, Marshall concluded his reflections on class and citizenship by arguing that the balance achieved between these two great forces in the twentieth century by no means promised a simple stable future. In Marshall's view, bow long the current balances lasts cannot easily be determined. And, he concluded, 'it may be that some of the conflicts within our system are becoming too sharp for the compromise to achieve its purpose much longer'. Marshall appears to have been quite sensitive to the potential instabilities which might wreck any period of social equilibrium. Written four decades before the epoch of Reagan and Thatcher, and the new Right's attack on welfare rights, this certainly was an insightful observation.

A third set of criticisms Giddens makes is concerned with Marshall's threefold classification of rights. Giddens objects in particular to Marshall's treatment of civil rights as a homogeneous category. He emphasizes that the civil rights of individual freedom and equality before the law were fought for and achieved in large part by an emergent bourgeoisie. These rights helped consolidate industrial capitalism and the modern representative state. As such, they are to be distinguished from what Giddens calls 'economic civil rights' or 'industrial citizenship', as Marshall put it. This latter group of rights had to be fought for by working-class and trade-union activists. The right to form trade unions was not gracefully conceded, but was achieved and sustained only through bitter conflicts. The same applies to the extension of the activities of unions in their attempt to secure regularized bargaining and the right to strike. All this implies that there is 'something awry in lumping together such phenomena with civil rights in general'. If individual civil rights tended to confirm the dominance of capital, economic civil rights tended to threaten the functioning of the capitalist market.

More fundamentally, Giddens maintains that each category of citizenship right should be understood as an area of contestation or conflict, each linked to a distinctive type of regulatory power or surveillance, where that surveillance is both necessary to the power of mauling class and an axis around which subordinate groups can seek to reclaim control over their lives.

The bundles of rights have quite different origins, conditions of existence and institutional mechanisms of support, from the local community to the courts or parliament. Why, and in what particular ways, types of rights are linked to particular forms of power and locale is not sufficiently elaborated. And while there is much to recommend Giddens's emphasis on the achievement of rights through contestation, it does not separate him as decisively from Marshall as he claims. Marshall does grant conflict a central place in the achievement of rights.

However, underpinning Giddens's concern with conflict, and the domains in which it is located, is a wider concern to develop a new explanatory framework for the development of rights. It is worth dwelling on this for a moment, for it has a number of advantages over Marshall's account, although, it is itself by no means fully satisfactory.

The roots of modern citizenship

In Giddens's view, the development of citizenship and of modern democracy in general has to be linked to the expansion of state sovereignty or the build-up of administrative power from the late sixteenth century. The development of the state's 'apparatus of government' was made possible to a significant extent by the extension of the state's capacity for surveillance; that is, the collection and storing of information about members of society, and the related ability to supervise subject populations. As the state's sovereign authority expanded progressively and its administrative centres became more powerful, the state's dependence on force as a direct medium of rule was slowly reduced. For the increase in administrative power via surveillance increased the state's dependence on cooperative forms of social relations; it was no longer possible for the modern state to manage its affairs and sustain its offices and activities by force alone. Accordingly, greater reciprocity was created between the governors and the governed, and the more reciprocity was involved the more opportunities were generated for subordinate groups to influence their rulers. Giddens refers to this 'two-way' expansion of power as 'the dialectic of control' (1985, pp. 201ff.).

The struggle for rights, Giddens argues, can be understood in this context. The expansion of state sovereignty helped foster the identity of subjects as political subjects—as citizens. As Giddens puts it, 'the expansion of state sovereignty means that those subject to it are in some sense—initially vague, but growing more and more definite and precise—aware of their membership in a political community and of the rights and obligations such membership confers' (p. 210). Nationalism is a critical force in the development of this new identity. In fact, Giddens contends, nationalism is 'the cultural sensibility of sovereignty' (p. 219). The conditions involved in the creation of the modern state as a 'surveillance apparatus' are the same as those that help generate nationalism. Nationalism is closely linked to the 'administrative unification of the state'. And citizenship mediates this process. The development of citizenship, as pertaining to membership of an overall political community, is intimatley bound up with the novel (administrative) ordering of political power and the 'politicization' of social relations and day-to-day activities which follows in its wake.

The pursuit of equal membership in the new political communities reconstituted the shape of the modern state itself. Although the struggle for citizenship took a variety of forms, the most enduring and important was, Giddens claims, class conflict: first, the class conflict of the bourgeoisie against the remnants of feudal privilege; and, second, the class conflict of the working classes against the bourgeoisie's hold on the chief levers of power. These conflicts shaped two massive institutional changes respectively. The first of these was the progressive separation of the state from the economy. It was the establishment of civil and political rights by the bourgeoisie which first and foremost helped free the economy, and more generally civil society, from the direct political interference of the state. The 'separation' of the state from the economy remoulded both sets of institutions. As Giddens exaplins it, the new rights and prerogatives should not be seen as being created 'outside' the sphere of the state, but as part and parcel of the emergence of the 'public domain', separated from 'privately' organised economic activity. Civil rights thus have been, from the early phases of capitalist development, bound up with the very definition of what counts as 'political'. Civil and political citizenship rights developed together and remain, thereafter, open to a range of divergent interpretations which may directly affect the distribution of power.

The second massive institutional change was linked, after the general achievement of the franchise, to the success of the working classes in the late nineteenth and twentieth centuries struggling for 'social rights', or for what Giddens sometimes prefers to call 'economic rights'. This second set of struggles produced the welfare order—the modern welfare interventionist state. Social or economic rights cannot be regarded as a mere extension of civil and political rights, for they are in part the creation of an attempt to ameliorate the worst consequences of the worker-citizen's lack of formal control of his or her activities in, above all, the work-place.

In sum, in Giddens's assessment, class conflict has been and remains the medium of the extension of citizenship rights and the basis of the creation of an insulated economy, polyarchy and the welfare state. The forging of state sovereignty was a critical impetus to the struggle for rights and to the remoulding of citizenship. The increase in state administrative power led to the creation of new aspirations and demands, and to the development of institutions which were responsive to them. These were major historical changes. But there is nothing inherent about them, Giddens notes, which would prevent their erosion in different political or economic circumstances. They remain fragile achievements.

There is much that is compelling about this position. In particular, Giddens's emphasis on the way in which an increase in state power led to the progressive reliance of the state on new relationships with its subjects—relationships based on consent, rather than force—

has much to recommend it as a basis for explaining why new forms of political relations were called into being in the modern era. Likewise, his emphasis on the contingent nature of these developments has much to be said for it, especially if one is seeking to explain the different forms citizenship has taken, and the complex articulation of these forms with industrial capitalism. None the less, it is our view that the value of Gidden's analysis is weakened considerably by a number of difficulties. It will be our contention that problems in Giddens's position derive from accepting too much of Marshall's initial terms of reference, and from lack of precision in central formulations. The upshot of these problems is a fundamental underestimation of the complexity of citizenship: its multidimensional roots and the way the struggle for different types of rights is 'inscribed' into, or embedded in, changing conceptions of citizenship. A few reflections on the nature of citizenship provide a useful starting-point from which to highlight these shortcomings.

Citizenship, Rights and Obligations

From the ancient world to the present day, all forms of citizenship have had certain common attributes. Citizenship has meant a certain reciprocity of rights against, and duties towards, the community. Citizenship has entailed membership, membership of the community in which one lives one's life. And membership has invariably involved degrees of participation in the community. The question of who should participate and at what level is a question as old as the ancient world itself. There is much significant history in the attempt to restrict the extension of citizenry to certain groups: among others, owners of property, white men, educated men, men, those with particular skills and occupations, adults. There is also a telling story in the various conceptions and debates about what is to count as citizenship and in particular what is to count as participation in the community.

Citizenship is about involvement of people in the community in which they live; and people have been barred from citizenship on grounds of gender, race and age among many other factors. To analyse citizenship as if it were a matter of the inclusion or exclusion of social classes is to eclipse from view a variety of dimensions of social life which have been central to the struggle over citizenship. In light of this fact, the debate about citizenship initiated by Marshall requires elaboration and modification.

The argument against Marshall and Giddens can, thus, be put as follows. Class conflict may well be an important medium for the development of citizenship rights but is by no means the only one which requires detailed examination. If citizenship involves the struggle for membership and participation in the community, then its analysis involves examining the way in which different groups, classes and movements struggle to gain degrees of autonomy and control over their lives in the face of various forms of stratification, hierarchy and political oppression. The post-Marshall debate needs to extend the analysis of citizenship to take account of issues posed by, for instance, feminism, the black movement, ecology (concerned with the moral status of animals and nature) and those who have advocated the rights of children. Different social movements have raised different questions about the nature and dimensions of citizenship. As one commentator aptly put it, 'citizenship rights are the outcome of social movements which aim either to expand or to defend the definition of social membership...The boundaries which define citizenship...ultimately define membership of a social group or collectivity'. The struggle over the nature and extent of citizenship has itself been a, if not the, central medium of social conflict—the medium through which various classes, groups and movements strive to enhance and protect their rights and opportunities. The very meaning of particular rights cannot be adequately understood if the range of concerns and pressures which have given rise to them is not properly grasped.

Now, it is the case that Giddens does acknowledge a range of movements which have been significant in shaping the struggle for citizenship rights. But this acknowledgement has come 'late' in the sense that it leaves the impression of being tacked on to his existing explanatory framework. This is the case for at least two reasons. First, whenever Giddens offers substantive expanations of the development of citizenship, class conflict is the major determining factor. Second, little attention is devoted to understanding the nature and activities of social movements, and particular movements' advocacy of certain rights is not properly explained. Giddens's attempt in his most recent work to provide a 'conceptual map' that links together diverse sources of social protest with particular sets of institutions and particular forms of rights does not solve the problems. Significant movements are missed out altogether (such as the anti-racist movements), and the connections between those that are there and particular struggles for rights seem tenuous. For example, many would argue with the view taken within Giddens's scheme that social rights are the prime objective of the labour movement, that political rights are the prime concern of the 'free speech movement', that civil rights are the main focus of the peace movement and that 'moral imperatives' are the preoccupation of the ecological movement. Moreover, different movements changing orientations over time (from civil concerns to perhaps wider political and social issues), their different institutional locations at any given moment (economy, polity, local community, etc), and their different views of the meaning of rights cannot be accommodated on a map which essentially plots static relations between phenomena. In short, although Giddens acknowledges different clusters of movements and rights in the struggle for citizenship, this is not elaborated into a coherent framework.

But apart from these broad sets of rights, there are other categories which neither Marshall nor Giddens develops, linked to a variety of domains where, broadly speaking, (non-class- specific) social movements have sought to reform power centres according to their own goals and objectives. Among these is the area of struggle for reproductive rights—at the very heart of the women's movement. Reproductive rights are the very basis of the possibility of effective participation of women in both civil society and the polity. A right to reproductive freedom for women entails making the state or other relevant political agencies responsible not only for the medical and social facilities necessary to prevent or assist pregnancy, but also for providing the material conditions which would help make the choice for women if they are to be 'free and equal'. Giddens's lack of attention to reproductive rights is symbolic of his disregard of the whole question of the social organisation of reproduction, and of women and gender relations moe generally. He has not made the latter an integral component of his work and the inevitable result, and it is a major lacunae in his conception of the conditions of involvement of women (and men) in public life.

Marshall's and Giddens's accounts of rights suffer, in addition, from a further limitation: a strict focus on the citizen's relation to the nation-state. While this is unquestionably important, the whole relation of rights to the nation-state has itself become progressively more problematic in the twentieth century. For a gap has opened up, linked to processes of globalization, between the idea of membership of a national political community, that is citizenship, and the development of international law which subjects individuals, non-governmental organisations and governments to new systems of regulation. Rights and duties are recognized in international law with transcend the claims of nation-state and which, whilst they may lack coercive powers of enforcement, have far-reaching consequences. For example, the International Tribunal at Nuremberg (1945) laid down, for the first time in history, that when international rules that protect basic humanitarian values are in conflict with state laws, every individual nust transgrees the state laws. The legal framework of the Nuremberg Tribunal marked a highly significant change in the legal direction of the modern state; for the new rules challenged the principles of military discipline and subverted national sovereignty at one of its most sensitive points: the hierarchical relations within the military. In addition, two internationally recognized legal mainstays of national sovereignty—'immunity from jurisdiction' and 'immunity of state agencies'—have been progressively qustioned by Western courts. While it is the case that national sovereignty has most often been the victor when put to the test, the tension between citizenship, national sovereignty and international law is marked, and it is by no means clear how it will be resolved.

A satisfactory account of the meaning and nature of citizenship today must transcend the terms of reference which Marshall and Giddens have set down. The study of citizenship has to concern itself with all those dimensions which allow or exclude the participation of people in the communities in which they live and the complex pattern of national and international relations and processes which cut across these. Neither Marshall nor Giddens has provided an adequate basis for such a study.

The restricted conception of citizenship in Marshall's and Giddens's work has serious sociological and political implications for central areas of inquiry. The section below will explore these implications in relation to Giddens's treatment of the ideological nature of rights, the critical dimensions of the state, the social structure of post-war society and contemporary political directions.

When setting out the meaning of citizenship rights, Giddens criticizes Marshall from a Marxist perspective ad then uses Marshall against Marxism, pursuing the question: are rights an ideological sham or of real significance? In recent writings, Giddens has affirmed that capitalism is, as Marx argued, a class society. Pivotal to Giddens's analysis is the capitalist labour contract, the basic concept, he suggests, for analysing the class structure of capitalism from the eighteenth century to the present time.

The creation of a market-place for both labour power and capital involved two fundamental developments. The first of these was the progressive separation of the economic from the political. The creation of a distinctive sphere of the political was effected by the overthrowing of feudal courtly power, and by its progressive replacement by parliamentary representative government. The struggle for civil and political rights consolidated this development, giving distinctive form to the public domain. While the separation of the economic from the political was in many respcts a progressive development in political terms, it served also to undercut the new-won freedoms. For although the new freedoms were universal in principle, they favoured the dominant class in practice. The rights of the citizens to elect or stand as representatives were not extended to work and, accordingly, the sphere of politics was not extended to industry. Once citizens entered that factory gates, their lives were fully determined by the dictates of capital. To quote Giddens: 'the capitalist labour contract...excludes the worker from formal rights over the control of the workplace. This exclusion is not incidental to the capitalist state, but vital to it since the sphere of industry is specifically defined as being "outside politics". 'In substantial degree', Giddens argues, 'Marx was surely right'. Many of the new freedoms were 'bourgeois freedoms'.

In prior types of society it was taken for granted that the worker or peasant had a significant degree of control over the process of labour. But with the birth of industrial capitalism this substantial degree of control was lost and had to be won all over again. The formation of the labour movement, and of trade unions in particular, created a minimum basis of power for workers in the industrial sphere. Labour and socialist parties were able to build on this despite often bitter opposition. Together, unions and socialist parties took advantage of and fought for the development of political and social rights. It is very important, Giddens concludes from this, to see the different kinds of citizenship rights distinguished by Marshall as contra Marx and Marxism 'double-edged'. Citizenship rights do serve to extend the range of human freedoms possible within industrial capitalist societies; they serve as levers of struggle which are the very basis on which freedoms can be won and protected. But at the same time they continue to be the sparking-points of conflicts. In the final analysis, therefore, citizenship rights have not simply been bourgeois freedoms. To use Marshall against Marx is, according to Giddens, to recognize that Marxism has failed to understand, and anticipate, the very way in which certain types of citizenship rights have been actualized within the framework of liberal industrial capitalist society. As he puts it:

> Among the industrialized societies at least, capitalism is by now a very different phenomenon from what it was in the nineteenth century and labour movements have played a prime role in changing it. In most of the capitalist countries, we now have to speak of the existence of 'welfare capitalism', a system in which the labour movement has achieved a considerable stake and in which economic [social] citizenship rights look large. Citizenship rights helped cement the industrial capitalist order while at one and the same time creating new forms of politics linked to new rights for all its citizens.

There is a fundamental ambiguity in Giddens's analysis. This ambiguity derives from his attempt to reconcile three different positions. First, he wants to argue that Marx was right: citizenship rights have been so much ideology—a sham. Giddens affirms the view that citizenship rights have for long periods largely been the province of the bourgeoisie and can legitimately be referred to as 'bourgeois freedoms'. Second, he argues that Marx was only partially right. Marx was right about the extent to which citizenship rights served to legitimate and cement the industrial capitalist order. But Marx was wrong as well because citizenship rights have proven to be 'double-edged'. Third, Giddens argues that Marx was simply wrong about the nature of rights. The fact that rights are double-edged—the fact that citizenship rights can be actualized within the framework of liberal democracy—seems to him to imply that the revolutionary socialist project is quite unjustified. To support this view Giddens singles out the fact that citizenship rights have been actually developed and extended within the sphere of industrial capitalism modifying and altering industrial capitalism itself. Giddens's overall equivocation on this issue, and the consequences this equivocation has, can be highlighted by considering his appraisal of the political significance of the separation of the 'political' and 'economic'.

For Giddens, the separation of the political and economic is linked fundamentally to the nature of modern domination—the rule of capital. While Giddens is surely right to stress the way the institutionalized separation of the economic from the political creates the very basis for the development and expansion of capital—and secures the interests of the capitalist class—his analysis fails to explore systematically the ways in which this separation also creates a significant space for the realization of political rights and freedoms. The relative separation of the political and economic means that there is a realm in which the citizen can enjoy rights unavailable to those in societies where this separation has not been established. What this amounts to, among other things, is the necessity to recognize the fundamental liberal notion that the 'separation' of the state from civil society is (and must be) a central feature of any democratic political order; without it, a number of critical modern political innovations—concerning the centrality, in principle, of an 'impersonal' structure of public power, of a constitution to help guarantee and protect rights, of a diversity of power centres within and outside of the state, of mechanisms to promote competition and debate between alternative political platforms—cannot be enjoyed. While one consequence of th differentiation of the economic and political is to give the economy relative freedom and, thereby, to produce and repoduce massive asymmetries in income, wealth and power, as Giddens rightly maintains, another is to create a space for the enjoyment of civil and political rights. The significance of this requires detailed comparative investigation (between countries West and East, North and South) which is missing in Giddens's work.

An additional problem of analysing and assessing citizenship rights primarily in terms of their ideological significance for class relations and capitalist society is that the very diverse origins of rights and the distinctively modern conception of citizenship gets put aside. The modern conception of citizenship is inseparable from a series of multiple and complexly overlapping conflicts. Struggles between monarchs and barons over the domain of rightful authority; peasant rebellions against the weight of excess taxation and social obligation; the spread of trade, commerce and market relations; the flourishing of Renaissance culture with its renewed interest in classical political ideas including the Greek city-state and Roman law; the consolidation of national monarchies in Europe (England, France and Spain); religious strife and the challenge to the universal claims of Catholicism; the struggle between church and state—all these played a part in the emergence of the modern idea of the state, the citizen and citizenship. The idea of the individual as a citizen is, moreover, an idea deeply connected with the doctrine of freedom of choice, a doctrine which raises questions about choice in matters as diverse as marriage, economic and political affairs. If the modern idea of citizenship crystallized at the intersection of a variety of struggles, it did so in the context of struggles concerned with rights which are fundamental to most aspects of choice in everyday life. The significance of these rights goes far beyond that which can be embraced in an analysis which simply places class first.

Giddens's emphasis on separating out the formal rights that people enjoy from the actual capacities they have to enact rights is important. But this insight is not original, and his use of it is marred by terms of reference which are too narrow and do not permit the adequate specification of the diverse range of rights that emerge with the development of modern citizenship. The right to freedom of choice in marriage, the right to choice about one's religion—these and many other rights cannot simply be understood or their meaning explicated within the framework of concerns 'rights: sham or real'? They suggest a diversity of issues, and a diversity of conditions, which need much more careful analyses than Giddens has hitherto provided. They also require a much more sophisticated classificatory scheme of rights if many of them are to be given adequate treatment at all. A satisfactory theory of rights, which attends to the diverse range of rights which have been essential to the shaping of the modern world, will require an analysis which goes far beyond that provided by Marx, Marshall or Giddens.

6

Citizenship and Minority Rights

There is no more dynamic social figure in modern history than the citizen. Citizen and citizenship are powerful words. They speak of respect, of rights, of dignity. We find no pejorative uses. It is a weighty, monumental, humanist word.

The last twenty years have witnessed a remarkable upsurge of interest in two topics amongst political philosophers: the 'minority rights-multiculturalism' debate, and 'the 'citizenship-civic virtue' debate. Surprisingly, these two debates have developed independently of one another, with only a few isolated discussions of their interconnection. There has not been any serious attempt to connect these two topics in a more systematic way. There is an urgent need to explore how emerging theories of minority rights and multiculturalism affect the virtues and practices of democratic citizenship, and to see how emerging theories of citizenship and civic virtue affect the rights and status of ethnocultural minorities.

There are potential tensions between these two concerns. In fact, defenders of minority rights have often been suspicious of appeals to some ideal of 'good citizenship', which they see as reflecting a demand that minorities should quietly learn to play by the majority's rules. Conversely, those who wish to promote a more robust conception of civic virtue and democratic citizenship have often been suspicious of any theory of minority rights, which they see as reflecting the sort of divisive politics of narrow self-interest that they seek to overcome.

Despite these long-standing mutual suspicions, it is increasingly recognized that any plausible or attractive political theory must attend to both the claims of ethno cultural minorities and the promotion of responsible democratic citizenship.

Discourse on Minority Rights

In recent years a new debate has emerged amongst political philosophers concerning the rights of ethno cultural groups within Western democracies. The theory of minority rights in a loose way refers to a wide range of public policies, legal rights, and constitutional provisions sought by ethnic groups for the accommodation of their cultural differences. Groups claiming minority rights include immigrant groups, indigenous peoples, national minorities, racial groups, and ethno religious sects; and their claims range from multicultural policies to language rights to respecting treaties with indigenous peoples. Other theorists use different terms to describe these sorts of claims –e.g. 'multiculturalism', 'groups rights', or 'differentiated citizenship'.

Minority rights is a heterogeneous category. Minority Rights has become an umbrella term. There are different types of minority rights. Nevertheless, all minority rights share two important features: (a) they go beyond the familiar set of common civil and political rights of individual citizenship which are protected in all liberal democracies; and (b) they are adopted with the intention of recognizing and accommodating the distinctive identities and needs of ethno cultural groups.

In the recent years political philosophers have shown a great deal of interest in the normative issues raised by such minority rights. What are the moral arguments for or against such rights? In particular, how do minority rights relate to the underlying principles of liberal democracy, such as individual freedom, social equality, and democracy? Are they consistent with these principles? Do they promote these values? Or do they conflict with them?

The philosophical debate on these questions have evolved dramatically over the past two decades. In the mid-1980s there were very few political philosophers or political theorists working in the area. Indeed, for most of this century issues of ethnicity have been seen as marginal by political philosophers. Today, however, after decades of relative neglect, the question of minority rights has moved to the center stage of political theory. There are number of reasons for this. First, the collapse of communism in 1989 sent waves of ethnic nationalism ripping through Eastern Europe, with dramatic consequences for the process of democratization. Optimistic assumption that liberal democracy would emerge smoothly from the ashes of communism were challenged by issues of ethnicity and nationalism. Second, there have waves of Western backlash against immigrants and refugees in many Western countries especially France, Britain, Germany and the United States. Third, the resurgence and political mobilization of indigenous peoples, resulting in the draft declaration of the Rights of Indigenous Peoples at the United Nations. Fourth, ongoing, even growing threat of secession within some of the most flourishing Western democracies, from Quebec to Scotland, Flanders, and Catalonia.

All of these factors, at the beginning of the 1990s, suggested that Western liberal democracies had not in fact met or overcome the challenges posed by ethnocultural diversity. It is not surprising therefore, that political theorists have increasingly turned their attention to this issue. For example, in the last few years we have seen the first philosophical books in English on the normative issues involved in secession, nationalism, immigration, multiculturalism, and indigenous rights.

The first task confronting any defender of minority rights, therefore, was to try to overcome this presumption, and to show that deviations from 'difference-blind' rules that are adopted in order to accommodate ethnocultural differences are not inherently unjust. Several authors like Young, Parekh, Tully, Taylor, Harrow and Spinner took up this task, attempting to defend the justice of certain kinds of multicultural accommodations or groups-specific rights. These authors used a verity of arguments to make their case, most of which can be seen as resting on a common strategy. They all claim that while difference-blind institutions purport to be neutral amongst different ethnocultural groups, they are in fact implicitly tilted towards the needs interests, and identities of the majority groups; and this creates a range of burdens, barriers, stigmatizations, and exclusions for members of minority groups. The adoption of certain minority rights, it is argued, helps to remedy the disadvantages the minorities suffer within difference-blind institutions, and in doing so promotes fairness. Minority rights do not constitute unfair privileges or invidious forms of discrimination, but rather compensate for unfair disadvantages, and so are consistent with, and may indeed be required by, justice.

It is not that ethnic groups have always been successful in getting their claims accepted and implemented. But defenders of minority rights have successfully redefined the terms of public debate in two profound ways: It is now widely recognized that difference-blind rules and institutions can cause disadvantage for particular groups. Whether justice requires common rules for all, or differential rules for diverse groups, is something to be assessed case-by-case in particular contexts, not assumed in advance; (b) as a result, the burden of proof has shifted. The burden of proof falls solely on defenders of difference-blind institutions, who must try to show that the status quo does not create injustices for minority groups and their members.

The first wave of minority rights theorists have, in other words, unsettled the complacency with which liberals used to dismiss claims for minority rights, and have successfully levelled the playing field when debating the merits of the claims by particular ethnic groups. It is an interesting question why minority rights theorists have been so successful in changing the public debate so quickly. In part, this is built on a growing acknowledgment of the many ways that mainstream institutions implicitly favour the majority by using the majority's language, calendar, and symbols. Moreover, it is difficult to see how all of these biases could be overcome. The idea that public institutions could genuinely be neutral amongst languages or religious calendars seems increasingly implausible.

But there is also growing awareness of the importance of certain interests that had typically been ignored by liberal theories of justice; e.g. interests in recognition, identity, language, and cultural membership. So the original justice-based grounds for blanket opposition to minority rights have faded. This has not meant that philosophical and political opposition to minority rights has disappeared, or even significantly diminished. But it now takes a new form.

Discourse over citizenship

It is at this point that the debate over minority right merges with the debate over the virtues and practices of democratic citizenship-a debate that has been developing independently over the last decade. Indeed, there has been an explosion of interest in the concept of citizenship amongst political theorists. In 1978 it could be confidently stated that 'the concept of citizenship has gone out of fashion among political thinkers. By 1990 Derek Heater claimed that citizenship had become the 'buzzword' amongst thinkers on all points of the political spectrum.

There are a number of reasons for this growing interest in citizenship throughout the 1990s. One reason is related to the rise of minority rights. Debates over multiculturalism have often been factious, and have put a considerable strain on the norms of civility and good citizenship. Some people fear that the tyranny of 'political correctness' and culture wars have made it difficult for people to participate as citizens; others fear the inevitable backlash that has accompanied the increased presence or visibility of minority groups. But there are several other recent political events and trends throughout the world that point to the importance of citizenship practices. These include increased voter apathy and long-term welfare dependency in the United States, the erosion of the welfare state, and the failure of environmental policies that rely on voluntary citizen co-operation.

These events made it clear that the health and stability of a modern democracy depends, not only on the justice of its institutions, but also on the qualities and attitudes of its citizens; their sense of identity, and how they view potentially competing forms of national, regional, ethnic, or religious identities; their ability to tolerate and work together with others who are different from themselves; their desire to participate in the political process in order to promote the public good and hold political authorities accountable; their willingness to show self-restraint and exercise personal responsibility in their economic demands, and in personal choices that affect their health and the environment; and their sense of justice and commitment to a fair distribution of resources. Without citizens who possess these qualities, 'the ability of liberal societies to function successfully progressively diminishes'.

It is not surprising, therefore, that there should be increasing calls for 'a theory of citizenship'. Political theorists in the 1970s and 1980s focused primarily on what Rawls called the 'basic structure' of society: constitutional rights, political decision-making procedures, social institutions. Today, however, it is widely accepted that political theorists must also pay attention to the qualities and dispositions of the citizens who operate within these institutions and procedures. Hence political theorists in the 1990s focused on the identity and conduct of individual citizens, including their responsibilities, loyalties, and roles.

The need for such a theory of citizenship received dramatic support from Robert Putnam's influential study of the performance of regional governments in Italy. He showed that these regional governments, set up in the post-war period, performed very differently, despite having more or less identical institutions. And it appears that the best explanation for the variation in performance was not differences in the income or education of the citizens, but rather differences in their civic virtue, what Putnam calls their 'social capital'—their ability to trust, their willingness to participate, their sense of justice.

The first task for theorists of citizenship was to specify more concretely the sorts of civic virtues required for a flourishing democracy. According to William Galston's prominent account, responsible citizenship requires four types of civic virtues (i) general virtues: courage; law-abidingness; loyalty; (ii) social virtues: independence; open-mindedness; (iii) economic virtues: work ethic; capacity to delay self-gratification; adaptability to economic and technological change; and (iv) political virtues: capacity to discern and respect the rights of others; willingness to demand only what can be paid for; ability to evaluate the performance of those in office; willingness to engage in public discourse.

Other authors offer a slightly different list, but Galston's account captures a core set of concerns in the citizenship literature. Indeed, it is difficult to imagine anyone really disagreeing with the desirability of these sorts of qualities. The hard questions arises when we ask what exactly governments can or should do to promote these virtues. This is where the real disputes arise. They focus more on describing desirable qualities of citizens, and less on what policies should be adopted to encourage or compel citizens to adopt these desirable virtues and practices.

And some important differences have emerged in how political theorists would approach citizenship promotion. In particular, political theorists disagree about the role of ethnic and religious groups in promoting citizenship. Some theorists like Glendon and Walzer say that the best 'schools of citizenship' are the voluntary associations and organizations of civil society, including ethnic and religious groups, and that the best thing the state can do is simply to let these organizations alone. Others argue that the sort of socialization provided by ethnic and religious groups can inhibit, as well as promote, responsible citizenship, and that mandatory citizenship education in the schools is needed to supplement and correct the lessons learned in civil society.

This disagreement about how best to promote responsible citizenship reflects another emerging trend in the literature—namely, the need to adapt theories of citizenship to the realities of modern pluralistic societies. Much of Galston's list recalls discussions of civic virtue in the city-states of ancient Greece or Renaissance Italy. And indeed several authors like Skinner Pocock and Oldfelid, explicitly describe them as trying to recover and retrieve the classical republican tradition of political thought, drawing on thinkers such as Aristotle, Rousseau, and Machiavelli. But it is increasingly recognized that the sorts of civic virtues required for a large pluralistic modern society, and the appropriate means to promote them, may differ from those required for a small, homogeneous city-state. The goals of citizenship, and the means of promoting, it must take into account the levels and forms of ethnic and religious pluralism.

This idea helps explain the growing attention paid to the need to engage in public discourse. The decision of government in a democracy should be made publicly through free and open discussion. This is necessary now as it was in the democracies of the ancient world. But in a modern pluralistic society the virtue of public discourse is not just the willingness to participate in politics, or to make one's views known. It also includes the willingness to listen seriously to a range of views which, given the diversity of liberal societies, will include ideas the listener is bound to find strange and even obnoxious. The virtue of political discourse also includes the willingness to set forth one's own views intelligibly and candidly as the basis for a politics of persuasion rather than manipulation or coercion.

Stephen Macedo calls this the virtue of 'public reasonableness'. Liberal citizens must give reasons for their political demands, not just state preferences or make threats. Moreover, these reasons must be public reasons; for example, reasons capable of persuading people of different ethnic or religious groups. In ancient Greece or in seventeenth-century New England towns it might have been enough to invoke tradition or Scripture. But in a modern pluralistic society liberal citizens must justify their political demands in terms that fellow citizens can understand and accept as consistent with their status as free and equal citizens. This requires a serious effort to distinguish those beliefs that are matters of private faith from those that are capable of public defence, and to see how issues look from the point of view of those with differing religious commitment and cultural backgrounds.

Vote-centric theories see democracy as an area in which fixed, pre-existing preferences and interests compete through fair decision procedures or aggregation mechanisms such as majority vote. But it is now widely recognized that such a conception cannot fulfill norms of democratic legitimacy, since the outcomes can only represent winners and not a common will; and ethnocultural or other marginalized minorities may be permanently excluded from real power within the system.

The shortcomings of the vote-centric approach have compelled democratic theorists increasingly to focus on the process of deliberation and opinion formation that precede voting. Theorists have shifted their focus from what goes on in the voting booth to what goes in the public deliberations of civil society. It will be through participating in the formation of public opinion, rather than through winning a majority vote. It is voice rather than vote is the vehicle of empowerment.

In one debate it is increasingly accepted that minority rights claims cannot be dismissed as inherently unjust, and instead are sometimes consistent with, if not required by, principles of justice. In the other debate most theorists now accept that the functioning of society depends not only on the justice of its institutions or constitution, but also on the virtues, identities, and practices of its citizens, including their ability to co-operate, deliberate, and feel solidarity with those who belong to different ethnic and religious groups.

The obvious question then becomes: how are these two issues related? In particular, how do minority rights affect the virtues and practices of democratic citizenship? It is often supposed that minority rights will have a negative impact on citizenship practices, or will inhibit the state's ability to promote citizenship effectively. Many critics worry that minority rights involve the 'politicizatin of ethnicity', and that any measures that heighten the salience of ethnicity in public life are divisive. Over time they create a spiral of competition, mistrust, and antagonism between ethnic groups. Policies that increase the salience of ethnic identities are said to act 'like a corrosive on metal, eating away at the ties of connectedness that bind us together as a nation'. On this view, liberal democracies must prevent ethnic identities from becoming politicized by rejecting any minority rights or multiculturalism policies that involve the explicit public recognition of ethnic groups.

The strong version of this critique treats minority rights as the first step on the road to Yugoslavia-style civil war. A more moderate version states that while minority rights may not lead to civil war, they will erode the ability of citizens to fulfil their responsibilities as democratic citizens by weakening citizens' ability to communicate trust, and feel solidarity across groups differences.

How valid is this fear? To what extent does it justify denying or limiting what would otherwise be legitimate claims to minority rights? Until recently, many defenders of minority rights have simply dismissed this worry, and expressed skepticism about appeals to citizenship. This is understandable since in many multi-ethnic and multinational states the rhetoric of citizenship has been used historically as a way of advancing the interests of the dominant national group. The discourse of citizenship has rarely provided a neutral framework for resolving disputes between the majority and minority groups; more often it has served as a cover by which the majority nation extends its language, institutions, mobility rights, and political power at the expense of the minority, all in the name of turning supposedly 'disloyal' or 'troublesome' minorities into 'good citizens'.

Minority rights theorists provide evidence of historical misuse of citizenship talk to justify the assimilation or oppression of minorities. It is not surprising that many minority groups are skeptical when members of a majority oppose minority rights on the grounds that they erode our sense of citizenship. Yet we believe that concerns about the impact of minority rights on citizenship cannot be ignored. There are legitimate interests that are tied up with the promotion of a sense of common citizenship in multi-ethnic countries. Multi-ethnic countries are as much in need of the virtues, practices, and institutions of democratic citizenship as mono-ethnic countries. Multi-ethnic countries are more in need of such things as public reasonableness, mutual respect, critical attitudes towards government, tolerance, willingness to participate in politics, forums for shared political deliberation, and solidarity.

And there are legitimate concerns that some minority groups, perhaps in response to the rigid conception of citizenship advanced by the majority, have appealed to notions of identity and difference that leave little room for the promotion or nurturing of these aspects of democratic citizenship and social unity. Some groups may sometimes retreat to a notion of citizenship that is little more than passive obedience to the law, and reluctant acceptance of the status quo. And there is a fear that various forms of minority rights could encourage and entrench these passive, inward-looking, and resentful forms of groups identity that inhabit wider political co-operation, dialogue, and solidarity.

These sorts of concerns are legitimate, and deserve serious consideration. However, we believe that this worry cannot be evaluated in the abstract, or through armchair speculation, as if it were a purely conceptual issue. Rather, we need to evaluate these potential conflicts between citizenship and diversity through careful examination of specific contexts and case-studies, and in light of a deeper understanding of the various patterns of ethnic relations.

One natural place to look for answers to our questions about citizenship in diverse societies is in the ethnic conflict literature. Although the potential tensions between minority rights and citizenship have not yet attracted adequate attention from political philosophers, this problem has been the focus of a very active debate among social scientists engaged in ethnic-conflict studies. These studies have been largely historical and descriptive in nature: looking at actual ways governments—both democratic and non-democratic –have tried to manage ethnic conflicts, and attempting to give explanations for successes and failures. It may, therefore, be instructive to have a survey of the broad range of policy options open to states with inter-ethnic tensions, as viewed through the lens of ethnic-conflict theory. John McGarry and Brendan O'Leary's taxonomy of the macro-political forms of ethnic conflict regulation is very illuminating.

Methods for eliminating differences:- genocide, forced mass-population transfers, partition and/or secession and assimilation.

Methods for managing differences:- hegemonic control, territorial autonomy, non-territorial autonomy and multicultural integration.

This typology provides a healthy reminder that there are many methods of ethnic-conflict resolution, widely used around the worlds that fall outside the bounds of contemporary theorizing about minority rights and democratic citizenship. It goes without saying, for example, that the first two methods for eliminating differences—genocide and forced mass-population transfers or ethnic cleansing—are without defenders amongst contemporary Western political theorists.

The first system for managing differences, namely, hegemonic control, also has few defenders. With hegemonic control the ruling class does not attempt to eliminate or merge the identities of minority groups, but is merely content to make any 'overtly violent ethnic contest for state power either unthinkable or unworkable on the part of the subordinated communities. Hegemonic control is possible even in formal conditions of democracy and equal citizenship. Where there are two or more deeply established ethnic communities, and where the members of these communities do not agree on the basic institutions and policies the regime should pursue, then "majority rule" can become an instrument of hegemonic control'. Indeed, many ethnic-conflict theorists consider this to be the most commonly used method for achieving stability in multi-ethnic societies, democratic and non-democratic.

These methods of regulating ethnic conflict fall outside the bounds of political theorizing, not, also because they are uncommon or unfeasible, but because amongst Western political theorists no one disputes that these are unjust and illegitimate.

The legitimacy of the remaining forms of ethnic-conflict regulation, is however, a matter of considerable debate. For example, the third option for eliminating differences, secession, has been the subject of growing debate in recent years, and has been vigorously defended by several theorists with honest liberal credentials. However, even defenders of a right to secession rarely claim that it will eliminate ethnic conflict. It is generally recognized that secession merely relocates issues of ethnic conflict and minority rights to the successor states, often with brutal consequences. With some 5000 to 8000 ethnocultural groups in the world, and only around 200 states, simply arithmetic dictates that over 90 per cent state are inevitably going to be shared by more than one ethnic group, and often by dozens. This means, in effect, that whatever the legitimacy of secession, it does not eliminate the need for the other methods for managing ethnic conflict.

There has also been a major dispute about the legitimacy of assimilation, the last method for eliminating difference. Assimilation as a method for eliminating difference encourages the idea of trying to eliminate difference within the state by seeking to integrate or assimilate the relevant ethnic communities into a new transcendent identity. This can be done more or less coercively: at the more coercive end the assimilationist state can ban associations and publications that seek to foster or reproduce a minority identity, or compel all citizens to stop using surnames that reflect a minority background; at the less coercive but refuse to accede any recognition or support to minority background; at the less coercive end the assimilationist state can respect the individual civil rights of citizens, but refuse to accord any recognition or support to minority languages and cultures, and insist that all public schools, government institutions, street signs, and public holidays reflect the dominant language and culture. In either case, the goal over time is to compel or pressure all citizens to see themselves as members of a single, common national culture that merges all pre-existing ethnic differences.

It is important to distinguish assimilation from multicultural integration. Both involve fashioning a new transcendent identity—the identity of citizenship, or full, equal membership in the state. And both seek to integrate people from various ethnic background into common social and political institutions. However, multicultural integration does not have the intent or expectation of eliminating other cultural differences between subgroups in the state. Rather, it accepts that ethnocultural identities matter to citizens, will endure over time, and must be recognized and accommodated within these common institutions. The hope is that citizens from different backgrounds can all recognize themselves, and feel at home within such institutions.

The relative merits of assimilation and multicultural integration are still a matter of some debate. There is complete rejection of the more coercive forms of assimilation that have been pursued by unsavory dictators and ruling classes throughout the modern era as they banned minority languages and religions and rewrote history in the attempt to assimilate minority groups into the larger nation.

In recent times most political theorists, at least in the English-speaking world, believe that some forms of recognition and accommodation of minority groups are justifiable in at least some circumstances. As a result, assimilation has gone out of favour amongst Western theorists. Hence, most political theorists working on these issues, focus on one or more of the last three methods for managing differences from the above taxonomy; namely, territorial autonomy federalism, non-territorial power-sharing, or multicultural integration.

This points to an important feature of the contemporary debate. Most democracies, historically, have adopted strategies to mange ethnic conflict that we now view as morally indefensible—from the forced movement of indigenous peoples to hegemonic control to assimilation. As these approaches have gradually been rejected as either unworkable or morally indefensible, people have gradually been rejected as either unworkable or morally indefensible, people have been looking round for other models or paradigms of ethnic relations. And the three best-known alternatives—federalism, consociationalism, and multicultural integration—all involve significant elements of minority rights.

Many scholars in the ethnic-conflict field advocate one or more of these three options as having proven success in managing ethnic conflict. It is important to note that normative political philosophers are likely to have somewhat different criteria for evaluating the success of these approaches. In the context of ethnic-conflict studies, the focus is on explaining how state governments can control ethnocultural conflicts and maintain political stability. The aim is to avoid violence and instability. Political philosophers, by contrast, are likely to care not only about the absence of violence, but also about the extent to which society meets norms of justice, individual freedom, and deliberative democracy. A multi-ethnic society could be relatively stable, and yet score very poorly in terms of the virtues and practices of democratic citizenship. Political philosophers will want to know if and when apparently successful forms of managing diversity involve the erosion of cherished values of democratic citizenship: and this sort of information is not always available in the ethnic-conflict literature which is primarily concerned with descriptive, not normative issues.

Moreover, many of the minority claims being advanced today go beyond traditional forms of federalism, consociationalism, or multicultural integration. These forms of managing diversity are all undergoing transformations as a result of such factors as new migration flows, global communications, and the influence of human rights and post-colonial ideologies. Indeed, ethnic relations in most Western democracies are in a state of flux, as old assumptions and expectations are being questioned and challenged. Nineteenth century policies aimed at hegemonic control or assimilation may be out of date, but so too are nineteenth-century forms of federalism or consociationalism. The demands of indigenous people, transnational migrants, African-Americans, and other groups cannot easily be satisfied by these traditional mechanisms.

Much of the debate in political theory concerns these new and untested, claims for minority rights. Precisely because many demands are untested and given that ethnic relations are in a general state of flux, they raise fears that cannot be placated by pointing to the historic success of more traditional forms of minority rights. It is not clear, for example, that traditional safeguards and limitations will apply to new forms of minority rights. This fear is exacerbated by the widespread perception that these claims are grounded in a more absolutist, exclusive, and non-negotiable conception of identity than earlier forms of minority claims. The underlying logic of modern identity claims, it is said, make compromise, tolerance, and deliberation particularly difficult to achieve. As a result there is a concern that the sorts of minority rights being claimed today may put us on a particularly steep and slippery slope.

This suggests that there is still a key role for political philosophers to play in assessing the relationship between minority rights and citizenship. First, in so far as it is important to look at the impact of minority rights—not only on stability, but also on norms of democratic citizenship—then philosophical work needs to be done to clarify the relevant normative standards of citizenship. Secondly, in so far as many minority rights claims are relatively new and untested, philosophical work is required to clarify the underlying logic of these new claims, and to identify the extent to which they entail or engender an undesirable absolutist or non-negotiable conception of culture and identity. And thirdly, if there is some conflict between respecting the legitimate claims of minorities and promoting desirable citizenship virtues and practices, what sorts of trade-offs between these values are appropriate and morally defensible?

In order to identify the underlying logic and social implications of minority rights claims, we need first to consider what sort of groups exist within the state. Different kind, of groups face very different kinds of challenges finding their place within the larger state, and therefore, demand different kinds of special accommodations. A persistent source of confusion in both academic and popular discussions of multiculturalism is to assume that all kinds of cultural minorities are demanding the same kinds of rights for the same reasons. For example, many critics fail to notice that while national minority groups like the Scottish typically seek autonomy from the central government to govern their own affairs, immigrant groups tend to ask for measures that will make it easier for them to participate in the central institutions of the state.

There is no single definitive typology of forms of ethnocultural diversity. However, there are some significant ways of distinguishing kinds of groups that clarify our understanding of the political stakes in a great number of culturally diverse states. The following list provides a rough and preliminary typology of minority groups, focusing on the sorts of ethnocultural communities.

(1) **National minorities.** Although the word 'nation' is often used to refer to states, we follow all contemporary scholars of nationalism in using it to refer to a specific type of community or society that may or may not have its own state. For more than a century political philosophers and social scientists have debated the question. 'What is a nation?' It is often noted that for any list of the defining features of nationhood, there are indisputable examples of nations that do not meet all of the conditions. For example, nations typically have a common language that distinguishes them from their neighbours, though Germany and Austria are certainly distinct nations with the same language, and the Swiss share a common national identity despite speaking four different national languages. Partly for this reason, many scholars follow Max Weber in thinking of nations as 'communities of sentiment'. In effect, communities qualify as nations when they think of themselves as nations. And as it turns out, these groups tend to be historical communities, more or less institutionally complete, occupying a given territory or homeland, and sharing a distinct language and mass culture.

(a) **Stateless nations,** or nation without a state in which they are the majority—exist in all parts of the world. They find themselves sharing states with other nations for a variety of reasons. They may have been conquered and annexed by a large state or empire in the past; ceded from one empire to another; or united with another kingdom through royal marriage. They typically mobilize along nationalist lines, using the language of 'nationhood' to describe and justify these demands for self-government. While the ideology of nationalism has typically seen full-fledged independence or demographic reasons make this unfeasible for many national minorities. Moreover, the historical ideal of a fully sovereign state is increasingly obsolete in today's world of transnational institutions and economics.

(b) **Indigenous peoples** also meet the criteria of minority nationhood and exist on all the inhabited continents. Typically their traditional lands were overrun by settlers and then forcibly, or through treaties, incorporated into states run by outsiders. Indigenous peoples usually seek something rather different: the ability to maintain certain traditional way of life and beliefs while nevertheless participating on their own terms in the modern world. In addition to the autonomy need to work out that sort of project, indigenous peoples also typically require of the larger society's long-overdue expressions of respect and recognition to begin to make amends for indignities they suffered for decades or centuries as second-class citizens with examples drawn from Australia, New Zealand, North America, South Africa, and elsewhere. We can explore issues about the best way to balance structures of self-government for indigenous people with their need to participate effectively in the institutions of the larger state.

(2) **Immigrant minorities.** A second source of ethnocultural diversity is immigration, that is, the decision of individuals and families to leave their original homeland and emigrate to another society, often leaving their friends and relatives behind. This decisin is typically made for economic reasons, although sometimes also for political reasons: to move to a freer or more democratic country. It is essential to distinguish two categories of immigrants-those who have the right to become citizens and those who do not. We add refugees as a third category with special needs and motivations, even though in practice they will fall into one or the other of these categories in different states.

(a) **Immigrants with rights of citizenship.** These are people who arrive under an immigration policy that gives them the right to become citizens after a relatively short period of time subject only to minimal conditions like learning the official language, and knowing something about the country's history and political institutions. This has been tradition in the United States, Canada, and Australia—and also, to varying degrees, in former colonial powers like Britain, France, and the Netherlands, which allowed large number of former colonial subjects access to citizenship.

(b) **Immigrants without rights of citizenship.** Some migrants are never given the opportunity to become citizens, either because they entered the country illegally or because they entered as students or 'guest-workers' but have overstayed their initial visas. When they entered the country, these people were not conceived of as future citizens, or even as long-term residents and indeed in most cases they would not have been allowed to enter in the first place if they had asked to be permanent residents and future citizens. Borrowing a term from ancient Greece, Michael Walzer calls these groups 'metics'—that is, long term residents who are none the less excluded from the polis. Metics raise different challenges from those of immigrant citizens. They face enormous obstacles to integration—legal, political, economic, social and psychological—and so tend to exist at the margins of the larger society.

(c) Refugees. Many parts of the world, including Eastern Europe, Africa, and Central Asia, most of the migrants today are refugees seeking asylum, rather than voluntary immigrants admitted under an immigration policy. This raises important questions about the aim of multicultural integration. Western democracies accept many refugees in addition to other immigrants. But in the West it has been possible to treat refugees, for all intents and purposes, as if they were immigrants. Government and the general public expect that refugees, like immigrants, will settle permanently and take out citizenship in their new country; and this expectation has been borne out in practice. One reason why this has been possible is that refugees in Western democracies tend to arrive in small numbers from distant lands, usually as individuals or families rather than in large groups. It is, therefore, easier for them to integrate, and more difficult for them to return to their country of origin. However, in Eastern Europe, Central Africa, Central Asia, and elsewhere, refugees often come in great numbers from short distances, which makes integration more difficult and the prospect of return more likely.

In most case, if refugees stay in their new country for many years, it will become their new home. They may cling to the hope of returning to their country of origin. But if they have stayed long enough to get a job and to start raising a family in their new country, they are very unlikely to leave. When they do decide to stay, the only viable and just long-term solution is to allow and encourage their integration into the mainstream society. This is the only way to avoid the injustices and conflicts associated with the marginalization of metics. Adopting such a policy not only avoids the dangers of marginalization, but also allows a country to take maximal advantage of the skills and education of the refugees, so that they become a benefit to their new country, not a drain.

(3) **Religious groups**. There are many ways one could distinguish religious groups for the sake of clarifying questions about special rights. Whereas most immigrants wish to participate in the

larger society, there are some small immigrant groups that voluntarily isolate themselves from the larger society and avoid participating in politics or civil society. This option of voluntary marginalization is only likely to be attractive to religious sects whose theology requires them to avoid most contact with the modern world—such as the Hutterites in Canada, or the Amish in the United States, both of whom came to North America from Europe to avoid persecution for their pacifist religious beliefs. The Hutterites and Amish are unconcerned about their marginalization within the larger society and polity, since they view its worldly institutions as corrupt and seek to maintain the same traditional way of life they had in their original homeland. Indeed, they have demanded the right to take their children out of school before the legal age of 16, in order to protect them from such corrupting influences.

Such groups are 'partial citizens', because they voluntarily waive both the rights and responsibilities of democratic citizenship. They waive the right to vote and to hold office as well as their right to welfare benefits but by the same token they also evade their civic responsibility to help tackle the country's problems. Moreover, they are often organized internally in illiberal ways. For this reason, many people have thought that the state should intervene in such groups, at least to ensure that children are adequately informed about their opportunities in the outside world. However, in practice, most democratic states do tolerate these groups, so long as they do not harm people inside or outside the groups, and so long as members are legally free to leave.

Isolationist religious groups are quite rare in the Western world. Much more common are religious communities whose faith differs from either the religion of the majority, or the secular beliefs of the larger society and state institutions. Members of these communities may share the same ethnocultural background or citizenship identity as the majority—as is typical of many fundamentalist Protestants and devout Catholics in North America. By and large, these groups are seeking not to remove themselves from mainstream society, but rather to shield themselves or their children from very specific aspects of mainstream culture that are at odds with their faith, and to exempt themselves from certain general rules that seem to discriminate against them. A classic example now is the case of Sikhs, who seek exemptions from certain military and police dress codes concerning appropriate head gear, not because they wish to withdraw from mainstream society, but because they wish to participate in these central institutions like everyone without having to compromise their beliefs for the sake of an arbitrary regulation.

(4) **African-Americans.** They not fit the voluntary immigrant pattern, not only because they were brought to America involuntarily as slaves, but also because they were prevented from integrating into the institutions of the majority culture through racial segregation, laws against miscegenation, and the teaching of literacy. Nor do they fit the national minority pattern, since they do not have a traditional homeland in America in which they are a majority, or a common language that distinguished them from the majority. They came from a variety of African cultures, with different languages, and no attempt was made to keep together those with a common ethnic background. On the contrary, people from the culture were typically split up once in America. Moreover, before emancipation they were legally prohibited from trying to re-create their own cultural structure. The situation of African-Americans, therefore, is virtually unique, although the use of 'race' to define subordinate groups is certainly more common. Given their distinctive situation, it is widely accepted that they will also have distinctive demands which cannot be captured by either the immigrant model of integration or the national minority model of self-government, although they may draw elements from both.

Respecting Diversity

It is important to note that different sorts of groups have different histories, needs, aspirations, and identities; and these differences influence the sorts of claims that they tend to make on the state. Of course, at one level we can say that all of these groups are engaged in 'identity politics', 'the politics of difference', or 'the politics of recognition'. However, if our aim is to see how minority rights claims affect the practice of democratic citizenship, we need a more sophisticated account that helps us to identify the underlying nature and logic of these claims.

In liberal reqimes there have been many policies and prorates for prospecting and promoting cultural rights. We will briefly describe each of these kinds of cultural rights.

1. **Exemptions from laws that penalize or burden cultural practices.** Exemption rights are individually exercised negative liberties granted to members of a religious or cultural groups whose practices are such that a generally and ostensibly neutral law would be a distinctive burden on them. Such exemptions have a long history in Western democracies, with a standard example being special consideration for Jewish shopkeepers with respect to Sunday-closing laws. As such, these rights are typically justified with arguments highlighting freedom of conscience and religion, and the unfair burden placed on those whose religious obligations differ from the majority's.

2. **Assistance to do things the majority can do unassisted.** Assistance rights are also a familiar feature on the landscape of most liberal democracies. Often justified on grounds of equality in the face of special disadvantages, they are routinely accorded to members of 'non-cultural' groups, such as the mentally or physically disabled, and cultural groups alike—most controversially in the form of affirmative-action policies.

3. **Self-government for national minorities and indigenous communities.** Self-government rights are in may ways the ultimate minority rights, and can even include demands by groups to secede from the larger state in order to escape the status of being a minority altogether.

4. **External rules restricting non-members' liberty in order to protect members' culture.** It is uncontroversial for all but radical cosmopolitans that nation-states can act in certain ways to protect their culture by limiting the liberty of non-citizens, especially non-residents-for example, by imposing restrictions on immigration or on foreign ownership of mass media. It is usually a matter of high controversy, however, when a cultural groups within a democratic state demands the right to limit he liberty of fellow citizens who are not members of their groups. In general these rights are justified in the name of protecting potentially fragile elements in minority cultures; and the need to protect cultures is often justified with the idea that a healthy cultural context is a necessary condition for individual autonomy and self-respect. Probably the most widely discussed example of such external rules concerns the infamous Quebec language laws which, among other things, have banned the

use of languages other than French on commercial signs within Quebec, a province with more than 1 million non-francophone citizens.

5. **Internal rules for members' conduct that are enforced by ostracism and ex-communication.**

What is interesting about these rules is that they would usually be clearly unjust if imposed by the state. For example, a state may not exclude women from decision-making offices, yet the Catholic church is allowed to, and Catholics who challenges this principle may be subject to informal or formal but non-coercive sanctions by the church. However, it is increasingly recognized that these internal sanctions, even if informal or non-coercive, can none the less have a very significant impact on the freedom and well-being of group members. It may therefore be necessary for the state to intervene to protect vulnerable members of groups from particularly oppressive internal rules.

6. **Incorporation and enforcement of traditional or religious legal codes within the dominant legal system.** There is nothing inherently contradictory about having two or more systems of law operating within a single political jurisdiction: it happens in Canada and the United States—where the former French colonies of Quebec and Louisiana have retained civil law traditions alongside the common law of the larger state-as well as in the United Kingdom, Switzerland, and of course the European Union. Arguments for incorporation of minority legal systems are closely linked to arguments for self-government, especially in the case of indigenous territories. In religiously divided societies, like the Ottoman Empire or modern-day Israel and India, differentiating family law among religious communities can be justified as a form of consociational autonomy or multicultural toleration.

7. **Special representation of groups or their members within government institutions.** This form of groups right is as old as representative government itself, where it has always been entirely without controversy that territorial units are given representation in major government institutions, particularly within decision-making bodies. It is rather more controversial when cultural or religious groups or women demand special or guaranteed

representation in the same government bodies. Nevertheless, these claims to representation are unlikely to fade, issues of 'voice' and 'public reasonableness' have become central to debates about democratic citizenship, and these are inextricably tied to representation.

8. **Symbolic recognition of the worth, status, or existence of various groups within the larger state community**. This is a catch-all category for a wide variety of forms of groups recognition within the institutions, symbols, and political culture of the larger state. At stake are such matters as the name of the polity, its flag, its coat of arms, its national anthem, its public holidays, the name by which a cultural groups will be known, or the way a group's history is presented in schools and textbooks. Even such apparently functional issues as the distribution of federal powers may carry symbolic importance if a national minority controlling one of the provinces interprets as asymmetrical distribution of powers in its favour as recognition that it deserves special status as being more than 'just another province'. From the minority culture's perspective, the absence of interpreters at a particular government office might be viewed as an inconvience, whereas the elevation of the majority tongue to the official status, or the denial of the status to the minority language, might be viewed as an open declaration that some are not wanted as members of the state.

Symbolic gestures granting or denying recognition can have profound and continuing effects within a political culture in ways that directly affect the well-being and self-respect of citizens of minority cultures, as well as their enthusiasm to participate in the political life of the larger state.

We should also remember that symbolic recognition is not simply a mater of members of the majority acknowledging the special status of minority groups with whom they share a state. It also requires members of the majority to rethink their own group's identity and relation to the state. So an Englishman would recognize not only that Britain now contains large numbers of citizens of Asian, African, and Caribbean descent in addition to the Scots, Welsh, Northern Irish, but also that this requires rethinking what it means to be British-probably in ways that would have been inconceivable for his grandparents fifty years earlier. He may have to distinguish more clearly than he had before between an ethnic English identity and a civic British identity, and to recognize that 'Britishness' must be defined in a way that is accessible to both the new immigrants and the historically settled peoples who share the British Isles.

Issues and tensions in the Face of Minority Rights

Fears have been expressed about how minority rights affected democratic citizenship. This is not a simple question, since talk about citizenship, particularly in the English language, can refer to an astonishingly wide variety of ideas, concepts, and values. More to the point, talk about disintegration, fragmentation, or weakening of citizenship can be expressing any number of quite distinct political worries.

At the individual level talk of a person's 'citizenship' can refer to three distinct ideas or phenomena: (a) her status as a legal citizen, defined largely by a panoply of civil, political, and social rights as well as a relatively small number of duties (e.g. to obey the law, pay taxes, perform military service); (b) her identity as a member of one or more political communities, an identity that is often contrasted with her other more particular identities based on class, race, ethnicity, religion, gender, profession, sexual preference, etc.; or (c) her activity or civic virtue. These three ideas are conceptually and empirically linked in a variety of ways. Obviously, the exact rights citizens have will partly define both their citizenship status and identity, as well as the range of political and social activities available to them. The form of citizenship identity will have an impact on their motivations to participate virtuously in civic and political activities; and so on. Similarly, if one of these aspects of citizenship is eroded, then the others may be affected as well.

This aspect of citizenship that is clearly about multiculturalism and cultural rights. This is an ideal or goal of citizenship that applies, not at the individual level, but at the level of the political community as a whole: it is the ideal of social cohesion, which may include concerns about social stability, political unity, and civil peace. All of the worries about the vulnerability of one or more of these four ideas: citizenship status, citizenship identity, citizenship activity, and citizenship cohesion.

Minority rights usually involve some form of differentiated citizenship status: they grant certain groups or their members rights or opportunities not available to other groups or citizens. But when does differentiated status become unequal status? Some people contend that the very idea of 'differentiated citizenship' is an oxymoron. According to these commentators, citizenship is, by definition, a matter of treating people as individuals with equal rights under the law. This, it is sometimes said, is what distinguishes democratic citizenship from feudal and other pre-modern views that determined people's political status by their religious, ethnic, or class membership.

However, we believe that this claim, that minority rights are inherently in conflict with the very concept of citizenship, is untenable. Virtually every modern democracy recognizes some form of group-differentiated citizenship. One result of the new-found interest in minority rights has been an explosion of work uncovering the myriad forms of special-status or asymmetrical rights or group-specific exemptions accorded to indigenous, ethnic, racial, or ethnoreligious groups in most Western democracies. Bhikhu Parekh has rightly put it, citizenship in fact 'is a much more differentiated and far less homogeneous concept than has been presupposed by political theorists'.

So differentiated citizenship is not a contradiction in terms, nor even particularly uncommon. Our question is, when do differentiated rights involve some real disadvantage or stigmatization in citizenship status—some inequality in respect, or in life chances, or in influence over government policy? That is, when does differentiated status starts to create first and second class citizens? Members of the majority often complain that the special rights for minorities reduce others to being second-class citizens. If this perception is deep and widespread, it can erode the sense of common identity and solidarity.

Some critics argue that this may indeed be the case. In some cases, this threat arises for reasons internal to a particular policy of minority rights. Shachar explains, for example, how allowing religious communities to control some aspects of family law—such as rules for marriage and divorce—can have devastating implications for the rights of women in ways that are clearly incompatible with the norms of equal citizenship in a liberal democracy. Similar arguments were made against Quebec's language law, which at one stage banned the use of English on shopkeepers' windows. These cases both suggest that minority claims to cultural recognition threaten equal citizenship status when the costs and benefits of minority protection are unfairly distributed-i.e. when one subgroup within the minority (e.g. women), or when selected non-members (e.g. Anglophones in Quebec), are asked to bear most or all of the costs of cultural reproduction, while others enjoy the benefits.

In other cases, the threat to equal citizenship status may arise as an unintended consequence of the minority right. For example, Mansbridge ponders the implications for democratic citizenship of having selective electoral districts to ensure the election of more African-Americans. Her worry is not that these are inherently unfair but rather that there is evidence that this policy leads to a loss of influence for minority groups outside these districts, and hence may be reducing political equality for members of designated groups in the process of trying to enhance it.

These threats to equal citizenship should be of major concern. But there is no reason to think that they are intrinsic to all minority rights claims. On the contrary, most defenders of minority rights insist that it is the denial of minority rights that poses the greater threat to real equality. They argue that minority rights are needed to prevent the ongoing stigmatization of ethnocultural minorities, and to remedy the disadvantages they suffer in the larger society. For example, the strengthening of official language rights for French Canadians, along with a substantial degree of autonomy for the French-speaking province of Quebec, have surely played an important role in the transition for French Canadians from being an economically disadvantaged and politically under-represented group in the 1950s, to being roughly in a position of social, economic and political equality with English-speaking Canadians today. Similarly, while certain forms of groups representation may unintentionally erode a group's political equality, Mansbridge and others have argued that other forms of groups representation are vital to genuine political equality. Levy has argued that in so far as the historic conquest of indeigenous peoples and the stripping of their self-government rights were grounded in racist and imperialist ideologies, then restoring rights of self-government can be seen as affirming the equal standing and worth of indigenous peoples. In these and other ways, one can argue that, far from eroding equal citizenship status, 'the accommodation of differences is the essence of true equality'.

Some have pointed out the negative impact of cultural rights on the citizenship identity that citizens share as members of a political community. This identity will always coexist for every individual citizen with numerous other identities based on class, occupation, region, race, ethnicity, religion, gender, sexual preference, generation, mother tongue, hobbies, and so on. And, furthermore, it will differ in relative importance for each individual. Civic republicans would like to insist that the citizenship identity be each individual's primary and highest identity, and its is a major aim of the politics of civic republicanism to try to bring this about. But we know that this will never be true for many people. If forced to choose, some religious people would flee their country rather than give up practicing their faith. Moreover, it is hard to think that there is anything politically sinful about people deciding to have these sorts of priorities with respect to their different identities, or that a modern state should be permitted to act in a heavy-handed way to make its citizens all fervently patriotic.

None of this is to deny, however, the significance of common citizenship identities in a democratic state—particularly in states shared by groups that already have strong identities based on different religions or ethnicity. It may be unreasonable to expect people to cherish their citizenship identity more than any of their other identities, but it is important for people to be motivated to act as citizens first and foremost when debating and acting in the public realm, at least for a broad range of issues. It would be an obvious sign of ill health in a democracy if a politician could publicly justify his actions in parliament by announcing that he knew a certain policy was bad for the country, but that he supported it because it would enrich his family. It would be equally worrying if political leaders could declare that a policy they supported was bad for the country but in their own ethnic groups best interest.

One could question how tight the connection really is between having a strong citizenship identity and being motivated to act as a responsible citizen. For example, identifying themselves as 'an American' seems quite important to most Americans, at least as important as their other social identities.

Still, it is surely true that if ethnic, regional, or religious identities take priority over a common citizenship identity, there will be difficulty maintaining a healthy democracy. And many critics worry that this sort of fragmentation of identity is a likely consequence of multiculturalism. It has been argueds that multiculturalism can be interpreted as picture of society as a "mosaic" of several bounded, *nameably*, individually homogeneous and unmeltable minority uni-cultures which are pinned onto the backdrop of a similarly characterized majority uni-culture'. In such a society, where there is no common citizenship identity bridging or transcending the various groups identities, politics is likely to be reduced to a mere *modus vivendi* amongst groups that barely tolerate, let alone co-operate with each other. There is little hope for the sort of mutual understanding, deliberation, trust, and solidarity required by a flourishing democracy.

There is some evidence that the fluid and inclusive nature of these immigrant identities exists, not in spite of multicultural policies, but rather because of them. Precisely because they have secured public recognition and support for their ethnic identity, they have the confidence to interact with others in an open way; whereas those groups whose identities lack this sort of public recognition tend to be more defensive about their culture, and more fearful about he consequences of cultural interchange. This shows, once again, that the impact of minority rights on identity cannot be deduced a priori, but requires actual empirical investigation.

It has been argued that the weakening of citizenship identity will hinder the cultivation of the various of democratic citizenship as well as the motivation or capacity to participate in wider public deliberation. A classic example is the fear that allowing or funding schools for particular religions will destroy one of the most effective forums of citizenship education—the state school system, where children learn to play and work with children whose parents have different religions, ethnic backgrounds, and values. This is a general worry about conflict between rights to religious education and the promotion of citizenship virtues necessary for deliberative democracy.

One reason why this is a classic case is that it combines several different possible threats to citizenship. First, religious schools are seen as potentially eroding children's motivation to act as citizens, by privileging a particularistic religious identity at the expense of a common civic identity. Secondly, even if religious schools actively encourage their students to affirm a large civic identity, and hence their motivation for citizenship, they may potentially erode children's capacity for good citizenship, since the curriculum of these schools may not teach the virtues of tolerance and public reasonableness. Thirdly, even if these schools promote both the motivation and capacity for citizenship, they can be seen as eliminating the opportunity to act as citizens since all students share the same faith, there is no need or opportunity for students to step outside their role as religious believer and adopt instead their role as citizens.

What is interesting to note, however, is that concern for citizenship virtue and participation is often invoked by advocates of minority rights. They argue that special attention must be paid to the circumstances and needs of diverse groups if they are to feel like full members of the society, and to acquire the capacity and opportunity to participate in society. In most of the case concerns about threats to citizenship are overstated. The impact on citizenship of minority rights, in most cases, is mixed and ambiguous, both enhancing and threatening aspects of democratic citizenship. Under these conditions, it is clearly unhelpful to talk as if there is a zero-sum relationship between minority rights and citizenship; as if every gain in the direction of accommodating diversity comes at the expense of promoting citizenship.

But there is one case where this sort of zero-sum approach may seem applicable—namely, the case of territorially concentrated national minorities who may contemplate secession. If the cultural identity for most members of a minority group is stronger than their citizenship identity in the larger state—e.g. if they feel more Scottish than British or more Catalan than Spanish—then it may come to feel natural for them to have their own state, or at least most of the autonomy of an independent state. The goal of minority nationalist is precisely to legitimize and strengthen this sense of separate nationhood. Providing rights of self-government or extending federal autonomy gives minority leaders institutions and legislative jurisdiction with which they can progressively strengthen the minority cultural identity at the expense of the statewide citizenship identity.

But the ethnic-conflict literature suggest that the most common response to this threat, even in democratic countries, has been to deny national minorities the kinds of autonomy and recognition that would encourage the development of their own identities. However, this presents an incomplete picture of the mechanisms that lead to strengthening or weakening citizenship attachments among the citizens belonging to national minorities. Coulombe, Reaume, and Baubock all emphasize that refusal to grant recognition and autonomy to such groups is often likely to provoke even more resentment and hostility from the members of the national minorities, alienating them further from their identity as citizens of the larger state. In addition, Coulumbe highlights the way minority nationalist movements can be driven not only by minority led regional governments exercising their powers of self-government, but also by heavy-handed attempts from the central government to promote a statewide identity that national minorities find threatening. Finally, both Baubock and Smith emphasize the importance of balancing the centripetal forces of recognition and autonomy with other federally guaranteed individual rights and non-territorial group rights. Such a 'cocktail' of rights would reduce opportunities for injustice and could reinforce the sense of citizenship in the larger state for members of national minorities as they come to see both the central and regional governments as guarantors of their rights.

In sum, whether we are concerned with citizenship status, identity, virtue, or cohesion, the relationship between minority rights and citizenship is more problematic then it might initially appear. We can see legitimate worries about the potential impact on citizenship, but also countervailing arguments showing that some minority rights can actually enhance citizenship. It is impossible, therefore, to make any sweeping generalizations for or against the impact of minority rights on citizenship.

This is not, of course, an argument for ignoring or discounting the relevance of citizenship when evaluating minority rights. It is important to determine not only whether particular proposals for minority rights are consistent with principles of justice, but also whether they would enhance or erode desirable qualities of democratic citizenship. The shift from justice based to citizsenship-based arguments about minority rights is a useful and necessary broadening of the debate. Our argument is simply that this question must be examined empirically, in specific contexts, rather than prejudged on the basis of a priori speculation or anecdotal evidence.

In any event, the concern that minority rights will hinder out a common citizenship identity presupposes that such a common identity already exists, or would exist were it not for the presence of minority rights. But of course, in many contexts, this is not true. Many members of minority groups—whether they be new immigrants or conquered national minorities—do not identify with the state in which they live, and instead feel quite alienated from it. This is particularly true of groups that have faced discrimination or prejudice, and who therefore feel unwanted. Granting such groups minority rights can hardly erode a sense of common citizenship identity, since it does not yet exist. Indeed, minority rights may be the best way to encourage alienated groups to come to identify with the larger political community. Coulombe, Reaume, Baubock, and Modood have forcefully argued that the refusal to grant recognition and autonomy to such minorities is likely to provoke even more resentment and hostility, alienating them further from their identity as citizens of the larger state. By contrast, minority rights may confirm for minorities that they are full members of the larger society whose contributions will be welcomed. In all of these ways, then, minority rights have the potential to enhance, as well as to erode a common citizenship identity.

We cannot rest content with the sort of rhetorical generalizations that characterized the 'culture wars' of the 1980s and early 1990s. Defenders of minority rights can no longer claim that concerns about civility and civic identity are simply illegitimate attempts to silence or dismiss troublesome minorities.

Arguments for Group Rights

Citizenship is s status and privilege. It can be exclusive as well as inclusive. The most obvious way that citizenship operates as a privileged status is through the denial of membership to non-nationals. While citizenship remains closely tied to the nation-state, such exclusion is inevitable. But this relationship is becoming increasingly problematic as globalisation challenges the boundaries of states. We can consider a different form of exclusion that occurs within the borders of the state. In its liberal form, citizenship claims to embody the ideal of universalism. All individuals who can legitimately claim to be citizens of the state are supposed to share equally the rights and responsibilities of citizenship. For some critics, however, ironically it is this very claim to universality that acts as a powerful exclusionary discourse. A notion of a universalized citizenship, it is suggested, simply cannot be sustained in the context of plural societies. In addition to individual rights, special group rights are therefore required to ensure that some individuals are not excluded from the benefits of citizenship because of their gender, race or any other aspect of their identity. The works of Iris Young Bhikhu Parekh and Will Kymlicka are generally acknowledged as powerful contributions to this debate.

The essence of Young's case against liberal citizenship can be found in her analysis of the universality that it embodies. Young identifies three meaning of universality that are associated with liberalism. The first ideal of universality is that all members of a society are able to participate politically in the shaping of their lives. This is clearly a desirable end, and should be a goal for all democrats. Many of the barriers to this ideal concern the unequal distribution of resources such as money, time and information.

However, the inequality of resources is only part of the problem. Even if we could overcome the material inequalities between citizens, the two other kinds of universality that liberalism entails would ensure, argues Young, that citizenship remains unequal in practice. This is because liberalism embraces a conception of citizenship that denies social differences. Young contends that liberalism advocates not just universality in the sense of an equality of participation but also in the highly abstract sense of individuals adopting a universal point of view. Citizenship demands that individuals 'leave behind the perception they derive from their particular experience. In short, citizens are required to deny their very identity when exercising their rights and responsibilities.

The third meaning of universality is the practical implication of this. The laws that are made by citizens or their representatives apply to everyone, regardless of the diverse needs and inequalities that exist in society. Thus the structures of decision-making within liberal society prevent all voices from being heard effectively. Liberalism represents not equality between different individuals but the domination of the ideal of equality over difference: the diversity that characterizes society is scarified in the name of an abstract and unattainable conception of citizenship.

Young contends that because individuals are not abstract rational creatures, but are products of cultural and social structures, they cannot achieve the kind of objective viewpoint that liberal citizenship demands. So any democratic institutions based upon such an abstract view of individuality must be faulty and unresponsive to people's needs. This by itself is a serious problem. In addition however, for Young, liberalism's approach to citizenship masks a set of unequal power relationships. These inequalities hide the fact that citizenship is defined in terms of, and therefore works in favour of, a particular social identity, namely that of white males. This bias is extremely deep-rooted and is historically bound up with imperialism and patriarchy. Citizenship has often been seen in the liberal tradition as for 'civilised' peoples only. Moreover, citizenship is theorized in liberalism in terms of objective reason and in opposition to emotion and the body. Thus women, who in the liberal tradition are the personifications of the irrational and emotional, are perceived as unable to fulfil the responsibilities of citizenship. Because of the deep roots of these inequalities, Young is correct to argue that they are often reproduced at an unconscious level.

Young insists that to understand why citizenship serves to further the interests of some while excluding the needs of others we must have a more developed theory of power. It is the structures of power, such as the class system for example, which pervade liberal institutions and which result in material and cultural inequalities Young discusses such structures of power through her development of a typology of oppression. She identifies 'five faces of oppression' exploitation, marginalisation, powerlessness, cultural imperialism and violence. Any group that experiences one or more of these is the victim of oppression. By focusing upon individuals and ignoring the structural aspects of power, liberals tend to overlook or misunderstand how citizenship fails to serve all person equally. This is true also of many republican thinkers who have as their ideal a civic unity enshrined in the status of citizenship. Young contends that 'this ideal of the civil public excluded women and other groups defined as different, because it s rational and universal status derives only from its opposition to affectivity, particularity, and the body'.

Young insists that an inclusive citizenship must take group identity seriously, for it is groups that constitute individuals. Moreover, social groups are so diverse that non-members of a particular group cannot fully understand the nature of that group's oppression. Young pleads for the need to acknowledge a 'politics of difference'. By this, Young means that group identities must be incorporated into the decision-making institutions of the community.

"Groups," according to Iris Marion Young, constitute individuals. A person's particular sense of history, affinity, and separateness, even the person's mode of reasoning, evaluating, and expressing feeling are constituted partly by his or her group affinities. On this point, Young agrees with communitarians such as Michael Sandel. But Young does not equate groups with communities, at least not if "community" is taken to mean a political community or a society. In her view, societies consist of many groups that are largely defined by differences from one another—hence the need for "the politics of difference". Moreover, neither the definitions of these groups nor the identities of the individuals they constitute are fixed or stable. Instead, Young sees group differentiation as multiple, cross-cutting, fluid, and shifting. The culture, perspective, and relations of privilege and oppression of these various groups, moreover, may not cohere. Thus individual persons, as constituted partly by their group affinities and relations, cannot be unified, themselves are heterogeneous and not necessarily coherent.

A politics of difference must therefore work to preserve and enhance heterogeneity or diversity.

But that, on Young's account, is precisely what liberalism and republicanism fail to do. Liberalism, with its emphasis on impartiality and equal respect for individuals, reduces plurality to unity and denies difference: the ideal of impartiality generates a dichotomy, between a general will and particular interests. The plurality of subjects if not in fact eliminated, but only expelled from the public realm; the concrete interests, needs, and desires of persons and the feelings that differentiate them from one another become merely private, subjective. As for republican theorists, their desire to establish a "civic public" leads to the same denial of difference:

This ideal of the civic public excludes women and other groups defined as different, because its rational and universal status derives only from its opposition to affectivity, particularity, and the body. Insofar as he is a citizen even man leaves behind his particularity and difference, to adopt a universal standpoint identical for all citizens, the standpoint of the common good or general will. In practice republican politicians enforced homogeneity by excluding from citizenship all those defined as different, and associated with the body, desire, or need or passion that might veer citizens away from the standpoint of pure reason.

Young's politics of difference direct us to preserve and enhance heterogeneity and diversity. Young's answer contains three parts. First, we must recognize two distinct sets of rights: a general system of rights that are the same for all, and a more specific system of group conscious policies and rights. The second level is necessary to ensure that group-conscious policies cannot be used to justify exclusion or discrimination against members of a group in the exercise of general political and civil rights. Next, we must identify oppressed groups. In the case of the United States, Young includes in this category, among others, the following: women, Blacks, Chicanos, Puerto Ricans and other Spanish-speaking Americans, American Indians, Jews, lesbians, gay men, Arabs, Asians, old people, working-class people, and the physically and mentally disabled". The third part of the program is to accord group representation to these oppressed and disadvantaged groups.

Such group representation implies institutional mechanisms and public resources supporting (1) self-organisation of group members so that they achieve collective empowerment and a reflective understanding of their collective experience and interests in the context of the society; (2) group analysis and group generation of policy proposals in institutionalized context where decision makers are obliged to show that their deliberations have taken group perspectives into consideration; and (3) group veto power regarding specific policies that affect a group directly, such as reproductive rights policy for women, or land use policy for Indian reservations.

This is clearly a program for radical change. It is also, as a number of more and less sympathetic critics have pointed out, troublesome in several ways. There are a host of problems involved in deciding what counts as a social group, let alone an oppressed group that deserves special representation. Should the list of such groups include "Nazis, fundamentalists, or even the Amish, all of whom could claim to be victims of oppression as Young describes it? Should Asian Americans, for example, count as a group, or should there be separate group representation for Japanese Americans, Korean Americans, and so on? Could group representation even serve to entrench some forms of oppression? If working class people receive special representation, for instance, their representatives could include men who, on Young's account, oppress women; if women receive special representation, their representatives could include white women who oppress blacks; if blacks receive special representation, their representatives could include heterosexuals who oppress lesbians and gay men; the representatives of all of the above could oppress old people; and so on.

Another set of difficulties arises when we ask how the politics of difference will generate decisions. Presumably all previously silenced voices will be hard in a "heterogeneous public where participants discuss together the issues before them and come to a decision according to principles of justice. Group representation nurtures such publicity by calling for claimants to justify their demands before others who explicitly stand in different social locations. But how will the representatives reach these decisions when their claims come into conflict? Unless we assume that all oppressed groups always agree with one another or will quickly see the justice of one another's position, there must be more to a politics of difference than granting groups representation as groups. Young does say, of course, that some groups should have "veto power regarding specific policies" that affect them directly, but this is more likely to forestall than to generate decisions. Surely someone who presents herself as a champion of progressive causes cannot rest easy with the anti-democratic and conservative implications of "stall decision making."

This last set of difficulties points to the superiority of republican liberalism to the politics of difference. Republican liberalism encourages people to search for common ground by acting as citizens; the politics of difference tells them to "stand in different social locations," which leads directly to "stalled decision making." Young's point, to be sure, is that the search for common ground serves to justify the dominance of a particular group. But if there is no common ground or common good, how are public decisions, including those of the "heterogeneous public," to be justified?

Young obviously believes that some policies are better than others and can be justified as such. This belief, however, follows from two premises that provide the implicit underpinnings of her politics of difference. The first trades on an appeal to the ideal of autonomy. Why else should we care that "all oppressed people suffer some inhibition of their ability to develop and exercise their capacities and express their needs, thoughts, and feelings". The point of acting to end oppression is precisely to enable people "to develop and exercise their capacities" –which is, at the least, closely akin to autonomy. In the end, groups are important and deserve recognition and respect because they "constitute" or "are major constituents of individual identity". In the end, that is, it is the ability of individuals to develop and exercise their capacities that is important.

The second implicit premise of Young's argument is an appeal to solidarity or civic virtue. For all her talk of particularity, diversity, and heterogeneity, Young also needs something "like a common good" to serve as a basis for agreement: "In a society differentiated by social groups, occupations, political positions, differences of privilege and oppression, regions, and so on, the perception of anything like a common good can only be an outcome of public interaction that expresses rather than submerges particularities". For all of her distrust of "a mythical 'common good'", Young's politics of difference no more escapes the need to find this good and to persuade people to act to realize it than any other theory.

The politics of difference relies on the implicit appeal to autonomy and solidarity, then subverts itself by stressing difference and particularity rather than the sense of common ground—of sharing the benefits and burdens of a cooperative endeavor—that fosters solidarity. Autonomy does involve independence, but it is not the independence of the "lone rights-bearer," the person who is thoroughly self-sufficient. Instead, autonomy is something that we can develop and exercise only with the aid and cooperation of others, and these others will frequently be found in the groups and communities that do indeed partly constitute our individual identities. A proper regard for autonomy therefore demands that we recognize the extent of our interdependence and our obligations to others who themselves have a right of autonomy.

Young is keen to distinguish her theory of democratic citizenship from that of classical pluralists who see democracy as a compromise between predetermined positions represented by pressure groups. According to her definition, unlike in classical pluralism, social groups are determined not just by mutual interests but because their members share a particular way of life. Young's essentially cultural definition of the social group is reinforced by her argument that ideological groups do not count as social groups as she defines the term. Later in her argument, Young further narrows the definition of those social groups which are entitled to special rights. Young asserts that 'specific representation' is only for 'oppressed or disadvantaged groups'. This principle, she argues, will prevent the proliferation of groups asserting their own case for rights.

In several ways, Young's theory of citizenship marks a break with the liberal tradition. Young contends that universalized notion of citizenship asserted by liberals has led to the oppression of minorities and the denial of difference. It is only by asserting what she calls 'differentiated citizenship', built upon group rights that pluralist societies can maintain order and move towards a just polity. In terms of the four dimensions of citizenship context, extent, content and depth Young envisages a more extensive citizenship than liberals. The content of citizenship must emphasise group rather than individual rights. The context of citizenship is not that of the homogenous community but a society that celebrates and protects difference rather than seeking to transcend it. Finally, it could be argued that Young's citizenship is thick rather than thin since it is rooted in the identities that constitute the individual, and as such is more significant status than the narrowly public-orientated citizenship of liberalism.

Will Kymlicka attempts a somewhat different strategy to defend group rights in contrast to Young. He remains more firmly rooted in the liberal tradition. However, like Young, Kymlicka also advocates a differentiated citizenship. He advanced a theory of, argues for what he calls, 'multicultural citizenship' that recognizes the importance of culture to an individual's sense of place and identity. Kymlicka notes that liberals have tended to see the relationship between the state and ethnicity as synonymous with that of the state and religion. According to this perspective, the best way to tackle the pluralist realities of modern society is to separate ethnic identity from the state in the same way that the church should be separated from the state. Particularistic identities should be confined to the private world. Citizenship should remain public, universal and cultural-blind. The result of this approach has, however, been 'to render cultural minorities vulnerable to significant injustice at the hands of the majority, and to exacerbate ethnocultural conflict'. The traditional liberal defence of natural rights cannot solve the problems of differences within the state. Advancing theory of minority rights Kymlicka insists, that comprehensive theory of justice in a multicultural state will include both universal rights, assigned to individuals regardless of their group membership and certain group-differentiated rights for minority cultures.

It is important to note that Kymlicka uses the term culture interchangeably with the term 'nation' and 'a people'. He has in mind then ethnic groups, rather than groups based on class or gender. However, he is careful to argue that the national groups he discuses are not defined in terms of race or descent. The importance of ethnic identity is that it provides the 'cultural context' in which individuals develop and therefore 'sets the parameters for individual choice'. Kymlicka contends that 'the availability of meaningful options depends on access to a societal culture, and on understanding the history and language of that culture'. Given the importance of the context national culture provides for citizenship, Kymlicka considers it essential that the polity supports all those ethnic cultures that its members consider important. Kymlicka envisages three kinds of group rights to achieve this objective and goal.

First, self-government rights involve the devolution of powers to minorities within the state. This is likely to lead to some form of federal polity. Second, there are polyethnic rights, which protect group identity through legal and public financing of minority cultures. Third, there are special representation rights that give guaranteed representation for minorities in the community's political institutions. Self-government rights are obviously more extensive and are one step away from secession. Polyethnic and representation rights, however, more clearly involve the integration of minorities into the polity; not through the denial of cultural differences but rather through the recognition of those differences as an essential part of a stable multicultural state.

Such an accommodation of difference acknowledges that liberal citizenship is traditionally defined 'by and for white, able-bodied, Christian men', and recognizes that citizenship is an inherently 'group-differentiated notion'. In a world where citizenship is determined by the state, decisions about who is entitled to the status are based on an individual's group membership. It is Kymlicka's contention that we should apply the same principle to groups within states and seeks to accommodate their needs accordingly. Although their arguments differ, Young and Kymlicka both arrive at the conclusion that citizenship must be rooted in a notion of the social group. Citizenship cannot be purely an individual status because citizenship only has meaning to the individual in the wider cultural context of the group.

Young and Kymlicka undoubtedly raise important and difficult questions concerning the universality of citizenship. Both are correct to identify how liberal theories of citizenship have tended towards highly abstract conceptions that deny the social character of the individual. A disembodied and atomistic definition of the citizen ignores the barriers that exist to the effective exercise of rights and responsibilities. In focusing their attention upon the experience of minorities or oppressed groups in general, both authors begin to identify how the inequalities inherent in liberal society negate the promise of meaningful citizenship. The neglect of the context of citizenship ensures the danger that universality can crush social differences.exist. Vulnerable groups are at risk of having their needs ignored and their voices left unheard. Both Young and Kymlicka meet the challenge of inequality by advocating a change in the content of citizenship to include group-differentiated rights alongside individual rights. They avoid the temptation to reject entirely the emancipatory potential of citizenship. Such a rejection is often explicitly made in postmodern accounts of social life which, while often insightfully deconstructing the assumptions that lie behind many apparently neutral concepts such as justice, state and citizenship, fail to advance the alternative conceptual tools that are necessary to deal with the inherent human problem of governance. A more constructive postmodern approach is to build upon the strengths of liberalism and to make its promises real by identifying and overcoming the barriers to their fulfillment. The theories of Young and Kymlicka must then be welcomed as bold attempts to overcome the problems of modernity. But the theories of Young and Kymlicka force a number of problems.

The first problem with a citizenship centred upon groups is ascertaining what groups can legitimately claim to be special cases and are therefore deserving of additional entitlements not available to other members of a polity. Young's definition of groups as being constituted by those who "share a particular way of life" is unsustainable. In seeking to transcend what Young sees as the essentialist individualism of liberal citizenship, she merely replaces it with an equally essentialist definition of the social group. Young quite rightly wishes to argue against defining individuals in static terms, which denies them the capacity to grow and to change. But in identifying women, for example, as necessarily having a shared experience and thereby classifying them as a social group is to commit the very error that Young accuses liberals of. The denial of the internal differences that exist within the various social groups overlooks the fact that every individual has multiple identities and social roles. All of these identities may be equally important to the individual. Moreover, one aspect of an individual's identity might be tension with another: one's identity as a black woman could at certain moments be in tension with one's identity as a member of the working class and so on. We cannot define individuals in terms of any single part of their identity. A theory of citizenship based upon groups rights risks freezing social differences and creating an uncommunicative, fragmented and highly static politics. This is hardly likely to lead to the transcendence of oppression that Young seeks.

Another problem with Young's formulation is this: what is to prevent a proliferation of new groups demanding rights and thereby fragmenting the polity still further? Young's answer can be found in her discussion of the five faces of oppression, which she considers to be 'objective criteria' for ascertaining the legitimacy of rights claims. What makes a group's claim legitimate is that it is subject to one or more of these five aspects of oppression. Young's definition of oppression, however, is clearly far from objective, is contradictory, and therefore unhelpful in identifying the forms of oppression particular social groups experience. Her wish to differentiate between forms of oppression leads Young to some bizarre conclusions. She states that 'working-class people are exploited and powerless but if employed do not experience marginalization and violence'. This conclusion is so clearly unsustainable that it requires little comment. Does a working-class person who works in a tedious, insecure, unsafe manual job and who lives on a rundown, crime-ridden council estate not experience marginalisation and violence? In addition, the bases of oppression change, as do the ways that individuals identify their interests. In recent years people of mixed parentage in the USA have been arguing strongly to be classified as a group worthy of special treatment. Interestingly this has been opposed by many ethnic leaders. What this illustrates is the largely arbitrary nature of awarding rights according to groups membership. It also shows the potential tension that exists between groups competing for special status. Joppke has argued that in fact many of the official 'victim' categories in the USA, such as Asian or Hispanic, are extremely artificial constructs. Moreover, the strategy of multicultural citizenship has other dangers. For instance, in the context of calls for greater multiculturalism in France, 'the new racism of Le Pen emulates the multicultural right to be different'. In other words, the politics of group identity can play into the hands of the powerful.

Oppression, then, is a more complex problem than Young acknowledges. Crucially, oppression is relational in character. Hegel's famous discussion of the master-slave relationship illustrates that the oppressor is also enchained by his or her oppression. This is also Marx's point when he argues that capitalism is alienating for the capitalist as well as for the worker. Young builds her defence of group rights on the idea that only those who experience oppression can understand that oppression. Only those who are oppressed are truly authentic and can claim special rights. Anne Phillips, despite developing a strong critique of Young's ideas herself, defends Young on the grounds that Young wishes a polity where 'we acknowledge others as being of equal account'. However, this is just what Young effectively denies in her emphasis upon oppression as an experience that cannot be understood except by the oppressed. This has serious implications for Young's approach to democracy.

Given the discredited status of classical pluralist theory, Young is keen to distance herself from it. However, Young is unsuccessful in differentiating her theory from the interest groups of pluralism of writers such as Dahl. This is largely because, like the pluralists, the social groups arrive at the democratic assembly with their minds already largely made up. Their status as oppressed groups gives their arguments a moral force and an understanding of power that groups representing white males lack. It is implicit in her argument, therefore, that some voices are more authoritative than others. Moreover, in her defence of veto powers, Young effectively removes some crucial issues from the political agenda. For example, she argues that women have the sole right to reproductive rights. However, the only logical reason for defending this position is because of women's biological differences from men. Given Young's critique of essentialism, this marks an important contradiction in her argument for it seeks to base rights claims on predetermined, naturalistic criteria.

Group perspectives and experiences can have very dangerous implications for the quality of deliberation: it sets the limits of democracy before a word has been spoken. If, for example, men can never understand women's oppression, what incentive is there to encourage men to develop empathy and to adopt a critical stance towards their own behaviour? It is particularly crucial for those who suffer most from domination to transform the way that others see that oppression. Politics then becomes little more than a method through which groups difference is affirmed. For this reason, Young's essentialist theory is unlikely to lead to a deliberative democracy.

Miller rightly argues that Young fails to identify how or why diverse groups will be reconciled. She appears to assume, observes Miller, that 'when the groups she identifies as oppressed make their case, this case will overwhelm the opposition'.

Young's naivety in these matters is compounded by her romanticized view of social groups. Phillips contends that 'the oppressed have no monopoly on good behaviour, being a victim is not a guarantee of right'. The response of oppressed groups to their situation can be negative as well as positive. Historically it has resulted in separatist movements, terrorism and vengeance, as well as more constructive alternatives. In addition, to judge individuals by their group membership is to risk violating those individuals' freedom. This problem is inherent in all collective identities. An obvious example of how an individual can suffer from his or her group membership is that of hostage-taking for political reasons. Thus the British hostage John McCarthy, who was held captive by Islamic fundamentalists in the Middle east for several years, was apparently told when captured that this was not his problem, but 'his country's problem'. By inviting others to treat us as members of a particular group we risk creating a tension between individual rights and this collective identity.

Like Young, the basis for group rights in Kymlicka's theory is cultural. However, the shared way of life that Kymlicka identifies as constituting a group worthy of special rights is not determined by oppression, as such, but by national identity. Crucially, to justify his theory, Kymlicka makes what he calls an analogy to states. His logic is as follows. States are the pre-eminent political organizations in the world. It is nation-states that therefore define who is a citizen and who is not. Consequently, citizenship is an inherently group-orientated idea since it is linked to the membership of a culturally defined collectivity. This means that logically we cannot deny group rights to national groups that do not enjoy statehood. However, just as Young's acknowledgement of the multifaceted and overlapping nature of social identities is in tension with her defence of clearly defined groups for the purposes of determining special rights, so Kymlicka's theory too falters on his definition of culture. The problem is that while rights are comparatively concrete things in that they bestow certain material benefits, culture is clearly fluid and ever changing. Indeed, it could be argued that a culture that is unchanging is a dead culture.

In basing his theory of citizenship on national culture Kymlicka runs into the same problems that we find in Miller's theory of nationality. He assumes that choices that citizens make are meaningful only in the context of the nation. Kymlicka asserts that 'individual freedom is tied to membership in one's national group'. But why must we accept this? The concept of national culture hides many division such as class and gender. What is more, national discourse are often used by elites to gloss over these differences and excuse them from tackling the roots of inequalities. Kymlicka, in linking meaningful choices to national culture, also runs into the problem of distinguishing between meaningful and meaningless choices. It may be that the identities that an individual most values are not their ethnicity or nationality but the ideological or lifestyle choices they make.

Kymlicka appears to favour national identity above other sources of meaning because of its basis in history. Yet, historical nationality has had an ambiguous relationship to citizenship. The reality is that often a defence of one's national identity is made and sustained in opposition to another's sense of identity. Thus in Northern Ireland, for instance, the very essence of many Unionists' sense of national identity is to be found in their anti-Catholicism and hostility to the civil rights claims of Catholics living in the North. National identity cannot be so easily detached from religion, sectarianism, and ethnic hostility as Kymlicka seems to suggest. Kymlicka writes that 'the primary good... is the cultural community as a context of choice, not the character of community or its traditional way of life'. However, national characteristics and the values so dear to many nationalities often stand in tension with citizenship's emphasis upon human agency. It is essential to the practice of citizenship that we remain critical of the received wisdom of the past. This leads us into highly controversial territory. Kymlicka attempts to tackle this problem by advocating a distinction between internal and external cultural restrictions. Liberals should, he argues, defend group rights because they recognize the reality of cultural differences and promote diversity as a social good by protecting minority cultures from the majority. However, liberal should argue against internal restrictions that infringe the civil rights of members of a cultural group. This clearly stands in tension with Kymlicka's argument that what matters is not the nature of a culture as such, but rather the necessary context any culture, however oppressive, provides for the choices we make as citizens. Like Young, his theory is compromised by his reliance on a predetermined cultural identity as a basis for citizenship.

Young and Kymlicka identify some real problems with liberal citizenship. They are right to worry about the implications for citizenship that the neglect of important social differences entails. It is tempting to seek to defend vulnerable minorities through the development of group rights. However, there is non-arbitrary way of determining which groups deserve such special provision. Young and Kymlicka assert a particularistic and essentialist definition of culture which amounts to a denial of the human agency that citizenship must recognize if it is to be truly inclusive. Young's argument for group rights, based as it is upon a shared sense of oppression, is likely to meet with increased hostility to minorities, as well as leading to the further fragmentation of society. By uncritically embracing the state as the only plausible polity and linking this to a national culture, Kymlicka unwittingly advocates conditions that can only exacerbate the tensions between majorities and minorities. Indeed Kymlicka acknowledges that 'the state unavoidably promotes certain cultural identities, and thereby disadvantages others'. He is also aware that globalisation has made the myth of a culturally homogenous state even more unrealistic He is, however, unwilling to develop the logic of such development into a post-statist theory of citizenship. Kymlicka's defence of state sovereignty serves only to highlight further the contradictions at the heart of liberal citizenship between equal rights and national sovereignty.

Citizenship, Equality and Difference

We consider the relationship between equality and difference, which seems to be the most crucial issue raised by theories of differentiated citizenship. This discussion will lead naturally to a consideration of how citizenship can be enhanced. Pateman observes that the problematic relationship between equality and difference has bedeviled much feminist analysis of citizenship in particular. Women have often appeared to be faced with the choice of whether to argue for incorporation into an inherently masculine conception of citizenship, an incorporation that can only be achieved by denying their differences from men, or whether to assert a politics of difference, which challenge ideas of universal citizenship and argues instead for special rights and responsibilities. However, there is no reason to suppose that equality and difference are inherently in opposition. The dominant liberal perspective of citizenship could be understood in terms of its dualistic logic. Because of the assumptions liberals make about the relationship between the individual and community, and in their eagerness to preserve a market-dominated private sphere, liberal citizenship is abstract in form. The opposition between equality and difference can be seen as a product of this abstracted individualism. Equality and difference is another false dichotomy that we must seek to deconstruct and dissolve. Pateman shows in fact how early campaigners for women's citizenship such as Mary Wollstonecraft argued for equal rights and for their differences with men to be acknowledged. The only way this can begin to be achieved is through adopting a relational rather than atomistic theory of citizenship. As Pateman rightly holds, the choice between equality and difference is a false one. The main barrier that prevents the development of a relational citizenship, which sees equality and difference as complementary, is that of domination.

Young's emphasis upon oppression and her advocacy of group rights are clearly attempts to problematise domination and move beyond it. However, Young's approach to domination is not a relational one. She doubts that the oppressors can understand their own natures and thereby empathize with the oppressed. Implicitly, then, Young takes up a position on the question of equality and difference which favors an assertion of the latter over the former. Kenan Malik has eloquently pointed to the problems with such a strategy. Malik argues that equality must remain the essential goal for radicals if emancipation is to be achieved and citizenship is to be inclusive of diverse identities. In classical liberalism, Malik observes equality was naturalized and rights granted by God. Marx however more persuasively rooted equality firmly in social relations. The danger of a politics of difference is that the assertion of diversity becomes the very rationale for politics. Of course, politics presupposes difference. Without diversity and conflicts of interests, we would have no need for politics. However, the whole point of politics is to look for areas of compromise, to build common interests and to create systems of governance that are able to accommodate differences peacefully. To place too much stress upon difference and to deny the ability of humans to understand each other's position is to reject implicitly the possibility of equality. Citizenship is a shared project that involves diverse, but intrinsically social, individuals building common institutions that sustain their lives. The general perspective on social issues that Young rejects as unrealizable is in fact just what citizenship requires us to develop. It is only by looking beyond our own experiences that we can deliberate effectively and can thereby hope to maintain social order. A politics of difference cannot achieve the emancipation of excluded groups. The philosophy of difference is the politics of defeat, born out of defeat. It is the product of disillusionment with the possibilities of social change and the acceptance of the inevitability of an unequal, fragmentized world. The consequence has been the celebration of marginality, of parochialism and indeed of oppression. Transcending such an outlook requires not simply intellectual conviction but political aspiration.

However, such political aspiration towards equality need not deny difference. As Young herself observes, difference need not mean 'a complete absence of relationship or shared attributes'. Logically, an aspiration towards equality presupposes difference. The aim of equality is precisely to recognize and protect diversity by respecting the rights of all individuals, regardless of their beliefs of identity. This is why it is potentially dangerous to base an individual's citizenship on any single aspect of their identity or membership. Kymlicka's position on this question is particularly revealing because, while Young is explicitly critical of the whole liberal tradition, Kymlicka seeks to justify his theory according to liberal values. By tackling the difficult questions of equality and difference in liberal terms Kymlicka unwittingly reveals the real source of the problem, namely the state.

Again we come back to Kymlicka's definition of citizenship as an inherently group-based concept. It is because Kymlicka defines citizenship in this way that he is able to argue that individual rights are complemented and not jeopardized by the addition of group rights for some minorities. However, Kymlicka mistakes expediency for principle. Citizenship is only defined culturally because of the existence of the state which determines social membership by nationality. However, classical liberals were highly suspicious of the state. Kymlicka, in contrast, makes a virtue of the state by arguing that one of its essential function is to preserve cultural difference. Yet elsewhere Kymlicka contends that 'cultures do not have fixed centres or precise boundaries'. The result of this contradiction is that by linking rights to ethnic groups, we ground citizenship on constantly shifting foundations. Waldron argued that humans undoubtedly need some cultural context, but why should we assume, as the logic of Kymlicka's theory implies, that 'the social world divides up neatly into particular distinct cultures'. It is because Kymlicka is so attached to the state that he fails to see that an alternative and more fruitful path to justice would be to ensure that individual rights are not violated by states. This, of course, would require a basic rethinking of the nature of political community and would inevitably require the development of institutions of global governance beyond the state. It is this position that is consistent with liberalism, however, not the group-based model of citizenship that Kymlicka advocates.

Kymlicka is right to argue that human rights discourses have so far failed to tackle the problem of minority cultures, but this is precisely because the state that Kymlicka defends prevents human rights from being applied equally. Moreover, minority cultures can be as oppressive of their members as majorities can oppress minorities. This is particularly a problem for women, who have often found that a defence of cultural practices means condoning such acts as female circumcision or the forced abduction and rape of young girls as a legitimate method of acquiring a wife, a practice that occurs in parts of Southern Ethiopia. This is why during South Africa's transition to democracy, women's groups fought so hard to have civil rights embedded in the constitution so as to override tradition and customs that have often involved discriminatory practices against women.

Kymlicka himself is aware of the fact that many cultures are illiberal and present considerable problems for individual liberty.

However, once we accept the logic that groups can have rights there is no reason to prevent new groups, potentially undesirable in their beliefs, claiming such rights. Kymlicka does attempt to address aspects of this problem. He believes that immigrants to liberal states, because they have entered voluntarily, are in no position to demand rights to self-government. However, this is a very naïve view of the reasons why migration occurs. The push and pull factors of migration very often involve poverty, political persecution, religious discrimination, and so on. A purely voluntaristic theory of immigration is hardly realistic. This reveals Kymlicka's failure to address the problem of how the states system and its promotion of neo-liberal market reforms has undermined the rights of many across the developing world and has intensified migratory flows. Kymlicka argues that group rights are essential to a fair society. He also contends that the expedient rejection of such rights by political elites often sacrifices justice for stability. Logically then, Kymlicka cannot sustain an objection to voluntary immigrants demanding group rights where they have been the victims of state injustice.

Kymlicka does in fact accept that unjust acts by the state do alter the legitimacy of rights claims when he writes that a 'country forfeits its rights to restrict immigration if it has failed to live up to its obligations to share its wealth with the poorer countries'. Having conceded this, however, it is difficult to see how immigrants cannot justly demand special rights given the fact that the majority of Western governments clearly have not fulfilled their obligations to the global community. This problem is even more acute if we consider groups who are acknowledged as ethnic groups, worthy of self-government rights, but who clearly have not arrived voluntarily. At various times in its history this movement has advanced a separatist and overtly racist, particularly anti-Semitic position. And yet, as an ethnic group that has arrived largely in America as the result of slavery, any claim they might make for self-government rights is hard to resist if we accept Kymlicka's position that group rights represent compensation for past injustices. Elsewhere Kymlicka slides from his defence of group rights based on justice, to a denial of rights in the name of stability. In considering the United Nations' defence of 'self-determination' of peoples, he argues that to put this principle into practice would be 'destabilizing'.

A consideration of the relationship between equality and difference shows that group-differentiated citizenship presents major problems for building the kind of communicative politics necessary to constitute equality and to preserve diversity. In Young's theory, group rights risk freezing individuals into fragmented groups that can only ever represent part of any individual's identity, and offer little hope for developing a common citizenship that aims not at homogeneity but solidarity. The national groups that Kymlicka makes central to his theory of citizenship can also be oppressive of individual rights, for such identities often privilege cultural unity over individual choice. Despite Kymlicka's valiant attempt to defend group rights from a liberal perspective, it seems to be that group rights are inherently opposed to the individual rights advanced by liberalism. The key to understanding why the liberal promises of security, autonomy and equality are not fulfilled is to be found in the liberal assumptions of the inevitability of the nation-state, and in their assertion of the superiority of the market over democracy in allocating the resources necessary to the practice of citizenship.

There are many reasons for welcoming a multicultural society. The distinctively "liberal" reason, urged forcefully by Will Kymlicka over the past decade and more, is couched centrally in terms of "choice."

"Culture," Kymlicka maintains, is necessary to provide agents with a "context for choice," and hence tor exercising the sort of autonomous agency so central to liberal values. "Culture" in turn is inherently communal, the product of collective activity. So to foster and protect the cultures that make autonomous individuals possible, Kymlicka concludes, we must foster and protect the communities that create and sustain those cultures in turn.

So far, that constitutes an argument for "culture" and "community" in the singular. If all that autonomous agency required were a "context for choice." then any culture would do and no more than one would be required. But suppose more than one culture happens to be extant in any particular place. Then there is an argument within this choice-based liberal framework for allowing all of them free play. To do otherwise would risk depriving autonomous agents shaped by one or another of those cultures of their own '"contexts for choice" and the autonomous agency that proceeds from it. This is a result that liberals would clearly wish to avoid. Thus, Kymlicka writes. "The liberal value of freedom of choice has certain cultural preconditions." and "liberals should care about the viability of societal cultures, because they contribute to people's autonomy." Failure to protect those cultures "will create new tragic cases of groups which are denied the sort of cultural context of choice that supports individual autonomy."

Kymlicka's own original, and distinctively liberal argument for multiculturalism was thus in terms of facilitating the autonomous agency of individuals. But that case for protecting the autonomy interests of individuals in minority cultures soon started sliding into being a matter of protecting minority cultures as such. Whereas Kymlicka's original argument about protecting people in minority cultures would have better expressed, strictly speaking, as an argument for "the rights of cultural minorities." the title of his own subsequent collection was. tellingly, *The Rights of Minority Cultures.* The conclusion of the argument had been remembered, while the premises have been all but forgotten.

For the issue of "individual autonomy" does conspicuously arise in connection with "illiberal cultures". This is what Susan MollerOkin had in mind when asking *Is Multicultumlism Bad for Women?* If the distinctively liberal rationale for multiculturalism were to promote people's autonomy, then that rationale would provide no grounds for multicultural acquiescence in cultures that systematically impair the autonomy of many of their members.

Kymlicka had anticipated that objection. From the start, he conceded the fact that there were some awfully illiberal cultures. The question, for him. was merely what to do about that fact. Where critics saw certain cultures as essentially and irredeemably illiberal, Kymlicka saw cultures a always in flux and hence as always potentially liberalizable.

Who is right on this issue of the malleability of cultures. The important point, for present purposes, is the sheer fact that even so committed a multiculturalist as Kymlicka is not necessarily nonjudgmental among alternative cultures. It is, for Kymlicka, a criticism of some cultures that they are illiberal. Kymlicka is perfectly prepared to endorse attempts to reform them. The fact that he is judgmental in all those ways is in no w ay vitiated by the fact that he stops short of endorsing attempts at active suppression of those cultures.

Thus, liberals conspicuously including the most prominent liberal multiculmraiists—prioritize autonomous agency. They are prepared to adjudge cultures that better promote autonomous agency as superior cultures. They demur only as regards how best to attain those superior cultural results.

Liberals clearly prefer cultures that facilitate rather than undermine people 's autonomy, understood as their "capacity to choose." So too do they prefer cultures that afford people a wide range of options among which to choose, "The value of diversity within a culture," for liberal multiculturalists such as Kymlicka, "is that it creates more options for each individual, and expands her range of choices."

One must at least have an "adequate range of options" to qualify as "autonomous" at all.' Beyond a certain point, additional options doubtless become a burden rather than a blessing. But up to that point, having more options among which to choose, while not exactly making one "more autonomous," makes one's autonomy "more valuable." So say liberals in general, and liberal multiculturalists along with them.

Arguing against Kymlicka's claims about culture and choice, Jeremy Waldron asks us to imagine someone not unlike himself:

> A person who lives in California, but came there from Oxford via Edinburgh, and came in turn to Oxford from the other side of the world, the southwestern comer of the Pacific Ocean, whither his English and Irish ancestors emigrated in the mid-nineteenth century. Someone who did not associate his identity with any secure sense of place, someone who did not take his cultural identity to be defined by any bounded subset of the cultural resources available in the world. He did not take his identity as compromised when he studied Greek, ate Chinese, wore clothes made in Korea, worshipped with the Book of Common Prayer, listened to arias by Verdi sung by a Maori diva on Japanese equipment, gave lectures in Buenos Aires, followed Israeli politics, or practiced Buddhist meditation techniques.

Understood (as Waldron pretty clearly intended it to be understood) as an argument that he is participating in many cultures at once, Kyralicka is unpersuaded. He doubts that Waldron's example could be all that common. More fundamentally, Kymlicka doubts that the lifestyle Waldron describes really amounts to "living *in a* kaleidoscope of cultures." studying Greek does not make you Greek, nor does practicing Buddhist meditation techniques make you a Buddhist. You are not genuinely "living in" any of those cultures when you merely borrow bits from them.

What Waldron describes, Kymlicka thinks, is merely someone who is "enjoying the opportunities provided by the diverse societal culture which characterizes the Anglophone society of the United States."- That is to make two claims at once: (1) that there is a singular the Anglophone U.S. "societal culture," and (2) that that single "societal culture" is itself internally diverse, being comprised of a pastiche of fragments borrowed from many other "societal cultures" from around the world.r

If so, then, on the point at issue between them, Kymlicka would be right and Waldron wrong. Anglophone residents of the United States do indeed have a "secure framework of a single culture to which, in some deep sense, they belong," just as Kymiicka had said. That singular Anglophone U.S. societal culture just happens to be internally diverse, in the various ways that Waldron memorializes.

Bhikhu Parekh and Multiculturalism

Parekh's thesis stems firstly out of a rejection of relativism and monism and subsequently from the claim that liberal attempts to respond to the fact of multiculturalism do not take the concept of culture seriously enough. In identifying the faults of these theories he lays the ground for an argument about the nature and importance of culture to human existence and argues for a politics based on intercultural dialogue. In doing this Parekh engages with the very thorny issue of intercultural evaluation of disputed practices such as arranged marriages, polygamy, female circumcision, ritual slaughter of animals, issues of customary dress and participation in aspects of public education, all of which have aroused different degrees of concern and anxiety over the years. Parekh also addresses the relationship between minority cultures and the 'operative public values' of society. It is a comprehensive work by a contemporary British political theorist, who is also a member of House of Lords and a very senior figure in the UK Commissioin for Racial Equality and the chairperson of the Commission on the Future of Multi-ethnic Britain.

The very basis of Parekh's political theory is the attempt to give adequate expression to the interplay between these three features. Relativism and monism are clearly to extreme. We must not overemphasise difference and we must not overemphasise similarity. It is a balancing act that Parekh also believes that contemporary liberal responses to diversity have failed to pull off. Parekh's critique of Rawls is similar in scope and content to that offered by Kymlicka- One chief concern is that Rawls's assumption that political liberalism does not presuppose comprehensive liberalism is unconvincing- Indeed, Parekh believes that political liberalism is 'conceptually an substantively parasitic upon comprehensive liberalism' in that presupposes a conception of human individuality that is not to be found in other traditions of thought. As a consequence of this, Parekh believes that Rawls's work is deeply inhospitable to cultural plurality. He argues that Rawls's political liberalism unduly restricts political discourse. Allowing people into society provided they leave their moral and religious baggages at the door, is to bar important resources from political debate. To offer only a unitary concept of individual citizenship is to deny cultural pluralism a voice from the outset.

From Pareksh's point of view, Kymlicka's liberal multiculturalism does not fare much better. Parekh explicitly picks up on the point that there appear to be no general or undisputed principles that inform Kymlicka's hierarchy of national refugee and immigrant minority rights. If culture is a primary good in that it is a necessary condition for the good life, then are we right to deny immigrants access to their culture? Parekh also believes that Kymlicka 'absolutises liberalism'. Kymlicka's pervasive suggestion that national minorities are tc be given self-government rights provided they govern themselves within certain liberal parameters fails to take cultural diversity seriously enough.

Will Kymlicka and Joseph Raz-have expressed sympathy with the demands of national minorities for self-determination. In this context Kymlicka explicitly distinguishes between the rights of national minorities and the recent demands by some ethnic minorities for self-determination in terms of the recognition fo their mother tongue and state support for separate ethnic institutions.[56] For Kymlicka the claims of immigrant groups to self-determination are considerably weaker than those of national minorities, because not only have immigrants voluntarily chosen to leave their own national community, but, unlike long-standing and indigenous groups, they lack viable cultural structures which they can claim a rigtht to preserve. Hence, in order to succeed, immigrants ought to be encouraged to integrate into the wider society. However, as Parekh notes,[57] these objections are open to question. Immigration occurs for a wide variety of reasons and the decision to leave one's country does not necessarily 'signify a decision to leave one's culture'.[58] Furthermore, while immigrant cultural life may lack 'the cohesion and continuity charactersitic of indigenous and longestablised groups' it is not 'devoid of a cohesive cultural structure.[59] On the contrary, immigrant groups often form their own distinct communities and neighbourhoods and, even where these are absent, 'they tend to form nationwide and communal institutions to sustain their way of life'.[60] Parekh's objections suggest that in principle the demands for *self-determination* on the part of ethnic *minorities* may at least in some instances be on par with those of national minorities and hence should be given serious *consideration.*

Instead of relativism, monism and the attempts of liberals such as Rawls and Kymlicka to develop a minimum universalism, Parekh's theory takes the form of 'pluralist universalism'. Pluralist universalism entails a particular view of human nature, of culture and of morality itself. We share certain attributes as members of the same species and this has some normative force but it is very thin. We share a physical and mental structure, have the same basic needs and common condition of growth. But our nature is formed not merely from these basic characteristic but in tandem with our active participation in nature.

This is what Parekh means when he says that humankind are culturally embedded. It is important to note here that because of the important place of culture in this dialectice, and because culture is by definition a social or group concept, we need to be able to conceive of people not merely as individuals but as part of a collective group or groups. For Parekh, the rights of cultures are 'primary collective rights.'

7

Feminism and Citizenship

During the last few years, citizenship in general, and women's citizenship in particular, has occupied the center stage in feminism, both theoretically and politically. What unites women all was recognition of the interdependence of analytical and political commitment, of situated knowledge and of the intersectionality of gender, race and ethnicity, class and other social divisions. Many, although not all of the feminists, felt that the notion of citizenship might be a useful tool to both analyze and promote women's position – however, heterogeneous this category may be in contemporary society.

In the ancient, medieval and early modern eras women were not, nor were considered ever likely to be citizens at all. The first is late fifth – to early fourth-century BC. Athens. Although they were excluded from citizenship in the proper sense of the term, the matter of women's political interest, capacity and influence was certainly being aired. Aristophanes wrote two plays on the theme, namely *Lysistrata* in which the women are peace-asking heroines and *Women in Parliament*. Some years later Plato, writing about his concepts of guardian and ruler classes in *The Republic*, had this to say: 'for the purpose of keeping watch over the commonwealth, woman has the same nature as man, save in so far as she is weaker'; and, of the elite rulers, 'All I have been saying applies just as much to any women who are found to have the necessary gifts'. But, more commonly held contrary opinion was voiced unequivocally by Aristotle.

The second example is taken from the haphazard system of parliamentary representation in England in the Middle ages and the early modern period. Candidates were often chosen by the constituency landowners; and because of the limited franchise this sometimes meant effectively nominating the MP. In the Middle ages abbesses are known to have named representatives, and in the reign of Elizabeth I two women who 'owned' boroughs returned the MPs. Not unit 1644 did the distinguished lawyer Sir Edward Coke lay it down that 'all they that have no freehold and all women having freehold should be barred from the electoral process'.

The reference to property ownership is crucial. As a virtually general rule two considerations precluded women from being citizens in the full sense until a century or so ago. One was that women could rarely legally own real estate, while the ownership of property was the precondition of the franchise. The other was that women were considered incapable of engagement in politics. Aristotle proclaimed the latter opinion with conviction: 'The slave', he declared, 'is entirely without the faculty of deliberation; the female indeed possesses it, but in a form remains inconclusive." Furthermore, the prejudice of women's intellectual inferiority was later sustained for centuries in the western world by the views of the Christian churches. Women's emancipation had to overcome these two impediments, both legal constraints and psychological assumptions.

The rejection of even the very occasional opportunity for women to involve themselves in elections in England was paralleled on the continent from the Middle Ages to the sixteenth century by a gradual exclusion of women from forms of civil and economic citizenship, which they had sometimes formerly enjoyed. This resulted particularly from the firming up of the guild system, which denied women membership. Not until the eighteenth century women in some countries demanded rights alongside men and started effectively to participate in political affairs, for it was not only the men who were enthused by and swept up in the radical and revolutionary atmosphere, especially in France and Britain. In 1792 the first thorough exposition of the feminist case was published; this was Mary Wollstonecraft's *Vindication of the Rights of Women.*

Wollstonecraft was clearly wrestling with what has been referred to as her 'dilemma' – a dichotomy in her feminist theory which still burdens the minds and consciences of feminist writers. On the one hand, she insists: 'When I treat of the peculiar duties of women, as I should treat of the peculiar duties of citizen or father, it will be found that I do not mean to insinuate that they should be taken out of their families. On the other hand, she asserts that 'in order to render their private virtue a public benefit, they must have a civil existence in the state, single or married.' How, then faithfully to discharge the duties of the two personae? She tries to resolve the dilemma by declaring that a 'wife also an active citizen' – notice the echo of Sieyes – 'should be equally intent to manage her family, educate her children, and assist her neighbors'. The bias, even so, is more towards the domestic than the public role.

In the nineteenth century concerns about the condition of women found expression in two main forms. One was the contribution of European socialists, including Marxist thinkers. The other was the practical campaigning for women's rights, confined mainly to the USA, Britain and Scandinavian countries. But even in those countries, advocacy and achievement alike were slow, hesitant and piecemeal. Various objectives were defined: to promote female leadership for the achievement of moral reform; to open up much fairer educational and employment opportunities for women; to liberate married women from their legal subordination to their husbands; and to acquire full rights of political participation. The last two of these items are especially germane to any definition of citizenship and therefore warrant a little detail.

In his exposition of the English law and constitution in the mid-eighteenth century, Blackstone bleakly declared: 'By marriage the husband and wife are one person in law; that is, the very being or legal existence of the women is suspended during the marriage or at least is incorporated and consolidated into that of the husband'. Naturally this 'civil death' of the women on entering the marriage contract included the loss of any right personally to hold property. Not until 1882 in England was this particular position reversed.

However, male-dominated societies and institutions, including, of course, legislatures, were not always by any means sympathetic to improving the position of women. The notable exception to this widespread male attitude was John Stuart Mill, who wrote *The Subjection of Women* in 1861 and who, six year later, moved a proposal unsuccessfully in the House of Commons that the franchise be extended to women. Suffragist movements in Britain and the USA succeeded in publicizing their cause; but it was the contribution of women to the war effort during the First World War that effectively won them their rights – by the Nineteenth Amendment to the US Constitution in 1920 and by British acts of Parliament in 1918 and 1928. Yet these changes had been preceded by reforms in New Zealand (1893), Australia (1902) and Norway (1913). In France, in contrast, where women proudly bore the title 'citoyenne' during the Revolution and where Marianne is the symbol of national pride, women had ironically to wait until 1945 –6 for political equality: 'equal rights with men in all spheres' was the formula written into the Preamble of the Constitution of the fourth Republic. Meanwhile, in Switzerland, where the cantonal system had become a byword for male democracy, female suffrage was lengthily delayed until 1971.

However, the right to vote - a basic civic right, needs to be supplemented by the representation of women in legislatures if they are to arrive at full citizenly stature. Except in the Nordic countries, women have been slow to seek and/or gain election. For example, in 1994 women accounted for 41 percent of the Swedish Riksdag, compared with only 9 per cent of British MPs.

Some feminists, nevertheless, would not now place such heavy emphasis on civil and political citizenship. This is partly because the campaigns in these fields have been largely won; but partly too because the characteristic nature of their sex and their child-bearing function tends to focus women's attention on the social and economic facets of citizenship. Since the mid-1960s, indeed, a great deal of thought has been devoted to the feminist agenda. It is scarcely surprising that women became especially conscious of their condition of second-class citizens at this time; after all, so many individuals, groups and peoples with grievances protested and rebelled in 1968.

Three main strands of feminists thinking may be traced from the 1960, sometimes referred to as the 'second wave' to distinguish the period from the nineteenth century. The first strand is liberal feminism, which derives its concern for women's freedom and individualism from the strategy laid down by the likes of Wollston craft and Mill. Secondly, socialist feminism takes its inspiration from Fourier, Engels and Marx, accusing the male-dominated family and capitalist production system as the sources of women's suppression.

Thirdly, we may identify radical feminism, which develops the socialist agenda by attacking the whole structure of society as patriarchal, that is, entirely determined by male interests.

The importance of political and constitutional developments for the feminisation of citizenship needs to be spelled out. The legitimacy of the political community is often grounded discursively in certain human qualities, regarded as foundational for the constitution of citizenship and the public sphere, here defined broadly as encompassing both civil society and the state. In opposing the entrenched privileges of the Church and the aristocracy, the philosophers of the Enlightenment stressed individual rationality, autonomy and equality as the central sources of legitimacy for the democratic political community and its public sphere. Historically, these human qualities came to be defined as masculine. Indeed, one of the central paradoxes of modernity has been that the moment of male emancipation was also the moment of gender reification and exclusion, of course, not all men were emancipated either. This was nowhere more evident than in France where the naturalization of male privileges in the name of universal rights sexualized the public/ private divide in almost pornographic terms. Whereas in England and America attempts were made to confine women to the domestic sphere by constructing them as virtuous mother and carers, in need of protection from a dangerously sexualized male world, in France women were constructed not only as irrational but as sexually rapacious and violent. Before the French revolution, women were very much a part of the opposition to absolutism, and their activity took more or less overtly political forms. The salons run by elite women sponsored the discussions that contributed to what became a critical and dissenting 'public opinion'. This public included women but only those of wealth, education and social grace.

Women were active in oppositional journalism. Indeed, with the exception of Rousseau who was strongly anti-feminist many of the French Enlightenment male philosophers such as Montesquieu, Diderot, Voltaire and Condorcet were sympathetic, or actively supported women's rights. Some women, at least, were no longer confined to domestic spaces – so much so that Sombart proposed that one of the defining features of post-Renaissance developments in Europe was the rise in consumption linked to the seculrisation of women.

By contrast, following the Revolution and its declaration of equality, liberty and fraternity, a rigid separation of the sexes into two spheres became embodied in a sexual imagery, establishing the physical boundaries of masculine and female bodies. Crossing the threshold from the hearth to the forum led to hermaphrodism, the men charged, the loss of distinguishing features of male and female. The danger of androgyny was a sexually indecipherable, hence monstrous body. Political women were depicted in caricatures as ugly, comical, funny-looking, masculine imitators. Women with monocles, cigars and beard; and men in skirts. Transgrssion was depicted as castration – as a threat to the sign of men's difference and the symbol of his power, now equated with political rights rested on segregated spaces.

At the end of the nineteenth century, women for French thinkers such as Le Bon became a metonym for the crowd, the loss of self, the unconscious, 'the emotionally shallow, lacking in creativity. They were constructed as violent furies or suppositious handmaidens of priests. Emile Durkheim used morphological evidence to argue that women evolved through civilization to have smaller brains than in primitive societies. All these qualities excluded women, naturally and essentially, from active citizenship in the public sphere.

Of course, France was a democracy only intermittently and partially in the years following the Revolution, and women suffered badly under repressive and authoritarian regimes. The law of 28 July 1848, for example, excluded women from participation in clubs, whether as observers or members. This was at a time, it should be noted, when Anglo-American women's philanthropy was reaching new heights, with hundreds of thousands of women participating in organized charitable works or mobilising for political rights campaigns. In the very year of the Seneca Falls Convention, the Constituent Assembly in France agreed that women must be barred from political activity. Violent attacks on female meetings were condoned. The French government undertook welfare reform top-down. All this meant that a fully-fledged women's movement never developed in France. Women finally got the vote in 1944. Yet in the USA, too, the process of democratisation, of full adult emancipation, was only achieved in the late 1960s, following the civil rights movement.

Under these circumstances it is hardly surprising that leading French feminists from the very beginning stressed their 'difference' as legitimising grounds for their participation in the public sphere. They drew upon the exemplary figure of the Virgin Mary as mother, an epitome of autonomy, duty and obligation. Jeanne Derrain, a leading French feminist in the mid-nineteenth century constructed the symbolic and distinctive meaning of womanhood in her time into a justification for political rights.

The point is, however, that without the philanthropic army of indefatigable women charitable workers, with their spectacular fund-raising capacities, evident organisational skills, ability to hold office and deliver public speeches; without the pamphleteering and parliamentary lobbying, such sentiments lacked political force. In England, by contrast, women moved into the public sphere at the same time that they legitimised their inclusion as full citizens in the political community in terms of their special qualities as mothers. While some continued to espouse radical Enlightenment ideas about gendered equality, there was also a move among Christian evangelicals such as Catherine Beecher to promote the 'notion of female superiority that was accepted not only by women but by many of their male supporters. This led many later feminists 'to believe that it was woman's mission to re-shape the whole society.' This stress on difference and uniqueness was usually based on notions of gendered complementarity. As Ellice Hopkins put it:

> May we not find in the larger family of the State, that the work of the world is best done by the men and the women together, each supplying what is lacking to the other, the man the head of the woman, the woman the heart of the man.

This stress on difference and complementarity has been transformed, of course, by second-wave radical feminists into an argument against 'masculine' individual rationality and 'abstract' universalism. Privileged are the 'unique' qualities of women: compassion, particularism, sociality, obligation. In some instances, this latter feminism represents, however, a move away from political motherhood. Political motherhood as conceived here rests on as encompassing relationship: women are responsible to their families and the political community in its entirety, including men, with regard to issues of universal and humanitarian concern. In line with this, Sara Ruddick defines maternalism as a protective relationship open to men as well, and rejects an apriori 'mythical division between women's peacefulness and men's wars' Nevertheless even as they deny so-called 'abstract' 'masculine' universalism, western maternalists and peace activists take for granted what Third world political mothers cannot ignore the existence of a stable, liberal democracy; freedom of speech and association; habeas corpus, the rule of law. Moreover, as Yuval-Davis perceptively argues, to create peace with the enemy, motherhood must transcend its own particularities.

The strength of political motherhood as an evolving social movement has been to introduce now human qualities into the public sphere, and to define them as equally foundational in the legitimation of the political community. The point is not thus whether men are compassionate and loyal or women rational and objective; the point is that all these qualities embody and objectify the ideal of citizenship and their absence delegitmises the state and its political authority. It is in this sense that without subscribing to essentialist definitions of intrinsic male and female qualities, we plead for the 'feminisation' of citizenship. Arguing against the existence of two contrasting, gendered ethics, Susan Okin proposes that the qualities they jointly espouse are inseparable. She argues that the best theorizing about justice has integral to it the notions of care and empathy, of thinking of the interests and well-being of others who may be very different from ourselves.

Similarly, Carol Gilligan speaks of a convergence of 'male' and 'female' ethics which recognises the dual contexts of justice and care. Not only feminism but socialism, anti-racism or multiculturalism introduce new human qualities of economic egalitarianism, tolerance or the right to cultural recognition into the discourses of legitimation that permeate the public sphere. These new values continuously reconstitute what it means to be citizen.

The discussion so far has underlined the fluidity of the private/public divide as a constantly shifting and contested demarcation. Lister remarks perceptively that the public-private divide can be understood as a shifting political construction, under constant renegotiation, which reflects both historical and cultural contexts as well as the relative power of different social groups. The public and private define each other and take meaning from each other.

The semantic fuzziness and terminological confusion arising from the widespread deployment of concepts such as private and public in scholarly and public discourses has undermined the analytic rigour. Partha Chatterjee contends that the line between public and private is a completely inadequate tool for analysing constructions of civil societies in post-colonial nations and that a non-west centric analysis of gender relations cannot assume the boundary between private and public as given.

It is sometimes necessary to hold on to a distinction while continually questioning its very possibility. This strategy of writing against the grain from within a discourse displaces conceptual distinctions, and revealing the implicit ideological baggage they carry. In line with this, recent feminist philosophers draw on Habermasian discourse ethics to argue against any substantive division between the private and public spheres. The point is elegantly put by Seyla Benhabib in a reevaluation of Hannah Arendt's thought and of overly juridical or static liberal theorizations of citizenship. Benhabib defines the public sphere as, very broadly, a political space of discursivity in which contested issues are addressed. It is a permeable arena continuously responsive to new issues, moral challenges and new modes of discourse. Feminism as a social movement and mode of active citizenship has forced certain issues, such as familial power imbalances, into the public sphere. While recognising the basically liberal framework which allows discourse to flourish, Benhabib argues against a topographical or spatial definition of the division between public and private. Any site, however likely, can become a site of discourse, and hence part of the public sphere. Moreover, against the liberal view that sees the constitutional framework as basically fixed, she argues that even procedural and constitutional frameworks are open to ethical scrutiny and moral debate.

Benhabib's work points to the fact that the public sphere is a complex and stratified political space, only partially and sometimes implicitly oriented towards the state and state policies. This is particularly evident in 'motherist movements' which often start from very local concerns, and expand their vision and sphere of publicity in the context of a broadening struggle.

In coining the term political motherhood, Jennifer Schirmer highlights the ability of 'motherist' movements in Latin America not only to break into the public sphere, but to create transnational links beyond the nation-state. Motherist movements in Latin America are united in the *Organisation of Latin American Countries for Relatives of the Disappeared,* one of the most powerful indigenous transnational networks and human rights lobbies in the world. This forum includes 17 countries and has support groups throughout the West carrying out fuind raising and acting as political watchdogs for human rights abuses. Schirmer shows that the organizers of the movement began as mothers whose maternal role as protectors of their homes and family had been violated, and who sought restitution from the state. As the women moved into public political activism, however, they became targets of state violence. They were jailed, kidnapped, raped and tortured; their headquarters were bombed and their lives threatened. Many of the women started in Christian groups espousing liberation theology, a holistic ideology which promotes both economic well-being and political equality and freedom. Hence, Schirmer argues, the political consciousness which the women developed was transformed in action, to encompass many different dimensions of their activism, some of which could be defined as 'feminist' (campaigns against rape, domestic violence, the struggle for equal rights in the home and in the public sphere), some as economically pragmatic or class-oriented (such as women's education) and some as universalist (such as fighting for human rights alongside men.)

Importantly, the women, Schirmer argues, rejected radical Western feminisms that start from sharp gender oppositions, even while they recognized that militarism and state terror were forms of domination and torture perpetrated by some men. She thus rejects the revolutionary distinction posed by feminist scholars such as Kaplan and Molyneux between 'female' consciousness (practical and traditional) and 'feminist' consciousness (radical and strategic,) with its implication that the latter is more 'advanced' than the former. Instead, she proposes that women's consciousness is contingent and contextual, arising from the articulations of different dimensions of their activism and their long-term ideals and goals. Women's collective experience, in other words, evolves through and in action, determining the specificity of their feminism.

Moreover, feminist consciousness responds to the broader national and civil context in which the battle for women's specific citizenship rights takes place. As others, too, have argued in the face of poverty, underdevelopment and severe abuses of human rights, women outside Western democracies have been able, despite the multiple oppressions they suffer, to transcend their narrow interests as women and work for wider and more complex causes, creating alliances by drawing upon all their multiple identities: as mothers, wives, democrats, peasants, workers and patriots, as well as women united in a global sisterhood. During the colonial era, women mobilised against specific cultural practices that were particularly oppressive: polygamy, child marriage, widow burning, feet binding or female seclusion, while fighting for the right to property, education and divorce, much like their counterparts in the West. Indeed, extensive networks of women activists between Asia, the Middle East and the West developed during the nineteenth century. Asian and Middle Eastern women were influenced by missionary women and theosophists while, simultaneously, they also joined the anti-colonial and independence movements. They fought with and against colonialism. Mahatma Gandhi, in his espousal of non-violent resistance, developed his own version of political motherhood, exhorting women to 'extend their hearts and interests beyond the narrow confines of their homes' and arguing that the principle of 'non-violence' (ahimsa) and political non-violent resistance were suited to women by nature, that women's courage and self-sacrifice were superior to men's.

Though there is no existence of an apriori necessary link between subject positions, there are constant efforts to establish between them historical, contingent and variable links. This type of link, which establishes between various positions a contingent, unpredetermined relation is what Mouffe says 'articulation'. Even though there is no necessary link between different subject positions, in the field of politics there are always discourses that try to provide an articulation from different standpoints. For that reason every subject position is constituted within an essentially unstable discursive structure, since it is submitted to a variety of articulatory practices that constantly subvert and transform it. This is why there is no subject position whose links with others is definitively assured and, therefore, no social identity that would be fully and permanently acquired. This does not mean that we cannot retain notions like 'working class', 'men', 'women', 'blacks' or other signifiers referring to collective subjects.

The acceptance by feminists of such an approach has very important consequences for the way we formulate our political struggles. The central issues become: How is 'woman' constructed as a category within different discourses? How is sexual difference made a pertinent distinction in social relations? And how are relations of subordination constructed through such a distinction? The whole false dilemma of equality-versus-difference is exploded since we no longer have a homogeneous entity 'woman' facing another homogeneous entity 'man', but a multiplicity of social relations in which sexual difference is always constructed in very diverse ways and where the struggle against subordination has to be visualized in specific and differential forms. To ask whether women should become identical to men in order to be recognized as equal, or whether they should assert their difference at the cost of equality, appears meaningless once essential identities are put into interrogation and contestation.

As a consequence, the very question of what a feminist politics should be, has to be posed in completely different terms. So far, most feminists concerned with the contribution that feminism could make to democratic politics, have been looking either for the specific demands that could express women's interests or for the specific feminine values that should become the model for democratic politics. Liberal feminists have been fighting for a wide range of new rights for women to make them equal citizens, but without challenging the dominant liberal model of citizenship and of politics. Their views have been criticized by other feminists who argue that the present conception of the political is a male one and that women's concerns cannot e accommodated within such a patriarchal framework. Following Carol Gilligan, they oppose a feminist 'ethics of care' to the male and liberal 'ethics of justice'. Against liberal individualist values, they defend a set of values based on the experience of women as women, that is, their experience of motherhood and care exercised in the private realm of the family. They denounce liberalism for having constructed modern citizenship as the realm of the public, identified with men, and for having excluded women by relegating them to the private realm. According to this view, feminists should strive and struggle for a type of politics that is guided by the specific values of love, care, recognition needs and friendship. One of the clearest attempts to offer an alternative to liberal politics grounded in feminine values is to be found in 'Maternal Thinking' and 'Social Feminism' principally represented by Sara Ruddick and Jean Bethke Elshtain. Feminists politics, they argue, should privilege the identity of women as mothers and the private realm of the family. The family is seen as having moral superiority over the public domain of politics because it constitutes our common humanity. For Elashtain 'the family remains the locus of the deepest and most resonant human ties, the most endearing hopes, the most intractable conflicts'. She considers that it is in the family that we should look for a new political morality to replace liberal individualism. In women's experience in the private realm as mothers, she says, a new model for the activity of citizenship is to be found. The maternalists want us to abandon the male liberal politics of the public informed by the abstract point of view of justice and the generalized other and to adopt instead a feminist politics of the private, informed by the virtues of love, intimacy and concern for the concrete other specific to the family.

An excellent critique of such an approach has been provided by Mary Dietz who shows that Elashtain fails to provide a theoretical argument that links maternal thinking and the social practice of mothering to democratic values and democratic politics. Dietz argues that maternal virtues cannot be political because they are connected with and emerge from an activity that is special and distinctive. They are the expression of an unequal relation between mother and child which is also an intimate, exclusive and particular activity. Democratic citizenship, on the contrary, should be collective, inclusive and generalized. Since democracy is a condition in which individuals aim at being equals, the mother-child relationship cannot provide an adequate model of citizenship.

A different feminist critique of liberal citizenship is provided by Carole Pateman. It is more sophisticated, but has features in common with 'Maternal Thinking'. Pateman's tone bears the traces of radical feminism, for the accent is put, not on the mother/child relation, but on the man/woman antagonism. Citizenship is, according to Pateman, a patriarchal category: who a 'citizen' is, what a citizen does, and the arena within which he acts, have been constructed in the masculine image. Although women in liberal democracies are now citizens, formal citizenship has been won within a structure of patriarchal power in which women's qualities and tasks are still devalued. Moreover, the call for women's distinctive capacities to be integrated fully into the public world of citizenship faces what she calls the 'Wollstonecraft dilemma': to demand equality is to accept the patriarchal conception of citizenship that implies that women must become like men, while to insist that women's distinctive attributes, capacities and activities be given expression and valued as contributing to citizenship is to demand the impossible because such difference is precisely what patriarchal citizenship excludes and exiles.

Pateman sees the solution to this dilemma in the elaboration of a 'sexually differentiated' conception of citizenship that would recognize women as women with their bodies and all that they symbolize. She declares that this capacity of motherhood should be granted equal political relevance for defining citizenship as that which is usually considered the ultimate test of citizenship – a man's willingness to fight and to die for his country. She considers that the traditional patriarchal way of posing an alternative, where either the separation or the sameness of the sexes is valorized, needs to be overcome by a new way of posing the question of women. This can be done through a conception of citizenship that recognizes both the specificity of womanhood and the common humanity of men and women. Such a view that gives due weight to sexual difference in a context of civil equality, requires the rejection of a unitary masculine conception of the individual, abstracted from our embodied existence and from the patriarchal division between the private and the public. What feminists should aim for is the elaboration of a sexually differentiated conception of individuality and citizenship that would include 'women as women in a context of civil equality and active citizenship'.

Patemen provides many very interesting insights into the patriarchal bias of the social contract theorists and the way in which the liberal individual has been constructed according to the male image. But Mouffe considers that Pateman's solution, however, is unsatisfactory. Despite all her arguments about the historically constructed aspects of sexual difference, her view still postulates the existence of some kind of essence corresponding to women as women. Indeed, her proposal for a differentiated citizenship that recognizes the specificity of womanhood rests on the identification of women as women with motherhood. There are for her two basic types of individuality that should be expressed in two different forms of citizenship: men as men and women as women. The problem according to her is that the category of the 'individual' while based on the male model, is presented as the universal form of individuality. Feminists must uncover that false universality by asserting the existence of two sexually differentiated forms of universality.

Mouffe agrees with Pateman that the modern category of the individual has been constructed in a manner that postulates a universalist, homogeneous public that relegates all particularlity and difference to the private, and that this has very negative consequences for women. But she rejects the remedy to replace it by a sexually differentiated, 'bi-gendered' conception of the individual and to bring women's so-called specific tasks into the very definition of citizenship. She insists that such a solution remains trapped in the very problematic that Pateman wants to challenge. Mouffe affirms that the separation between public and private is the founding moment of modern patriarchalism because 'the separation of private and public is the separation of the world of natural subjection, i.e., women, from the world of conventional relations and individuals, i.e. men. The feminine, private world of nature, particularity, differentiation, inequality, emotion, love and ties of blood is set apart from the public, universal and masculine – realm of convention, civil equality and freedom, reason, consent and contract. It is for that reason that childbirth and motherhood have been presented as the antithesis of citizenship and that they have become the symbol of everything natural that cannot be part of the 'public' but must remain in a separate sphere. By asserting the political value of motherhood, Pateman intends to overcome that distinction and contribute to the deconstruction of the patriarchal conception of citizenship and private and public life. As a result of her essentialism, however, she never deconstructs the very opposition of men/women. This is the reason that she ends up, like the maternalists, proposing an inadequate conception of what should be democratic politics informed by feminism. This is why she can assert that the most profound and complex problem for political theory and practice is how the bodies of humankind and feminine and masculine individuality can be fully incorporated into political life.

Mouffe's view is quite different. She argues that the limitations of the modern conception of citizenship should be remedied not by making sexual difference politically relevant to its definition, but by constructing a new conception of citizenship where sexual difference would become effectively irrelevant. This, of course, requires a conception of the social agent as the articulation of an ensemble of subject positions, corresponding to the multiplicity of social relations in which it is inscribed. This multiplicity is constructed within specific discourses, which have no necessary relation but only contingent and precarious forms of articulation. There is no reason why sexual difference should be pertinent in all social relations. Today many different practices, discourses and institutions do construct men and women differentially and the masculine/ feminine distinction exists as a pertinent one in many fields. But there is no reasons why this should remain the case, and we can well imagine sexual difference becoming irrelevant in many social relations where it is currently found. This is indeed the objective of many feminists.

Mouffe is not arguing in favour of a total disappearance of sexual difference as a valid distinction; she is not saying either that equality between men and women requires gender-neutral social relations, and it is clear that, in many cases, to treat men and women equally implies treating them differentially. Her thesis is that, in the domain of politics, and as far as citizenship is concerned, sexual difference should not be a valid distinction. She agrees with Pateman in criticizing the liberal male conception of modern citizenship, but she believes that what a project of radical and plural democracy needs is not a sexually differentiated model of citizenship in which the specific tasks of both men and women would be valued equally, but rather a truly different conception of what it is to be a citizen and to act as a member of a democratic political community.

Besides, the public realm of modern citizenship was constructed in a universalistic and rationalistic manner that precluded the recognition of division and antagonism and that relegated to the private all particularity and difference. The distinction public/ private, central as it was for the assertion of individual liberty, acted therefore as a powerful principle of exclusion. Indeed, through the identification between the private and the domestic, it played an important role in the subordination of women. Recently, several feminists and other critics of liberalism have been looking to the civic republican tradition for a different, more active conception of citizenship that emphasizes the value of political participation and the notion of a common good, prior to and independent of individual desires and interests. Nevertheless, feminists should be aware of the limitations of such an approach and of the potential dangers that a communitarian type of politics presents for the struggle of many oppressed groups. The communitarian insistence on a substantive notion of the common good and shared moral values is incompatible with the pluralism that is constitutive of modern democracy. The problems with the liberal construction of the public/private distinction would not be solved by discarding it, but only by reformulating it in a more creative way. Moreover, the centrality of the notion of rights for a modern conception of the citizen should be acknowledged, even though these must be complemented by a more active sense of political participation and of belonging to a political community.

Debates about human rights point to the complexity and heterogeneity of the modern democratic public sphere: it extends globally, beyond the boundaries of nation-states, and reflects the politics of a heterogeneous public. This implies, according to Iris Young, that 'no persons, actions or aspects of a person's life should be forced into privacy; and (b) no social institutions or practices should be excluded apriori from being a proper subject for public discussions and expression'.

Young refers to the work of feminist political philosophers such as Seyla Benhabib who draws on Habermas's theory of communicative ethics to construct a 'discursive model' of the public sphere. Like others, Benhabib too starts from the recognition that the women's movement has made issues previously considered private into public matter of justice. It has thus extended egalitarian morality into sphere of life controlled by tradition and custom. This does not deny rights to privacy. It does, however, imply a critical feminization of rights discourses and bureaucratic procedures.

The feminist slogan 'the personal is the political' implies that any issue can become the proper subject of public debate. This is so because, as anthropologists too have recognized, all spheres of life, from the family through voluntary associations to the political arena proper, are inflected by competitive power relations, unequal access to human and symbolic capital, and agonistic dialogue. Post-liberal feminists such as Young and Benhabib recognize the fluid boundaries separating private and public, while also stipulating the need to retain foundational human, civil and political rights. Yet even these basic rights, Benhabib argues, can be the subject of moral scrutiny and debate, while being the very condition of such critical dialogue. In similar vein Chantal Mouffe has urged that the private/public distinction can no longer be grasped as corresponding to 'discrete, separate spheres' because both private acts and public performances are framed by 'ethico-political' principles. The further key point is that these foundational principles, the grammar of liberty and equality, are interpreted variously from different perspectives.

The denial of a substantive divide between public and private means that there are no specific spaces or places which occupy the 'public sphere'. Public participation is engaged in critical dialogue on a range of normative issues, from the local to the transnational. The public sphere comes into existence whenever people engage in practical dialogue, so that there may be as many public spheres as there are controversial general debates – a plurality of public spaces around contested issues of general concern. Although in many senses this seems merely to redescribe the liberal conception of civil society, its strength is in privileging the dialogical openness and porousness of the public sphere and its responsiveness to inequality and difference.

Much civic participation, especially by women, is local and Lister defends a broader, more inclusive notion of the political which embraces such grassroots activisms. For many women, she argues, 'involvement in community organizations and social movements can be more personally fruitful than engagement in formal politics which is often more alienating then empowering. Local activism strengthens self-esteem and develops political consciousness and a sense of personal agency, both essential attributes of citizenship. This is a feature of local activism emphasized also by Parry who adds that, in Britain at least, local campaigns often seem actually to work, which reflects well on the responsiveness of the political system.

The spaces from which women's activism is first fostered are theorized by Pnina Werbner as a key to understanding the way women's political consciousness develops. She draws parallels between first wave 'motherist' and contemporary peace movements in the Anglo-American West and their counterparts in post colonial nations - in Latin America, South Asia and Israel, and among diasporic Pakistanis in Britain. Werbner's central argument is that women's active citizenship often starts from pre-established cultural domains of female power and rightful ownership or responsibility. These culturally defined domains, or the attack upon them create the conditions of possibility for the movement of such women into the public sphere, and their progressive defiance of authoritarian structures of power, usually controlled by men. Although women's activism is locally embedded, it reaches beyond the nation to create transnational networks of economic support, peace and human rights.

Historically, Werbner argues, political motherhood challenged established notions of civic legitimacy and created the conditions for the feminization of citizenship: the reconstitution of citizenship in terms of encompassing qualities associated with women's role as nurturers, carers and protectors of the family and its individual members. Rather than dualistic theories of gendered opposition, these qualities came increasingly to be defined as critical to justice and hence to the continued legitimacy of the wider political community. Although reforms were achieved piecemeal, they came over time to effect a radical transformation in the values of the public sphere and attitudes to it.

Werbner's analysis supports anthropological and sociological accounts which recognize that women in post colonial nations are not simply victims but active agents of their own destiny; they can exercise their rightful claims vis-à-vis male members of their families while sustaining viable female cultural worlds. They can also draw upon indigenous traditions of cultural resistance and a strong sense of concern for family and community. Analyzing global 'integrative feminisms', Angela Miles makes the point that many Third World Women can call on important resources in their action that feminists in North America often lack. They often have more intact women's subcultures, identities and organizations; less mystified and romantic notions of male-female relations; and clearer understandings of male power.

Women's subscultural resources have been mobilized to generate the present enormous efflorescence of local, national and global women's organizations. According to Miles, women's global empowerment first became visible at the Nairobi Forum in 1985 where women became the overwhelming presence, setting the pace and breaking down barriers between North and South. The level of organization of Third World women at the Fourth World Conference on Women in Beijing in 1995 was so striking as to lead one African-American participant to speak of the 'humbling' experience of confronting Southern women's power, solidarity and vision by comparison with her own fragmented North American delegation. The women's movement, as Virginia Vargas and Cecilia Olea put it, 'appropriated' the conference. Miles highlights integrative feminists' stress on diversity and dialogue across difference: between North and South, and between traditional women and feminists of various persuasions.

The present period has been one in which democracy and citizenship became the banners of the women's movement in Peru, seen as crucial to the development of diversity, the negotiation of different interest and the visibility of social inequalities; a buttress against conservative forces. These arise from the pluralisation and fragmentation of the movement as it has gained presence and new forms of expression in different public arenas. New laws and institutions have been created specifically for women. There are now visible women leaders. Under the circumstances, the problem has been one of preserving a radical outlook and meaningful autonomy while entering democratic alliances and intervening in state policies. 'Identity' is no longer simply an expression of resistance but a 'project' which needs to be defined. In this regard Vargas and Olea object to a tendency to marginalize women as engaged in an 'ethical' politics, not in the 'real' politics of the political arena proper. The goal of the movement should be to expose any politics, they say, that infringes upon women's claims to full citizenship. At present, however, feminist NGOs dissipate their collective power because of lack of coherent overall agenda. The need, Vargas and Olea argue, is to demand from the state clear rules and mechanisms of accountability and participatory democracy. While women should recognize the many advances made, they should aim to achieve further specific reforms in reproductive, social and economic rights and to open up the movement to new actors and further diversity.

Moreover, as many feminist writers have argued in different ways, the very compositeness of modern subjectivities opens up paths towards local, national and even global dialogue across bounded identities, creating the grounds for a new politics of solidarity.

Globalisation and Feminism

This section is to bring critical globalisation literature into productive conjunction with feminist critiques of the gendered impact of globalisation; and to ask whether feminist notions of citizenship can be utilised to think about, and organise in these globalising times. Feminist critiques and politics have revealed that citizenship, both as a status and as a basis for claim, has historically been problematic for women and for men outside dominant groups. Now, in the wake of intensifying globalisation, state transformations and rising exclusivist identity politics, citizenship needs to be rethought as a possible tool for feminist use within a global frame.

Citizenship constructs a public status and identity-long presumed to be male-that rests in ambiguous ways on the private support world of family, home and women. It has always been a difficult construction for women, much debated in feminist literature and conferences. But it has provided spaces for feminist politics. While first-wave feminists and anti-colonial nationalist women struggled for suffrage and legal rights later movements used formal citizenship rights as platform to actualize rights promised to them as citizens. Debates around formal citizenship enabled feminists to expose the contradiction between states' constitutional declarations of equal citizenship and treatment of women as the possessions of their husbands or communities, relegated to the ambiguous space of personal law, for example. These debates also demonstrated that women's and men's memberships of other collectivities, including racialised, ethnic, religious and sexual minorities, continue to affect their access to and experience of citizenship.

Citizenship claims are most often made against the state. Indeed, one way of understanding citizenship is to define it as a person's relationship with their state. But the state has always been an ambiguous and difficult issue in feminist politics. Feminists have revealed 'gendered states', and it seems that state consolidation projects, earlier in Western and more recently in Third World states, frequently reinforced masculinist power. Feminists continue to debate the possibility of a woman-friendly state, and note the irony of appealing to a masculinisty state for protection from, for example, male violence. Yet feminists continue to address all kinds of claims towards the state, and articulate these claims in terms of women's formal citizenship and social rights. And while many feminists are ambivalent about approaching the state, the state that feminists address is itself changing dramatically. In recent decades, intensifying globalisation processes have been accompanied by a transformation of states, which have, willingly or unwillingly, disowned many obligations to their citizens. Might we be looking to sites of state which are now vacated, or fundamentally changed, as a consequence of globalisation processes?

To devise effective feminist politics, then, we need to ask where power is located these days. Fears of global power and its blatant unaccountability underlie some feminist attempts to reclaim the state and citizenship, as still difficult, but more accessible than global power. What possibility is there to agree for an inclusive state-based right collectivity which extends to all those resident in it? What do we make of citizenship when we shift our focus beyond state boundaries, in a search for transnational and tranformative feminist alliances?

Globlaisation is a shorthand for many different and often contradictory shifts in relations of power, wealth and identity. A helpful distinction is between globalisation as process and as ideology. As process, it refers to transformations in relations between politics and economics, capital and labour, states and markets, and international and state politics. These transformations were ushered in by the rising fortunes of East Asian states, the floating of the US dollar in the 1970s, the oil shocks as OPEC states flexed their muscles, and the steady growth in indebtedness of many Third World states, which allowed increasing intervention by international financial institutions. The transformations were accelerated by developments in technology and communications, enabling instantaneous and deteritirialised organisation and decision-making. They were effectively universalized in 1989, with the collapse of state socialism as a practiced or imagined alternative to capitalism.

There is much in contemporary globalisation literature detailing deregulation of trade, finance and banking, and the remarkable growth in 'the "symbol" economy of capital movement, exchange rates and credit flows. Financial transactions now massively outpace trade in goods and services. A key feature is 'quicksilver capital'-the hyper mobility of capital. Transnational production is increasingly spread over different sites and states, and new corporate management strategies now instantaneously link different parts of the globe, independently of state boundaries and agents.

Whereas the twentieth century has witnessed a growing density of inter-national relations many of the new transactions or relations bypass states or cross boarders beyond state control. Time, place and space are all reconfigured. National economies deregulate and liberalise trade and investment. It is not so much that there is a free market; rather almost every aspect of national economic activity is now subjects to international supervision. It is increasingly difficult to demarcate boundaries between the international and the national. Almost nothing is simply 'domestic' anymore: the globalised market impacts on individuals as well as states. Feminist politics, too, must be played out in the increasingly, contradictory spaces between the supposedly still sovereign 'nation-state' and the powerfully generative 'global system'.

There is considerable dispute in the literature concerning the extent and nature of globalisation, including between 'hyperglobalists' who perceive globalisation as a massive, irresistible force which will result in homogenization, McDonaldisation or the total integration of the world into a single hierarchically organised set of domination-subordination relations; and the 'globalisation sceptics', who argue that the continuing significance of national and international economy, and note the rise in regionalism rather than globalism. Clearly, though globalisation is not a uniform, unilinear or inevitable process. It impacts unequally and differentially on different regions, classes and people. It is currently marked by growing disparities of wealth within and between states. Power and wealth are concentrated among the 'triad' of North America, Western Europe and East Asia. Within these states, too many experience increasing poverty and reduction of social welfare. Many of those most severely affected are women, including women who are racialised migrants and/or without access to formal citizenship. In the process, class becomes an increasingly transnational phenomenon: a tiered hierarchy of new transnational elites, middle classes who services are rewarded by global servicing, and a vast transnational underclass. While no region or state can escape the impact of the capitalist world market, whole states and regions, notable in Africa, are bypassed, except as suppliers of raw materials or of migrant labour for the rich states and regions. In these new configurations of power, we might expect class to have become a more powerful rather than a less effective basis for mobilizing. So we need to ask what class means in view of the changing global division of labour – and, more particularly, what class means to feminists these days.

An effect of globalisation as ideology is to naturalise the process, to impute magical qualities to 'the market', to depoliticise and so distract from the myriad political and economic decisions and practices that propel it. Economic rationalism or neoliberalism is the carrying card of the current phase of globalisation. Shifts in the nature and location of power generate a new political geography, within which transnational companies, international financial institutions and some state elitres are now major players.

Globalisation as ideology reminds us of the politics, power relations and material interests that underpin the process. Globalisation as process reminds us that globalisation is always in process still becoming: and that it is a contradictory and contested process. Critical globalisation literature stresses the importance of recovering agency and sometimes class as spaces for resistance to globalistation. Much of this literature make reference to but do not pursue as central the gendered effects of globalisation, and only hint at or roll-call women's movements or feminism as resistance. Bringing these writings into productive conjunction with feminist critiques which document the gendered effects of globalisation can generate strategies that politicise, denaturalise and gender globalisation – rather as feminist critiques politicised, denaturalised gendereded 'the private' in previous and ongoing struggles.

Transforming States

Globalisation signals the transformation of the state to the point where it now plays a near-universal role as local manager or facilitator for global capital. Many political leaders are either unable or unwilling to direct the national economy, or to abide by the national social contract which guided different states in the post war years. Samir Amin notes that the 'three ways' of this contract – Keynesian managed capital with its safety net, Sovietism with its worker citizen, and the Bandung or national development state-all assumed some state responsibility for economy and society. Western states have now begun to re-privatise those responsibilities which worker and women's struggles had exacted. The collapse of European state socialism means the market rules. In the residual Third World, post-developmentalism flourishes in debt-ridden states, now dominated by international financial institutions, conditionality and structural adjustment policies. Even states still formally Communist like China and Vietnam have opened their economy to 'the market'.

States appear to have lost crucial aspects of their sovereignty. It is a mistake, however, to imagine states as yet another victim of globalisation. Particular state elites in the West/North (Reagan's US, Thatcher's Britain, now Howard's Australia, for example) embraced neoliberalism with glee, and others too became active agents in their own state's transformation. Some states, especially in East and Southeast Asia, historically welcomed integration into the global economy while simultaneously attempting to maintain control over the direction of national economies, leading to capitalisms, or at least to state or regional variants. The futility of these attempts only became clear in the late 1990s. Thus today neoliberalism takes a somewhat different form in different states. East and Southeast Asian states embraced growth and the market, but in more authoritarian or interventionist ways than their Western counterparts. They were held up as models of growth, until the sudden and unexpected 'Asian crisis' spread from mid-1997. Ideas about cultural difference and Asian values, until recently deployed to explain success, were rapidly mobilized to explain failure, allegedly caused by distortions and the feeding of 'crony capitalism'.

The crisis in a number of Asian countries was triggered by the devaluation of the Thai baht in July 1997, followed by currency crash through most Southeast Asian states. Capital flight from the region was accelerated by harsh IMF intervention, which has the effect of spreading a sense of panic, along with bank and company failures and rapidly rising unemployment. Indonesia was the most severely affected: there the crisis wiped out three decades of growth, reducing some 17 million families to poverty and threatened starvation. The dislocations generated political unrest which saw the overthrow of the Suharto regime and rioting, including rape, the primary targets were ethnic Chinese. The crisis demonstrated the power that resides in the IMF and other financial managers of global capital; it also confirmed that scapegoats will be found, most likely those who are perceived as not really belonging to the state, even if their families have been citizens of generations.

While states appear to be surrendering some aspects of their sovereignty, or having these taken away from them, they are simultaneously charged with implementing those very policies that facilitate openness and competition, and are approved of by international capital and its managers. They must also manage internal dissent and contain the pain, for political instability will also frighten off investors, and risk further disciplining from the outside. Across the globe, the lure of neoliberal ideology and the power of globalising interests forced the states to facilitate the best fit possible with the global market, becoming more open and cutting back on 'unproductive social expenditure' – precisely those sites and roles of state that were pushed and galvanised and prodded into action by feminist mobilization.

While interrogating state transformation, of course requires specificity-which state? which women or men within that state? There is a global trend towards a redefinition of political economy, away from a nation-state base. This trend is characterized by a renegotiation of relations between state and society as often the latter becomes more economy than society; a shift in language from social rights to competition, productivity, and efficiency; and a shift from public to private and from social to family or individual responsibility. These changes dramatically reduce the political space for citizenship or social rights, including rights for women. And they are profoundly gendered in their consequences.

Gendered Transformations

Intensifying globalisation processes and state transformations are highly gendered-in part because women were already positioned in relation to the state, citizenship and the labour market differently from men. Women are especially hard-hit when the state reduces, or withdraws from, or charges for, social support. Women are disproportionately represented among state workers in those areas most under attack, like health and education. The withdrawal of food subsidies and focus on production for export rather than subsistence or local consumption generate a massive crisis in reproduction, where the conditions necessary for sustaining everyday living are unavailable to so many. Women in their domestic and reproductive roles must compensate for state retreat, or for state failure to provide social infrastructure and support. In many states, too, girl children are more likely to lose chances and choices as education, for example, becomes much more expensive.

Feminist critics of citizenship have long argued that active citizenship requires material conditions which support and enable women's participation in the public/political sphere. In recent decades, feminists have publicized private lives and family secrets, challenging the public/private boundary line in the process. They have insisted on expanded notions of the political. Feminist activism in very different forms and places convinced states to assume some responsibility for women's safety or interest, though often with conditions of heightened surveillance or dependence. But even where resources or choices were conceded, they were never beyond question. Now hard-won feminist gains are under renewed attack almost everywhere, under the impact of neoliberalist state ideologies. This is especially marked in formerly state socialist countries, and in states where fundamentalist movements dominate or influence the state, but it is painfully evident, too, in Western states.

Global deregulation and restructuring forces push women figuratively and sometimes physically back 'home', even though some one third of households do not have a male breadwinner, and more women than ever before officially work outside the home. Alongside this 'return' of women to their presumed place as wives, mothers and carers of citizens, and reduced state attention to their needs, another kind of privatization – marketsing – further undermines women's gains and claims. These shifts accompany the growing disorganisation of labour, and a 'new mythology' which identifies private power with personal freedom. States appear to be seeking a new kind of citizen, a consumer whose roles and expectations fit better with global capital and state transformation.

Women as workers have long been caught between their productive and reproductive roles, in ways that disadvantage them in the labour market. That market is segmented along lines of nationality, race, ethnicity, gender and often age, as well as class. International processes, including colonization and migration, have informed these divisions within states. Now globalisation compounds these disconnections, and makes access to citizenship a crucial determination of difference. And globalisation of the labour force makes it more likely that workers must negotiate state borders and join transnational flows in search of work.

Gender and the Global Division of Labour

The changing global division of labour is marked by a predominantly male core of skilled workers, and a vast global assembly line of casualised, feminised labour. Transnational corporations (TNCs) are 'on the global prowl' for cheap labour, or more accurately for 'labour made cheap.' The vast majority of workers in export processing zones (EPZs) are young women. Women in First and Third World work in flexibilised, low-paid, risky conditions in factories and sweatshops. They have become part of a globalised feminised working class.

Women's labour has long been cheapened through ideologies. Women's work is seen as temporary, filling in before marriage; as supplementary, as if only men are family providers; and natural, as women are expected to have caring and domestic skills. Women are also constructed as patient and less trouble, in ways that deny them politics and agency. Gender is racialised, too; commodifying 'Asian women', for example in ways that launch many of them into particular kinds of work along transnational circuits of exchange-as workers in the EPZs or sex tourist sites, or as international domestic workers.

Women as labour migrants participate directly in globalisation flows, even as their decision to move often reflects the impact of restructuring or other aspects of global change on their and their families' lives. They may be seen to be out of place: beyond the protection/control the community expects,or as transgressors of other spaces. They may be subject to harassment or violence. Yet the globalisation of labour and the feminisation of the global division of labour mean that more and more women move across state boundaries in search of work. This place them beyond their state's legal reach, and means they often lack even formal citizenship or legal rights. This is more so where they enter another state illegally, or become illegals through, for example, overstaying a work or tourist visa.

Globally, migration is increasingly in the form of labour migration, including the strictly policed worker contract system of oil-rich Middle Eastern and growing East and Southeast Asian states. For example, more than four million people, close to one in six of the Philippines' workforce, are working overseas. Between one and 1.7 million women from poorer South and Southeast Asian states are employed as domestic workers in a lucrative regional trade. There is an internationalized service class of female employees and an extraordinary transfer of reproductive labour across state borders. How states are often unwilling defenders of citizen rights, when they are dependent on remittances from overseas workers, and often on employer states' foreign and investment, and when they have little regard for women's or workers' right at home.

Globalisation has reconfigured but not reduced the hierarchies of states, whose reputation or standing might support or reduce a citizen against another state. So recent reports of abuse against national as international demestic workers have become a focus for and protest in the Philippines.

While women are especially hard hit by globalisation processes and state transformation, different women are affected differently.

Not all women are poor; although nowhere are women as well off or well paid as men are. And rising neotraditionalist and familialist movements impose more traditional family and gender roles on many women, subjecting them to renewed surveillance and control. That particularist identity movements are on the rise in an age of globalisation is less a paradox than it might at first appear. Indeed, they reflect in part reactions against modernization, the secular state, and the dislocations of power, wealth and meaning that accompany contemporary social change. State unwillingness, or inability, to 'deliver', their close association with particular interests and/or exclusion of others, trigger reactive politics that mobilise along other associational lines. In migrant-receiving states, migrants or racialised/ethnic minorities become targets in old industrial heartlands, as competitors or threat. 'Besieged' members mobilise against 'outsiders' and claim the state as theirs only.

There identity politics have especially bad consequences for women. As markers of community boundaries, signifiers of cultural difference and as reproducers both physically and culturally, women become vulnerable to boundary policing by both in-group and other men and women. Here we need to distinguish between the symbolic uses made of women in identity politics, and the ways in which actual women negotiate identity; not forgetting too those women who are agents in exclusive politics.

This gendered identity politics are often transnational, engaging diasporic networks and using new global technologies to transmit meanings, grievances and funds. Within these deterritorialised identity politics, women can also become the territory. Policing women's mobility, relations and bodies become part of a national project of boundary maintenance. Culture, identity, difference and community are mobilised, making it even more difficult to give feminist accounts of difference that do not become complicit with the uses that masculinist states and identity movements make of women and cultural difference.

Boundary Defence/Boundary Transgressions

While states almost universally continue to liberalise in terms of production, trade and finance, and communications and new electronic technologies override borders, states at the same time act to maintain or reinforce their control of people flows. Border police entry, residence, state services and success to citizenship is their sovereign right. State protection against other people ironically makes illegals and labour migrants unprotected. So we need to ask of each state: Who has trouble getting in, staying in, accessing work and belonging?

The sovereignty story is built upon the nation-state, presuming a coincidence of people, territory, authority and identity that migration disrupts. Citizenship is a territorially based identity, one that rests on state sovereignty, and on the state as container of its citizens' identities. Globalisation erodes sovereignty and territoriality, further confusing the inside and the outside, and making citizenship seem in some senses anachronistic. As we have seen, one dimension of change is the massive transfers of population which have characterisd recent decades. Well over 100 million people now live outside their country of birth or citizenship. Millions of women are resident in countries where they have no citizenship rights, and either no or uncertain residence and work rights. Every state assumes the right to treat citizens and non-citizens differently. So it is a test of the possibilities of feminist politics to take seriously the rights of non-citizens too. In these days of rising racism and anti-immigrant feelings, citizen-based claims which do not attend to the many people in the state who are not citizens easily become complicit with exclusivist or racist politics.

But why, in these days of transnational and global power, of new market citizenship, do states still expect a singular, primary loyalty from 'their' citizens? So many people are out of place, living, traveling along diasporic or other circuits; identities, too, are often transnasional, mobile, and hybrid. Why is it still that most of us do not give 'global citizenship tied to a state, or a collection of states?

Some states posit a multicultural policy, unsettling the hyphen between the nation and the state, while continuing to 'man' the gates of entry, residence and citizenship against most would-be migrants. Multiculturalism has been described as a top-down labour import and management strategy; though such policies have usually also emanated from mobilised migrant and social right movements from below, and sometimes from foreign policy and other state pressures, too. But multiculturalism usually imagines difference in terms of home state and new home. Increasingly, postmigratory identities are more multiple, fluid and multinational, and are negotiated within complex transnational webs of association and communication. Thinking about home, and about citizenship becomes much more complicated as globalisation processes recast the relationship between people, place and identity. Nevertheless, ideas of place and home live on in the imaginings of many diasporic collectivities, and these ideas have very real implications for notions of self and citizenship.

Resisting Identities/Resisting Globalisation

Capital has been a lot more successful at globalising than labour, or feminism. But globalisation impacts directly on people everywhere, in gendered effects. Most globalisation analyses and narratives still invisibilise women, and do not admit their experiences as evidence. How do different women understand, and respond to global power? Is it possible to use transnational spaces for feminist resistance against the devastation of globalisation and state transformation?

Chin and Mittelman ask, What is the meaning of resistance in the context of globalisation? Part of the power of globalisation as ideology is to naturalise the process, to contibute to its own production through making market domination seem not only desirable but inevitable. Part of the politics of resistance is to challenge this market-imposed 'death of politics' to put the politics back into 'economics', to trace the power relations', including gender relations, that are embedded in these processes. This means exposing the myth of government and state powerlessness in the face of global forces, and insisting on notions of public accountability and political responsibility. It means reactivating the possibility of a more inclusive political economy, and of a revitalised civil society within states. It also means extending notions of radical and participatory democracy to include global politics, while never losing sight of power relations, of class, gender and other axes of difference that shape global politics too.

Does citizenship have a role to play in enabling resistance, in particular feminist resistance to market domination and neoliberal states? Citizenship is two-edged weapon-simultaneously inclusive and exclusive and its long association with dominant group masculinity power make it a difficult concept to utilise. Furthermore, its close association with the state, and with territory and place, make it almost impossible to imagine a citizenship which is degterritiorialised.

Is seeking global civil society hopelessly idealistic? Transnational social movements do now imagine, and act within the world as a political field. Intensifying golbalisation and state transformation have proceeded at such a pace that it can now be argued we live in post-nationstate times. Transnational power demands and produces transnational resistance. There are now extensive networks, dialogues, organisations and alliances within international NGOs,. Interrogating these agents, sites and discourses that are resisting globalisation reveals many of them are not progressive, and may be overtly anti-feminist. It is necessary to forge alliances beyond feminism, though feminists themselves are by no means united in their understandings or strategies of resistance in the face of global power.

Feminists have been organising transnationally – for women's rights, for peace, for example – for more than a century. Now, gendered analyses and feminist politics contest the complex power/wealth/identity of the new global gender regime. There are many example of good feminist transversal practice, like *Women Against Fundamentalism* and *Women Living Under Muslim* Laws, whose members include women who have crossed borders as migrants, dissidents or refugees. Others more specifically address globalisation effects, for example the South-based DAWN group. Feminist politics in the processes around international conferences, especially the 1993 *Vienna Human Rights Conference*, the 1994 *Cairo Population and Development Conference*, and the 1995 *Beijing Women's Conference*, produced connections, contests and writings which reveal something of the difficulties and opportunities of transnational feminist alliances.

Feminist theories and practices around difference have generated many insights into intra-state, or First World/Third World, or Eastern/Western European divides. Feminists have delved deep into questions of identity and subjectivity and self-recognised difference remains a key site for negotiating power and other relations between women, as well as between men and women. Nationality and citizenship, and whether or not we reside in the state where we have at least formal claim to citizenship, are crucial aspects of women's identity too. The contemporary revival of interest in citizenship, including among some feminists, reflects in part a reaction against global power and state assaults on social, including women's rights. It is also a reaction against the mobilisation of exclusivist citizenship politics against racialised and minoritised 'others'. But what can we make of citizenship as a tool for feminist resistance ot the damaging effects of globalisation processes, state transformations and exclusivist identity politics, especially in our focus on international or transnational feminist politics?

Conclusion: The Way Forward

Both as a political imaginary and as a set of practices citizenship is caught between the normalizing forces of modernity and the essentialising forces of nationalism and exclusion. These are played out historically in conjunctures that impact in culturally specific way on women's membership in their political communities. Yet citizenship, we have argued, holds a promise for the future: of personal autonomy and the protection of collective difference and diversity even beyond the nation-state. The women's movement has played a key role in articulating this future vision of citizenship that combines both equality and difference and is based on more inclusive forms of dialogue. In summary, then, we present many discourses and discussions, practices and theovies. Despite its gendered history, it is possible to recast citizenship in a feminist and plural perspective as an important political tool. The language of citizenship provides women with a valuable weapon in the fight for human, democratic, civil and social rights. However, we need to be vigilantly aware of the double-edged nature of citizenship – the fact that it is not only emancipatory and socially progressive but simultaneously exclusionary and often tied to essentialising cultural discourses. These need to be challenged if the full potential of citizenship is to be realized. In a globalising world in which the economic, political and military power of nation-states is increasingly being eroded, there is a need to re-imagine citizenship from a gendered perspective in progressive terms. To the extent that states are deterritorialised, we need to open up our thinking about political accountability. Supranational states such as the European Union have to be evaluated in terms of their gains and losses for women and disadvantaged minorities.

Without new forms and procedures of political accountability we cannot contemplate transnational, supranational or global forms of citizenship. At the same time, in a globalising world the women's movement cannot be only territorial. The challenge is to create movements that are genuinely international at the grassroots level. To the extent that nation-states have been weakened, this has resulted in an attack on their weakest members and this has occurred in the absence of any counter-attack by progressive forces or the Left. Hence the women's movement must fight to defend those vulnerable groups that are most disadvantaged and marginalized in the current political climate. A separation of the women's movement and an exclusive focus on women's interests can lead to a privileging of white professional women at the expense of these vulnerable groups. To avoid this we need to bring feminism into conjunction with other social movements and non-governmental organizations, to ensure grassroots participation, and work closely with the labour movement and with other disadvantaged groups, irrespective of gender.

Women have a proven capacity for transnational networking and for creating alliances across cultural,class and national differences. In building such alliances, women should aim to work with stat, suprastate and UN agencies, in order to persuade them to incorporate ideas formed in the women's movement. At the same time, the women's movement must guard its own autonomy and retain its innovative and subversive power. The private/public division is fluid, historically and contextually determined, contested and constantly struggled over and redefined. It is culture and gender-specific. Women need to fight to reclaim civil rights to privacy, protection and autonomy vis-à-vis the state, while challenging current state welfare reforms that are undermining social citizenship entitlements and a whole range of achievements gained by a prior generation of women activists. As public spaces have been democratized and have come to be open to women and minorities there has been a tendency to privatize real decision-making power by shifting it away from the public sphere and to privatize public spaces. Women must struggle to keep power in the public sphere, to retain its openness and to fight against this dual tendency.

Community-level women's activism is not only a way of raising consciousness and self-confidence, and opening new spaces in which women's voice can be heard. It is the pre-political base for social movements and it has the power to effect real long-terms changes in mainstream politics. The importance of this intermediate sphere must therefore not be underestimated. Like citizenship, multiculturalism is a double-edged sword that often excludes the interests of women and economically disadvantaged groups by privileging cultural, regional or national divisions.

We need to challenge the corporatising tendencies of pluralist politics which obscure class, gendered and racial disadvantages and ignore the predicaments experienced by the disabled, by non-citizens and by stigmatized minorities. Women must continue to fight to expose universalistic claims that disguise particularistic interests and for the right to participate in the determination of the social categories which are deemed relevant in the making of social policy, and the circumstances in which these policies and categories are applicable. The struggle will be a long one. We will have to go miles and miles before we reach destination.

8

Expanding Citizenship

Undoubtedly citizenship has great potential as an idea that challenges injustices within and across societies. It was liberalism that began to extend the reach of citizenship through its defence of equality and individual rights. These liberal ideals moved citizenship beyond the exclusive connotation citizenship had in the pre-modern world. However, we want to reconstruct the idea of citizenship in ways that transcend the limits of liberalism. This means building upon the foundations of liberalism, rather than seeking a completely new basis for citizenship. The challenge is to look for ways in which the promise of liberal citizenship can be fulfilled.

Citizenship and Political Community

Citizenship is a status that mediates the relationship between the individual and the political community. Citizenship also provides a framework for the interactions between individuals within civil society. The advantage citizenship has over other social identities is that it has an inclusive quality that other identities such as class, religion, gender or ethnicity lack. The recent popularity of citizenship amongst radicals can in part be explained by the widespread realization that social struggles based upon exclusive identities have an inherently authoritarian character. Phillips argues that there is a tendency amongst Marxists to see social differences as a distraction to the primary conflict between classes. It follows from this that identities other than class must be suppressed if communism to be achieved. The danger of such group exclusivity, whether it is based upon class or ethnicity, is the main reason why may scholars have argued against the notion of group rights. It is hazardous to attribute positive or negative characteristics to individuals on basis of their membership of a social group. We must instead building upon liberals emphasis upon citizenship as an individual status.

The relationship between the polity and its citizens, as well as between citizens themselves, are reciprocal and interdependent however, even if this is not always recognized by the individuals involved. This means that rights and responsibilities of citizenship are logically closely related. Rights imply responsibilities, since rights do not exist in a vacuum. Others must recognize and respect our rights and we have a responsibility to do the same. To make the rights effective rights also depend for their existence on the maintenance of the political community that sustains them. Consequently, we have a responsibility to exercise our rights, where these rights are fundamental to the good of the community. A healthy polity, then, needs an active citizenry. Active citizenship begins with the individuals, since it is through individual actions that the structural conditions of citizenship are reproduced and improved. Political reform must therefore look to improve the opportunities for citizens to exercise their rights and responsibilities by promoting an ethic of participation. It is only by actively exercising citizenship rights that the false opposition between rights and responsibilities can be dissolved. Reform must also aim at increasing awareness of the relational nature of individuality. One of the most damaging effects of an emphasis upon natural rights in liberalism has been to encourage atomism and instrumentalist attitudes towards our rights. This is where communitarian critics of liberalism have a point. Our belief that our rights are unrelated to the communities in which we live, then will endanger the very existence of our entitlements.

One of the purposes of citizens' responsibilities is to strengthen the ties that bind individuals together and to thereby offset the atomistic tendencies of liberalism. In liberal societies today, the opportunity structures for the exercise of citizenship are clearly failing to do this. Studies of political participation show a worrying decline in the faith citizens have in their political systems and in their representatives. Voting turnouts have fallen in most democratic countries in the last few years and many political parties have experienced declining membership. This at a time when mass higher education and the enormous increase in the influence and range of information media have enchaned citizens' general political awareness. Since the Second World War, many societies have also witnessed a consistent increase in instances of anti-social behaviour, with crime being an obvious example. Such behaviour can be explained in part by the alienation people feel towards their communities. It has been rightly pointed out that these problems go a long way towards explaining the growing significance of the communitarian movement. Communitarians have stressed the need for society to demand greater responsibilities from its citizens as a corrective to the entitlement revolution.

Communitarians are right to stress the need for a greater sense of citizen responsibility. However, this cannot happen at the expense of rights. Neither can we attribute society's problems to the cultural sphere, as many communitarians have been tempted to do. The kinds of development that Etzioni and others identify as negative, such as the sexual liberation of the 1960s and changes in family structures, reflect the struggles for equal citizenship by women and sexual minorities. Turner has rightly argued that the apparent postmodern cultural conditions can be interpreted as the logical consequence of liberalism, with its stress upon individuality and equality. Indeed, the values of liberalism have facilitated the most diverse and pluralistic communities in history. We cannot, and should not, resist the positive and egalitarian social changes that have taken place in many post-war societies in the areas of sexuality, gender politics, music and art. In the context of late modern social conditions a return to tradition is no longer possible.

Beck detects a process in Western society which he calls individualization. The breakdown or decline of traditional reference points such as religion, class, nation or stable employment mean that individuals 'must produce, stage and cobble together their biographies themselves'. One interpretation of individualization is that advanced by those who advocate a 'politics of difference'. Extreme individualism could lead us to the conclusion that the many different interests within society are simply too diverse to be reconciled through a universal citizenship. However, the irony is that writers who subscribe to such a view have often tended to advocate group identity as the main agent of politics, and such deny the very individuality they claim to defend. Nevertheless, the fragmentation of an increasingly individualized society must be tackled in some way.

The ties that bind the community together cannot be cultural in form, since there is no reason to suppose that diverse individuals will have an attachment to their ethnicity. We must therefore enhance channels of communications between citizens politically, through a commitment to a universal ideal of citizenship. This does not necessarily mean, as some advocates of the politics of difference have argued, that all citizens share the same conception of what constitutes the good life. What it does mean, as Oldfield argues, is that the good life for one is not necessarily the good life for another, but the good life for each must include activity which sustains the political community. Linkages between citizens in the form of reciprocal rights and responsibilities underpin the political community in at least two ways. First, they build solidarity between the members of a society. It is important here to distinguish between solidarity between diverse individuals joined together by the institutions of governance and a stifling conformity that some communitarian theories imply. Second, the exercise of citizenship is an educative process. Individuals learn about the techniques of politics through practicing them. This means recognizing the close relationship between citizenship and democracy. Indeed, citizenship can be seen as a precondition of democracy. Even if not formally constituted, rights and responsibilities are implied by a democratic system of governance. Democracy involves the idea of equal rights to participate. It also implies those civil rights that are necessary to the expression of opinion such as the right to free speech, association and protest. Conversely, democracy transforms membership of a polity from subjecthood into citizenship. It is only by recognizing individual as autonomous agents capable of self-governance that active citizenship is possible.

In the context of contemporary social conditions, democracy becomes all the more important to stable governance. One of the positive contributions postmodern theory has made to social science is to help to expose the teleological assumptions that underpin many modernist theories of human emancipation. Thus, classical Marxism embraces a theory of change that romanticizes one social group – the proletariat and postulates an end to history where the need for politics and citizenship to mediate between conflicting positions disappears. However, the inevitable victims of revolution are individual rights. For as Engels contends, 'a revolution certainly the most authoritarian thing there is'. Postmodernism, in contrast, has emphasized the socially constructed nature of truth claims. A logical implication of this is to defend the institutions of democracy as the only possible method for reconciling differences and arriving at policy decisions that the majority of the population can live with. Democracy does not aim at a universal truth, but seeks instead to build relationship between diverse citizens. Postmodernists are right to be concerned with perfectionist theories of politics, if perfectionism means that political deliberation aims at a final solution to human conflicts which denies difference. Democracy replaces teleological or evolutionary theories as the means to emancipation, which must be an ongoing and dynamic process.

Arguments against compulsory voting are normally of two kinds. The first argument is that compulsion violates an individual's right not to take part in the process, whether because of apathy or out of protest. Second, compulsory voting would give politicians the excuse of getting what amounts to a 'donkey' vote where people have to be led by their ears to the polling booth! However, the first objection is met by the argument that voting is a civic responsibility as well as an individual right. Moreover, we could allow individuals to register their dissatisfaction by including the option of 'none of the above' on the ballot paper. The argument that by compelling people to vote is to undermine its significance is not a convincing one. In fact, there is a good chance that an element of compulsion would encourage citizens to participate politically in other ways and to ensure that they are politically informed. Currently, politicians are able to ignore many citizens' preferences because these citizens opt out of elections. Levels of non-participation are also closely linked to socio-economic status. The danger is that parties will increasingly ignore the needs of the poorer sections of society and will gear their policies towards satisfying the middle class. Compulsory voting would address the problem of inequalities in participation and would mean that parties could not ignore the millions of citizens who currently do not take part in elections.

Another policy, which would address the balance between rights and responsibilities, is that of community service. Many countries do require citizens to perform national service in the armed forces. There is no reason why the principle of devoting some time to the community's needs should not be extended to other areas of social life. These might include offering support to the disabled or the elderly, contributing to the maintenance of the environment, or working to enhance the community's cultural activities. The important point is that community service would build solidarity between citizens, particularly if it designed in such a way as to ensure a good social mix occurred between classes and ethnic groups. Community service would help maintain the civic community and provide valuable services to citizens. As Dauenhauer argues, community service would also be an important aspect of the education for citizenship which society needs to provide for its citizens. Dauenhauer proposes a year of service directly after school as a bridge between childhood and the adult world. It certainly would be important to link community service closely to educational programmes on citizenship, which should be compulsory during school years and which should also play some part in higher education as well. Currently the emphasis in education tends to be towards individual self-development and preparation for jobs. Education needs also to build civic responsibility and a sense of sociability.

Ideally, of course, citizenship responsibilities should take the form of voluntary obligations. However, obligation does not develop in a vacuum. Community is the structural context to expect all citizens to take some responsibility for its maintenance. Critics worry that such duties as compulsory voting and community service are a violation of individual liberty. However, individual liberty is more likely to be imperiled by a one-sided view of citizenship that stresses only abstract rights. Once we accept that our rights depend on maintaining common institutions, we are more likely to accept the need for an enhancement of duty. The kinds of proposals we have discussed here would hardly destroy individual choice. The fact is that in liberal societies the polity makes very few demands on our time. Apart from the duty to obey the law, pay our taxes, and possibly serve on a jury, citizens have few duties to perform. It is nonetheless right to be worried if greater responsibilities come at the expense of rights. If citizenship is to be enhanced, we must address the question of social rights as well.

Rethinking Social Rights

Citizenship not only needs the opportunity and the responsibility to participate politically, but they also require the resources to enable them to participate. The community has a duty to provide for every citizen's basic needs. According to Marshall's liberal account of citizenship, the state accepted this responsibility in the post-war period through the institutionalization of social rights. The welfare state was to guarantee that no one, regardless of his or her condition of employment, would live in poverty. The rights of social security would ensure that capitalism was civilized and inequalities legitimized. Social rights, for Marshall, give citizenship real substance because they ground citizenship upon publicly funded resources. However, social rights have always had an uneasy relationship with the other rights of citizenship. Barbalet has argued that we must question whether 'social rights can be rights of citizenship'. He sees citizenship as 'right of participation' in the polity. Social rights are a means to facilitate this participation, rather than a constitutive part of citizenship as such. In addition, 'citizenship rights are necessarily universal. Social rights, on the other hand, are only meaningful when they are substantive and substantive rights can never be universal'. Lastly, because social rights depend upon a bureaucratic and fiscal basis they are not rights at all, but instead are 'conditional opportunities'.

Certainly, social rights are deeply flawed in the form that they have taken in capitalist society. Barbalet is right to identify a tension between an ethic of participation, which is intrinsic to active citizenship and the passive nature of social rights as constituted by the welfare state. The implementation of social rights has depended upon arbitrary and discriminatory decision of welfare providers. Social rights have often stigmatized recipients rather than empowered them. Many social benefits therefore go unclaimed. The administrative decisions that are associated with social rights have had negative implications for individuals' civil rights and are detrimental to benefits through more harsher and more intrusive policing of benefits. In turn, the whole status of social rights is diminished. Social rights, as constituted in the welfare state, fail to build bridges between citizens. Instead, they create divisions between active citizens who are able to exercise their market rights through employment, and 'passive' citizens who are constantly labeled as 'undeserving' or members of an 'underclass'.

We do not have to accept Barbalet's argument that social rights are inherently in tension with civil and political rights however. The key to understanding why social rights have failed to achieve the functions that liberals like Marshall hoped for, is that social rights have been understood as supportive rather than subversive to the logic of capitalism. The link between citizenship and the welfare state that emerged after 1945 was therefore comparatively a weak one. The primary relationship between individuals is seen as market interaction governed by contract, rather than the reciprocal relationship of rights and responsibilities. Social right have tended to be seen as compensation for unemployment, rather than as an intrinsic part of citizenship. The linkage between paid employment and social rights has meant that social citizenship has been biased towards men, who are more likely to be in full-time work and are thereby able to claim the higher rates of benefit associated with graduated tax contributions. Social rights are not inherently selective as Barbalet argues. It is the link between work and social benefits that creates this impression. The third tension between social rights and citizenship rights that Barbalet identifies reveals that the logic of his position is underpinned by an assumption that civil and political rights are in some sense prior to community. The argument that social rights are resource-dependent is of course true. But this is the case for all rights. It is only if we accept the abstract logic of liberalism, which privileges and naturalizes those rights that underpin market relations, then we are able to argue that social rights are of a different nature from the other rights of citizenship.

The danger of reifying civil and political citizenship and denying their necessary linkage to social rights is that social rights become extremely vulnerable to erosion. Indeed, following the neo-liberal backlash against social welfare in the 1980s and 1990, a huge literature has developed on the crisis of the welfare state. Concerns about the negative influence a culture of dependency has upon morality, the detrimental effect high taxation supposedly has for business competitiveness and the problems of an ageing population have all been high on the political agenda in western societies. Cox detects a significant weakening of the relationship between welfare benefits and citizenship, even in the most advanced welfare systems. This is somewhat ironic as politicians such as Tony Blair and Bill Clinton have made great use of the language of citizenship in their attempts to plot a 'third way' to govern society that avoids the 'statism' of socialism and the 'market fundamentalism' of neo-liberalism. However, the language of citizenship as used by advocates of the third way often plays down rights as unconditional claims and instead maintains that rights can be denied to those who do not accept duties, primarily to work or at least to seek work. This once again highlights the weakness of a social rights regime that is subordinate to market imperatives.

Responsibilities then become stratified on the basis of wealth. As Jordan contends, 'the only way to create a citizenship obligation to work would be to create a common interest in the provision of certain goods through all contributing part of their working lives to producing this good'. The weak connection between entitlements administered by the welfare state and political citizenship marks social rights vulnerable to the kind of discursive strategies deployed by politicians eager to cut back welfare bills and to maintain their economy's competitive edge in the global market place. If social rights are to have a more secure basis, we must rethink the function they serve and their relationship to citizenship more broadly. Social rights take on a very different form from the welfare rights defined by Marshall and Barbalet if we priorities the political and egalitarian relationship of citizenship over the unequal market relationship of contract.

Intimate Citizenship

Another area in which citizenship might be enhanced is conveyed by Ken Plummer's useful phrase, 'intimate citizenship'. In our reading of the term, intimate citizsenship refers to the application of the principles of citizenship to interpersonal relationships. In the liberal tradition, citizenship has been seen as a strictly public affair, where reason holds sway. The private sphere is based on family life and market exchanges that are governed by the laws of supply and demand. In the discussion of social rights above, have already suggested that a citizenship subservient to market imperatives is undermined. The introduction of intimate citizenship would be a major step towards tackling this problem. Here we want to discuss how the idea of citizenship can be applied to such questions as family relationships and the management of violence.

Ontologically the private sphere is depoliticised in liberal theory. It is the sharp divide between a political public world and a non-political private realm that has been challenged by feminists. The slogan 'the personal is political' captures nicely the idea that the private realm does involve power relationships that are deeply political. Moreover, a sharp divide between private and public is itself a political construct that favours men's interests. Such a divide has the effect, feminists argue, of hiding from public gaze the violence, particularly towards women and children that often occurs in family life. An important aspect of a holistic citizenship is the appliation of its ideals to this private sphere. This does not mean that the relationships entailed by citizenship form the totality of human relations. Neither does it mean dispensing with a public-private divide completely. There is a good case, however, for applying the idea of reciprocal rights and responsibilities to human relationships in general. A deep sense of citizenship does imply that we cannot have a sharp divide between our identity as human on the one hand and citizen on the other. In a different context, this was very much the point that Marx was driving at in his *On the Jewish Question.* The idea that the rights and responsibilities of citizenship can be limited to a narrow set of human relationships risks undermining the importance of citizenship completely. We cannot rationally deliberate and compromise in a public assembly and then return home to abuse our family. A citizenship beyond liberalism is more demanding than that. It requires us to respect the rights of all those with whom we have relations, and to honor our responsibilities towards them.

Such questions are inevitably raised by the development of more individualistic and yet egalitarian societies. As such, a holistic approach to citizenship is consistent with the core principles of liberalism. As women, sexual minorities and other previously excluded groups struggle for recognition, the public/private divide is inevitably problematic. At times, the relationship between public and private seems even paradoxical. What this means is that we cannot assume a neat, unchanging divide between the personal and political. In fact, such a divide presupposes exclusion and the suffocation of legitimate claims to rights. The struggle homosexuals have had, first to have their sexuality decriminalized, and then to seek equality with heterosexuals, is a good example of what were traditionally private questions of morality entering the public domain.

A loosely related point, and a crucial component of intimate citizenship, is the democratization of the private sphere. Two writers who have considered this question are Giddens and Hoffman. Giddens is in little doubt that 'the family is becoming democratized' and in ways which are closely related to processes of democratization generally. Greater equality between men and women and more sensitivity to the rights of children inevitably lead to a renegotiation of personal relationships based on principles of deliberation and, crucially, freedom from violence. Ideas of rights and responsibilities pervade these relationships, whether rights and responsibilities are formalized in law or not. Giddens believes that social policy must aim to firm up intimate citizenship by providing a network of rights and responsibilities between family members. For example, he suggests that as more couples are having children outside of marriage, what is required is a contractual commitment to children that is separate from the marriage contract. Such a contract would give both parents equal responsibility for their children's welfare.

Giddens contends that, by applying the ideas of citizenship to personal relationships, we raise questions about the role of violence in social life generally. By gearing social policy towards encouraging compromise between individuals, we care a political framework that can work to remove violence from all human relationships. Giddens insist that individuals who have a good understanding of their own emotional make up, and who are able to communicate effectively with others on a personal basis, are likely to be well prepared for wider tasks of citizenship.

Despite making close analogies between personal relationships and public life, Giddens is nevertheless unwilling to follow the logic of his theory: a critique of violence in human relationships should lead us to a critique of the state. Giddens is trapped in a dualistic logic that refuses to go beyond a static view of the public and private. On the one hand, he sees the way in which violence within the family destroys reciprocity and democracy. On the other hand, he maintains that a society without the state, which rests its power upon violence, would lead only to chaos. Indeed, Giddens appears to see violence as the only basis for social order. He writes 'where states have no enemies, but face only diffuse threats, a potentially but not actually hostile international environment, disintegrative tendencies internally might again become strong'. In direct contrast to his plea for democratic families, Giddens is arguing here that to ensure peace, states must prepared for war!

John Hoffman's ideas have been ground-breaking because he has made the necessary link between the state and human relationships in general, which Giddens, because of his statist assumptions, refuses to make. Hoffman argues that for citizenship to fulfill its emancipatory potential, it is necessary to move beyond the state. This is because the democratic ideals closely associated with citizenship oppose violent solutions to political problems which the state, with its claim to a monopoly of force and violence, implicitly endorses. The use of violence is relational in its effect because it dehumanizes the perpetuator as well as the victim.

Tensions between what is public and what is private are inevitable, argues Hoffman. What is crucial, however, is that these tensions are resolved democratically and not by force. The democratization implied by intimate citizenship, and the development of more representative political institutions and new forms of political participation are all part of the same movement towards a post-statist citizenship. Central to Hoffman's theory is a distinction between force and coercion. Force involves the negation of choice. Coercion on the other hand refers to non-violent social pressures that may be aimed at individuals who refuse to respect others' rights and who display anti-social behaviour. Critics may argue that this aspect of Hoffman's theory is utopian. However, Hoffman's theory meets the charge of utopianism on at least three counts. First, Hoffman's theory moving realistically towards a progressive future for citizenship beyond the state relates to the question of globalisation, which is creating a momentum towards global systems of governance.

Second, by problematising the relationship between democracy and the state, Hoffman's theory implies that any movement towards democracy undermines the state's reliance upon force. The state does not disappear overnight but it is nonetheless increasingly challenged by the process of democratization both within the personal and the global spheres.

Third, by accepting the need for coercion that falls short of force, Hoffman allows for the fact that all societies have norms and values which govern social interaction and which require some form of regulation. Of course, some value systems are conservative and oppressive. However, like the question of the pubic-private divide, the key to addressing this problem is to ensure that the mechanisms through which norms are decided and put into practice are democratic and deliberative. It is true that all societies, whether they are governed by a state or not, require constraints upon members' activities. Hoffman's argument that stable government requires social coercion does not violate individual liberty but is an important aspect of freedom, where freedom is conceived in social terms. The consistency of Hoffman's theory with liberal principles is supported by the fact that liberals such as J.S. Mill hold similar views on the role of social pressure which falls short of actual force. In his famous tract *On Liberty*, Mill argues that we must respect the rights of others to choose how to lead their lives as a matter of principle. However, this does not prevent us from applying pressure upon an individual who is acting in a way that may harm themselves or others. Indeed, in many cases we are morally obliged to try to persuade others that their actions may have negative consequences. More recently, communitarians have also stressed the importance of informal constraints upon citizens' actions. Etzioni contends that the measure of good societies is the 'extent to which they rely on informal social mechanisms- the moral voice versus the state and its coercive tools of law enforcement'.

The idea of coercion as used by Hoffman can be conceptually linked to the ethic of care, which many feminists have advocated as a way of civilizing citizenship. This is possible because Hoffman clearly has a view of coercion that is constructive and compassionate, rather than narrow-minded and moralistic in the negative sense of the term. A positive view of coercion, as a concern for others' welfare, is therefore close to the ideal of care. By introducing notions of care and compassion into debates concerning intimate citizenship, feminists seek to bridge the dualism between reason and emotion which so concerns postmodern critics of liberalism. Bubeck's view is that, while we must avoid naturalizing women's behaviour, it is nevertheless the case that women's experiences of mothering and caring for dependants make them more likely than men to have a relational view of politics that is sensitive to others' needs and concerns. Bubeck argues that the both care and politics are muddling through types of activities which involve the welfare of others. An ethic of care also implies interdependence rather than the abstract form of independence advanced by liberalism. As such, by bringing the values of care to citizenship we are more likely to build consensual relationships in both the public and private domains. Critics like Ignatieff are right to be concerned about linking care to citizenship if this means neglecting the question of formal social rights. Nonetheless, when Ignatieff writes that 'welfare is about rights, not caring' he presents us with a false choice. A purely formal expression of rights can easily lead us into the abstract logic of instrumentalism that sees no connection between our rights and our obligations to others. The challenge that intimate citizenship presents us is to combine a strengthening of traditional expressions of rights and responsibilities informal terms with a sense of compassion and obligation that informs all relationships in both the public and private worlds.

In this chapter, we have presented some ways in which citizenship can be enhanced and the strengths of liberalism such as individual rights and equality built upon. Rights and responsibilities must be attached to all diverse individuals who nonetheless share an interest in the maintenance of common institutions, to build a sense of solidarity and mutual endeavor. We have suggested that in the increasingly individualistic context of liberal society, we should be required to perform more duties than is currently the case in many communities. Compulsory voting and community service are examples that may encourage the ethic of participation, which we have argued is crucial to a coherent definition of citizenship. Experiments in deliberative methods of policy-making such as citizens' juries are another way in which political rights can be made more meaningful and collaborative. A holistic approach to citizenship must also acknowledge, however, that an effective ethic of participation must be supported by a material foundation. Traditional approaches to social rights have failed to secure individual autonomy. In contrast, a citizens' income is a policy that remove citizenships' dependence upon the market and decommodifies rights in ways which are likely to encourage a more activist and progressive citizenry. Finally, we have argued that a thick conception of citizenship requires us to rethink our personal as well as public relationships. Developing intimate citizenship is crucial to the further democratizations of society and to the conceptualization of a citizenship beyond the state.

World citizenship and morality

The feeling of a universal identity and the acceptance of a universal morality are so closely linked. The world 'cosmopolitan' in general parlance means a person who feels at home in a number of countries. The usefulness of its more specific political connotation of trans – or supra-national has only recently come to be again recognized by scholars. However, in origin it had neither of these meanings. The Greek word *'cosmopolites'* should properly be rendered as 'citizen of the cosmos' or 'universe'. A person thus described was therefore someone conscious of being part of the whole universe, the whole of life, the whole of nature, of which all human beings, let alone just the community of the person's political state, were but tiny portions.

This insight, of course, has been revived in our own times, though in the more restricted, planetary sense. Most akin to the ancient Greek view is the Gaia hypothesis that the entire planet is a living, organic system. More simply, the increasing numbers of people who are concerned about man's impact on the environment not only speak in terms of ecological interdependence, but also in terms of humankind's stewardship of the planet. The massive impact and control that we have must be tempered by respect for other life-form and for the needs of future human generation.

All this adds up to a moral consciousness which can, perhaps justifiably, use the vocabulary of citizenship. For citizenship entails the ethical element of responsible behaviors towards and obligations to one's fellow citizens and the state or community which provides us with the citizenly status.

Even so, human beings are a special, identifiable part of the total order of nature. And because they are, they must have features which they share in common and which set them apart, as the Greeks saw it, from the gods and beasts. This recognition was revolutionary step in Greek thought. From the primary human communities of families and clans came the remarkable leaps to the political organization of the state. In ancient Greek practice and thought the *polis* provide the political organizations; and the sense of distinctiveness, indeed superior to the non-Greek-speaking 'barbarians', provided the sense of a common culture. Yet as early as the eighth century BC the comprehension that the whole of humankind shared something in common was starting to emerge. And slowly the idea gathered strength.

The key to the distinctiveness that humans share and that sets them apart from other animals, as the philosophers explained, was *logos,* the capacity for reasoned speech, which also embraced the capacity to comprehend the universal Divine or Natural Law. All human beings are capable of forming a bond by means of obedience to the common Natural Law and by communication. The possibilities for realizing this potential for the uniting of the human race were limited in the ancient world. Nevertheless, with economic globalization, the spread of English as a lingua franca and the communicative power of the Internet, the dream of Heraclitus, who understood the full implications of *logos* in the sixth century BC, may be nearing g realization.

The link between the concept and human unity was stated unequivocally by Locke, seventeen hundred years later: by the law of nature, he wrote, 'common to them all, a man and all the rest of mankind are one community, make up one society distinct from all other creatures'. Through the concept of Natural Law Locke derived the principle of natural rights, These rights, incorporated most distinctly in the eighteenth-century American Declarations and in the twentieth-century UN International Bill of Rights, may in a sense be thought of as the world citizen's equivalent of the rights of the citizen *vis-à-vis* the state.

A citizen, however, owes duties as well as enjoying rights; and we must 'think globally'. Let us take three examples of recent proposals to improve humankind's sense of responsibility. In the 1980s an Australian cabinet minister, Gareth Evans, articulated the idea of 'good international citizenship' as 'an exercise in enlightened self-interest: an expression of idealistic pragmatism.

The Commission on Global Governance has urged the adoption of a global civic ethic as the moral foundation for a more effective system of global governance than the current pattern. In addition to reinforcing the established lists of fundamental human rights, it has outlined some half-dozen matching responsibilities. These include: to consider the impact of one's actions on the security and welfare of others, to promote equity, including equality of the sexes, and to protect the interests of future generations. A distinguished group of former heads of state and government, calling themselves the Inter Action Council, has drawn up Universal Declaration of Human Responsibilities in a conscious attempt to balance the Universal Declaration of Human Rights.

World law and the citizen

From Locke to the French Revolution the belief that the general notion of Natural Law could be translated into an outline of specific natural human rights became widely accepted. But the protection of those rights was seen to be the responsibility of the state, not of international society; so human rights were closely associated with citizens' rights What interests us here is how these rights, in expanded form, came to be thought of as universal rights, proclaimed and guarded by the international community of states. For, by this transition, human rights assumed a semblance of the rights of the world citizen. Furthermore, they have the status of law in so far as they are incorporated into documents signed and ratified as treaties by ration – states.

As early as the revolutionary age, indeed, there was an understanding that in principle the American and French Declarations were being propounded not just for the sake of their own people: Jefferson, for instance, wrote about the Declaration of Independence, 'we are acting for all mankind'.

What has attra:ted the attention of scholars more from this period is Kant's conception of a cosmopolitan law or code of right, expounded in his *Perpetual Peace*. His image of this form of law is very restricted, merely the right of abode anywhere on earth. The result of its practical application, however, was already an intermingling of people and the opening up of the prospect for 'a universal right [i.e. law] of humanity' – the flowering of world citizenship. 'The peoples of the earth', Kant declared, 'have thus entered in varying degrees into a universal community, and it has developed to the point where a violation of rights in one part of the world is felt everywhere'. From the perspective of the second half of the twentieth century – form the Holocaust to Bosnia, Rwanda and Kosovo – it was a perceptive remark.

However, little was done to draw up the details of such cosmopolitan law of rights until the mid-twentieth century. The universal protection of human rights assumed unambiguous status in international law through the Charter of the United Nations. Art. 55 states that 'the United Nations shall promote universal respect for, and observance of, human rights and fundamental freedoms for all', while Art. 56 pledges all member states to assist in this task.

These rights were articulated in the *Universal Declaration of Human Rights*. This document, however, has no legal force. On the other hand, subsequent supporting document do. These are: the *International Covenant on Economic, Social and Cultural Rights*; the *International Covenant on Civil and Political Rights*; and the *Optional Protocol* to the latter. These four documents are collectively called the *International Bill of Right*. By signing the two Covenants, about half the world's states are party to agreements having the force of international law. And the rights relate to both individuals and groups, notably ethnic groups.

So, just as the individual *qua* state citizen is conceived as having civil, political, social and economic rights, so the individual *qua* human being or world citizen is conceived as having a parallel set of rights necessarily enjoyed and enforced in practice as the ideal documents commend and command. However, if citizens have rights, they also have concomitant obligation not to infringe the rights of other citizens. Therefore, the same principle of reciprocity must apply to persons in their capacity as world citizens. This precept was made explicit in the *Charter of the International Tribunal* set up after the Second World War to try German leaders charged with crimes against humanity. The Tribunal made in it transparently clear that an individual's duty to adhere to this universal moral code transcends his duty of obedience to the state where that state demands the contravention of the higher law.

And the principle was still being upheld at the end of the twentieth century AD with the prosecution at The Hague and Arusha of those persons indicted for war crimes in the gruesome Bosnian and Rwandan civil wars respectively.

World governance and the citizen

Protection of and obedience to the law is a rather passive form of citizenship, though none the less vital for all that. A potentially stronger form is the exercise of political rights. How does this aspect of the status translate into world citizenship? One is to participate in civil society organizations with a global reach. A second is to be involved in the supra-national political institutions that already exist. And thirdly, there is the advocacy of new opportunities and institutions to enhance the reality of political world citizenship.

In state context, civil society organizations can be effective channels though which to exercise citizenly behaviour and wield influence on government policies. It is becoming increasingly evident that what can be termed global civil society is playing a similar role in a transnational setting. Many people are now acting as world citizens by participating in organizations which are devoted to publicizing global problems and exerting pressure especially on governments and multinational companies to change their policies and activities. Humanitarian and environmental concerns have generated most support.

Humanitarian organization includes specialist bodies such as *Medicine sans Frontiers.* More generalized humanitarian activities by global civil society relate to two main denials of human rights, economic and civil – through poverty and political persecution respectively. Bodies like *Save the Children* and *Oxfam* work in the first field; organizations like *Amnesty International* work in the second. Amnesty International was established in 1961, the centenary of the emancipation of Russian serfs and the American Civil War. In terms of world citizenship this body is of especial relevance because it is confronting national governments with transgressions against the UN Charter and International Bill of Rights.

Awareness of resource depletion and environmental degradation has spawned a large number of organizations at the national level.

Some, however, most conspicuously perhaps, Greenpeace, are global bodies; but many national associations also, by the very nature of their purposes, have global agenda.

In United Nations parlance substantial bodies of this kind are called NGOs or INGOs (International Non-Governmental Organizations). These increased in number during the twentieth century: in 1909 there were 176 INGOs; eighty years later there were 4,624. A large proportion of these work on behalf of the planet's environment. In 1992 the UN *Conference on Environment and Development* met in Rio de Janeiro. Representatives from more than 1,400 NGOs attended and thousand more participated in the unofficial Global Forum which was convened in tandem with the official UN meeting. This NGO collaboration with the UN continued thereafter in conferences on other topics.

Stress has been placed on the world role of individuals who are active participants in the global organizations. Yet many more behave as world citizen at lower level of commitment. But then that is true, as well, of state citizens. Signing petitions for and donating charitable contributions to such organizations must surely count as acts of world citizenship.

Finally, and not so obviously, are the influences that are subtly linking individuals into global networks and leading some perhaps to think less nationalistically and xennophobically, even endowing them with a positively cosmopolitan mentality, reminiscent of Kant's cosmopolitan law.

Cosmopolitan Democracy

The felt need for the system of world governance to be rendered more democratic by means of an elected body or bodies take us, in fact, to the heart of what are widely believed to be both urgent and reasonably practicable proposals at the turn of the century. We need to discuss this general proposal at the turn of century. We need to discuss this general requirement in its two major forms. One is for the creation, as highlighted in the world federalists' agenda, for a second UN assembly, the other, incorporating this scheme in its more ambitious agenda, is the developing concept of cosmopolitan democracy.

'We the peoples of the United Nations have resolved to combine our efforts,' these words from the Preamble to the UN Charter have occasioned cynical remarks from commentators who bemoan the utter lack of opportunities in the UN's institutions for the peoples to combine their efforts for any purposes at all. The world's states control the Security Council and the General Assembly. Only one tiny loophole exists in the Charter through which the spirit of democratic world citizenship might be able to infiltrate and thus challenge this dominance. The loophole is Art. 22, with this provision: 'The General Assembly may establish subsidiary organs as it deems necessary for the performance of its functions.'

The word 'subsidiary' is a catch, but at least this statement opens up the possibility of transforming the UN into a bicameral institution, with an assembly elected by 'the peoples'. It is an obvious idea. In fact, the shock of the First World War led, especially in the USA, to the composition of plans for world government, which included provision for an elected assembly. After the founding of the UN, the British Parliamentary Group For World Government advocated such a plan as early as 1952. The idea has received considerable support in more recent years through specially founded movements for UN reform – the Campaign for a More Democratic United Nations and the International Network For a UN Second Assembly.

The creations of an Assembly of Peoples would undoubtedly strengthen the principle of world citizenship. Individuals would be enfranchised, be able to vote for their representative to a supra-national parliament on a global level just as the citizens of the European Union exercise their right of suffrage at the sub-continental level. Such a constitutional adaptation would also be symbolic: it would signal acceptance that citizens as well as states are entitled to act on the international stage.

The cosmopolitan democracy pattern is envisaged as a gradual evolution of more effective and additional regional institutions and global bodies as well as a reformed UN and the current global civil society citizens to be protected by improved juridical systems and to participate in a variety of processes of direct democracy, representative democracy and referendums. In the words of David Held, the leading exponent of the idea, of a cosmopolitan democratic system:

> People can enjoy membership in the diverse communities which significantly affect them and, accordingly, access to a variety of forms of political participation. Citizenship would be extended, in principle, to membership in all cross-cutting political communities, from the local to the global

The cosmopolitan democracy thesis is, however, much more complex than just the functioning of the citizen in the proposed web of institutions and activities. It spans legal and economic structures as well as political. In political terms, for example, the arrangements would increase the accountability and therefore legitimacy of decision-making processes at all levels. In terms of role of the citizen specifically, the mode reveals how the principle and practices of multiple citizenship could be knitted together into a rather more coherent pattern of identities, duties and rights than the current, historically ad hoc, patchwork. Furthermore, the linking of cosmopolitanism with democracy has truly modernized the idea of the cosmopolites, who, in Greek thought, were merely the few furnished with the wisdom to perceive the universal law of nature. Multiple citizenship, it is evident, is rapidly becoming a reality. Yet it is complicated and difficult for the individual to cope with. Modern citizens must wear so many civic hats. Multiple citizenship presents the demands of multiple understanding, multiple identities, multiple loyalties, multiple rights and multiple duties. In the Aristotelian and Rousseauan ideal states, the political environment in which the citizen would operate was compact and intimate and possessed of simple sets of participative rules. In today's real world of manifold civic contexts, the citizen is required to possess knowledge, acquire understanding and develop skills pertinent to the several citizenly identities. The conscientious discharge of even a singular citizenship role is difficult enough. Multiple citizenship multiplies the difficulties.

We may also question whether multiple citizenship is compatible with the traditional state-centred concept of citizenship at all. What happens to the virtue of a citizen of the European Union finds his or her twin allegiances are pulled in opposite directions by irreconcile differences? We have come full circle and return to Cicero's principle of incompatibility.

The problem is highlighted by the current growing requirement for loyalty to institutions and agendas on supra-national domains, competing with traditional powerful national ties. This consideration leads to compelling objections concerning the building of supra-national layers of citizenship.

Many temperamentally find the idea of a supra-national identity uncongenial. Comments uttered in France across two centuries against perceived threats to national identity may be taken as illuminating examples of this standpoint. Reacting against the cosmopolitanism of the philosophers in 1772, Rousseau acidly declared: 'Today there are no longer Frenchmen, Germans, Spaniards, on even Englishmen, whatever is said; there are only Europeans. All have the same tastes, the same passions, the same customs. They are at home wherever there is money to steal and women to seduce'. In 1974 the French sociologist Raymond Aron, reacting against the cohering agenda of the European Community, asserted with forthright conviction: 'There are no such animals as European citizen There are only French, German or Italian citizens'.

The problem is that there is no similar culture, history or mythology that is fully universal in scope and in which may be embedded in a firm cosmopolitan identity. Even the more plausible efforts to emphasize the common European inheritance of the members of the EU – a kind of cultural highest common factor – is having only limited success.

These problems are compounded by the conflation of culture and politics. It has often been asserted, world citizenship is undesirable: a homogenized world culture and a world state present a vision of dystopica. Creativity and freedom alike would be seriously impaired; world citizens would headly be motivated and organizd to act as guardian of the quality and liberties of human life.

We must, indeed, recognize the very real differences between the ancient Stoics' imagined cosmopolis and the modern blueprints for a world state. The Stoic could manage to balance their loyalty to the state in their adherence to a universal morality by separating them into virtually distinct public and private spheres. A full-fledged modern world state, in contrast, might well require a transfer of civic allegiance from the state to the universal polity.

9

Citizenship and Globalisation

Globalisation as a buzzword has occupied the center stage in political discourses of late modernity. The popularity of the concept is reflected in the proliferation of articles, books and political speeches exploring the notion that a combination of advanced communications systems, the growth of world markets, and the pervasive reach of multinational corporations are steadily eroding the boundaries that have hitherto defined social membership. Could it be that he concept of citizenship is becoming redundant, since its close association historically with closed political communities is inappropriate to the porous boundaries of a new global age? Many defenders of nationality such as Miller insists that without the psychological barriers between citizen and stranger citizenship can be no more than a superficial concept. Citizenship which fosters a distinct national culture is unlikely to engender the values of civic virtue necessary to good governance. In sum, globalisation appears to challenge the contemporary relevance of citizenship because it eases the boundaries, both material and psychological, which have made citizenship significant in modernity.

While the economic and cultural effects of globalisation are often exaggerated or misinterpreted, globalisation, particularly in the form of planetary risks, has indeed hung a question mark over traditional assumptions about social membership. In particular, the tension between universal rights and sovereignty is being highlighted by these processes. Traditional international relations theory is unable to conceptualize the nature of contemporary social changes that are creating a more interdependent world. We must therefore move beyond traditional conceptions of security if we are to remodel citizenship in a way that is relevant to the requirements of a global age.

Some authors, such as Yasemin Soysal, have suggested that in the context of globalisation, citizenship is being replaced by human rights; the protection of these universal rights is now the key to securing individual autonomy. But others have raised the question of whether human rights are indeed superseding citizenship in the way that Soysal suggests.

Globalisation and Citizenship

Globalisation is generally said to involve processes of social change which are cultural, economic and political in form. Waters provides a succinct definition of globalisation: 'a social process in which the constraints of geography on social and political arrangements recede and in which people become increasingly aware they are receding'.

Spectacular innovations in information and communications technology, including satellites, computers, jet travel and digital television, have made access to other cultures easier and more instantaneous than in previous eras. A consequence of this, argues Ohmae, is the development of a global culture that is moving people beyond narrow national self-interests. As consumers of cultural symbols and signs, as well as material products, individuals are now looking beyond the boundaries of the state and making choices according to personal taste rather than national identity. The world of the global consumer is facilitated by the growth in world trade and the constitution of a global market place. The principal vehicle of these market forces is the multinational company, which is increasingly breaking its links with the nation-state and is instead seeking new opportunities across the globe, regardless of the dictates of national interest. The significance of the rise of multinationals is, however, disputed by those who consider globalisation as concept to be ill-defined and overstated. Hirst and Thompson, for example, have presented a critique of the idea of economic globalisation. They argue persuasively that world trade and investment pattens are still heavily concentrated within Europe, Japan and the USA, and that multinational companies are very much reliant upon the framework of laws, training, education, research, and general infrastructure provided by the nation-state.

Many have argued that polarization, rather than globalisation, may best describe aspects of world trade, since whole regions are more or less excluded from the benefits of capital accumulation. Countries in Africa, Latin America and Eastern Europe, for instance have in recent years seen their share of world markets decline. Such evidence contradicts the optimistic account of globalisation presented by Ohmae, who considers the triumph of capitalism on a planetary scale to bring benefits for all. The reality is that it is the Western states that are benefiting from the liberalization of trade in many areas. Moreover, in areas of commerce such as the control of technology innovations and copyright, where the West has vested interest in maintaining control, tight regulations remain. International patent rights have been extended to genetic materials such as seeds and natural medicinal which means that a few companies have effectively obtained monopoly rights over genetic research on an entire species and on any useful products of that research. For these reasons, then there is a lot of truth in the argument that globalisation, rather than marking the demise of the state, in fact represents a particular state strategy that aims at securing and protecting the interests of political and economic elites of liberal states.

There is also good reason to doubt the triumph of global culture. In effect, Ohmae's idea of global culture represents the spread of liberal values of individualism, market forces and Western consumer tastes. Many cultures have in fact responded negatively to the apparent triumph of liberalism following the ending of the cold war. Often these reactions take the form of fundamentalist reactions against the superficial and unsatisfying values of consumer capitalism. The rise of Islamic fundamentalism in parts of Africa and Asia, the huge range of ethnic conflict in the former Soviet Union and eastern Europe, and the continued dominance of the communist party in China are all evidence that contradicts any simple global cultures thesis.

Fukuyama, the American social theorist sees in globalisation the triumph of liberal values. In Fukuyama's case, however, it is processes of democratization in such regions as Asia, Africa and Eastern Europe, as well as the spread of market principles, which are cited as evidence that the alternatives to liberal democracy are collapsing.

A consideration of Ohmae's and Fukuyama's arguments helps throw light upon the nature of the processes associated with globalisation in ways that take us back to the internal tensions within liberalism. These tensions have helped shape the form and development of citizenship. Ohmae sees little place for democratic citizenship in his vision of a global age. Like many neo-liberals, Ohmae is highly skeptical of the values of democracy and instead sees the market as the surest way to govern society and to distribute resources. Fukuyama sees a much closer relationship between the values of the market and democracy and believes that the two institutions of capitalism and citizenship in combination create the most favourable conditions for individual's freedom and stable government. But there are in fact strong contradictions between the values of capitalism and citizenship. Globalisation is making this contradiction more acute in several ways.

First, while the world economy cannot actually be described as global in an inclusive sense of the term, it has become more internationalized. States compete for market shares in an international system that is only minimally governed. Institutions such as World Bank, Organisation for Economic Co-operation and Development (OECD), and the International Monetary Fund (IMF) attempt to give some structure to the world economy, but overwhelmingly these institutions are dominated by advocates of neo-liberalism. So, as competition between states grows stronger, the tension between states interest and universal rights and between capitalism and democracy becomes more intense.

Second, the dominance of the market over citizenship is an important element in the development of global risks. These risks are the most important aspect of global change. Unlike the advantages of the global market or the values of abstract individualism, risk can truly be said to be planetary in its impact. The idea of global risk refers to problems that cannot be managed successfully by any single state. They include migration, infectious diseases, international crime, nuclear power and ecological damage: none of these problems respect the boundaries that states defend. Modern communications technology has intensified these problems and made states and individuals more aware that these problems exist. The development of global risk has huge implications for the role of the state and its ability to guarantee citizenship. In classical international relations theory, the state which concentrates force in the form of sovereignty is seen as the only plausible method by which order can be maintained. The primary justification the state has to rule is its promise to provide security to its citizens. It is this Hobbesian logic that is being challenged by contemporary social changes associated with globalisation.

Realists have argued that since states are the only viable institution of governance, the claims of individuals outside of the jurisdiction of any individual state must be balanced by the state's primary duty to its own citizens. In effect, realists postulate an inherent opposition in the international sphere between order and demands for justice. However, with the intensification of planetary risks, this opposition can no longer be sustained. Many of the problems associated with risks are closely related to the high levels of global inequality that exist between states. The processes associated with economic globalisation have increased this inequality. The deregulated, and therefore unstable nature of financial markets, for example, impacts negatively upon the maintenance of citizenship rights, particularly in poorer countries. In turn, this leads to greater poverty, which increases the possibility of instability and war. Given the increase in the destructive capability of modern weaponry, warfare is much harder to contain within a single state or even a geographical region. Environmental damage, which is inherently of global importance, is also linked to poverty, as developing states struggle desperately to increase industrial productivity rather than seeking sustainable methods of development may be less profitable in the short term.

The effects of these inequalities of basic rights and liberties are increasingly impacting directly upon rights as well as poor countries. Migration and international crimes are linked to this inequality, for example. The phenomenon of economic refugees, who seek to leave the poor regions of the world and search for a place at the high table, is alarming liberal states. This problem is set to become one of the key political issues of the twenty-first century.

In the context of globalisation, however, where risks are both more dangerous and more transparent, states cannot convincingly claim to guarantee their own citizens' rights if they do not also consider the rights of individuals in other communities. It is for this reason for some writers are arguing that human rights are replacing citizenship as the primary guarantee of individual autonomy.

Human Rights and Citizenship

Soysal is one of those who detects an enhanced role for human rights in late modernity. In her book, *The Limits of Citizenship,* she advances a sophisticated argument which has at its centre the assertion that 'a new and more universal concept of citizenship has unfolded in the post-war era, one whose organizing and legitimating principles are based on universal personhood rather than national belonging'. The context of this shift is the development of a global system that encompasses international law, the United Nations network, global civil society, and regional governance, as found in institutions such as the European Union.

Consequently, the language of human rights is becoming increasingly popular to the national government as respect for the person and challenges the idea that states are sovereign in relation to their citizens and that other states or international bodies have no rights to interfere in this primary relationship. Soysal's evidence for this transformation is focused upon the experience of so-called guest workers in Europe. These are individuals who live and work in a foreign country, often for years, without ever acquiring citizenship status. The growing importance of human rights, however, means that the benefits of citizenship are becoming less important. Organizations representing guest workers have been able to mobilize support for the extension of basic social and civil rights. Thus the significance of citizenship has been reduced to the point where 'non citizens' rights do not differ significantly from those of citizens. As such, social membership is increasingly post-national and based upon personhood rather than citizenship. Even groups such as Muslims, who have historically lived in tension with liberal values, are utilizing discourses of human rights in ways which speak to modern individuals needs, such as rights to worship and to cultural recognition.

Importantly, Soysal rejects arguments that seek to understand the experience of guest workers as beneficiaries of the extension of the territorial reach of citizenship, which now includes denizens as well as citizens by augmenting the criteria for rights based upon nationality with the additional criteria of residency. Such perspectives, contends Soysal, 'remain within the confines of the nation-state model'. Instead, what is happening to guest workers reflects a more 'profound transformation in the institution of citizenship, both in its institutional logic and in the way it is legitimized. To locate the changes, we need to go beyond the nation-state'.

We agree that Soysal's argument is convincing. There is the urgent need to reconceptualise citizenship in ways which break the link with the state. It is only in this way that the rights of citizenship can be extended in a manner consistent with liberal notions of the equal worth of individuals. Soyal is also right to identify the growing importance of human rights in world politics. Sine the Second World War, international law governing human rights has been expanding rapidly. *The UN Declaration of Human Rights*, which was adopted unopposed by the UN General Assembly in 1948, is the centerpiece of human rights law. Since then, other conventions covering such matters as the outlawing of torture, discrimination against women and children, and the promotion of the rights of migrants have gained widespread international support. In 1993, 171 governments at the *World Conference on Human Rights* in Vienna supported a statement to the effect that economic, social and cultural rights are 'universal, indivisible, and interdependent and interrelated'. Moreover, within Europe in particular, cases of injustice within states are increasingly likely to be decided at a level beyond the individual state. An excellent example of this occurred on 27 September 1999, when the *European Court of Human Rights* in Strasbourg ruled in favour of four gays who had objected to the fact that Britain's armed forces exercised a ban on homosexual and lesbian recruits. The Court ruled that the British Government was contravening the basic human right to enjoy a private life, the nature of which should have no bearing upon eligibility for employment.

There is evidence, then, to suggest that states are becoming aware of the problems of global risks and how abuses of human rights by states are likely to impact beyond state boundaries. Turner has observed that risk has helped to create common interests and an awareness of the frailty of human existence. Risk has thereby created the basis for a high degree of agreement on the need for human rights. Frailty has become a universal feature of human existence. Turner insists that globalisation means that 'the debate about human rights might begin to replace the debate about citizenship in both academic and political life'.

Human rights by themselves do not ensure the development of the participatory networks that are necessary to sustain common institutions of governance. Such networks are also crucial in building bridges between immigrant groups and the dominant culture within the polity. It is right to seek to detach citizenship from nationality. A post-national model of citizenship, as expressed in Habermas's notion of "constitutional patriotism", nonetheless requires that all members of a community participate in and display loyalty to their governmental institutions. It is hardly healthy for any democracy to have large groups of individuals working and living in a community, but without the opportunity to make decisions about that community's future: membership of a polity involves responsibilities as well as rights. It can only fuel hostility towards minorities if some groups are seen to benefit from the social aspects of citizenship without playing their part in the community. Human rights, then, do not address the question of reciprocity of obligation. Crucially, it is because citizenship involves participation and responsibilities that human rights cannot simply supersede citizenship in the way Soysal suggests. Joppke has rightly observed that citizenship is tolerable in the interim, but not in principle.

In any case, Soysal is over-optimistic about the extent to which immigrants do in fact enjoy social and civil rights. Immigrants' standing within the community may well be challenged and undermined by shifts towards more draconian immigration or asylum policies. Bhabha has commented that racial harassment and violence persist across EU member states. Discriminatory police behaviour and visible ghettoisation characterize European metropolitan cities. Widespread racism in employment and in the provision of public services remains a matter of acute public concern across the EU. Despite formal legal entitlements to an extensive range of state benefits, in practice, Europe's third country nationals do not enjoy the full civil rights to which the 'native' population has access. Such evidence rebuts Soysal's optimism that the promotion of human rights in Europe is a panacea, resolving the division that has accompanied the delineation of Europe.

Countries outside Europe conform even less to the post-national model of citizenship that Soysal outlines. In the USA, for example, changes in welfare legislation in 1996-limited eligibility of immigrants to virtually all cash benefits. Schuck remarks that this legalisation has increased sharply the value of American citizenship while reducing the value of permanent legal resident statues. Schuck also makes the point that there are around 5 million illegal immigrants in the USA who play a crucial role in the economy as low-paid factory and domestic workers. These persons feel little benefit from the post-national order described by Soysal.

The guest worker's experience in Europe cannot be easily generalized into a widespread shift to a post-national citizenship. Joppke argues that by focusing upon the experience of these workers, Soysal is in danger of elevating 'the fringe into the core experience'. Also, in those countries such as Germany where guest workers are numerous, there is an ongoing debate over the desirability of denying citizenship to long-standing residents. In 1999 Chancellor Schroder's Social Democratic Government passed a new citizenship law which cut the link between German blood and nationality and thereby paved the way for guest workers to seek citizenship. The new Act gives automatic citizenship to children born to foreign residents. This shows that there is a strong strain of opinion in states like Germany, with a high number of guest workers that does consider it a problem to have millions of non-citizens residing on a long-term basis in the state. Moreover, Joppke observes that the vast majority of people do not choose to migrate and rely upon their own state to protect their rights. However, human rights are abused by states in many parts of the globe and a stable post-national order will need to address the institutions of governance that guarantee rights globally. This will require a more critical engagement with the powers of the state, if human rights are not to remain secondary to sovereignty.

The question of human rights cannot then be detached from the wider political question of governance. The central paradox that is shaping world politics in late modernity is 'a deterritorialized expansion of rights despite the territorialized closure of politics'.

The point is, however, that human rights rest upon shaky foundations unless mechanisms can be found to move beyond state-centric definitions of politics. In her eagerness to proclaim the post-national order, Soysal in effect defends a highly abstract view of rights which distances these rights from the social and political structures that sustain them. A sustainable post-national mode of citizenship must in fact be more than an abstract defence of human rights, because governance requires participation and responsibilities as well as rights. In this sense, Soysal can identify the 'limits of citizenship' only because she defines the concept in a very narrow and passive way.

Citizenship beyond the State

Despite the importance of human rights doctrines, citizenship retains a salience when considering the problem of governance. This is for two main reasons. First, although globalisation has altered the context in which states govern, it is the state that remains the institution most able to concentrate economic, military and communicative power. The state therefore forms the primary context for the individual citizen. Rights and responsibilities are still exercised mainly at the level of the state. International actors such as MNCs and bodies like the World Bank and the IMF are not rootless actors but rely upon a frameworks of rules determined by states. Second, citizenship expresses a relationship between rights, responsibilities and participation which is crucial to any form of governance. The problem with human rights is that they are not tied to the idea of political community and lack effective mechanisms through which they can be fulfilled.

Moreover, not all analysts of international politics accept the arguments advanced by Soysal and Turner that universal rights are sustainable or even desirable. Recently Samuel Huntington offered a new perspective on a state-centred model of world order by arguing that the pursuit of universal standards of justice, in the form of human rights, is counter-productive. Huntington's neo-realism represents a second possible strategy to the question of how we understand the relationship between citizenship and globalisation that contrasts starkly with the human rights model. Huntington maintains that since the world is divided into distinct civilizations, which are mutually and inevitably suspicious of one another, it would be impossible to ground global governance on the foundation of universal human rights. Instead, 'the security of the world requires acceptance of global multiculturalism'. The chief protectors of these civilizations are states. Therefore, attempts to undermine sovereignty through the promotion of human rights are likely to lead only to further conflict. Huntington contends that the communications technology of the global age has accentuated rather than diminished the differences between cultures.

Huntington is motivated by a fear of the rise of aggressive alternatives to liberalism in the form of fundamentalism, and in particular militant Islam. What Huntington fails to fuly acknowege, however, is the far more dangersous impact of western fundamentalism in the form of neo-liberalism. It is an obsession with liberalization in world trade that has fuelled radical alternatives to liberalism in the form of religious or ethnic fundamentalism. Of course, Huntington is right to argue that human rights cannot simply be imposed upon states suspicious of Western calls for democratic reform.

Huntington fails to see that it is the state that is the problem, not diverse cultures. This is illustrated by the fact that many of the conflicts in world politics since 1945 have been between states who Huntington says share the same culture; for example the Korean war or the two Gulf wars of the 1980s and 1990s. The reality is that conflict is inherent in the states system. This is built upon mutual suspicion between states, even where states may share a common culture or ethnic origin. Huntington also ignores how advocates of human rights have attempted to build upon universal rights, even in states which have very different cultures.

In 1999, for example, a US-led NATO intervened militarily to stop human rights abuses by Serbia against the people of Kosovo, who are predominately Muslim. Again, it is difficult to understand such actions within the logic of Huntingtn's clash of civilizations thesis. The central problem with Huntington's theory is that it is culturally deterministic. A world of multiple cultures is of course both inevitable and desirable, but if these differences are to be reconciled peacefully it is the nature of political and economic links through which states interact that are crucial. This is also true of relationships within the state between different cultural groups. Given Huntington's rejection of multicultural institutions as a way forward for liberal states, it is difficult to see how, for example, the 20 million or so Muslims who reside in Western states can be considered as equal citizens. In this regard, Huntington underestimates the culpability of liberal states in their hypocritical advocacy of human rights while at the same time promoting the further deregulation of world trade which undermines basic rights. The West has also given considerable support to authoritarian regimes, such as Saddam Hussein's Iraq during the 1980s. Such hypocrisy, and the subsequent inequalities that derive from such actions, will only drive already alienated minorities towards fundamentalist reactions against liberal values. The self-contradiction of liberal ideology is total. If all humans have equal rights, we cannot maintain the kind of inegalitarian system that the capitalist world economy has always been and always will be.

A third and more potentially fruitful alternative to Soyal's passive view of citizenship and Huntington's rejection of universal human rights theories does exist. This approach argues that the roots of citizenship lie within individual communities, and rights and responsibilities will be expressed largely within this local context. However, globalisation demands that the roots of citizenship grow outwards to encompass obligations to other communities and the exercise rights within a variety of contexts. Lister has advanced an inclusive notion of citizenship, which attempts to live up to liberal aspirations to equality of all persons. He insists that it must necessarily be both internationalist and multi-layered. Citizenship is best thought of, suggests Lister, in terms of a 'spectrum that extends from the local through to the global'. This is what Heater has called multiple citizenship. A conception of multiple citizenship underscores the need to separate citizenship from limiting cultural identities such as nationality. The flexibility of mind required by a multi-textured view of citizenship also makes multiple citizenship incompatible with a citizenship based upon group identity such as advocated by Kymlicka and Young. Heater argues that 'it is necessary to accept as perfectly feasible the notion that an individual can have multiple civic identities and feel multiple loyalties'.

This third approach to citizenship is central to theories of cosmopolitan democracy advanced by such writers as David Held.

Cosmopolitan democracy seeks to theories a citizenship that is global in its orientation and involves not just the protection of rights but also the extension of responsibilities beyond the state and the development of global institutions of governance. It is only by extending the responsibilities that diverse cultures have to respect each other's rights, together with the construction of more participatory institutions of global governance, that rights will be sustainable. This is because human governance is concerned with the problem of order and the distribution of material and cultural resources. As threats to social order increasingly occur at the level beyond the state, new political institutions are therefore required to meet these challenges. Similarly, globalisation has intensified levels of inequality across the globe and made the inequity in the distribution of resources more apparent. Held observes that the key challenge in political theory today is how institutions and concepts previously associated with the state can be adapted to the management of such global problems.

Rights remain central to any constructionist model of cosmopolitan democracy. Rights are the best mechanisms we have for signifying human dignity and autonomy. The problem, however, with the liberal tradition is that the rights it has defended have been highly abstract and disembodied. Given that in practice liberals have also embraced the state as the basic unit of politics, rights have been disconnected from an interdependent view of human relations and have tended to be enjoyed only by privileged individuals within privileged states.

However, processes of globalisation are beginning to change our perception of the nature of rights. First, the new security dilemmas associated with across-border threats such as nuclear annihilation or ecological disaster are making states more sensitive to the rights of others. Injustices and rights violations within states can no longer be so easily contained, and state sovereignty is undoubtedly being challenged by the extension of arguments for human rights and by a more vigorous UN. The UN Charter makes no mention of humanitarian intervention and yet the UN is increasingly intervening in the internal affairs of states to protect basic human rights. Although UN operations in Iraq, Rwanda, Somalia and Bosnia in the 1990s have had mixed results, the important principle of intervention on humanitarian grounds is being established. In

1994 the International War Crimes tribunal was set up by the UN to investigate and prosecute perpetrators of crimes against humanity carried out in the war in Bosnia that followed the break-up of Yugoslavia. This body followed a precedent established after the Second World War at the Nuremberg trials, where Nazis responsible for atrocious acts of genocide found that a defence based upon following the orders of one's government was not acceptable.

Regional bodies that are attempting to manage the problems associated with globalisation, such as the European Union (EU) are also extending citizenship rights beyond the boundaries of individual states. In fact the EU is unique amongst regional economic bodies because unlike, say, the North American free trade agreement or association of Southeast Asian nations, it has looked to create political and not just economic institutions of cooperation. In the 1990s in particular the EU has made significant strides towards political union. At the centre of the project has been the creation of European Union citizenship, established formally through the Maastricht Treaty of 1992. This innovative development extended civil, and some political rights to all individuals who were members of EU countries. Citizens of member states can also vote to send representatives to the European Parliament, a body that has seen its powers of scrutiny and policy-making grow in the 1990s.

The second way that globalisation is challenging an abstract view of rights is by enhancing awareness of threats to the eco-structure and therefore humanity's vulnerability to ecological damage, degradation and disaster. This is why Turner's argument that an ontology for rights at the global level could be provided by the acceptance of human frailty is so useful. This idea captures the relational nature of citizenship in a way that the atomistic logic of liberals such Hobbes and Locke fails to grasp. A relational view of rights demands not only that we find ways to extend the benefits of rights to all peoples, regardless of national boundaries. Global citizenship must involve responsibilities as well as rights. The rapid growth of ecological political thought in recent years has helped sensitizes us to this issue in relation to the conservation of natural resources and a shift towards sustainable development which does tackle such phenomena as global warming or acid rain. An ecological dimension to citizenship involves extending the ethic of care, central to many feminist accounts of citizenship.

First, the ecological citizen is increasingly 'aware of his or her organic process of birth and growth out of the earth as a living organism'. Such a conception of citizenship challenges the male-dominated, disembodied perspective on citizenship which has been central to liberalism and which has encouraged an atomistic approach to the question of rights and responsibilities.

Second, ecological citizenship means extending our understanding of citizenship beyond material concerns with welfare rights and rights to property and market exchange. A consideration of ecological citizenship helps us to see the conceptual links between intimate citizenship and global problems. By taking care to be responsible in our own relationships, consumer patterns, and in the way we treat our environment generally, individuals can begin to make the shift away from purely quantitative measures of human success towards deeper and more qualitative assessments – such as the quality of the air we breathe, natural beauty and the enjoyment of freshly produced food. Understood in this way, citizenship makes an important challenge to the semiotic dominance of market-oriented language that has stressed narrow economic criteria as the primary measurement of human achievements.

Third, the idea of limitless progress associated with liberalism, scientific innovation and economic growth is clearly being challenged by globalisation, which is revealing the limits of modernity. Ecological citizenship requires that we treat issues of conservation as at least as important as issues of progress in science and economics. Thus the responsibilities we have as citizens extend not only to those with whom we currently share our community or planet, they also extend towards other species, the environment, and future generations of citizens. Citizenship needs to be underpinned by ecocentric as opposed to anthropocentric values.

Rethinking citizenship in response to worries about the environment is a good example of how global risks are demanding that we detach citizenship from its association with limiting concepts such as the nation-state or the public-private divide. As implied by the idea of intimate citizenship, ecological citizenship will also involve taking the notions of rights and responsibilities more seriously in non-conventional settings, such as in the family, in the supermarket and in the context of the workplace. Ecological citizenship represents a deeper conception of citizenship than that offered by classical liberalism. Many of the responsibilities associated with this form of post-liberal citizenships will be voluntary obligations rather than enforceable duties. The current world order is structured firmly around the interests of states, and international law is still concerned with the activities of states rather than individuals. An important step towards a more global citizenship must therefore be a greater willingness for states to exercise global obligations and build stronger links with other countries. Western states in particular must recognize the ways in which the world's political and economic systems are organized in ways that favour their interests over those of the rest of the globe. Appalling levels of poverty, debt and political instability in Africa, for example, are largely the legacy of the slave trade, colonialism and the unethical practices of Western companies.

There are many ways in which states can recognize their obligations. Western states could write off the debts that developing countries owe to them. As of 1999, for every £1 given by rich countries in the form of aid, poor countries return £4 in debt repayments. Many of these debts are the result of the legacy of imperialism and the low prices that the raw materials – the production of which many developing countries rely upon fetch on the world markets. These prices themselves reflect the inequality of power between buyer and seller. Agriculture in the developing world is also jeopardized by such policies as the Common Agricultural Policy (CAP) in Europe, which pays huge subsidies to farmers and thus creates unfair competition to Third World farmers. By writing off debt, aid to developing countries would become meaningful and could help to encourage sustainable development. By the end of 1999, there were some positive signs in this regard; President Clinton announced his intention to cut debts to zero provid more money was directed towards health and education programmes by Third World governments. Debt cancellation must also be accompanied by much more generous aid provision, which not only will help to stimulate economic activity in developing countries, but will also help to maintain political stability.

Dauenhauer has rightly argued that rich states can also help development in poorer countries by avoiding adding to the 'brain drain' whereby skilled workers are poached by Western states. States must be more open and consistent in immigration policy and should shift towards criteria based upon the needs of immigrants rather than purely assessing applicants in terms of their financial viability. The record of liberal states here, however, is still poor in most cases. A good example of cynical immigration policies occurred when the British government, following the ending of Hong Kong's status as a British colony, chose to bestow citizenship only upon a few thousand of the most skilled and wealthy members of Hong Kong in the 1990 Nationality Act. Instead of seeking only to import more expertise into wealthy countries through selective immigration policy, technologically advanced states should instead be more ready to share their innovations with others. This is one of the few areas of world trade that requires further liberalization. Currently, the technology used by many MNCs is shrouded in secrecy and host states are prevented from sharing in such expertise, even though their citizens are employed by MNCs. Poorer countries cannot hope to compete in an increasingly technological and knowledge-driven market if they are denied access to inventions by strict copyright and patenting laws.

States can exercise global citizenship by respecting the rights of other peoples, honouring existing responsibilities and looking to extend obligations that build trust between diverse communities. Unless rights and responsibilities of global citizenship are linked to the democratization of decision-making bodies that govern world affairs, however, their existence will remain precarious. Noam Chomsky gives many examples of how human rights have been used by the West as a propaganda tool against perceived opponents of liberalism while a blind eye has been turned to abuses in countries that are seen as important political lackeys or economic partners. Thus the USA, for instance, has been prepared to commit large crimes in response to Iraq's invasion of Kuwait in 1990s, but has failed to put sufficient pressure on Israel to abide by several UN declarations to withdraw from the West Bank and other territories that Israel holds illegally. As long as institutions of global governance such as the UN, the World Bank and the IMF are dominated by a small group of states, it is unlikely that the reciprocal trust that must underpin the rights and responsibilities of citizenship can extend to meet the challenges of globalisation. Threats that conservatives like Huntington identify to world order, and particular all forms of fundamentalism, are largely an understandable reaction by the non-

Western world to the exclusionary practices, hypocrisy double standards and the hostility of Western policies in the international arena, rather than the result of fixed and conflicting cultures as Huntington suggests. Yet, democracy and human rights are powerful and emancipatory ideas, and authoritarian governments have found it hard to suppress popular demonstrations in favour of these principles in countries like East Timor, China and Iran. In each of these three examples, there have been mass demonstrations during the 1980s and 1990s in favour of democratic reform and the protection of basic rights.

In seeking to build systems of global governance, however, it would be unwise to aim at the creation of a world state. Arendt has rightly remarked, that 'the establishment of one sovereign world state would be the end of all citizenship'. Advocates of cosmopolitan democracy appear to recognize the problem that the states system arises for global governance and the security of rights. Merely recreating the state form at a higher level of organization would not tackle the problem that violence, concentrated primarily in the state, raises for democratic citizenship.

Crucially, multiple citizenship does not entail the destruction of separate political communities but rather seeks to transform the nature of the relationship between these communities. Held uses the term 'overlapping networks of power' in contrast to the concentration of power in the state that has set the limits of citizenship in modernity. According to the principles of cosmopolitan citizenship, the individual will increasingly become used to exercising rights and responsibilities in a number of contexts and political communities. This suggests the need to transcend the concept of sovereignty, which a deep sense of citiznehsip must be opposed to, rather than seek to divide sovereignty as Held suggests. Hoffman has shown how Held's position is in fact inconsistent. Hoffman notes that while Held's theory has an underlying post-statist logic, Held is unwilling to detach sovereignty from the state. He insists that the modern state is not defunct but rather that "its idea" must be adapted to "stretch across borders". The danger of reforming, but retaining the concept of the state can be illustrated by the EU's attempt to construct political union through the extension of citizenship to the supranational level. The ambiguity of the EU project in general, and its associated form of citizenship in particular, symbolizes the wider tensions that are increasingly shaping global politics.

The EU appears to represent a unique attempt in modernity to extend the rights of citizenship beyond the state. This is a step in the right direction towards a multiple citizenship model suggested by cosmopolitan democracy. Through the growing powers of the European Parliament in particular, European citizenship is being linked to new forms of political participation that are encouraging closer cooperation between political parties, pressure groups and social movement across national boundaries. However, such positive developments must be balanced by an acknowledgement that for many policy makers in the EU, the citizenship project of the Union retains a distinctly statist and exclusive character. This can be demonstrated by the EU's approach to questions of third country nationals.

Unfortunately, the creation of EU citizenship at Maastricht failed to take an excellent opportunity to sever the link between nationality and citizenship. According to EU law, member states can still assert their right to determine citizenship of their communities and, in turn, EU citizenship is limited to those individuals who are legitimate citizens of member states.

It is this exclusive aspect of the EU that helps to highlight the weakness in the arguments of Soysal, who sees in the EU 'post-national membership in its most elaborate legal form and that illustrates the contradictions inherent in the idea of divided sovereignty as advanced by Held. It can be argued that far from being a post-national organisation, the EU, is in fact attempting to encourage an exclusive and mythical European identity that sets cultural as well as legal limits on the expansion of citizenship. The Amsterdam Treaty of 1997 has further highlighted the negative implications of an EU superstate for asylum seekers and immigrants, by firming up common border controls. The Maastricht Treaty asserted the EU's support for human rights. However, at Amsterdam, it was agreed that the European Court of Justice would have no jurisdiction in the area of 'law and order and safeguarding of internal security', the 1997 treaty asserted that EU citizenship was to complement and not supersede national citizenship.

The future of citizenship turns up the ways in which the problems raised by innovative but contradictory institutions of governance such was the EU are tackled. Richard Falk is surely right to state that in considering the future of citizenship, we cannot be overly constrained by what appears to be 'realistic' in the short term: 'global citizenship of a positive variety implies a utopian confidence in the human capacity to exceed realistic horizons, but it is also rooted in the highly pragmatic conviction that what is currently taken to be realistic is not sustainable'. Falk puts his finger on the challenges globalisation raises for citizenship. Advocates of global citizenship are not abstract utopians. They seek to build upon actual social changes that are making a modernist approach to citizenship untenable.

We should not give way to false optimism, however. Globalisation is a double-edged weapon. Globalisation without doubt presents us with opportunities to extend the egalitarian thrust of liberal citizenship to its logical end, but globalisation also brings with it coniserable dangers:- four possible scenarios for the future, ranging from an inclusive world citizenship, a disintegrative scenario of trade wars and ethnic violence, a globe dominated by a large political bloc involving the West and former Communist states, and the development of an exclusive Western regional fortress.

We have advanced an argument that a conception of citizenship in a global age must be postmodern in character. In terms of guaranteeing rights and ensuring the fulfillment of the responsibilities that any form of stable governance requires, it is no longer possible to retain the link between citizenship and the closed and exclusive form of political community that is the state, whether that state be national or regional in character.

Before the formation of modernity, citizenship was invariably an exclusive status. In some cases, particularly in the ancient Athenian polis, citizenship was undoubtedly deep, in the sense that citizens felt a strong commitment to common institutions of government and the obligations that citizens were expected to perform were extensive. Citizens themselves were entrusted to be rulers, as well as the ruled, and the polis's democratic and highly participatory system of governance reflected this. But in the pre-modern world the extent of citizenship was never broad in its scope, as it did not include large sections of the population. Women especially were excluded from citizenship. In pre-modern society, the division between citizen and non-citizen signified inequalities that were taken to be natural and immutable.

The development of liberalism from the seventeenth century onwards marked a profound shift in the meaning of citizenship. Thinkers such as Hobbes and Locke introduced the notion of equality into debates concerning the relationship between the individual and state. For Locke and Paine, all individuals have indivisible rights to life, liberty and property. It is the main task of the political community to guarantee and protect these freedoms.

The conception of equality defended by liberals has, of course, been abstract in character. But by identifying the inherent equality of worth that all humans share, liberals did create the conceptual space for radicals to exploit. Socialism is also a post-liberal theory precisely because socialism challenges liberal society to make its promises of equality, security and justice real for everyone. A post-liberal approach to citizenship entails the identification of the political, economic and social barriers that prevent the rights and responsibilities of citizenship from being fairly distributed. Thus, socialists in the twentieth century have struggled to extend the franchise and to make markets more accountable to government. Post-liberal then, take the context of citizenship more seriously than do liberals. They recognize that the structures of decision-making, economic production, and social institutions, such as the family, all play a significant part in determining the content, extent and depth of citizenship. The limits of citizenship in its liberal form can be explained, above all, by liberalism's neglect of this social context of rights and responsibilities. Why do liberals overlook the barriers to citizenship?

It has been sufficiently recognized how a liberal defence of rights rests upon a set of assumptions that privileges the self-interest of the rational, egotistical individual over the needs of political community. Because liberals assume that we are autonomous actors, even before the formation of the state, arguments for liberal rights, crucial though they are, must be rooted in a network of responsibilities between individuals and their communities. Like socialism, contemporary theories of republicanism and communitarianism are post-liberal because they stress the relational and non-hierarchical character of citizenship. Post-liberals, then, stress autonomy rather than liberty as a defining characteristic rather than merely a licence to pursue one's interests without regard to the requirements of civic duty. A post-liberal approach to citizenship demands that rights and responsibilities be treated as mutually supportive, rather than opposed as many liberals theories have implied.

Our individual rights are only meaningful when they are supported by a sense of obligation amongst others both to recognize our rights and to help us to build and sustain the social institutions that make rights possible. Postmodern societies are highly diverse and individualistic, and ways need to be found to create common interests and to develop social obligations. There must be a degree of consensus over the values that underpin citizenship, if modern societies are not fragmented further and thereby become increasingly hard to govern effectively. The object of increasing duties, such as the responsibility to vote or to perform community service is to create the conditions whereby legal sanctions might gradually be transformed into a sense of voluntary obligation between diverse individuals. By enhancing responsibilities, we also acknowledge citizenship as an active and not a passive status. Participation by all citizens, to the best of their ability, is essential if the content of citizenship is to be agreed democratically. By linking rights and responsibilities to an ethic of participation, citizenship can be reconceptualised as a holistic idea, as opposed to the dualistic conception of citizenship found in liberalism's defence of abstract rights.

Feminist and ecological critiques have highlighted how other aspects of liberalism's defence of abstract individualism have had negative implications for the practice of citizenship. Feminist accounts of citizenship have shown how liberal citizenship is a 'disembodied' notion. In liberalism, citizenship has tended to be concerned with contractual relationships, market exchanges and the independence of the individual. Thus, the relationships between individuals are understood in atomistic terms. Feminists in contrast, insist that the rights and responsibilities we have as citizens have to be linked to a recognition of the importance of the body. Lister argued that too often in traditional political theory the body, emotion and sexuality are seen as intrinsically female traits that hinder the application of reason, which must, liberals argue, lie at the heart of citizenship. Only once we realize that all individuals, regardless of their gender, have physical and emotional needs, we are likely to conceive of citizenship in terms of the values of interdependence and care. Moreover, these values, argue ecologists, must be extended beyond direct human need. In particular, humans must acknowledge their obligations to the environment, to other species, and to future generations. A postmodern approach to citizenships draws upon such post-liberal theories as socialism, feminism and ecologism.

A Postmodern Citizenship

In modernity the nature of citizenship has been determined by a paradox. The identification of citizenship with the nation-state has limited the universality and egalitarian ideals of liberalism. The French Revolution was the key event that fused the cultural idea of nationality with the political status of citizen. The pressures of war and revolutionary upheaval led to the abandonment of the more inclusive elements of the French Revolution, expressed in the defence of universal rights. Consequently, citizenship in the nineteenth and twentieth centuries has been closely associated with nation-building and military duty. Not only did the firming up of state boundaries mean a greater division between citizens and strangers, it also had major implications for the extent of citizenship within state boundaries. Writers such as Balibar and Yuvai-Davis have shown how the nation-state is defined in gendered and racial terms. Women, for example, are portrayed as the 'mothers of the nation' who must be protected and kept 'pure' by their male defenders. The widespread use of rape as a military tool, particularly in ethnic wars of the 1980s and 1990s in such countries as Yugoslavia, is an example of how women are perceived as symbols and possessions of the nation, rather than as full citizens equal to men. As well as being gendered, the state is also racialised. Most republican of states, such as, contemporary France, show how an apparent neutrality towards citizenship in fact masks a deep-seated racism and pathology towards immigrants.

The weakness of many traditional post-liberal and more contemporary postmodern theories are that they fail to identify the problem that the existence of the state creates for a universal citizenship. While reforms of the state, to enhance the democratic and inclusive nature of its institutions, are a necessary move, they are not a sufficient step towards fulfilling citizenship's potential. As long as we live in a world divided by territorial states, which are invariably defined in ethnic and gendered terms, citizenship's egalitarian logic will remain unfulfilled.

It is important to remember that the main function of citizenship is to govern society according to the principles of respect for others' rights and an obligation to play a part in the maintenance of common institutions that sustain these rights. Violence, concentrated above all by the states, negates these principles of citizenship. A consideration of intimate citizenship, where rights and obligations create consensual rather than oppressive relationship within the private sphere, must also be extended to a consideration of the wider problem of state violence. A recognition of the problem of violence for all human relationship means that a postmodern citizenship problematises both the state and the public-private divide. We cannot seek consensual relations in one sphere and rely upon force in the other. Postmodern citizenship is deep because it applies the values of rights and responsibilities to all human relationship, whether they be public or private in character.

In this context, Heater's notion of multiple citizenship seems to be the most appropriate form for citizenship, given both the plurality of modern society and the recent growth in the number and type of social and political institutions in which citizenship can be exercised. The flexibility of mind required to perform citizenship in a variety of contexts underlines the dangers of associating citizenship with only one narrow aspect of identity, such as nationality, ethnicity or group membership. Critics have argued against advocates of differentiated citizenship, where this means that we are asked to privilege one aspect of our identity over equally valued identities. The attractiveness of citizenship is that it does not force us to make a choice about what constitutes our essential nature. Instead it encourages us to conduct relationships with other citizens which are deliberative and open-ended. A citizenship based upon groups would most likely increase mutual suspicion and would endanger the rights of 'deviant individuals' within groups. Postmodern citizenship must build upon and not reject liberals' defence of individual rights. Only through individual rights can real diversity, based upon individual choice and not pre-determined cultural identities, be maintained.

The best form of political community, as Habermas has argued, is one where 'constitutional patriotism' rather than cultural ties, generates a sense of loyalty and obligation. This does mean that diverse cultures or even nationality disappear. For the foreseeable future, citizenship will still be exercised primarily at a local level. but what postmodern citizenship demands is that the boundaries between political communities are not perpetually closed, either materially or culturally, and that many of the rights and responsibilities of citizenship extend beyond administrative boundaries. Recent processes of social change, associated primarily with globalisation, appear to be creating the opportunity for the development of postmodern citizenship. Human rights, for example are undoubtedly much more pervasive in their influence than ever before. In the twenty-first century, abuses of individuals' basic rights by their own states are becoming increasingly difficult to defend. The international community has begun to take human rights abuses more seriously, witnessed by a growing number of humanitarian interventions in places like Iraq and Kosovo. We are also witnessing the embryonic growth of institutions of global governance, such as the UN, as well as a greater role for regional bodies like the EU that have at least the potential to move beyond statist models of citizenship.

The key aspect of globalisation which makes a postmodern citizenship more likely in the future is the threat posed by planetary risks. According to liberals like Hobbes, the security and social order upon which any stable conception of citizenship must rest is best guaranteed by the state. Global risk challenges this relationship between citizenship and the state by undermining the state's capacity to provide security to its citizens. Theorists of cosmopolitan democracy like Held assert that institutions of governance, as well as right and responsibilities, must extend beyond the state if the very basis of human society is not to be destroyed by ecological disaster or by nuclear calamity.

Shaw argues that globalisation has helped to creat a post-military society. Pre-modern and modern forms of citizenship have been associated closely with military duty. The coming of a post-military society challenges this. By post-militarism, Saw is not claiming that we have seen the end of armed conflict. But in the shadow of nuclear annihilation, total wars in the style of the First or Second World Wars are much less likely. Moreover, the mass conscription armies of the twentieth century, which are linked historically to the creation of the welfare state and therefore the extension of citizenship, are no longer necessary. Professional, high-tech armies now conduct warfare. This suggests that the long established link between military duty, masculinity and citizenship is being weakened. Opportunities for more care-oriented approaches to citizenship are created as the connection between violence and citizenship is increasingly problematised.

Even more importantly, globalisation has highlighted the problem material inequalities pose for the practice of citizenship. Global inequalities constantly threaten the rights of those living in the developing world. Furthermore, the communications revolution and the development of planetary risk have spread both the dangers and the awareness of these dangers to the Western world. Within the context of liberal society, we have to make the case for a new approach to social rights that seeks to strike a better balance between the imperatives of the market and the requirements of citizenship. The policy most likely to ensure that rights and responsibilities are not undermined by the inherent inequalities and exploitative tendencies of capitalism is a guaranteed citizens income. This is a matter of both justice and self-interest. In the context of globalisation, no community's citizenship can be assured if huge inequalities are allowed to continue. Migration, religious fundamentalism, terrorism, international crime, regional conflicts and environmental damage are all fuelled by inequalities and the effects of these new security risks will be increasingly felt by both the developed and developing worlds. Institutions of global governance must therefore abandon the divisive neo-liberal approach to economic management that currently informs such bodies as the World Bank and the IMF. Rich states must recognize that the world economic system is biased in their favour and many of their achievements have come at the expense of Third World countries. States and regional bodies like the EU must therefore be more willing to honour their responsibilities to developing countries and to offer more extensive aid to help develop the democratic institutions across the globe that are essential to the practice of citizenship everywhere.

Our approach to citizenship in this book has been 'critical postmodern' because it does not seek to reject liberalism, but rather to make its promises real. We also reject those postmodern discourses that are critical of the strengths of liberalism, in particular, equality, individual rights, perfectionism and universal citizenship. Citizenship does have a future in an increasingly global and postmodern age because its constituent parts – rights, responsibilities and political participation – are essential to human governance. We must recognize, however, that it is only by breaking the links modernity has forged between citizenship and exclusive notions such as the state and the market that citizenship's emancipatory potential can be realized, enriched and fulfilled.

Conclusion

Citizenship is a complex with various meanings. Its past political success does not imply that its currency has rested on clarity or unity of perception on the part of electorate, political leaders, or intellectuals. Various meanings reflect different usages. First, citizenship is a moral judgement. To be called a good or real citizen is a particular positive judgment about the morality of one's behavior. It: implies that the person is concerned with the collective interest and its well being. Second, it is a concrete, empirical, and descriptive term. In this sense, citizenship refers to a particular set of obligations and rights vested in eligible persons in a specific nation-state. Third, citizenship can be thought of as an analytic term. In this sense., citizenship encompasses the protection a state offers to its core members, the opportunities a state creates for its core members for political participation, or a combination of both these elements.

In any case, Aristotle's formulation supplies a symbolic and appropriate point of departure for our analysis. His views were linked to population size since he asserts the crucial importance of small size. Therefore, his perspective requires a fundamental explication to apply to contemporary mass society. But there is a powerful element of continuity between his formulation and that of T H. Marshall, one of the few contemporary sociologists who has written about citizenship.

Aristotle insists, "a citizen is one who permanently shares in the administration of justice and the holding of office". We shall make use of his definition of a democratic citizen and recognize that elements of citizenship are to be found in all nation-states, even in the most repressive totalitarian state. However, there is a crucial threshold separating democratic and non-democratic citizenship, even in the case of a benign non-democratic state. 'The difference, of course, is embodied in Aristotle's use of the term, permanent, which in sociological usage becomes an "ideal" term of reference.

Thus, in essence, in contemporary language a democratic citizen is a person who jointly, simultaneously, or in sequence, rules and is ruled. Aristotle himself uses timeless language: "citizens, in the common sense of that term, are all who share in the civic life of ruling and being ruled in turn". Only to be permanently ruled is to deny the person's citizenship, and to rule permanently is likewise destructive of citizenship. This means that citizenship is not reduced to residence or confined to rights or private law but involves constitutional rights and obligations under the system of public law.

However, this classical and political perspective on the purpose and context of citizenship can tend to become bypassed and obscured in the modern welfare state. Both for politicians and analysts of social policy and the welfare state, such things as education, leisure, and civility tend to be seen as cultural, and thereby peripheral aspects of welfare. As such they have been arguably less funded and less studied than other more material aspects, such as health-care, income-maintenance, and housing. Welfare states as major providers of cultural and material welfare, both intentionally and latently, are oriented to the needs of the advanced industrial and capitalist economy for the production and reproduction of variously skilled labor forces. In terms of classical ideals modern states tend to subject the notion of politics and political community to the rule of the problems of economics and economic association. They also tend to subject the notion of civility, and the rights and responsibilities associated with living a civilized life to the rule of achieving private goods and welfares, whether by public provision or the regulation of private provision. Perhaps these subjections of politics to economically based practices and values are unavoidable in anything other than the slave-economy of the classical polis.

Tendencies towards the economization of politics, in effect towards the depoliticization of the political community, have certainly appeared to be unavoidable in the long marches of capitalism and industrialism towards mass employment and labor-intensive economies. But the second perspective recognizes that the long marches are not over, that socio-economic change in modem social formations is endemic and incessant, and that this carries implications for both the theory and the political practices of citizenship. Ironically, contemporary economic changes may be seen as reversing the economization and de-politicization of politics and as providing opportunities for forms of political renewal and development in modern societies.

In the late twentieth century the continuing advances in the mechanical-slave economy of computerized and robotic economic production, and also in information and communications technologies, are beginning to assume the proportions of a new industrial revolution. According to some commentators such as Gorz and Toffler, this will usher in post-industrial forms of society and civilization in which, as in the classical polis, education and leisure, or at least "free-time," time free from employment, will be of considerably greater importance than at present. Social change is again determining the agenda for social theory in an analogous fashion to the way that the nineteenth century development of industrial capitalism provoked the development of classical social theory in the work of Marx, Weber, and Durkheim. Social change suggests that social formations based to important degrees around "producing," "marketing," and "consuming" information, education and leisure are in the offing. It is necessary then for social theory to begin to consider what implications such developments might have for its basic tools of trade. Such important descriptive-explanatory categories as "capitalism," "property," "social class," and "the state," together with related categories such as "political community" "civilization," and "welfare," not to mention "citizenship" - which have an additional explicitly normative dimension to them - are all prime candidates for a searching review and rethinking.

Marshall was optimistic about the progressive reduction of class inequality to be expected from the combined impacts of economic growth, of the development of social citizenship principles, and of the presumed redistributive characteristics of the welfare state. But history requires us not only to be sceptical about the state's power to change the reproduction of class inequalities in industrial -capitalist societies, but also to be aware of the diversity of inequalities in such societies and to be sensitive to the possible restructuring of inequalities in the transition to post-industrial societies. The post-war British class structure, in particular, has exhibited a notorious defensive traditionalism at all levels. It has successfully resisted differing pressures to change, whether emanating from techno-economic forces or from state policy. It may well be that now in a Britain in the painful throes of economic recession, economic decline, and economic reorganization, a restructuring of classes and other inequalities is underway. But the historic post-war class structure has been as fascinating by sociologists as it has been wondered at and gaped at by foreign tourists - captured by its picturesque tribalism. This graveyard of reformist optimism is well-trodden ground and readers will need no further rehearsal or reminder of its existence and pertinence. In any case the problematic of citizenship, with its presumptive formal egalitarianism, requires the study of other social divisions, categories, and forms of discrimination in modern societies besides those of class. Inequalities of gender, race, age, and employment status undoubtedly have various different, cross-cutting, and more or less important connections with the capitalist-industrial economic order. But their connections with social classes and with the system they form is less direct and they are certainly not readily reducible to or translatable into social class terms.

Against all of Marshall's hopes, the British version of the formally democratic state and the substantively egalitarian welfare state has, been complicit in the reproduction of old inequalities and the production of new ones in the post-war period. Marshall in hindsight, displays an optimistic complacency about class and its politics, and this helps in allowing him to appear to be generally relatively indifferent to citizenship as a primarily political status and political phenomenon. Perspective on citizenship concerned with its moral and ontological aspects of autonomy, reciprocity and public interest, directed in part against Marshall's complacency firstly about the fact that these aspects are necessary requirements of any notion of citizenship, and secondly about the fact that not only class inequality and many other social inequalities but also the operations of the democratic welfare state can compromise them.

Perhaps the most explicit example both of a denial of full citizenship not directly connected with class, and also of the British state's complicity in this, is in the area of immigration and race relations. But to update and criticize Marshall's analysis in respect of the position of blacks, or of women, the elderly, the unemployed, not to mention the working class in post-war Britain, would require major reviews of an equivalent set of social histories and sociological surveys.

The Revolt Against Politics

Sholars like Skinner have recently raised the question of whether the West's cherished and historic concept of the individual can much longer be retained. The same question can be asked of the concept of the citizen, our answer to both questions is an affirmative one, but only if the necessary mediating contexts, the social and moral walls of each, are maintained or, where necessary, created. We are inclined to think that a great deal of the revolt against politics we are now witnessing, not only in Watergate-ridden America but in each of the other Western and non-Western countries as well, rises from social needs of individuality and citizenship alike which have too long been ignored by a classical theory of democracy that finds its substance in the individual citizen and in internal political processes.

Two decades ago when Bernard Berelson, Paul Lazarsfeld, and William McPhee concluded their notable study of voting, they did so with some valuable reflections on the discordant relation they had found between this classical theory of democracy and the actual behavior of citizens in a democracy. Whereas in this theory the individual citizen is presumed to be, by nature, interested in politics, knowledgeable in some degree, and eager to participate, the facts tended to show otherwise. The typical citizen manifests almost none of these qualities. Looking at the individual alone, the authors could find little evident impulse to go out of his way to vote, much less become actively participant, practically no real knowledge of the issues presented in any election and quite dismally, no great interest in politics, at least as measured by the amount of time given. Berelson and his colleagues are not alone in their assessment. That remarkable Harvard economist, Joseph Schumpeter, with somewhat different point, was also struck by the yawning chasm between theoretical demand and actual response of the democratic citizen. As Schumpeter wrote in his *Capitalism, Socialism and Democracy:*

> He [the citizen] is a member of an unworkable committee, the committee of the whole nation, and this is why he expends less disciplined effort on mastering a political problem than he expends in a game of bridge

Classical theory of democracy does, however, work reasonably well, far from perfectly, but better than we would expect if we confined our attention to the individual voter alone and his relation to the political scene. The reason for this pragmatic effectiveness of democracy lies, the authors observe, not in the individual, not even in the political system as such, but rather in the interrelations of political, social, economic, and other institutions:

> The survival of political democracy depends on other features-the intensity of conflict must be limited, the rate of change must be restrained, stability in the social and economic structure must be maintained, a pluralistic social organization must exist, and a basic concensus must bind together the contending parties.

Fundamental to the liberal political community, in sum, is a whole constellation of forces which are not of democracy's making, which indeed are not even political in the strict sense of that word. They are forces which are inseparable from the social and economic and cultural roles we occupy, and these in turn are inseparable from such associations as family, neighborhood, voluntary group, social class, religion, and so on. Just as Protestantism was, at bottom, conceived by Luther and Calvin for minds already formed in the Catholic tradition, so it has to be concluded, that the democracy was designed for individuals well formed in the pre-democratic contexts of family, parish, township, religion, and other forms of intermediate association. The kind of discontinuity between the social and the political that was premised by Rousseau and Bentham in the interests of individuality and political justice alike turns out to be, not only deeply illiberal but thoroughly naive so far as the social psychology of citizenship is concerned.

It is the restoration of some kind of balance between the political and the social that we need above just about anything else at the present time. The political will no more sustain itself than will the economic. The capitalist dynamic Max Weber could see already beginning to lessen in intensity in his day, with capitalism and modernity generally becoming more and more of an iron cage, has its fit parallel in politics and the political community. Apart from the motivations which are anchored in pre-capitalist strata, Joseph Schumpeter wrote that capitalism must in time become a spent force; its capital will not save it. Marx was right in his conclusions, the conservative Schumpeter declared, wrong only in the reasons he assigned.

A good deal of the argument Schumpeter used with respect to capitalism seems apposite to the contemporary political state in the West. Precisely as Schumpeter could see capitalism's walls crumbling under the impact of the very dynamism of capitalism itself, is it possible to see the walls of the political community today crumbling, or beginning to crumble, under the weight of the sheer power we have put in the democratic state, a power assessable in terms of the bureaucracy that has become democratic man's chief object of hostility. Schumpeter thought that the fatal weakness of capitalism lay in its inability to attract the allegiance of the very intellectuals capitalism had helped to create in modern Western history. Capitalism alienates its own intellectuals Schumpeter observed.

For a long period, from the Renaissance down to World War II and its immediate aftermath, the political sphere captured the allegiance of the modern intellectual class as only the church had in earlier centuries. Around the state was built a clerisy very much like that which attended the church in the Middle Ages: a clerisy composed of scholars, scientists, philosophers, and technologists, as well as of those kings, assemblies, bureaucracies, and electorates - who actually managed the national state. What capitalism could never accomplish - winning the allegiances of intellectuals -the political state assuredly did, and, as Lord Keynes observed, a very great deal of hard, practical political policy in the West has its origins in the works of "some academic scribbler of a few years back." To a striking degree, the modern intellectual has been the political intellectual, often as confident of the capacity of political power and membership therein to save man from temptations of the flesh and other sinful impulses as the medieval intellectual tended to be of the capacity of the church and the city of God.

The State Versus the Market

The idea of a space between the state and the market, somewhere in civil society where citizens can make democratic initiatives is occupied politically by the new social movements (NSMs). Now it may be possible to construct new political forms by 'making state policy more accountable to civil society and by democratically expanding and reordering non-state activities within civil society itself.' This conceptualisation depends upon the retention of the distinction between civil society and the state and the idea of an area outside the state/market division in which public spaces can be freed-up.

There seems to be a fundamental difficulty with this civil society due in large part to its essentialist conception of democracy and rights. Firstly, the state/market couplet leads us into an intellectual *cul de sac* where collectivism and individualism, authoritarianism and freedom etc come to be depicted as discreet alternatives within capitalist social formations. This analytic distinction between the state and the market has a limited descriptive use at the level of organisational principle, but turns out to be of less use when confronting underlying power relations which underscore both state and market mechanisms. At one level it can be argued that both are underscored by the structural divisions of class, gender and race which take different forms through state and market mechanisms both organising social power in different ways. The history of state intervention in the provision of welfare in Britain, however, shows not the clash of opposites, but the interweaving of different mechanisms which often work in a complementary fashion. In fact the historically complementary relationship between the state and the market as different organisational forms of power is shown in the way in which these apparently opposing principles have been unable to act as real counterbalancing tendencies upon the operation of each other. The market has not been a democratising force against the bureaucratic collectivism of state control, and neither has collective welfare provision overcome the known problem of inequality and marginalisation associated with the market. Admittedly, there may be openings for the left to rethink new forms of welfare provision in the interstacies of these mechanisms, but there is a danger of disappearing down a chasm into a notion of civil society which itself fails to acknowledge power at the base.

The state and the market are more usefully thought of as different organisational forms within the totality of social relations which institutionalise social power. This enables us to understand why Marshall's idea of welfare citizenship has foundered on the rocks of a fragmented collectivism. The hoped for integration effect of the welfare state found in both Fabianism and the more functionalist brands of marxism has rightly been criticised by feminist and anti-racist writers for ignoring both the patriarchal and racist structures of state welfare which separate and disunify 'universal' interests and for its eurocentric and nationalist understanding of citizenship

The idea of freeing-up a space somewhere between the state and the market operates mainly on the ideological terrain. Indeed, according to Melucci, the actors in this space - the NSMs - operate largely on symbolic grounds, challenging the codes of contemporary discourse. However, these NSMs often have class, gender or racial positions which fragment their apparent unity or have histories of their own which situate them in very specific power relations. A careful attention must be paid to whether the NSMs challenge not only the symbolic codes of contemporary discourse, but the underlying structures of power organised through both the state and the market. When they do, for example in the case of Black urban protests in Britain in the early 1980s, they find this public space suddenly swamped by the repressive structures of state power.

Civil Society Versus the State

Secondly, the civil society/state distinction also proves problematic. The whole notion of civil society as a separate sphere, beyond the state in which citizenship claims might emerge, overlooks a number of important issues. Again, whether this analytic distinction bears any relationship to the lived reality of social relations seems doubtful. Almost all contemporary political philosophers seem at pains to point to the extensive intervention and regulation of private life via the apparatuses of the state, and indeed, the vast spread of state agencies and apparatuses is one of the dominant characteristics of late capitalist societies. How far there is life, 'beyond the gaze of the state' in western capitalist societies is not at all clear. Where there is a formal absence of regulation and control expressed in law and formal social policy, there is often the informal regulation through the back door. An obvious example is the way in which welfare agencies are often used to 'police' the implementation of immigration policies, through the requirement of citizenship proof. Civil society in which communities exist is structured through the power relations which underly both the state and the market.

The way in which community is often seen as an undifferentiated collectivity has been pointed out by feminist writers in particular. Their arguments about the gendered nature of community show us that the spaces of civil society are themselves riven by power relations. The patriarchal assumptions behind such notions as 'informal caring networks', for example, have been roundly exposed.

Membership of the assumed community of informal caring networks may serve, not only to reinforce certain gender role expectations, but to disenfranchise those carers. Precisely because they are informal, caring networks bring with them no formal basis for democratic control and accountability. There is no community basis within such networks, for the assertion of citizenship rights or of democratic control.

At a deeper level, a number of writers like Pateman, Benhabib, Cornell and Benton have mounted a serious critique of the concept of civil society as it has emerged in liberal philosophy. They point to the way in which the civic public of Locke, Rousseau and Utilitarianism, is a gendered realm, identified with reason and public virtue. This classic Enlightenment view of reason is tied, according to Young, to a notion of objectivity, of being detached in order to be 'public spirited'. This emerged in Western Europe along with the separation of the public and the private and the distinction between reason and desire in Enlightenment philosophy. These two spheres come to be identified increasingly with the male and the female respectively, as women are charged with the moral and emotional side of private life, and increasingly associated with desire, emotionality and irrationality, and a closeness to nature, unlike 'cultured' men. This becomes quite explicitly in the case of Rousseau, a reason for the exclusion of women from civil society Carol Pateman has shown how the ideal of citizenship as it developed in this tradition, involves the notion of 'fraternity' - an equality of brotherhood, in the modern patriarchy of equal men, as opposed to the traditional patriarchy of rule of the father in which the public is based on what she calls the 'fraternal social contract' and agreement amongst equals about the exclusion of women from the realm of public life.

Sarah Benton insists that the civil liberties we scrutinize today should not just be those of the Great Tradition, of freedom of speech and movement and assembly and against the state's invasion of privacy. There are 'privacies' the state must invade if women are to be full citizens. For they cannot begin to enjoy the classic liberties while their lives are curtained within the veiled area of private life cut off from the state's protectorate of men.

The intervention of the state into the private realm is, of course, more problematic than Benton perhaps implies. We know how the state is involved in the regulation of the private space of the family through a whole range of welfare and social measures which attempt to reinforce female dependency and gender roles. We know also how the state tries to regulate Black family life and attempts to restrict Black womens's fertility and keep Black family members apart. All of this, of course, is circumscribed by nationality, immigration and welfare legislation anchored in chauvinistic, eurocentric and racist practices which shape conceptions of citizenship.

Attempts to extend the realities of citizenship in civil society must not just seek extension of rights from the state, but must challenge the patriarchal and racist structures of state power and engage in a wider practice tied to the emancipatory struggles of those opposing such powers. Young offers a econstituted 'public space.' She contends that the Enlightenment ideal of the civic public where citizens meet, in terms of equality and mutual respect, is too rounded and tame an ideal of public. The ideal of equal citizenship attains unity because it excludes bodily and affective particularity, as well as the concrete histories of individuals that make groups unable to understand one another. She insists that an emancipatory politics should foster a conception of public which in principle excludes no persons, aspects of persons' lives, or topic of discussion and which encourages aesthetic as well as discursive expression. In such a public, consensus and sharing may not always be the goal, but the recognition and appreciation of differences in the context of confrontation with power. Young cites the 1984 Jesse Jackson campaign and the idea of a 'rainbow coalition' in USA as an example of this type of politics.

Citizenship and Nationalism

Writers from most perspectives on citizenship, whether pro-market or collectivist in orientation stress, the integrative aspect of citizenship, especially as it is tied to welfare. Welfare rights are often identified as a compensation for inequalities and a means to equal treatment. In this context the claims of citizenship in terms of a codified access to welfare through rights is increasingly argued as a counterbalance to the privatisation and marketisation of welfare in Britain. In this sense, there is a strong, anti-authoritarian element that can be used as a campaigning plank in liberal and democratic arguments about welfare provision.

However, we must be very cautious about the concept of integration, whether taken from the social administration tradition or from the more functionalist inspired marxisms of the recent years. It is not difficult to see the practical ways in which welfare mechanisms have failed to integrate many sections of a differentiated collectivity both formally and informally. The formal denial of welfare rights to women and to racialised groups both in the welfare legislation is well documented and the unofficial racism and sexism associated with the workings of welfare institutions is increasingly being exposed.

Citizenship, as a legal entitlement to rights and subjection to law, carries with it, not just the formal membership of a nation-state, but a whole set of socio-economic and ideological practices associated with nationalism. These amount to mechanisms of exclusion and inclusion of particular groups and categories of individuals. These groups comprise of most notably those without property, women, racialised groups and the differently abled, children and lesbians and gay men.

Citizenship, then, is related to the socio-economic and ideological construction of nation, nationality and of culture. Its task at the political level has been to construct a social formation, within which claims to rights can be judged according to the rule of law. Arguments around citizenship thus tend to be around an appeal to legal rights. This, however, abstracts these rights from their historical context and out of their international context in a world division of labour.

An instructive example of the exclusionary nature of citizenship is the case of the British Nationality Act, 1982. This piece of legislation which merely extends and codifies trends set in motion in earlier legislation, has been described as 'constitutionalising racism'. This Act established three categories of citizenship: British citizen, citizen of the British Dependent Territories, and British Overseas citizen, with different entitlements to abode and to rights. The last category carries with it no right of abode and is a completely worthless citizenship - for example it cannot be passed on to the citizens' children. A major intention of the legilsation is to exclude particular groups mainly black groups from right to reside and thus to make claims against the state.

Along side this must be placed the Immigration Act, 1988, which codifying the existing racist and sexist content of previous immigration legislation, extends the infamous 'no recourse to public funds' clause. Whereas the wives of British and Commonwealth men who settled in Britain on or before January Ist 1973 could be brought into the country by their husbands under the previous Immigration Act, 1971, it now has to be demonstrated that if they do come they can be supported themselves and will have 'no recourse to public funds.' This is not defined in the Act, but is interpreted to include public housing and the NHS, for example. Where a husband is already himself receiving 'public funds' such as in council housing, then right to entry is likely to be refused altogether.

These exclusionary practices are not arbitrary or accidental - nor are they the result merely of extreme 'new right' thinking. The basis for these exclusionary practices can be found in the immigration legislation of Labour governments in the 1960s and the Liberal legislation in the pre-First World War era. They were intimately bound up with the processes of British nationalism. The 'integrative' advantages of welfare policies for some sections has been inextricably linked to the denial of citizenship for others and the superexploitation of the underdeveloped nations. It is indeed very difficult to see the concept of citizenship outside its international context. Advances in the capitalist core have rarely led to advances for the periphery . In this context, then, arguments for citizenship must address the international division of labour and the processes of exclusion of racialised groups and of migrant labour. Failure to do this allows the formation of another set of interests - 'the national interest' above and beyond the abstract rights of individuals. This is then invoked to exclude those who do not find their lived experience of citizenship validated by the rule of law from challenging the power relations upon which rights are based. A concept of citizenship must, if it is to be genuinely liberatory, be internationalist and anti-nationalist. This may entail a radical rethinking of traditional forms of entitlement which have given rights to a particular set of citizens at the expense of others.

Citizenship and Need

Citizenship rights and entitlements must be tied to a fulfilment of need. Need in this respect can be seen as dynamic and differentiated, as against the universal and abstract basis of rights? The meeting of need implies not just set of rights but the power to achieve needs, in terms of access to resources. Needs can only be satisfied in an active process of human development both individually and socially. The concept of citizenship tied to the idea of the right to satisfy need becomes dynamic, political and comes into a confrontation with power. This means challenging the nationalistic and exclusionary practices associated with state power and the marginalisation effects of the market. This is going to bring those engaged in radical arguments about citizenship and needs into confrontation with the repressive apparatuses of the state. A political movement which fails to address this may find itself tolerated within the sphere of civil society, but unable to deliver anything beyond that already encompassed in present legislative programmes.

A dynamic concept of need, as an openly political issue, can address the fact that the formal equality of rights still remains situated within different power relations. It is possible to identify a universal set of principles which guarantee common human needs. Freedom is defined in a positive way as access to the social conditions necessary for individual development. This is premised on a notion of equality in terms of each individual's entitlement to the conditions necessary for human self-development. Alongside a concern with positive freedom goes the concern with negative freedom of the right not to be denied access to these conditions by others. This immediately raises the question of confrontation with those who have the power to deny access to resources. This means extending rights beyond the political sphere to the socio-economic sphere.

The well known limitations of traditional welfare citizenship theories associated with Marshall's work fail to extend the argument for rights into the economic sphere, into production as well as consumption. This Marshallian approach can be challenged using this need approach. Rights can only be meaningful if they raise the possibility of access to and control over the resources necessary to realise the human need for self-development. Thus the passive tradition of redistributive politics thorough welfare, is substituted by a politics which tackles issues of democratic control of production processes. This however must be situated in the context of an expanded view of production which is tied not solely to property relations but recognises the gendered and racialised basis of power in capitalist social formations.

From this perspective, arguments for welfare citizenship and for the extension of democratic rights, are extended beyond formal legal entitlements and the rule of law, to include political practices of a collective nature which challenge the structures of power inherent both within the state and market mechanisms.

An argument against the above position is the question of how do we arrive through a democratic decision-making process, at a calculation of need in a society divided by power? This philosophical argument fails to observe that in the most advanced countries the most basic of human needs for the conditions of self-development are not met for large numbers of people, and that in a world context, the most basic needs are constantly undermined and refused for large parts of the globe. These needs can hardly be said to have been met in Britain for those denied access to housing, the right to education or the rights and entitlements of citizenship through nationality legislation. In a world context it means an awareness of and a political alliance with those movements challenging the over-provision of 'wants' for a small number in the West on the basis of the super-exploitation of the underdeveloped world. In this sense, arguments for rights, which encapsulate access to the resources to meet needs, must be sensitive to the world distribution of resources, both human and natural and realise that a lebiratory politics cannot be simply nationalistic.

Need, in this respect, can be judged differentially in the context of an acknowledgement of power associated with existing exclusions from rights and practices necessary to have access to resources, both within and between nations. Acknowledging the right of marginalised or excluded groups to demand their own forms of collective action to achieve their needs is one step. This means that the universalistic rule of law criteria for forms of political organisation have to be very carefully thought out. What would be the attitude, for example, of a citizenship theory to the autonomous organisation and demands of republics, ethnic minorities or of racialised groups who express their demands in non-traditional forms of political organisation and protest? Citizenship theory has to be able to allow those autonomous movements, not just the public spaces of civil society, but the right to challenge the state and structures of market power.

The concept of citizenship has a radical purchase in opposing the authoritarian denial of civil rights and liberties. In the context of a restructuring of welfare state its appeal is clear: a reassertion of claims against the state and as a demand for just and equal treatment and demands for welfare rights. Directed towards an appeal to the rule of law however, its political effect is likely to be limited to an intellectual campaign. The abstract liberal tradition of rights must come to terms with feminist and anti-racist critiques which demonstrate the failure of citizenship rights vested in liberal democratic institutions to meet the needs of women and racialised groups and the socially and economically marginalised and disadvantaged. This is because the liberal traditions of citizenship are tied inextricably to a set of exclusionary practices associated with nationalism.

A radical movement inspired by the idea of citizenship must challenge its Eurocentric focus tied to the development of the capitalist core at the expense of the periphery and thus sees citizenship in an international context, and acknowledges the super-exploitation of the world division of labour. The movements of those fighting the exclusionary practices associated with citizenship rights both within and outside the core must be part of the struggle to realise a transformed notion of citizenship. Without this acknowledgement rights campaigns run the risk of a narrow and inward looking focus. A radical theory of citizenship would sensitize more European citizens and governments to the need for radically different policies and strategies towards Africa, Asia and Latin America.

The rights basis of citizenship, which must of necessity fix and abstract human actions into a set of legislative entitlements, should be tied to a dynamic concept of needs, as a set of conditions necessary for the individual and social fulfilment of human development. In a society fractured by divisions of class, gender and race and characterised by the marginalisation of social groups through age, differential ability, sexual orientation etc, such a movement will be confronted with relations of power crystalised through both state and market mechanisms. New forms of politics which acknowledge the different situation of groups within power structures and which allow diversity in terms of political organisation may become the basis for an assertion of citizenship based on need. A simple New Social Movements approach with its stress on autonomy and self-determination, may take us to the heart of the participatory democratic credo but a rhetorical demolition of hierarchies is one thing: getting rid of the state is quite another.

Liberal constitutionalism embraces a kind of integration, but not one that seeks to overcome all divisions and tensions within individual lives or society as a whole. We live in a diverse society, situated in a world composed of a dizzying array of cultural and religious communities. We need in our political arrangements with one another and with other societies, to cultivate not an exclusive attachment to our own ways, but a reflective willingness to pay others their due. Liberal justice, established through constitutionl structures, emphasizes the importance of a reflective respect for legitimate diversity But one whose character is too thickly constituted by more narrowly partisan commitments may lose precisely the ability to distance the self from one's own kind, and with it the ability to respect those who are different.

All of this suggests a certain division of political responsibilities, and a three-pronged program to promote liberal virtues, citizenship and community: greater emphasis on voluntarism to promote citizen initiative, federalism to beef up the possibilities for local diversity and participation, and a national politics of rights enforcement to protect the liberal right to choose.

Citizenship is as old as settled human community. It defines those who are, and who are not, members of a common society. Citizenship is a manifestly political enterprise, yet two general questions arise out of its practice which show that an appreciation of only the political dimension is insufficient for a proper understanding of it. The issue of who can practise citizenship and on what terms is not only a matter of the legal scope of citizenship and the formal nature of the rights entailed in it. It is also a matter of the non-political capacities of citizens which derive from the social resources they command and to which they have access. A political system of equal citizenship is in reality less than equal if it is part of a society divided by unequal conditions.

In its own terms the practice of citizenship contributes to the public good. But the structures in which citizens participate in their collective affairs have wider implications for the organization of society as a whole. Thus a second question raised by the practice of citizenship concerns the consequences of advances in citizenship rights, especially for the social relationships of citizens and non-citizens and for the social and economic institutions in which they live and work. In particular, disadvantaged groups in society might struggle for citizenship rights in order to improve their conditions. The question immediately arises of whether an expansion of citizenship participation can reduce class inequality, or affect the structure of relations between persons of different sex or race.

Citizenship is generally described as participation in or membership of a community. Different types of political community give rise to different forms of citizenship. These simple principles were elaborated nearly two and a half thousand years ago in the Third Book of Aristotle's *Politics*. The chief difference between citizenship in the classical Greek city-state and in the modern democratic national state is the extent or scope of the political community in each. Aristotle understood citizenship as the privileged status of the ruling group of the city-stale. In the modern democratic state the basis of citizenship is the capacity to participate in the exercise of political power through the electoral process. Thus participation by citizens in the modern nation-state entails legal membership of a political community based on universal suffrage and therefore also membership of a civil community based on the rule of law. For Aristotle the status of citizenship was confined to the effective participants in the deliberation and exercise of power; today national citizenship extends across society.

The expansion of citizenship in the modern state is both its growing achievements and the basis of its limitations. The generalization of modern citizenship across the social structure means that all persons as citizens are equal before the law and therefore that no person or group is legally privileged. And yet the provision of citizenship across the lines dividing unequal classes is likely to mean that the practical ability to exercise the rights or legal capacities which constitute the status of citizen will not be available to all who possess them. In other words, those disadvantaged and marginalised by the class system are unable to practically participate in the community of citizenship in which they have legal membership. The disability is a double one because in these circumstances citizenship rights which are only formal cannot influence the conditions which render the possession of citizenship ineffective, if not worthless.

The criticisms of modern democratic citizenship were clearly outlined in the 1840s by Karl Marx in his study of the constitutions of the American and French revolutions, through which modern citizenship first arose. Marx summarizes his objections to modern democratic, or bourgeois citizenship when he says that the state in its own way abolishes distinctions based on birth, rank, education and occupation when it declares birth, rank, education and occupation to be non-political distinctions, when it proclaims that every member of the people is an equal participant in popular sovereignty regardless of these distinctions, when it treats all those elements which go to make up the actual life of the people from the standpoint of the state. Nevertheless the state allows private property, education and occupation to act and assert their particular nature in their own way. Far from abolishing these factual distinctions the state presupposes them in order to exist.

Marx does not wish to be understood as rejecting the achievements of modern citizenship, for he describes them as 'a big step forward' and as the best that could be achieved 'within the prevailing scheme of things'. But this is precisely the point for Marx; he insists that mere political emancipation in citizenship is inadequate and instead he advocates a general human emancipation in which persons are freed from the determining power of private property and its associated institutions. According to Marx, then, the limitations of citizenship which arises through political transformation can be overcome only through a social revolution in which the class basis of inequalities in social conditions. and power is overthrown.

The alternative possibilities spelled out by Marx more or less constituted the parameters of political debate in nineteenth-century Europe. The choice seemed clear: either social inequalities were to be rendered irrelevant for membership in the status of citizen, or social inequalities were to be abolished through social revolution. Yet political debate is never conducted with words alone, and in the course of any debate its terms tend to be redefined. The nineteenth century debate on citizenship and revolution was fundamentally modified by the emergence of a labour movement which struggled for the right to form unions and the right to collectively bargain with employers over wages and conditions of work and employment. As a result of these struggles, either directly or indirectly, policies were developed which provided safety-nets against the effects of certain aspects of social inequality, and especially those connected with unemployment and old age. It is certain that during the last hundred years or so, the conditions of social inequality in Western capitalist societies have changed, and that these changes are associated with the participation of members of the propertyless and powerless class in the status of citizenship.

One type of response to this emerging situation has been to argue that changes in the social and economic circumstances of the working class have the effect of incorporating it in the structure of capitalism, thus undermining its revolutionary potential. But even if the argument about working-class incorporation is accepted on its own terms, it would not follow that the concept of citizenship does not require reexamination.. Precisely this point is implied when Lenin shows that the advent of adult male suffrage in the development of political democracy means that the compliance of the working class can only be bought with social reforms. This arrangement is one in which citizenship, against Marx's earlier expectation, does in fact lead to certain changes in the structure of social inequality.

Given the changes in the structure of social inequality brought about by developments in the concept and practice of citizenship, the question immediately arises of what these changes amount to. One approach which has taken different forms and appeared in left- as well as right-wing guise, postulates a direct relationship between the advance of citizenship and the retreat of class. In effect Stanislaw Ossowski, for instance, summarizing this approach says that when changes in social structure are governed by political forces, as with developments of citizenship, then 'the nineteenth-century concept of class becomes more or less an anachronism, and class conflicts give way to other forms of social antagonism'. It is a big step indeed which reaches from the point that aspects of social inequality are affected by extensions in the scope of citizenship, to the position that the class system itself is in decline. This approach tends to identify the class system with those disadvantages of class affected by the equalizing influence of citizenship. As systems of class inequality involve not only disadvantage but also privilege and the power to preserve it, it is unlikely that any changes brought to the class system through the development of citizenship, in which the powerful and privileged are included, would be fundamental. It has been argued that structures of social inequality are inherently highly resistant to change. Advances in the form of citizenship are likely to leave class structures intact, although class loyalty and class resentment may be affected by the removal of particular disadvantages. It should be clear that the question of the consequences of the development of citizenship on the structure of social inequality cannot be answered in the absence of a close re-examination of the issues involved.

References

Aallenbach, E. and Phillips, M. 1985: *A Citizen Legislature*. University of California Press, Berkeley.

Andrew, G. (ed.) 1991: *Citizenship.*: Lawrence & Wishart, London.

Anderson, B. 1983,: *Imagined Comunities: Reflections on the Origins and Spread of Nationalism* London:, Verso.

Arendt, H. 1973: *On Revolution*. Penguin, Harmondsworth.

Archibugi, D., and Held, D. 1995: *Cosmopolitan Democracy: An Agenda for a New World Order*. Polity Press, London.

Aristotle (trans. And ed. E. Barker) 1948: *Politics*. Clarendon Press, Oxford.

Aron, R. 1974: 'Is Multinational Citizenshp Possible?' *Social Research*, 41.

Barbalet, J.M. 1988: *Citizenship*. Open University Press, Milton Keynes.

Barber, B. 1984: *Strong Democracy: Participatory Politics for a New Age*. University of California Press, Berkeley.

Benhabib, Seyla 1992 *Situating the Self*. Rotledge, London.

Beiner, R. 1983: *Political Judgment*. Methuen, London.

Beiner, R. (ed.) 1995: *Theorizing Citizenshp*. University of New York Press, Albany.

Bulmer, M., and Rees, A. 1996: (ed.) *Citizenship Today: The Contemporary Relevance of T.H. Marshall*. University College London Press, London.

Brennan, T. 1981: *Political Education and Democracy*. Cambridge University Press, Cambridge.

Brinton, C. 1952: The *Anatomy of Revolution*. Prentice-Hall, New York.

Brubaker, W.R. (ed.) 1989): *Immigration and the Politics of Citizenship in Europe and North America*. University Press of America, MD.

Brubaker, W.R. 1992: *Citizenship and Nationhood in France and Germany*. Havard University Press, Cambridge.

Callan, E. 1997: *Creating Citizens: Political Education and Liberal Democracy*. Clarendon Press, Oxford.

Canovan, M. 1996: *Nationhood and Political Theory*. Cheltenham, Edward Elgar.

Cicero (trans. R. Gardner) 1958:. *In the Speeches*. Harvard University Press, Cambridge.

Carens, J. 1996-7: 'Dimensions of Citizenship and National Identity in Canada', *The Philosophical Fourm*, XXVIII: 111-24.

2000, *Culture, Citizenship and Community*, Oxford University Press. Oxford.

Cassidy, Y. 1991: (ed.) *Aboriginal Self-Determination*. Oolichan Press, Lantzville, BC.

Chambers, S. 1996: *Reasonable Democracy: Jurgen Habermas and the Politics of Discourse*. Cornell University Press, Ithaca.

Chesterman, J., and Galligan, B. 1998: *Citizen without Rights: Aborigins and Australian Citizenship*. Cambridge University Press, Cambridge.

Clarke, P.B. 1994: *Citizenship*. Pluto Press, London.

Cobban, A. 1964: *Rousseau and the Modern State*. Allen & Unwin, London.

Commission on Citizenship 1990: *Encouraging Citizenship*. HMSO, London.

Dagger, R. 1997: *Civic Virtues: Rights, Citizenship and Republican Liberalism*. Oxford University Press, Oxford.

Davies, I. And Sobisch, A. (ed.) 1997: *Developing European Citizens*. Sheffield Hallam University Press, Sheffield.

Dahl, R.A. 1992: 'The Problem of Civic Competence', *Journal of Democary*.

- 1997: 'On Deliberative Democracy', Dissent.

Dahrendorf, R. 1974: 'Citizenship and Beyond: The Social Dynamics f an Idea', *Social Research*.

Das, V. 1994: 'Cultural Rights and the Definition of Community' in O. Mendelsohn and V. Baxi (ed.) *The Rights of Subordinated People*. Oxford University Press, Oxford.

Delgado, R. 1995: (ed.) *Critical Race Theory: The Cutting Edge*. Temple University Press, Philadelphia.

Demaine, J. and Entwistle, H. (ed.) 1996: *Beyond Communitarianism: Citizenship, Politics and Education*. Macmillan. Basingstoke.

Etzioni, A. 1993: *The Spirit of Community*. Simon & Schuster. New York.

Favell, A. 1997: *Philosophies of Integration: Immigration and the Idea of Citizenship in France and Britain*. Martin's Prees, New York.

Faulks, K 1998: *Citizenship in Modern Britain*. Edinburgh University Press, Edinburgh.

Fukuyama, F, 1992: *The End of History and the Last Man*. Penguin, Harmondsworth.

Galston, W. 1991: *Liberal Purposes: Goods, Virtues, and Duties in the Liberal State*. Cambridge University Press, Cambridge.

Gardner. J.P. (ed.) n. d.: *Hallmarks of Citizenship. A Green Paper*. British Institute of International and Comparative Law, London.

Geertz. C. 973: *The Interpretation of Cultures*. Basic Books, New York.

Gilligan, C. 1982: *In a Different Voice*. Harvard University Press, Cambridge.

Green, L.C. 1987: 'Is World Citizenship a Legal Practicability'? *Canadian Yearbook of International Laws*, 25.

Habermas, J (1995) 'Multiculturalism and the Liberal State', *Stanford Law Review*, Vol. 47, No. 5, pp. 849-53.

Heater, D. 1991: '*Citizenship: A Remarkable Case of Sudden Interest*'. *Parliamentary Affairs*, 44.

- *Citizenship: The Civic Ideal in World History, Politics and Education*. Longman, London.

- *World Citizenship and Government: Cosmopolitan Ideas in the History of Western Political Thopught*. Macmillan, Basingstoke.

Hegel, G.W.F. (trans. T.M. Knox) 1967: *Hegel's Philosophy of Right*. Oxford University Press, London.

Held, D. 1989: *Political Theory and the Modern State*. Polity Press, Cambridge.

Held, D. 1995: (ed.) *Democracy and the Global Order*. Polity Press, Cambridge.

Ichilov, O. 1998: (ed.) *Citizenship, and Citizenship Education in a Changing World*. Woburn Press, Londong.

Ignatieff, M. 1995: 'The Myth of Citizenship', In Beiner, 1995.

Jowell, R. and Park, A. (eds) 1998: *Young People, Politics and Citizenship: A Disengaged Gerneration*? Citizenship Foundation, London.

Kymlicka, W. 1995: *Multicultural Citizenship: A Liberal Theory of Minority Rights*. Clarendon Press, Oxford.

Leader, S. 1996: 'Three Faces of Toleration in a Democracy', *Journal of Political Phiolosophy*.

Lister, R. 1997: *Citizenship: Feminist Perspectives*. Macmillan, Basingstoke.

Locke, J. 1962: *Two Treatises of Civil Government*. Dent, London.

Macartney, C.A. 1934: *National States and National Minorities*. Oxford University Press, Oxford.

Macedo, S. 1990: *Liberal Virtues*. Clarendon Press, Oxford.

Machiavelli, N. (ed. B. Crick) 1998: *The Discourses*. Penguin, Harmondsworth.

MacIntyre, Alisdair 1984 ; *After Virtue*, University of Note Dame Press, Indiana.

McLellan, D. 1997: *Karl Marx: Selected Writings.* Oxford University Press, Oxford.

Marshall, T.H. and Bottomore, T. 1992: *Citizenship and Social Class.* Pluto Press, London.

Mazzini, J. 1961: *The Duties of Man and Other Essays.* Dent, London.

Mead, L. 1986: *Beyond Entitlement: The Social Obligation of Citizenship.* Free Press, New York.

Meehan, E. 1993: *Citizenship and the European Community.* Sage, London.

Mendus, S. 1989: *Toleration and the Limits of Liberalism.* Humanities Press, Atlantic Highlands, NY.

Mill, J.S. 1910: *Utilitarianism, On Liberty, and Considerations on Representative Government.* Dent, London.

Montesquieu, Baron de (trans. T. Nugent) 1949: *The Spirit of the Laws.* Hafner, New York.

Mouffe, C. (ed.) 1992: *Dimensions of Radical Democracy: Pluralism, Citizenship, Community.* Verso, London.

Modood, T. 1993 : 'Muslims, Incitement to Hatred and the Law', in J. Horton (ed.) *Liberalism, Multiculturalism and Toleration.* MacMillan, London.

- 1993b: 'Muslim Views on Religious Identity and Racial Equality'. *New Community.*

- 1994: 'Establishment, Multiculturalism and British Citizenship', *Political Quarterly.*

Miller, D. 1995: *On Nationality.* Oxford University Press, Oxford.

Nkurmah, K. 1961: *I Speak of Freedom.* Heinemann, London.

Nussbaum M-1999 *Sex and Sinal Justice*, Oxted University, New Youk.

Oldfield, A. 1990a: *Citizenship and Community: Civic*

Republicanism and the Modern World. Routledge. London.

.. 'Citizenship: An Unnatural Practice'? *Political Quarterly, 61.*

.. Oliver, D. and Heater, D. 1994: *The Foundation of Citizenship*. Harvester Wheatsheaf.

Parekh. B. 1990: 'The Rushdie Affair: Research Agenda for Political Philosophy', *Political Studies.*

- 1995: 'Cultural Diversity and Liberal Democracy', in D. Beetham (ed.) *Defining and Measuring Democracy*, London, Sage.

- 1997: 'Dilemmas of a Multicultural Theory of Citizenship', *Constellations.*

2000: *Rethinking Multiculturalisn*, Palgrave, Basing stoke.

Pennock, J.R. 1979: *Democratic Political Theory*. Princeton University Press, Princeton.

Phillips, A. 1992: 'Democracy and Difference: Some Problems for Feminist Theory'. *Political Quarterly.*

- 1995: *The Politics of Presence: Issues in Democracy and Group Representation*. Oxford University Press, Oxford.

Plant, R. and Barry, N. 1990: *Citizenshp and Rights in Thatcher's Britain: Two Views*. IEA Health and Welfare Unit.

Plato (trans. F.M. Cornford) 1941: *The Republic of Plato*. Clarendeon Press, Oxford.

Plato 1970: *Laws*, Penguin, Harmondsworth.

Pitkin, H.F. 1967: *The Concept of Representation*. University of California Press, Berkeley.

Pogge, T. 1992: 'Cosmopolitanism and Sovereignty', *Ethics.*

Popkin, S.L. 1994: *The Reasoning Voter*. Chicago Press, Chicago.

Putnam, R. 1993: *Making Democracy Work: Civic Traditions in Modern Italy*. Princeton University Press, Princeton.

Raikka, J. 1996: (ed.) *Do we Need Minority Rights?* Kluwer, Dordrecht.

Raz, J. 1986: *Morality of Freedom*. Clarendon Press, Oxford.

- 1994: 'Multiculturalism: A Liberal Perspective', *Dissent.*

Reiss, H. (ed.) 1991: *Kant: Political Writings.* Cambridge University Press, Cambridge.

Riesenberg, P. 1992: *Citizenship in the Western Tradition: Plato to Rousseau.* University of North Carolina Press, Chapel Hill, NC.

Roche, M. 1992: *Rethinking Citizenship: Welfare, Ideology and Change in Modern Society.* Polity Press, Cambridge.

Rousseau, J. –J. 1911: *Emile.* Dent, London.

.. 1968: *The Social Contract.* Penguin, Harmondsworth.

Ruddick, Sarah 1980 'Maternal Thinking' *Feminest Studies.* 6: 342-67

Sapiro, V. 1984: 'Women, Citizenship and Nationality: Immigration and Naturalization Policies in the United States', *Politics and Society.*

Schuck, P.H. 1998: *Citizens, Strangers and In-Betweens: Essays on Immigration and Citizenship.* Westviews Press, Boulder, Colo.

Sevenhuijsen, S. 1998: *Citizenship and the Ethics of Care: Feminist Consideration on Justice, Morality and Politics.* Routledge, London.

Shafir, G. 1998: (ed.) *The Citizenship Debates: A Reader.* University of Minnesota Press, Minneapolis.

Sherwin-White, A.N. 1973: *The Roman Citizenship.* Clarendon Press, Oxford.

Shklar, J. 1969: *Men and Citizens: A Study of Rousseau's Social Theory.* Cambridge University Press, Cambridge.

- 1991: *American Citizenship.* Harvard University Press. Cambridge, MA.

Sinopoli, R.C. 1992: *The Foundations of American Citizenship and Civic Virtue.* Oxford University Press, Oxford.

Skinner, Q. 1992: 'On Justice, the Common Good and the Priority of Liberty', in C. Mouffe (ed.) *Dimensions of Radical Democracy: Pluralism, Citizenship and Community.* Routledge, London.

Smith, A.D. 1971: *Theories of Nationalism.* Duckworth, London.

Soysal, Yasaemin (1994) *Limists of citizenship*. Chicago University Press, Chicago

Spinner, J. 1994: *The Boundaries of Citizenship: Race, Ethnicity and Nationality in the Liberal State*. Johns Hopkins University Press, Baltimore.

Spivak, G. 1987: *In Other Worlds: Essays in Cultural Politics*. Methueun, London.

Stapleton, J. 1995: (ed.) *Group Rights: Perspetives since 1990*. Thoemmes Press, Boston.

Steiner, H. 1994: *An Essay on Rights*. Basil Blackwell, Oxford.

Stratton, L.C. 1992: 'The Right to Have Rights: Gender Discrimination in Nationality Laws'. *Minnesota Law Review*.

Symposium on 1995: 'Citizenship, Democracy and Education', *Ethics*.

- 1995: 'Democratic Education in a Multicultural State', *Journal of Philosophy of Education*.
- 1996: 'Citizesnhip: History, Theory and Practice'. *Australian Journal of Politics and History*.
- 1996: 'Nationalism'. *Critical Review*.
- 1996: 'Philosophical Perspectives on National Identity'. *Philosophical Fourm*.
- 1997: 'Citizenship in Feminism: Identity'. *Hypatia*.
- 1997: 'Sovereignty and Citizenship'. *Law and Philosophy*.

Taylor, C. 1992: 'The Politics of Recognition ', in A. Gutmann (ed.) *Multiculturalism and the Politics of Recognition*. Princeton University Press, Princeton.

(ed.) *Multiculturalism: Examining the Politics of Recognition*. Princeton University Press, Princeton.

Tocqueville, A. de. 1968: *Democracy in America*. Collins. London.

Trend, D. 1996: (ed.) *Radical Democracy: Identity, Citizenship and the State*. Routledge, London.

Tronoto, J. 1993: *Moral Boundaries: A Political Argument for an Ethic of Care*. Routledge, London.

Tully, J. 1995: *Strange Multiplicity: Constitutionalism in an Age of Diversity*. Routledge, London.

Turner, B.S. 1986: *Citizenship and Capitalism*. Allen & Unwin, London.

Turner, B. and Hamilton, P. (ed.) 1994: *Citizenship: Critical Concepts*, 2 Vols. Routledge, London.

- van Steenbergen, B. (ed.) 1994: *The Condition of Citizenship*. Sage, London.

Van Dyke, V. 1997: 'The Individual, the State, and Ethnic Communities in Political Theory'. *World Politics*.

- 1982: 'Collective Rights and Moral Rights: Problems in Liberal Democratic Thought'. *Journal of Politics*.

- 1995: 'The Individual, the State, and Ethnic Communities in Political Theory', in W. Kymlicka (ed.) *The Rights of Minority Cultures*. Oxford University Press, Oxford.

- 1998 : *A Theory of Citizenship: Organizing Plurality in Contemporary Democracies*. Westview Press, Boulder, Colo.

Vertovec, S. 1995: 'Multiculturalism, Culturalism and Public Incorporatioin'. *Ethnic and Racial Studies*.

Vogel, Ursula 1991 (ed.) *The Frontiers of Citizenship*. Macmillan, London.

Waldron, J. 1989: 'Religion and the Imagination in a Global Community: A Discussion of the Salman rushdie Affair'. *Times Literary Supplement*.

- 1992: 'Minority Cultures and the Cosmopolitan Alternative'. *University of Michigan Journal of Law Reform*.

Walzer, M. 1983: *Sphers of Justice: A Defense of Pluralism and Equality*. Basic Books, New York.

- 1992: 'The New Tribalism, :Notes on a Difficult Problem'. *Dissent*, Spring.

- 1995: 'The Civil Society Argument', in R. Beiner (ed.) *Theorizing Citizenship*. State University of New York Press, Albany.

- 1997: *On Toleration*. Yale University Press, Hew Haven.

Ward, C. 1991: 'The Limits of Liberal Republicanism: Why Group-Based Remedies and Republican Citizenmship don't Mix'. *Columbia Law Review*.

Warbner, Pnina 1990 *The Migration Process*. Breg Publishers, Oxford.

Wellman, C.H. 1995: 'A Defense of Scession and Political Self-Determination'. *Philosophy and Public Affairs*.

Wheeler, N.J. and Dunne, T. 1968: 'Good International Citizenship: A Third Way for British Foreign Policy. *International Affairs*, 74.

Wollstonecraft, M. (ed. M.B. Kramnick) 1975: *Vindication of the Rights of Woman*. Penguin, Harmondsworth.

Young, Iris Marion (1990) *Justice and Politics of Difference*. Princeton University Press, Princeton.

Zojavic, Stasa (1994) *Women for Peace*. Belgride.

Index